SCHOOL LAW

SECOND EDITION

SCHOOL LAW

SECOND EDITION

by

Madaline Kinter Remmlein, Ph.D., J.D.

*Consultant in School Law and
Professorial Lecturer at the
George Washington University;
formerly Assistant Director,
Research Division,
National Education Association
of the United States.*

Danville, Illinois: THE INTERSTATE PRINTERS & PUBLISHERS, INC.

© Copyright 1962 by

THE INTERSTATE PRINTERS & PUBLISHERS, INC.

First Edition, 1950

Second Edition, 1962
  First Printing, March 1962
  Second Printing, September 1964

Library of Congress
        Catalog Card Number: 62-7053

1   PRINTED IN U.S.A.

PREFACE

Twenty years ago, many classroom teachers and administrators appeared to be indifferent to the legal principles especially applicable to public education. This does not mean that they disregarded regulations; they usually conformed, however, because it was the custom or the local rule. They did not question the source or the principle underlying these standards. Today teachers are more likely to ask for the reasons behind school laws and rules.

Part of this awakening is the result of recent activities of the organized teaching profession. Teachers associations have sponsored legislation for the benefit of the schools; they have formed study groups to appraise the laws under which they are employed; they have engaged in litigation to redress situations thought to be inequitable. Through teachers organizations and teacher-education institutions, knowledge of the importance of school law and its many ramifications has spread to the rank and file, even to teachers in the most remote schools.

As a consequence, the body of school law, both statutory and case, has increased by leaps and bounds in the past two decades. Colleges and universities preparing prospective teachers have offered courses in school law, and state legislatures or state boards of education have prescribed training in school law as one of the prerequisites for certification. Nowadays there is not only more school law to be studied, but there are more students interested in learning the legal bases of their chosen profession.

Traditionally, school-law courses in teacher-training institutions have been taught by educators rather than by lawyers. Often they were confined to a reading of publications issued by the state department of education. Until recently, with few exceptions, these courses did not explore judicial interpretations or delve into legal principles underlying either statutes or court decisions. Even today some of the teachers college courses in school law offer little by way of real understanding of legal principles as they affect the public schools.

In the last twenty years, however, there has been a decided trend,

v

particularly in universities, toward engaging instructors in school-law courses who have legal training as well as experience in the field of education. Such persons naturally include in their courses the rulings of case law interpreting statutes on public-education matters, and also, to a greater or lesser extent, an explanation of legal principles in both statutes and court decisions.

There is no attempt anywhere to make lawyers of teachers or to give them legal training beyond their comprehension or their needs. Only sufficient theory need be included to provide an understanding of why a particular statute was enacted, its effect, and its probable interpretation; an acquaintance with court actions and the reasons why a particular court made a certain decision; a knowledge that the court may have been influenced by certain legal principles when it made an interpretation unexpected from the lay point of view; a recognition of when a teacher, faced with a legal problem, should seek the advice of an attorney. When exposed to them, students of education can and do grasp these issues. Experienced teachers who have had a well-rounded school-law course can serve more efficiently in the profession.

This text is designed to provide such a course. It gives the necessary background in legal principles. For the most part it leaves to individual instructors the further development of the various topics so as to reach larger issues of policy in school administration.

For almost twenty years the author has taught school law in departments of education of several universities. The classes have been composed mainly of graduate students who were teachers and administrators from a number of states. It was necessary to devise a method which gave each student general principles with applications to the state in which he was employed or expected to be employed. No textbook seemed to fill the need. Therefore, the first edition of *School Law* was prepared by this author to meet the needs of school-law courses; the book was published in 1950. The present publication is a revision of the 1950 text. It follows the same pattern as used in the first edition.

The legal principles involved in each subject are discussed briefly and illustrated by quotations from statutes and court decisions. Each student is expected to find for himself the statute and court decisions in his own state dealing with the same topics and to prepare a summary thereof as his class project. A work sheet at the end of each chapter aids the students by showing them what to research.

The material and method of teaching are not untried and have worked well with students of education. They are intrigued by some-

thing new—they are curious and interested. They enjoy comparing the statutes used as illustrations with those under which they are employed. Enthusiasm has developed in comparing the facts of an illustrative case with the facts of a similar situation within their own experience and in working through the principles to decide how a court might have decided the issue in these other circumstances. Debates among the students on the many angles of legal problems have made the procedure even more successful.

In the present text the body of each chapter consists primarily of *Statutory Material* and *Case Material,* which are excerpts from laws and court decisions, respectively. Preceding these quotations, the *Editorial Comment* explains the legal principles involved in the subject so that the student may understand and evaluate the materials quoted. *Statutory Note* and *Case Note* comments point out the principles involved in each quotation, why the court made the decision, and the prevailing or minority rule.

Illustrative statutes have been chosen, not as approved models of legislation necessarily, but to exemplify legislative language on a particular subject. Some statutes have been included because they are typical; others, because they are unusual. Similarly, in the case materials, cases have been selected because they illustrate a particular view, or because they are especially good judicial reasoning, or because they have made harsh law.

Since this text was not intended to be used in a particular state only, or in states with a particular type of school law, there are statutes and court decisions reported from many states. In fact, when there was no reason for preference of one state law over another on a subject, the example was chosen with regard to geographical spread. On a subject where several states have attempted to solve a problem in different ways, several statutory examples have been given.

The court decisions also come from a number of states. Where the courts of several states have decided a particular issue differently, illustrations of the several types of decisions are given, except in a few instances where there is such an overwhelming majority rule that the minority view is mentioned only in the case note.

In these quotations the author has not made editorial changes. Therefore, exact verbatim presentation shows inconsistencies in capitalization, punctuation, spelling, and paragraphing; sometimes such inconsistencies may be found within a single law or court opinion. Grammatical construction has not been corrected. Legislators and judges are not always expert in these matters.

Following the case material of each chapter is a section entitled *Sources of Further Information* containing citations to law books where other cases are reported on the subject. No similar compilations of statutes are available; hence the citations in these sources refer to court decisions or their discussion in the law books. By use of these citations, decisions on a subject may be found to within a month of any date; that is, the section numbers are perpetual identification numbers for a topic, rather than references to specific publications of a particular date. Appendix A gives detailed instructions on how to find school law, with exhibits from the law books, to show the type of publication referred to in some of the citations given in the *Sources of Further Information*.

More and more in recent years doctoral dissertations and masters' theses in the field of education have dealt with school-law subjects. The research involved in these studies will be greatly facilitated by application of the guides found in Appendix A which includes suggestions for statutory sources as well as references to case law. If the subject of the research is in teacher or pupil personnel, the case-law ground work has already been done for the investigator in the references listed at the end of each chapter as *Sources of Further Information*.

The final section of each chapter is a *Work Sheet* listing a project or a number of questions on the subject treated therein to be used by students in applying the principles to their own state and local laws and regulations. From this point on, they will have had the background necessary to evaluate their own statutes, to work out their own proposals for new legislation, to estimate the desirability of a test case in court, and—what is of even more value—to achieve the objective of a school-law course by molding their professional activities to conform to acceptable legal principles.

The subjects dealt with in this text have to do principally with classroom teachers and pupils. Other school-law subjects, such as alteration of district boundaries, are omitted because they have primary interest to school administrators and school board members only. School finance law is omitted because most schools of education provide a separate course in it, and, furthermore, the subject is too complex and broad for inclusion as a part of the present text.

The law of private schools is not included because the text is designed for public-school classroom teachers and administrators, but since the use of public funds for private-school pupils has been a controversial issue of considerable interest, especially in the past few

years, and does affect public-school teachers and pupils indirectly, some materials on this question are included in pertinent chapters.

Another type of information, given in Appendix B, is a glossary of legal terms used in the statutes and the court decisions of the text or their explanation. Definitions are given in nontechnical language for students of education; they are not intended to be suitable for persons with legal training. Fine distinctions, essential to a law student, are ignored in these definitions for students of education.

Appendix C is a short selected bibliography on school law, with a notation of publishers who can be expected to issue school-law publications from time to time. Inquiry of these publishers may be made to obtain current up-to-date information on any school-law subject included in the present text.

Quotations from statutes and court decisions were taken from official reports, not copyrighted. However, illustrative material in Appendix A was reproduced from copyrighted law books, with the permission of the publishers and copyright owners. The author is grateful to these firms for permission to use their material.

Madaline Kinter Remmlein

March, 1962

CONTENTS

	Page
Preface	v
List of Illustrative Statutes and Regulations, by States	xiii
Alphabetical List of Illustrative Cases	xv
Introduction	xix

PART I—PROBLEMS OF TEACHER PERSONNEL

Chapter

1.	Certification and Appointment	3
2.	Contracts of Employment and Tenure	23
3.	Loyalty Requirements	59
4.	Resignation and Abandonment of Contract	73
5.	Collective Bargaining	85
6.	Salaries	97
7.	Leaves of Absence	119
8.	Defamation of Character	129
9.	Benefits for Injuries and Other Disabilities	141
	A. Workmen's Compensation Benefits	141
	B. Disability Retirement Benefits	151
	C. Federal Social Security Disability Benefits	155
10.	Retirement and Social Security Benefits	161
11.	Miscellaneous Rights of and Restrictions on Teachers	179
	A. Health Requirements	179
	B. Residence Requirements	181
	C. Right to Engage in Political Activities	184
	D. Right to Appeal from School Board Decisions	187

PART II—PROBLEMS OF PUPIL PERSONNEL

Chapter   *Page*

12. Admission and Attendance 195

13. Transportation at Public Expense 227

14. Textbooks and Curriculum 245

15. Control of Pupils' Conduct 267

16. Redress for Injury through Negligence of Teacher or School Board 277

APPENDIXES

A. How to Find School Law 303

B. Glossary of Legal Terms 329

C. Selected Bibliography 337

Index 341

List of Illustrative Statutes and Regulations, by States

                                                                    Page

Arkansas Statutes, subsec. 80-1304 (b) (continuing-contract law) ... 29

Deering's California Education Code, secs. 903, 904, 906, 1041-1044
(liability for pupil injury) 282

Deering's California Education Code, secs. 12951-12958 (loyalty) ... 60

Deering's California Education Code, sec. 13525 (salary) 98

Colorado Revised Statutes, sec. 40-2-18 (corporal punishment) 269

General Statutes of Connecticut, sec. 10-151 (tenure) 29

District of Columbia Code. Title 36, sec. 501 (making the Longshoremen's and Harbor Workers' Compensation Act applicable to employees of the District of Columbia) 147

Laws of Florida, 1947. Chapter 24745, sec. 9 (tenure in Orange
County) 36

Florida Statutes Annotated, secs. 231.39-231.44 (leave of absence) 120

Code of Georgia Annotated, sec. 32-414 and 32-910 (right of appeal) 188

Burns Indiana Statutes, sec. 10-807 (corporal punishment) 269

Burns Indiana Statutes, sec. 28-4337 (residence) 182

Kentucky Revised Statutes, sec. 158.110 (pupil transportation) 228

Annotated Code of Maryland. Article 77, secs. 64, 99, and 102 (certification and appointment) 38

Maryland State Department of Education Bylaws, No. 14 (contract
of employment) 37

Maryland State Department of Education Bylaws, No. 73 (antifraternity rule) 269

Massachusetts General Laws Annotated. Chapter 71, sec. 40 (salary) 98

Massachusetts General Laws Annotated. Chapter 71, sec. 44 (political
activities) 185

Nevada Revised Statutes, sec. 392.440 (insurance for pupil athletes) .. 284

Revised Laws of New Hampshire. Chapter 51, sec. 3 (collective bargaining) 86

New Jersey Statutes Annotated, sec. 18:13-12 (abandonment of contract) 75

New Jersey Statutes Annotated, secs. 18:14-83.1, 18:14-85.1 through 18:14-85.3, 18:19-3, 18:19-8, 18:19-9 (curriculum) 249

New Jersey Statutes Annotated, sec. 18:19-1 (corporal punishment).. 268

New York Civil Service Law, sec. 108 (antistrike law).............. 75

New York Education Law, secs. 310-312 (right of appeal) 188

New York Education Law, Article 11 (teachers' retirement law) ... 165

New York Education Law, sec. 3023 (liability for pupil injury) 281

General Statutes of North Carolina, sec. 115-143 (health certificate) 179

General Statutes of North Carolina, sec. 115-193 through 115-197 (compensation for pupil injuries in transportation) 231

Baldwin's Ohio Revised Code, secs. 3329.01, 3329.05-3329.11 (textbooks) 247

Oklahoma Statutes Annotated. Title 70, sec. 9-7 (school bus insurance) 283

Oklahoma Statutes Annotated. Title 70, secs. 10-10 and 10-11 (compulsory attendance) 198

Purdon's Pennsylvania Statutes Annotated. Title 24, secs. 11-1121 through 11-1132 (tenure) 31

Purdon's Pennsylvania Statutes Annotated. Title 24, sec. 15-1516 (Bible reading) 251

Code of Virginia, secs. 22-203, 22-204, and 22-206 (certification and appointment) 5

Code of Virginia, secs. 22-284 through 22-294 (school bus insurance) 228

Virginia State Board of Education Regulations, No. 17 (control of pupils) 269

Revised Code of Washington, secs. 41.32.360, 41.32.540, 41.32.550, 41.32.560 (disability retirement) 152

West's Wisconsin Statutes Annotated, secs. 263.37, 263.38, 328.33, 331.05 (defamation) 134

United States Code Annotated. Title 33, Chapter 18 (workmen's compensation benefits applicable to employees of the District, of Columbia) 143

United States Code Annotated. Title 42, secs. 401-423 (disability provisions in Old Age and Survivors' Insurance program) 156

ALPHABETICAL LIST OF ILLUSTRATIVE CASES

Page

Adams v. State ex rel. Sutton, 69 So. (2d) 309 (Florida, 1954) 185

Adler et al. v. Board of Education, 342 U. S. 485 (1952) 64

Alston et al. v. School Board of Norfolk, 112 F. (2d) 992 (C.C.A. 4th, 1940) *cert. den.* 311 U. S. 693 (1940) 99

Anderson et al. v. State, 84 Ga. App. 259, 65 S. E. (2d) 848 (Georgia, 1951) 271

Backman v. Bateman et al.; Tanner v. Bateman et al., 1 Utah (2d) 153, 263 P. (2d) 561 (Utah, 1953) 10

Baron v. O'Sullivan et al., 258 F. (2d) 336 (C.C.A. 3d, 1958) 190

Beilan v. Board of Public Education, 357 U. S. 399 (1958) 69

Benson et al. v. School District No. 1 of Silver Bow County, _____ Mont. _____, 344 P. (2d) 117 (Montana, 1959) 93

Bower v. Industrial Commission, 61 Ohio App. 469, 22 N. E. (2d) 840 (Ohio, 1939) 149

Brown et al. v. Board of Education, 347 U. S. 483 (1954) 206

Brown et al. v. Board of Education, 349 U. S. 294 (1955) 208

Brown v. McCann, 36 Ga. App. 812, 138 S. E. 247 (Georgia, 1927) .. 137

Chapin v. Board of Education of the City of Peoria, Circuit Court of Illinois, Peoria, Illinois. No. 21255. December 9, 1939 87

City of Manchester v. Manchester Teachers Guild et al., 100 N. H. 507, 131 A. (2d) 59 (New Hampshire, 1957) 82

Cochran v. Louisiana State Board of Education, 281 U. S. 370 (1930) 251

Commonwealth v. Smoker, 77 Pa. Super. 435, 110 A. (2d) 740 (Pennsylvania, 1955). 216

Cooper v. Aaron, 358 U. S. 1 (1958) 210

Cotter et al. v. City of Chelsea, 329 Mass. 314, 108 N. E. (2d) 47 (Massachusetts, 1952) 102

Cuba Consolidated School District No. 1 v. Fox et al., _____ Mo. App. _____, 79 S. W. (2d) 772 (Missouri, 1935) 79

Dodge v. Board of Education of Chicago, 302 U. S. 74 (1937) 171

Dutcher v. City of Santa Rosa High School District; Rehe v. City of Santa Rosa High School District, 156 Cal. App. (2d) 256, 319 P. (2d) 14 (California, 1957) 290

Eastman v. School District No. 1 of Lewis and Clark County, 120 Mont. 63, 180 P. (2d) 472 (Montana, 1947) 43

Everson v. Board of Education of Ewing Township et al., 330 U. S. 1 (1947) 235

Floyd County Board of Education v. Slone, _____ Ky. _____, 307 S. W. (2d) 912 (Kentucky, 1957) 7

Fowler et al. v. Town of Enfield, 138 Conn. 521, 86 A. (2d) 662 (Connecticut, 1952) 107

French v. Board of Education of Unified School District of San Diego, 54 Cal. App. (2d) 148, 128 P. (2d) 722 (California, 1942) 77

Gandt v. Joint School District No. 3, 4 Wis. (2d) 419, 90 N. W. (2d) 549 (Wisconsin, 1958) 233

Greenup County Board of Education v. Harper, _____ Ky. _____, 256 S. W. (2d) 37 (Kentucky, 1953) 115

Groad v. Jansen et al., 13 Misc. (2d) 741, 173 N. Y. S. (2d) 946 (New York, 1958) 180

Guerrieri v. Tyson et al., 147 Pa. Super. 239, 24 A. (2d) 468 (Pennsylvania, 1942) 285

Hovland v. School District No. 52, 128 Mont. 507, 278 P. (2d) 211 (Montana, 1954) 45

Hughes et al. v. Caddo Parish School Board et al., 57 F. Supp. 508 (D. C. La. 1944) aff'd (per curiam) 323 U. S. 685 (1945) 274

Illinois ex rel. McCollum v. Board of Education of School District No. 71, Champaign County, Illinois, 333 U. S. 203 (1948) 260

Indiana ex rel. Anderson v. Brand, 303 U. S. 95 (1938) 54

Johnston et al. v. Rapp, 103 Cal. App. (2d) 202, 229 P. (2d) 414 (California, 1951) 111

Kaplan v. Independent School District of Virginia, 171 Minn. 142, 214 N. W. 18 (Minnesota, 1927) 257

Kuehn v. School District No. 70, Goodhue County, 221 Minn. 443, 22 N. W. (2d) 220 (Minnesota, 1946) 41

Lichtenstein v. Jansen et al., 4 A. D. (2d) 465, 167 N. Y. S. (2d) 31 (New York, 1957) aff'd (memorandum opinion) 184 N. Y. S. (2d) 857, 157 N. E. (2d) 728 (1957) 16

Livingston v. Regents of the New Mexico College of Agriculture and Mechanic Arts, 64 N. Mex. 306, 328 P. (2d) 78 (New Mexico, 1958) 286

Luce v. Board of Education of Village of Johnson City, 2 A. D. (2d) 502, 157 N. Y. S. (2d) 123 (New York, 1956) *aff'd* (memorandum opinion) 3 N. Y. (2d) 792, 143 N. E. (2d) 797 (1957) 294

Martin et al. v. Teachers' Retirement Board of City of New York, 70 N. Y. S. (2d) 593 (New York, 1947) 153

Meyer v. State of Nebraska, 262 U. S. 390 (1923) 253

Molitor v. Kaneland Community Unit District No. 302, 18 Ill. (2d) 11, 163 N. E. (2d) 89 (Illinois, 1959) *cert. den.* 362 U. S. 968 (1959) 296

Murphy v. School Committee of Lawrence, 321 Mass. 478, 73 N. E. (2d) 835 (Massachusetts, 1947) 101

Norwalk Teachers' Association v. Board of Education of City of Norwalk, 138 Conn. 269, 83 A. (2d) 482 (Connecticut, 1951) 89

Nyboe v. Allen et al., 10 Misc. (2d) 895, 175 N. Y. S. (2d) 334 (New York, 1958) *aff'd* (memorandum opinion) 7 A. D. (2d) 822, 181 N. Y. S. (2d) 132 (1958) 51

Parrish et al. v. Moss et al., 200 Misc. 375, 106 N. Y. S. (2d) 577 (New York, 1951) *aff'd* (without opinion) 279 A. D. 608, 107 N. Y. S. (2d) 580 (1951) 105

People v. Turner et al., 121 Cal. App. (2d) 861, 263 P. (2d) 685 (California, 1953) 202

Phelps v. Board of Education of West New York, 300 U. S. 319 (1937) 53

Pierce v. Society of Sisters; Pierce v. Hill Academy, 268 U. S. 510 (1925) 199

Povey et al. v. School Committee of Medford, 333 Mass. 70, 127 N. E. (2d) 925 (Massachusetts, 1955) 19

Schmidt et al. v. Payne et al., 304 Ky. 58, 199 S. W. (2d) 990 (Kentucky, 1947) 232

School City of East Chicago v. Sigler, 219 Ind. 9, 36 N. E. (2d) 760 (Indiana, 1941) 124

Scopes v. State, 154 Tenn. 105, 289 S. W. 363 (Tennessee, 1927) 255

Sestero et al. v. Town of Glastonbury, 19 Conn. Sup. 156, 110 A. (2d) 629 (Connecticut, 1954) 288

Sinton, Appeal of, 154 Pa. Super. 233, 35 A. (2d) 542 (Pennsylvania, 1944) 182

Slochower v. Board of Higher Education, 350 U. S. 551 (1956) 66

Spears v. McCoy, 155 Ky. 1, 159 S. W. 610 (Kentucky, 1913) 135

State ex rel. Lawson v. Cherry, 47 So. (2d) 768 (Florida, 1950) 8

State ex rel. Scoggins v. Vernon Parish School Board, ____ La. ____, 44 So. (2d) 385 (Louisiana, 1950) 122

State ex rel. Thomson, Attorney General, v. Giessel, 265 Wis. 558, 61 N. W. (2d) 903 (Wisconsin, 1953) 174

Suits v. Glover, 260 Ala. 449, 71 So. (2d) 49 (Alabama, 1954) 270

Sulzen v. School District No. 36 of City of Lecompton, 144 Kans. 648, 62 P. (2d) 880 (Kansas, 1936) 203

Thomas v. Bagwell et al., 123 Colo. 169, 226 P. (2d) 563 (Colorado, 1950) 40

Thompson v. Board of Education of City of Syracuse, 11 Misc. (2d) 603, 107 N. Y. S. (2d) 80 (New York, 1950) *aff'd* (memorandum opinion) 279 A. D. 621, 107 N. Y. S. (2d) 584 (1950) 114

Travis v. Teter et al., 370 Pa. 326, 87 A. (2d) 177 (Pennsylvania, 1952) 48

Tripp v. Martin et al., 210 Ga. 284, 79 S. E. (2d) 521 (Georgia, 1954) 13

Weinberg v. Fields et al., 114 N. Y. S. (2d) 238 (New York, 1952) .. 15

West Virginia State Board of Education v. Barnette, 319 U. S. 624 (1943) 217

Whitney v. Rural Independent School District, 232 Iowa 61, 4 N. W. (2d) 394 (Iowa, 1942) 148

Zorach et al. v. Clauson et al., 343 U. S. 306 (1952) 262

INTRODUCTION

Sources of School Law

The word "law" used as a general term means the body of legal rules which stem from all sources, and in this sense it includes much more than statutory enactments. The law of any phase of government or society is found in constitutions, statutes, and judicial precedents; so too is the "school law." This is the broad use of the word. When "law" is used in its specific meaning it refers to statutes, but the school law covered in this text gives as much emphasis to nonstatutory sources as to school laws enacted by legislatures.

Constitutions. The Tenth Amendment to the Federal Constitution reserves to the states all matters not delegated to the Federal Government. Education is not mentioned in the articles of the Constitution, and so, under the Tenth Amendment, is a reserved power of the states. Yet the Federal Constitution has had a profound influence upon the development of school law in this country.

The first ten amendments to the Federal Constitution, known as the Bill of Rights, were adopted in the first years of the life of the Constitution. They were promulgated primarily to put upon the Federal Government certain restrictions because the patriots of that day were afraid that the newly formed national government would take unto itself too much power. The Fourteenth Amendment made the restrictions of the first ten applicable to the states. Hence, no state may violate any of the first ten amendments, even in an area such as education which, under the Tenth Amendment, is within the province of the state. The Federal Constitution has therefore been called upon at times in challenging public-school policies or practices, and under the precepts of the Federal Constitution, certain state school legislation has been declared an invalid exercise of the state's power.

Within the boundaries of the Federal Constitution, school law has been developed by state constitutional and statutory provisions. Every state constitution contains some mention, at least, of public education. Some of the newer state constitutions contain many details

concerning the public schools, while some of the older state constitutions are more general in their references. Almost all state constitutions contain some provisions regarding the financial support of the schools; two-thirds of them refer to the use of public funds in connection with the schools, school lands, higher education, and the office of the chief state school officer; half of them include provisions for local and county organization and administration, including local financial support; school-age limits are established and the state board of education is created by constitutional provisions in almost half of the states.

No state constitutional provision may violate a provision of the Federal Constitution; if it does, it is void since the Federal Constitution is "the supreme law of the land."

Many other types of provisions are found in from one to ten state constitutions. For example, about a half-dozen states found it necessary to amend their constitutions in order to enact teacher retirement laws.

Statutes.[1] State legislatures have enacted thousands of school laws. The statute books of every state contain legislation more or less extensively prescribing how the public schools shall be operated. State statutes enacted by legislatures are therefore the most prolific source of school law.

Some aspects of the public-school program are spelled out in state statutes, leaving no foreseeable contingency unaccounted for. Some other aspects are merely mentioned, and the power to regulate details therein is delegated to the state board of education or chief state school officer. Still other aspects are ignored in the state statutes, but the general powers of the state board of education may be sufficiently broad to include them.[2]

In any phase of school management wherein the state board of education has been given powers of operation, the rules and regulations of the state board have the force and effect of law. However, being a creature of the legislature in most states, the state board has only the powers delegated to it or implied in the delegated powers. In the states where the state board is created by constitutional provision, its constitutional powers are usually general, and in specific instances it depends upon the legislature for its authority to act. In either case, if the state board acts outside its delegated or implied power, the

---

[1] Federal statutes, enacted by Congress, deal with certain phases of education, *e.g.*, vocational training, school lunches, military training, and financial aid. These aspects of school law are not included in this text.

[2] Comments regarding the state board of education apply to the chief state school officer in some states. Not all states have a state board of education.

rule or regulation is void. There is, however, a presumption of authority, and until challenged in court, all rules and regulations of the state board are presumed to be valid and are as enforceable as a statute enacted by the legislature.

Local school boards are subordinate agencies of the state. The legislature may delegate some of its authority in public-school matters to local school boards, or the state board may do so. Within the scope of its power, the rules and regulations of a local school board are legislation having legal force equal to state board regulations or state statutes.

Thus, statutory sources of school law are the enactments of the state legislature, rules and regulations of the state board of education, and resolutions of the local school board.[3]

Case law. Another source of school law lies in judicial opinions. Court decisions are primarily of two sorts: (1) interpretations of constitutional and statutory law and (2) the application of common-law principles. The latter comes about when a particular set of circumstances has not been legislated upon and the rights of the parties must be decided by the court on the basis of general principles handed down traditionally over many years.

Let us take an illustration or two of how case law affects the public schools. A state may pass a statute to the effect that a certain end must be achieved by all school districts and declares that the state board shall promulgate rules and regulations as to the details of the procedure. If the state board's rules do not fit into the general pattern of the state statute and an interested party challenges the validity of the state board rules, the court may declare that the state board has exceeded its authority. If the state board's rule is within the statutory prescription, the party may allege that a local school board has failed to follow the state board rule. There may be, in either case, a judicial question as to the meaning of the statute or the state board's rule and the court will construe or interpret it in deciding the merit of the complaint. Or, the party may challenge the statute, the state board rule, or the local school board practice, or all three, on grounds that some provision of the state or Federal Constitution has been violated. If such a violation can be proved, the statute, the state board rule, or the local school board practice, or all three, are wiped out as if never enacted; they are unconstitutional.

On the other hand, an interested party may challenge a local or state board practice when there is no statute on the subject, and the court

---

[3] Also federal statutes in particular areas. See footnote 1.

may have to resort to common-law principles in order to decide whether the practice is objectionable or not. Most of our school law is based on statutory law. The common law does, however, come into the picture on some occasions.

Statutory Construction

The technical parts of a statute are the title, the preamble, the enacting clause, the body of the law, exceptions and provisos, interpretation clauses, and repealing and saving clauses.

Constitutional provisions in many states prohibit legislation which covers subject matter not included in the title. When the body of a law is broader than its title, the part outside the scope of the title is invalid; the part within the scope of the title is valid provided it can stand alone without the invalid part. If the parts of the statute are so interrelated that they cannot be separated without destroying the intent of the legislature, or if the separation leaves an absurdity, the whole act will fail.

The preamble is the preface at the beginning of a statute giving the reasons for the enactment and the objects to be accomplished by it. The preamble is therefore sometimes used by courts when they subsequently look for the intent of the legislature. However, the preamble is not an essential part of a statute, and it is frequently omitted entirely.

The enacting clause is mere form: *e.g.*, "Be It Enacted by the General Assembly Duly Convened." The repealing clause is some such statement at the end, as "All acts and parts of acts inconsistent herewith are hereby repealed."

The title, preamble, enacting clause, and repealing clause are omitted by the compilers of statutes when the text of each law is included in the codified arrangement of the general code. Then, the body of the law only appears, and the other parts of the statute are mentioned in the annotations, if at all. All parts of the law are usually included in volumes of "session laws."

Where the school laws appear, in the compilation of general statutes in each state, is included in a recent publication which is notable not for that reason but because of a critical approach to their placement and content, with guides for their improvement.[4]

---

[4] Remmlein, Madaline Kinter and Ware, Martha L. *An Evaluation of Existing Forms of School Laws with Recommendations for Their Improvement.* Cincinnati, Ohio: W. H. Anderson Co., 1959. 253 p.

The first principle of statutory construction is that a court will attempt to interpret a statute according to the intent of the legislature. Sometimes that intent is obscure. Part of the obscurity comes from the legal phraseology traditionally used in writing legislative enactments.

Thomas Jefferson, speaking of the early Virginia acts, said that by "their verbosity, their endless tautologies, their involutions of case within case, and parenthesis within parenthesis, and their multiplied efforts at certainty by 'saids' and 'aforesaids,' by 'ors' and by 'ands,' to make them more plain, [they] are really rendered more perplexed and incomprehensible, not only to common readers, but to lawyers themselves."[5] Modern statutes are often just as difficult to understand, and school laws are no exception. It is therefore necessary to review briefly some of the rules of statutory construction in order to study school laws with more certainty of the intention of the legislators and also in order to understand judicial interpretations of statutes which are frequently the crucial point in the decision of a court action.

One of the cardinal rules of statutory construction is that the statute must be read as a whole; the language of one section may affect the interpretation of another. Sometimes therefore inconsistencies or discrepancies between sections of a particular law raise ambiguities which make it difficult for the courts to solve the facts of a case which brings into play more than one section of the law.

Furthermore, a law may be construed by reference to another statute dealing with the same or similar subject matter. After one law has remained on the statute books for a period of time and has been interpreted by the courts, a new law dealing with the same subject matter will be considered to have, by implication, incorporated these past understandings of the terms, unless the new law is explicit in stating a change. Or, a change in the new law may be considered by the courts as a deliberate intent on the part of the legislature to change the previously accepted meaning; otherwise, the court would say, no change would have been made in the new law.

If a law contains both general and specific provisions, the specific will control the general. Similarly, under the principle of *ejusdem generis* a series of particular words followed by a general term will limit the general term to the category particularized by the preceding specific words. Illustration may be found in many school laws re-

[5] Washington, H. A. (Ed.). *Jefferson, Autobiography; Writings of Thomas Jefferson*, Vol. 1, p. 44. Washington, D. C.: Taylor and Mawyr, 1853.

garding the causes for dismissal of teachers; *e.g.*, "immorality, incompetency, dishonesty, or 'other just cause.' " The general term "other just cause" would be interpreted as referring to causes in nature similar to immorality, incompetency, and dishonesty; that is, reasons derogatory to the teacher's personal reputation or professional capability.

There is a presumption that a law does not change the common-law tradition unless it is clearly meant so to do. Some statutes which have been enacted with the apparent intent to change the common law have been interpreted by the courts as merely a reiteration of the common-law principle, because the language of the statute was not sufficiently clear as to an intent to change the common law. For example, by common law a government is immune from suit for personal injury caused by its negligence. Statutes attempting to impose liability on certain governmental agencies have been construed by the courts not to have achieved this result because the legislation was not sufficiently clear in its intention to abrogate the common law. Any legislation abrogating the common law is strictly construed by the courts.

A statute operates prospectively and not retroactively unless it is clearly meant to apply retroactively. Certain kinds of laws cannot be retroactive under the constitutional prohibition against ex post facto laws. However, ex post facto does not apply to most kinds of statutes found in school-law materials. Many teacher welfare laws have been enacted with retroactive effect by allowing prior service credit to teachers in service at the time of the enactment. This kind of retroactivity, if there is no ambiguity, is not objectionable. The difficulty, however, lies in ambiguities which make the intent of the legislature uncertain.

A statute may set the effective date at some future time. There may be constitutional or statutory provisions which designate a time interval between passage of an enactment and the date when it becomes effective, *e.g.*, 60 days. If there are no constitutional or statutory provisions to this effect, and if the statute itself contains no reference to the date when it becomes effective, it will be considered to become effective immediately upon approval.

The effective date of an act is sometimes important, as when a beneficiary under the law attempts to obtain some right soon after its passage, or when one claims the power to act under the law. In such cases the decision may turn on a matter of hours.

Repeal of a statute does not imply the revival of a previous statute, unless the repealing law so states, except when the repeal is by the vote of the people by referendum petition. Nor is a previous statute

revived by the repeal of a subsequent enactment even when the repealing statute so states, unless the previous statute is reenacted in the repealing law. Legislation by reference is unconstitutional in most states. It is necessary therefore to set forth in full the material which is to be revived.

Words and phrases in statutory language are to be construed according to common usage. Technical words and those which have acquired a special meaning in law are construed according to their technical meanings. The singular may include several persons or things; plural may include the single. Masculine pronouns include the feminine, but "man" does not always include "woman."

Certain words must be watched in construing statutes. "May" designates a power but not a duty; "must" indicates a duty. However, "may" has frequently been interpreted as a duty when it applies to a governmental agency. One cannot therefore be certain of interpreting "may" as a permission only.

These rules of statutory construction have been enacted in from half to two-thirds of the states. In each state there are also other rules of statutory construction and usually a long list of definitions of terms contained in the general code of laws. Statutory construction has also followed many traditions in common law. All these many principles are used by the courts when the case before them involves a statute which must be construed before the rights of the parties can be settled.

Elements of Civil Procedure

Although school administrators and teachers are not intended to have a technical understanding of the legal procedure involved in court actions, an elementary knowledge of what goes on in the court is necessary for comprehension of the case materials contained in this text. The purpose of this brief section is not to make lawyers of school people, but only to provide the rudimentary knowledge necessary for an understanding of school law essential in the conduct of their school affairs.

Most of the school law based in court decisions is civil as opposed to criminal. There are some instances, however, where violation of school laws may result in a criminal action. If a person commits a crime, the state prosecutes him, and if found guilty, he is punished by fine or imprisonment. The justification is that the miscreant has wronged the state. If a person wrongs another individual, the latter

may sue him. Such a case is civil, not criminal. Some wrongs may be redressed by the individual injured and by the state also. In that situation the wrongdoer answers to the state in a criminal action and to the individual he has wronged in a civil action. They are separate cases.

Civil court actions may be "in law" or "in equity," although the two are frequently merged in modern court procedure. A successful law action results in damages for the injured party; an equity suit results in a court order or decree. Some payment of money damages may go along with the equity decree, but the principal end sought is the court order to the defendent forbidding him from doing some act, or by implication ordering him to do some act.

Law actions may be in tort or in contract. If a person breaches a contract, the injured person may sue for damages. This is a contract action. A tort action arises when a person is injured in body, in reputation, or in property.

The person who brings the civil action is called the plaintiff; the person against whom he brings the action is called the defendant. In certain types of actions, the plaintiff is called the petitioner and the defendent, the respondent.

The court in which the action takes place is the trial court. The plaintiff files his complaint charging the defendant with certain acts which wronged him, and "praying" the court for certain relief. The defendant "answers," either denying the allegations of the complaint or admitting some and denying others; or possibly admitting the facts but "demurring" as to the legal effect claimed by the plaintiff as a consequence of the admitted facts.

When the case goes to trial, the plaintiff presents his testimony to prove his allegations; the defendant then presents his testimony to prove his defense and to disprove, if possible, the plaintiff's allegations. When all the testimony has been received, the judge instructs the jury on the legal principles involved. It is the business of the jury to weigh the testimony and then decide the case in view of the court's instructions on the law.

If the evidence seems to be all in favor of the plaintiff, the court may give a directed verdict without giving the jury an opportunity to decide. If all the evidence seems to be in favor of the defendant, the court may dismiss the case without giving it to the jury. In some cases these directed verdicts and dismissals are appealed, and the appellate court may say that there was sufficient evidence on the other side to have allowed the jury to weigh it. Of course, some cases

are tried without juries, in which instances the judge will decide the facts as well as the law. In a civil case there need be only a preponderance of evidence to justify a decision; in a criminal case the evidence supporting a decision must be beyond all reasonable doubt.

Some cases are decided purely on procedural points, and the court does not go into the merits of the case. This means that the substantive facts of a case are not considered, but only the procedure. Procedural questions are decided before the merits of a case, and if the case can be settled on procedure the merits are not considered.

The loser in the trial court may appeal to an appellate court where he may be called the plaintiff or defendant the same as in the trial court. Or, the one who takes the appeal may be called the appellant, regardless of which side he was on in the trial court. The winner below is the appellee in the appeal. In some courts the loser in the trial court is called the plaintiff in the appellate court, even though he might have been the defendant in the trial court. This nomenclature is confusing in the abstract, but in each case it is clear who are the parties and which one brought the trial action. He is the one actually seeking redress.

Practically all the case materials in this text are excerpts from judicial opinions at the appellate level. Trial courts rarely record their opinions; frequently their cases are decided without written opinions. Therefore, cases which are not appealed are not recorded, except in the court's own records. They are not readily available to the public. Appellate courts, however, record their decisions with written opinions, usually, and these opinions are compiled for public records. These appellate court decisions are the foundation for case law which lawyers and judges follow in subsequent cases involving similar circumstances.

When a court decision has established a principle, it is a precedent for subsequent decisions until overruled, but the precedent value of the decision applies only within the same jurisdiction. In other jurisdictions, the courts are free to make different or contrary decisions, although they are sometimes influenced by the weight of prevailing views in other courts.

The Legal Status of the Local School District and School Board

Local school districts are territorial divisions of a state created for the express purpose of operating public schools. Sometimes the area is coterminous with a city or town, but the government is separate to a large extent if not entirely.

In some states school districting has been abandoned in favor of the county unit, in which case the entire county is a single school district and the governing agency is a county body. On the other hand, some large cities contain more than one school district. Also, high-school districts may be superimposed on common-school districts with separate governing boards, or elementary and high schools may be operated by a single agency.

Arrangements, therefore, differ from state to state, and even within states there are frequently differences depending upon the size or class of city or political subdivision. The particular districting arrangement is not so important as an understanding that the public schools are operated in subdivisions of the state which are usually legally separate from other civil units.

The governing authority is called the school board, the board of trustees, the board of education, the school directors, or in some of the New England states, the school committee. Whatever called in a particular state, the general term "school board" is used in this text, except in quotations from court decisions and statutes.

The school district and the school board are state agencies and are subject to the will of the state legislature and the state educational authorities, except in those matters left to local discretion. The school district is a territorial area populated by the residents thereof; the school board is composed of the locally elected or appointed officers chosen to operate the schools. In school law, however, the district must be thought of as a unit and the school board as a body, rather than as groups of individuals. School districts and school boards are corporate entities. Although there is considerable difference of opinion as to whether school districts are municipal corporations, quasi-municipal corporations, or even quasi-public corporations, in the sense that public corporation law is applicable, these differences are of no import here. The essential fact is that references to the school district or to the school board mean the corporate entity, not its composite parts.

Therefore, when there is a change in the personnel of the school board, the board itself continues as an entity regardless of the new members. Contracts, title to property, and other business is carried on in the corporate name of the school district—not in the names of the members of the board even though their names may appear on official documents as officers authorized to act for the district. If there is liability on the part of the school board, it is the board itself, not its individual members who are responsible (with some exceptions, such as when individual members misuse funds).

Occasionally, a defeated candidate for election to the school board contests the election of the winner on grounds of irregularity. Pending the judicial decision on the election contest the one presumed to have won serves as a regular member of the board. If the court decides that he was not properly elected his challenger takes over the office. However, during the period that the ousted board member served his actions are usually considered binding. He is called a *de facto* officer.

> It is the well-settled rule that the acts of officers *de facto* are as valid and effectual, where they concern the public or the rights of third persons, as though they were officers *de jure*, and that their authority to act cannot be questioned in collateral proceedings . . . subject to an exception that where a person is chargeable with the knowledge of the defect in the title of a claimed officer, to his office, that the general rule would not apply. . . . this legal protection is not afforded where the defects in the title of the officer are notorious, and such as to make those relying on his acts chargeable with such knowledge. What, then, may be considered notice sufficient to warn third persons and the public? The expiration of the term of an officer, and the appointment or election and qualification of his successor; the resignation of a public officer; the abolition of the office itself by an act of the legislature; the refusal of the board or legislative body of which the officer is a member to recognize him; or the judgment of a court against the title of the officer.[6]

School law pertaining to the powers and duties of school officers is not included within the scope of this text except as teacher and pupil personnel matters are involved. It is therefore unnecessary to go farther into the legal status of school districts and school boards for the purpose at hand.

The Legal Status of Public-school Teachers

A public position may be a public office or a public employment. The distinction between employees and officers is important because if teachers were school officers their status would be materially affected by the body of law dealing with public officers in general.

Five elements said to be indispensable in any public office are:

> (1) It must be created by the Constitution or by the Legislature or created by a municipality or other body through authority conferred by the Legislature; (2) it must possess a delegation of a portion of the sovereign power of government, to be exercised for

---

[6] *Heyland v. Wayne Independent School District No. 5 of Wayne Township,* 231 Iowa 1310, 4 N. W. (2d) 278 (Iowa, 1942).

the benefit of the public; (3) the powers conferred, and the duties to be discharged, must be defined, directly or impliedly, by the Legislature or through legislative authority; (4) the duties must be performed independently and without control of a superior power, other than the law, unless they be those of an inferior or subordinate office, created or authorized by the Legislature, and by it placed under the general control of a superior office or body; (5) it must have some permanency and continuity, and not be only temporary or occasional.[7]

The position of a public-school teacher is created by legislatures directly and by the state constitutions indirectly in provisions requiring the legislature to establish and maintain public schools. Education is a governmental function and is certainly concerned with the public benefit. The powers and duties of public-school teachers are fixed by law to a large extent. The position has permanency and continuity; the position is continuous regardless of turnover in personnel filling it and thus would be permanent in the eyes of the law.

Other definitions of public office have mentioned the requirement of an oath of office, and the salary fixed by law, as characteristic marks. Public-school teachers in many states are required to subscribe to an oath, and the salary is fixed by resolution of the school board within limits fixed by state laws.

There are, therefore, many characteristics in the position of the public-school teacher which suggest that the position is a public office. The line of demarcation between public officer and employee is "shadowy and difficult to trace." However, a number of courts have held that the most important and the decisive difference is that "an employment does not authorize the exercise in one's own right of any sovereign power or any prescribed independent authority of a governmental nature."[8]

So far as public-school teachers are concerned, absence of the authority to exercise sovereign power has been one of the chief distinguishing marks of the position. The courts have been almost unanimous in classifying teachers as employees rather than as officers.

---

[7] *State ex rel. Barney v. Hawkins*, 79 Mont. 506, 257 Pac. 411 (Montana, 1927).
[8] *State ex rel. Halloway v. Sheats*, 78 Fla. 583, 83 So. 508 (Florida, 1919).

Part I

PROBLEMS OF TEACHER PERSONNEL

Chapter 1.

CERTIFICATION AND APPOINTMENT

Editorial Comment

A teacher's certificate (sometimes called a credential or a license) is a document indicating that the holder has met the legal qualifications to follow the teaching profession. In some respects it is like a lawyer's or a physician's license. One great difference, however, is that teachers are employed while lawyers and physicians in private practice are self-employed. Therefore, a lawyer or a physician, upon obtaining his license, is free to open an office and practice his profession. On the other hand, holding a teaching certificate does not by itself give the holder the right to demand a position except in rare instances. Although a teacher who possesses all the legal qualifications required for a certificate may legally force the certifying agency to grant the certificate, there have been no modern cases where a certifying agency has been forced by court action to issue a certificate.

In addition to professional qualifications, there are frequently personal standards which must be met in order to qualify for a certificate. Citizenship is one such requirement, although an exception may be made in some states for those teaching foreign languages or on exchange from a foreign country. For other teachers, declaration of intention to become a citizen will suffice under a few laws, but if such a person does not follow through and become an American citizen within the specified time limit, the conditionally-granted certificate is revoked.

Age is another requisite, eighteen being the most frequently mentioned minimum age for eligibility. Evidence of good moral character and adequate physical condition is also required in some states. Signing a loyalty oath is prerequisite in almost all states.

State laws and state board regulations are abundant in the field of teacher certification with respect to professional qualifications. These

3

measures have been drafted to care for two kinds of prospective teachers: those who graduate from acceptable teacher education courses and those who seek certification by examination. Before specialized teacher education became prevalent, most teachers were certified by examination, usually administered by the county superintendent and valid in that county only. Today, the state department of education or an agency therein is usually made the exclusive certifying authority in the state, and the certificates it issues are valid throughout the entire state. An exception to this general practice prevails in a few large cities which are empowered by state law to conduct their own examinations and issue their own certificates, either in addition to or instead of the state certificate. Today, most certificates are granted on the basis of professional preparation. South Carolina is the only state that operates an examination plan for all its prospective teachers, regardless of graduation from an approved teacher education course.

Details of the kind, grade, duration, renewal, and revocability of teachers' certificates are included in the state law in some states; in other states, these details are left to the discretion of the state department of education, to be determined by rules and regulations under a general or at least a less detailed enabling act. Life certificates are given in many states, but usually only to experienced teachers who have had graduate training. Other states have abandoned the idea of a permanent certificate and require periodic renewals usually dependent upon experience and/or additional professional training. Some certificates expire by nonuse, and a teacher wishing to revive his certificate must meet professional standards current at the time.

A certificate of the proper kind is usually prerequisite to employment as a teacher. In most states, if a teacher without a proper certificate is employed for a position, the contract of employment is not binding. The teacher is said to be under a legal disability and his contract is void. In a few states, a qualified teacher may be employed without holding a certificate at the time, if it is obtained before the date set for service to begin.

In more than a dozen states, employment is prerequisite to issuance of the certificate. This practice is contradictory to the true meaning of the word "certificate."

Since, ordinarily, a certificate indicates only that the holder has met minimum qualifications and is eligible for employment, the question arises as to whether an employer may legally demand more than these minimum qualifications. The courts have universally answered af-

firmatively. Most cases arise, not because an applicant for a position has not met state or local qualifications, but because the employer did not follow proper procedure in arranging the employment.

Ordinarily, the school board must employ a teacher; in only a few states may the board delegate this authority to the superintendent. If there is no statutory authority for such delegation, employment by the superintendent may not be legal. In that event, the board is not bound by the superintendent's selection. Laws frequently prescribe that employment of a teacher by the school board must follow the nominations made by the superintendent, and in some states the function of a county board of education appears to be only to accept the recommendation of the county superintendent. In these instances, the board is prohibited by law from refusing to employ teachers recommended by the superintendent, unless it can show cause for refusal. Reasonable cause for refusing to employ a recommended teacher must be a legal disqualification, not some personal reason. In a few states local trustees recommend teachers who are to be approved by the county superintendent. In fact, the variations in procedure are many. However, under all laws the procedure which is laid down by the legislature or the state board of education must be followed to result in an enforceable contract of employment.

One procedural aspect is that, ordinarily, teachers must be employed by the school board when it is meeting as a body, and an appointment made informally by the members of the board approving separately, or together but not in a formally convened meeting, is not binding.

In a few large cities, written examinations are given to applicants for positions, in order to rank them with respect to scholarship and professional preparation. The grades of these examinations are used, together with evidence of character and general fitness, to assign applicants to eligibility lists from which appointments are made in order of rank on the list. Under this practice, the appointments must be made from the eligibility list and in the order in which the name appears on the list, or at least from among the top names.

Statutory Material

Virginia Code of 1950, secs. 22-203, 22-204, 22-206.

Sec. 203. The school board on recommendation of the division superintendent shall employ teachers and place them in appropriate schools and shall dismiss teachers when delinquent, inefficient or otherwise unworthy.

Sec. 204. No teacher shall be regularly employed by a school board or

paid from the public funds unless such teacher holds a certificate in full force in accordance with the rules of certification laid down by the State Board of Education; provided that any teacher, holding a degree from a four-year accredited college or university, whether in a public or private school, who acquires two years of teaching experience which is certified to be satisfactory by a division superintendent as to public schools or by a principal or equivalent officer as to private schools shall be deemed to have met requirements for having the collegiate certificate raised to collegiate professional, without being required to take more than nine semester hours in professional education, which hours may be waived or appropriately modified in the administrative discretion of the State Superintendent of Public Instruction upon the recommendations of the division superintendent of schools, or the chief administrative officer of a private school; and provided, that, in accordance with regulations prescribed by the State Board of Education a person not meeting the requirements for such certification may be employed and paid from public funds by a school board temporarily as a substitute teacher to meet an emergency.

Sec. 206. It shall not be lawful for the school board of any county, city or of any town constituting a separate school district to employ or pay any teacher or other school board employee from the public funds if such teacher or other employee is the father, mother, brother, sister, wife, son, daughter, son-in-law or daughter-in-law, sister-in-law, or brother-in-law of the superintendent, or of any member of the school board. This provision shall not apply to any such relative employed by any school board at any time prior to June 21, 1938. This provision shall not apply to any person within such relationship or relationships who has been regularly employed by any school board prior to the taking of office of any member of such board or division superintendent of schools, or who has been regularly employed by any school board prior to the inception of such relationship or relationships. If the school board violates these provisions, the individual members thereof shall be personally liable to refund to the local treasury any amounts paid in violation of this law, and such funds shall be recovered from members by action or suit in the name of the Commonwealth at the relation of the attorney for the Commonwealth. Such funds, when recovered, shall be paid into the local treasury for the use of the public schools.

Statutory note. Many states have antinepotism laws similar to Section 206 of the Virginia law quoted above. They are usually included in sections relating to the powers of school boards to employ teachers.

Although there is some ambiguity in the Virginia law as to whether teachers should hold their certificates at the time of signing the contracts, or need not necessarily until service begins, payment of salary to a regular teacher without a certificate is definitely prohibited. It would seem that the use of the word "employment" implies that the certificate must be held prior to signing the contract; however, the

general practice in Virginia is for the superintendent to send to the state department for certificates for teachers following employment.

The superintendent recommends and the board employs, under the Virginia law, but the law does not state that the contract of employment must be arranged in a formal board meeting. There is no provision to guide the superintendent in making his recommendations, other than certification requirements and nepotism prohibitions. Under such a general discretionary power, the superintendent could, if he wished, inaugurate some sort of merit rating scheme whereby applicants would be ranked and recommendations made from the rank order of an eligibility list. Many cities following the eligibility list system in the several states have no statutory authorization specifically, but rely upon the general powers of appointment in laws similar to that of Virginia.

Case Material

*Floyd County Board of Education v. Slone,*____*Ky.*____, 307 S.W. (2d) 912 (Kentucky, 1957). [Teacher denied salary for services rendered before eligibility for certificate.]

This action was instituted by the appellee, Ivonell Slone . . . against the appellant, Floyd County Board of Education, and also Palmer Hall, Superintendent of Schools and Secretary of the Board of Education of Floyd County, to recover salary claimed to be due her for teaching school in Floyd County in the fall of 1951. . . .

Miss Slone was assigned as a teacher in Subdistrict No. 14 in Floyd County by the County Superintendent on September 3, 1951. At that time she did not have a teaching certificate as required by KRS 161.020, nor was she eligible for such a certificate under KRS 161.040 because she had not reached her 18th birthday. Nevertheless she taught in Subdistrict No. 14 during the 1951-52 school year both before and after she became 18 on November 18, 1951.

On October 2, 1951, Miss Slone was paid $143.03 for the 16 days she taught in September. No further checks were issued to her until January 1, 1952, because of her statutory ineligibility. On January 1, 1952, she received checks for the fifth and sixth months of the school year, and from which had been deducted the $143.03 payment on October 2. Miss Slone was paid in full for the teaching she did after she became 18 and was issued a certificate. We believe the trial court erred in holding that she was entitled to salary for the time taught before she reached 18 years of age.

Apparently, the trial court's judgment was based on the proposition that, where parties to an illegal contract for services are not in equal fault and the transaction is only *malum prohibitum*, the innocent party may recover for value of the services actually rendered. . . . That appears to be a sound rule in cases of contracts involving individuals. It is not applicable to cases

involving payment by public agencies to public officers or employees—
where the rights of the officers or employees to compensation are incident
to and dependent upon their right to office or employment. See Flanary v.
Barrett, 146 Ky. 712, 143 S.W. 38, wherein it was said that one who is ineligible for a public office and therefore holds it without title is a volunteer
and cannot recover for services. That case involved the claim of a teacher
without a certificate making him eligible to teach in the type of school in
which he taught.

In the case at hand Miss Slone was ineligible for the office or position of
teacher because she held no certificate and she failed to qualify for such a
certificate under the provisions of KRS 161.040 during the period for which
her salary was withheld. It follows that she taught as a volunteer and was
entitled to no compensation during that period.

Case note. A contract signed by a party under a legal disability is
void. If the board had dismissed Miss Slone, she would have had no
redress. Acceptance of service by the board would not have cured
the defective contract, because void contracts cannot be ratified.

On the other hand, this case should be compared with *Williamson
v. Board of Education of Woodward*, 189 Okla. 342, 117 P. (2d) 120
(Oklahoma, 1941), in which a superintendent had a void contract
because it was oral whereas contracts in Oklahoma involving the
expenditure of more than $200 must be in writing. In the Williamson
case, the void contract was not cured by acceptance of partial performance under the principle of ratification, but Williamson was entitled to payment for service actually rendered before dismissal under
the principle of *quantum meruit*. Why did not the Kentucky court
allow Miss Slone to recover salary for service rendered before eligibility for certification under the principle of *quantum meruit*?

State ex rel. Lawson v. Cherry, 47 So. (2d) 768 (Florida, 1950).
[Power to nominate teacher not at the time holding a certificate.]

June 4, 1949, appellant Wilber Lawson was nominated by the School
Trustees of Clay County to be an instructor in Dunbar High School for
the school year 1949-50. When the school term began the County Board of
Public Instruction had not contracted with Lawson. On October 3, 1949,
Lawson appeared before the Board and requested to be advised why he had
not received his contract pursuant to the nomination of the trustees. The
response of the Board was that Lawson's nomination was conditioned on
the enrollment being sufficient to warrant his employment. On the following day the trustees made an unconditional nomination of Lawson. . . .

A sworn answer and return to the alternative writ tendered the following issues: (1) That Lawson was nominated on the condition that the enrollment warranted his employment. (2) That the county superintendent
recommended Lawson on the condition that enrollment warranted his em-

ployment. (3) That Lawson did not hold a valid certificate at the time he was nominated. . . .

There is no merit whatever to the contention that Lawson was disqualified as a teacher because he did not hold a valid teacher's certificate June 4, 1949, that being the date he was first nominated as an instructor by the trustees. The law, Section 231.14, Florida Statutes 1941, F.S.A., contemplates that a teacher have a certificate at the time he is employed. Lawson applied for his certificate late in June. For some reason unknown to him, its issuance was delayed. He was entitled to it on the date he applied for it and the rule seems to be that when issued it relates back to this date if that is material.

The important question here turns on the power and function of the trustees as against that of the county superintendent or the Board of Public Instruction with reference to the matter of nominating teachers for the public schools.

This court has consistently held that the power to select and nominate teachers for the public schools is vested in the trustees. . . .

It is true that under the school code the county superintendent may nominate or recommend a supervising principal and the trustees may not arbitrarily reject such a nomination. The power to nominate teachers generally is not in the superintendent, it is still a duty of the trustees and their nomination is final unless some moral or professional disqualification is shown. There is no suggestion whatever of Lawson's moral or professional qualification. An examination of the record discloses no basis for the Board's refusal to contract with appellant. The charge that Lawson's nomination was conditional is untenable and there is no finding of fact to that effect.

Case note. This case illustrates several points: (1) One type of procedure for the selection of teachers, as in Florida, is that school trustees nominate and the county board employs. Note, also, the distinction in Florida law between the procedure for employment of teachers and of supervising principals. (2) A nomination must be unconditional to be binding. In this case, even though the original nomination of Lawson may have been conditioned upon enrollment, the trustees later made an unconditional nomination. (3) Delay in issuance of a certificate to a qualified teacher, when the delay is no fault of his own, need not disqualify him. Courts of some other states would not have reached this decision. Strict courts under some statutes would have said that Lawson was not qualified for employment unless he had already been issued the certificate at the time of nomination or at least by the date he was given the contract. The opinion of the court did not disclose the date the certificate was issued, and the court implied that that date was immaterial. In that respect, this case is almost unique.

Backman v. Bateman et al., Tanner v. Bateman et al., 1 Utah (2d)
153, 263 P. (2d) 561 (Utah, 1953). [Application of antinepotism law.]

Original proceeding in this court to test plaintiffs' rights to continue as
school principal (Backman) and school teacher (Tanner) under a newly
enacted revision of our anti-nepotism statute.
The pertinent portion reads as follows:

"It is unlawful for any person holding any position the compensation for
which is paid out of public funds to retain in employment or to employ,
appoint, or vote for the appointment of, his . . . brother . . . [certain other
named relatives] when the salary . . . of such appointee is to be paid out of
any public funds; and it is unlawful for such appointee to accept or to retain
such employment in all cases where the direct power of employment or appointment to such position is or can be exercised by any person within the
degrees of consanguinity or affinity herein specified, or by a board or group
of which such person is a member. . . ."

The principles governing both cases being the same, they were consolidated. We first treat the suit brought by Ralph V. Backman. The facts
recited are based upon the statement of the plaintiffs, which the defendants
in their brief concede to be "accurate and complete."

Mr. Backman is 49 years of age, was born and has lived his life thus far
in Salt Lake City. He owns his own home where he presently resides with
his wife and five children; they are all integrated into various aspects of
community life. He has been employed by the Salt Lake City Board of
Education (hereinafter called the Board) continuously for the past 27 years.
He began as a teacher and has progressed by several upgrading steps until
he became principal of the South High School in 1948, in which position he
has since served. He has met the educational and other standards set up for
the various positions he has held to the satisfaction of the Board when he
was originally hired and on each renewal of his contract since. . . .

At a meeting of the Board a resolution was passed authorizing his continuance in his job for the next school year. His brother, LeGrand Backman,
who first became a member of the Board years after Ralph V. Backman
was hired, did not participate in this action. Ralph V. Backman had previously indicated his desire to be so employed. Therefore, he had a contract
to work for the school year 1953-54, except only if the statute in question
prevents him from being so employed. . . .

Mr. Backman contends that if this statute is interpreted and applied as
suggested by the defendants, it would have the effect of destroying his
employment and all of the advantages incident thereto—his preferred
position in grade, pay, seniority—and cause him to lose the benefits which
have accrued to him under the Teachers' Retirement Association. His argument is that for the law to thus forcibly compel him to uproot himself,
his family, his home and destroy the career to which he has devoted his life
because of a circumstance over which he has no control, is unreasonable
and arbitrary in the highest degree and is a violation of his constitutionally
guaranteed liberties, his right to work, and that it deprives him of property
without due process of law.

Generally speaking, the state may prescribe the conditions upon which it will allow work to be done in its behalf, yet regulations pertaining to public employment cannot discriminate against individuals or classes without a reasonable basis therefor related to the public good, nor deprive persons of their liberty or property without due process of law.

That Mr. Backman's interest in his employment involves a constitutionally guaranteed liberty seems so certain as not to admit of argument. . . .

Such right is indeed one of the most important of the liberties vouched safe to one in our society. It was so regarded by the framers of our state constitution. Article XII, § 19: "Every person in this State shall be free to obtain employment whenever possible."

It should be observed further that—under the facts here presented—Mr. Backman had a contract to work. Based on the tenure policy of the board he had every reason to expect that he could continue in his job so long as his work was satisfactory; the board had passed its resolution hiring him for the next year which he had accepted. This amounted to an agreement for his continuance in employment which vested in him a property right. . . . A property right existed also in the benefits which had accrued to him in the Teachers' Retirement Association, and which would be lost if his employment does not continue. . . .

The only basis upon which the proposed limitation of these rights could be justified would be under the police power to protect the public health, morals or welfare. It is true that when such matters are involved the police power is broad in its scope, but it is not without limit. It must be measured in relation to the above referred to constitutional rights. There must exist an evil of a substantial nature, the correction of which would serve the public welfare, and the law must be such as could reasonably be supposed to tend toward the accomplishment of that purpose. . . .

The vice at which anti-nepotism statutes are aimed is avoiding inefficiency in public office by preventing officials from favoring their relatives and appointing those who may not be qualified to serve. . . .

We agree that statutes which prohibit public officials from choosing and hiring their relatives, serve the salutary purpose of preventing selection of employees on the basis of favoritism to relatives rather than on merit. Such laws tend to make for better efficiency in public office, and are therefore a valid exercise of the police power. The authorities referred to, however, are concerned with anti-nepotism laws prohibiting the *hiring* of relatives in the original instance. Thorough research by ourselves and capable counsel has failed to discover any nepotism law which goes as far as this new Utah statute in that it proposes to *interrupt and destroy* the employment of persons who *had been lawfully hired* and had continued to work under the identical conditions for years. This presents a greatly different problem. . . .

As compared with the relatively negligible harm which might come from the sole fact of relationship as above discussed, far-reaching and drastic are the effects of this statute upon the lives and careers of plaintiffs and other capable and faithful public employees who have given many years to a particular job. . . .

Cognizant as we are that every doubt must be resolved in favor of constitutionality, we are nevertheless of the opinion, and hold that the retroac-

tive effect of this statute which would prohibit employees from continuing in their erstwhile lawful employments, solely because of relationship, where the relative does nothing to appoint or retain, nor has any power of supervision or control over the employee, would amount to an unwarranted infringement upon rights guaranteed to individuals under our constitution and is therefore invalid.

The same principles apply in the case of Mathias C. Tanner. The school boards are therefore at liberty to follow their desires in employing the plaintiffs.

Dissenting opinions: (1) Should the Board, in the example given above, refuse to continue a teacher in employment because of his close blood relationship to a member of the Board, it would no more divest such teacher of a vested right than such refusal based on an asserted personality defect or disagreement with a policy of the Board. And this is so because concededly a promulgation against nepotism may legally be made in furtherance of the public interest. It follows that a law which is enacted in furtherance of the policy which prohibits such employment is no more assailable than a resolution of the Board to the same effect.

(2) The majority, it seems, has gone on a semantic voyage, forgetting to take the statute along as a passenger. The majority sees no harm in continuing the employment of one whose relative becomes his employer. I may see little harm in it either but the legislature did, and it is no answer to say the bounds of reason were exceeded because we see no harm in the situation. The main opinion stresses the hardship that the act produces, but harsh results, as such, cannot render legitimate legislation impotent for that reason.

Case note. This was a test case to challenge the constitutionality of the revised antinepotism law in Utah. Though there are many antinepotism laws, none other than this has been interpreted to operate so as to require the dismissal of those in service before the election of their relatives to the school board. [See specific provision in Section 206 of the quoted Virginia law, page 6.]

The Utah court held that continuance in employment was a constitutional right of which the teachers could not be deprived because of the constitutional guarantee against deprivation of liberty or property without due process of law. Also, since Backman (and Tanner) held contracts for the ensuing year, their dismissal would have been a breach of their contract rights. Furthermore, the court emphasized their property rights in the retirement system. Rights such as these can be withdrawn under a reasonable exercise of the police power (which, by the way, is well defined by the court in this case), but retroactive operation of the antinepotism law here was held not to be a reasonable exercise of the police power. The court explained the purpose of antinepotism laws.

Two justices dissented from the majority opinion. One felt that no rights of the teachers involved would be impaired by the law. The other felt that the hardships which would be suffered by the teachers, were they to be dismissed, had unduly influenced the majority and that even though the court saw little or no harm in continuance of employment of teachers who have been in service before their relatives became school-board members, the legislature had.

Tripp v. Martin et al., 210 Ga. 284, 79 S. E. (2d) 521 (Georgia, 1954). [Superintendent's recommendation prerequisite to employment by board.]

Four of the five members of the Dodge County Board of Education filed an application for mandamus against Manning W. Tripp, as County School Superintendent, to require him to execute contracts with named teachers on behalf of the board. The defendant's demurrers to the petition were overruled, the demurrers to the defendant's answer were sustained, and the mandamus was made absolute.

The pleadings in this case present but one question for determination in this court. How are the teachers in the public schools of a county to be selected and employed?

The plaintiffs contend that the power to select and employ teachers in the public schools is vested solely in the county board of education. They rely on article 8, section 5, paragraph 1 of the Constitution of 1945, Code Ann. § 2-6801, which provides in part: "Authority is granted to counties to establish and maintain public schools within their limits. Each county, exclusive of any independent school system now in existence in a county, shall compose one school district and shall be confined to the control and management of a County Board of Education."

The writer has been unable to find any decision by this court construing Section 3 of the act of 1937, approved February 10, 1937 (Ga.L.1937, p. 882 et seq.), as it would apply to the right of the county school superintendent to recommed to the board of education the employment of teachers. Section 3 of the act of 1937 provided in part as follows: "For the purpose of this Act, the several counties of the State, and the various independent school systems established by law, shall be the local units of administration. In the local units of administration, the several teachers and principals shall be elected by the boards of education on the recommendation of the respective superintendents." . . .

Subsequently to the act of 1937, providing for the recommendation of teachers by the county school superintendent (which act was in effect at the time of the adoption of the Constitution of 1945), the General Assembly adopted an act known as the Minimum Foundation Program, approved February 25, 1949, Ga.L. 1949, p. 1406 et seq., wherein § 32-913 of the Code of 1933 was repealed.

There is no provision in the paragraph of the Constitution of 1945 providing for a constitutional board of education (Constitution, article 8, § 5, paragraph 1, Code Ann. § 2-6801), which prohibits the General Assembly

from requiring that teachers employed by a county board of education shall be recommended by the county school superintendent, nor is there any prohibition elsewhere in the Constitution of 1945 which would prevent the General Assembly from enacting such requirement.

Under the foregoing provisions of the Constitution, and in the absence of some constitutional limitation or prohibition, the general rule, long of force in this State, "that the general assembly of this state is absolutely unrestricted in its power of legislation so long as it does not undertake to enact measures prohibited by the state or federal constitution." . . . The Minimum Foundation Program Act, and § 4 thereof, which provides as follows: "In the local units of administration, the several teachers, principals and other school employees shall be elected by the boards of education on the recommendation of the respective superintendents. Contracts for teachers, principals and other professional personnel shall be in writing, signed in duplicate by the teacher in his own behalf, and by the superintendent of school on behalf of the board." The language of this section, "*shall be elected by the boards of education on the recommendation of the respective superintendents* [italics ours]," is mandatory and not directive.

Construing article 8, § 5, paragraph 1 of the Constitution of 1945, Code Ann. § 2-6801, with reference to schools being confined to the control and management of the county board of education, in conjunction with § 4 of the Minimum Foundation Program Act, Ga.L.1949, p. 1406 et seq., as they must be construed (since the General Assembly is conclusively presumed to know the provisions of the Constitution), it would be the duty of the county school superintendent to recommend to the board of education all teachers having the necessary qualifications, ability, and character. The board of education must select and employ those teachers needed from the number recommended by the county school superintendent.

The General Assembly having exercised a legislative power that is not in conflict with the Constitution, the trial court erred in making the mandamus absolute, so as to require the county school superintendent to execute contracts on behalf of the board of education with certain teachers whose employment was not recommended by the county school superintendent.

Judgment reversed.

Case note. Here is another procedure for the selection of teachers. In Georgia, and in many other states, the county school superintendent has the duty of recommending teachers and the county board of education must select and employ from those recommended by the superintendent. The Georgia procedure was enacted by the legislature in 1937. In 1945, Georgia adopted a new Constitution which gave general powers of control of the schools to the county boards of education. This board contended that the constitutional power superseded the statutory requirement. However, the court found no conflict between the constitutional power which was general and the statutory requirement which was specific, stating that the legislature

has plenary power over the schools so long as its enactments do not violate the constitution in any way.

Weinberg v. Fields et al., 114 N.Y.S. (2d) 238 (New York, 1952). [Examination for placement on eligibility list.]

Petitioner seeks a review order, Article 78, Civil Practice Act, of the action of respondents in failing him in that part of an examination called "Interview (Content)" taken by him for license to the position of First Assistant in Academic Subjects (Mathematics and Science) in Day High Schools in the city school system. He challenges the legality thereof on the ground that such result was unwarranted in fact and was reached by methods which were arbitrary, illegal and capricious, and in violation of the constitutional mandate that appointments and promotions in the civil service of the state "shall be made according to merit and fitness to be ascertained, so far as practicable, by examinations, which so far as practicable shall be competitive." . . .

The examination it was provided for consisted of several parts, four of which, to wit, written tests, supervision test, teaching test and the "oral English" part of the interview test, petitioner took and satisfactorily passed. He was failed on this so-called "Interview (Content)" test and, as a result thereof, he was not given the remainder which included a medical and physical examination, an appraisal of record and an evaluation of training and experience.

The interview test was comprised of "a separately conducted 'oral English' test and a separately conducted 'interview (content) test.'" The examining panel marked him "unsatisfactory" in the latter part and, as a result, failed him in all of it and in the over-all examination for the promotion sought.

Petitioner argues that the examination in the foregoing, and in other aspects, revolving to such an extent on the subjective reactions of the examiners, was lacking in those objective standards which the Constitution requires to insure competitive choice and which a reviewing body such as this must have in order to be able to weigh the soundness and fairness of the result.

But tests of the kind herein given in which the appraisal rests to an appreciable degree on "intangibles" have been upheld perhaps necessarily and rightly so. To draw a line of demarcation between objectivity and subjectivity is difficult.

Petitioner asserts that it was improper to include in the "interview" test an appraisal of him on "oral" English inasmuch as he had already taken and successfully passed a prior test devoted specifically to this. Respondents say, in reply (Jablonower affidavit, pp. 3 and 4), "The appraisal of the candidate's speech in this functional context is at least as important as the appraisal of it in the formal speech test where it is more likely to be guarded and less representative of the habitual speech pattern of the candidate. Furthermore, poor and illiterate speech is a hindrance to effective and convincing communication and affects for the worse the quality of the performance in the interview, whereas good and literate speech makes for

clarity, persuasiveness and other indispensable aspects of effective communication. In the 'content' portion of the interview test applicants are required to read aloud and discuss an appropriate excerpt from educational literature relating to the subject of the license sought. On the basis of such discussion by the candidate the Board of Examiners is in a position to pass judgment on the applicant's 'oral discussion' and 'personality.' Such discussion provides the basis for an evaluation of a candidate's mental celerity and resourcefulness, his readiness to clarify an issue by explanations, illustrations and applications, his ability to deal with contrasting views etc. Additional light may also be shed on the applicant's knowledge of his subject." . . .

None of the other objections made are of sufficient weight to serve as a basis to sustain petitioner's challenge. See also, in support of the view above set forth, Matter of Burke v. Fields, 279 App. Div. 674, 108 N.Y.S. 2d 313. The petition is dismissed.

Case note. The objective of the selection of teachers by use of eligibility lists is to ascertain the best fitted teachers among many applicants for appointment. Rarely are such examinations restricted to objective written tests; in practically every instance where eligibility lists are used, interviews and relatively subjective tests supplement the written tests. In this case the applicant passed several parts of the total examination but failed in what was called the "Interview (Content)" test. He alleged that the total examination pattern violated the prescription for selection on the basis of competitive examination because parts of it were not objective in nature. The court upheld the board in its practice of including appraisal tests based to a degree on intangibles, because the board was able to convince the court of the importance of the interview and also, incidentally, that the examiners were not completely subjective in their evaluation of candidates taking that test. The court added that it should not substitute its judgment for that of the examiners in the absence of evidence showing that the board had acted arbitrarily or capriciously. This is the typical reaction of courts; they will not interfere with the discretionary powers of school officials.

Lichenstein v. Jansen et al., 4 A. D. (2d) 465, 167 N.Y.S. (2d) 31 (New York, 1957) *aff'd* (memorandum opinion) 184 N.Y.S. (2d) 857, 157 N.E. (2d) 728 (1957). [Meaning of selection on competitive basis.]

Petitioner seeks an order directing the respondents to make appointments of principals and junior principals of elementary schools from eligible lists irrespective of sex. On May 10, 1954, the Board of Examiners of the Board of Education, at the direction of the Superintendent of Schools, announced two competitive examinations, one for the license of principal and the other for the license of junior principal of elementary schools. On December 20,

1956, the Board of Examiners certified to the Superintendent of Schools two lists of 161 persons who had passed the examination for the principal's license, one of 119 men and the other of 42 women, in the order of their ratings on the respective lists. On January 16, 1957, the Board of Examiners certified to the Superintendent of Schools the names of 343 persons who had passed the examination for the junior principal's license which were divided into two separate eligible lists, one consisting of 220 men and the other of 123 women, in the order of their ratings. Thereafter, the Board of Education decided to appoint 60 to fill the vacancies for principal, of which 44 were to be men and 16 were to be women; and to fill 59 junior principal vacancies, of which 38 were to be men and 21 women.

The gravamen of petitioner's objections is not so much that different numbers of women and men were appointed from the separate eligible lists, but that in announcing proposed appointments from the separate lists different ratings of eligibility were used. Thus, as to the principals' list, the Superintendent of Schools stated that in making appointments the last rating to be reached on the men's section of the list would be 76.53% and on the women's section of the list it would be 73.39%. Similarly, as to appointments from the junior principals' list, the last rating to be reached on the men's list would be about 76%, and on the women's section about 73%.

As a result, 5 women were to be appointed from the principals' eligible list whose ratings were lower than 30 men on such list who were not appointed; and 11 women were to be appointed from the junior principals' list whose ratings were lower than about 40 men on such list who were not appointed. (The briefs inform this Court that said appointments were actually made after the decision of Special Term.) It is this result which petitioner contends strikes at the very heart of the merit system of appointment in the civil service.

It is undisputed that it is the purpose of the Board of Education to make the appointments as if the men and women taking the two examinations were not in competition with each other but rather as if the men were in competition among themselves and the women likewise.

The petitioner challenges the promulgation of the two lists resulting from each of the two examinations and the manner in which the said lists were and are to be utilized in filling the said vacancies. Petitioner relies on Article V, Section 6, of the Constitution of the State of New York, which mandates appointments and promotions in the Civil Service of the State and the civil divisions thereof according to merit and fitness to be ascertained as far as practicable by competitive examination. The respondents justify their action by section 246 of the By-laws of the Board of Education providing "There shall be separate eligible lists for men and for women."

So far as is to be gathered from the opposing affidavits, the bases for the promulgation of separate lists for men and women are as follows:

"Education in our schools is and has been traditionally co-educational. By reason thereof there are many problems which continually arise in the schools, some of which can be more efficiently handled by men and others of which can be more efficiently handled by women. Furthermore, it has been found most desirable

for the efficient functioning of the school system that the teaching and supervisory staffs be fairly represented by both sexes. In addition, it has been found that as in other lines of endeavor, in the pedagogical field women excel in the performance of certain functions while men excel in others. The most desirable combination in an efficient school system is to have a fair balance of men and women on the pedagogical staff at all levels." (Affidavit of William Jansen, Superintendent of Schools.)

"Moreover, there is no question in this proceeding as to whether a particular school requires a man or a women principal or junior principal. Respondents contend that in the overall organization of the pedagogical staff it has been found as a result of more than a half century of experience that a fair proportion of men and women is essential and vital to an efficient and sound administration of the school system, and that the means for assuring and maintaining that balance is necessary." (Affidavit of Edmund J. Gannon, Associate Superintendent of Schools.)

We do not deem it necessary at this time to decide whether or not section 246 of the By-laws of the Board of Education is valid in the light of Article V, Section 6, of the Constitution of the State of New York. We assume the validity of the By-law, although the physical differences between the two sexes adverted to in People ex rel. Arden v. Gallagher, supra, concededly does not affect the ability of the men and women here involved to perform the duties of either principal or junior principal. We address ourselves to the validity of the proposed utilization of the lists on the facts of this case. It is obvious that the proposed appointments will not be made in accordance with the ratings, without regard to sex, of the candidates for the examinations. This represents a departure from the requirement of a competitive examination. The respondents have broad discretionary powers but they may not act arbitrarily. They are required to advance a rational basis for their procedure. People ex rel. Sweeney v. Rice, 279 N.Y. 70, 73, 17 N.E.2d 772, 773.

It is undisputed that the educational requirements, duties and salaries in respect of the two positions here involved are the same regardless of sex. It is also undisputed, as stated by the Associate Superintendent of Schools, that this proceeding does not involve the requirements of particular schools, as appeared in Fitzpatrick v. Board of Education, supra, or varying educational training depending on sex, as appeared in Schlivinski v. Maxwell, supra. The record does not demonstrate that the adherence to the merit system mandated by the Constitution precludes the representation by both sexes necessary for the sound administration of the school system, particularly in the light of the provisions of section 2573, subd. 10, of the Education Law, which enables appointments to the teaching and supervisory service from the first three persons on the appropriate eligible list. We are, therefor, of the opinion that the proposed action of the respondents is arbitrary and capricious.

Case note. Here a by-law of the board of education appeared to violate the constitutional mandate that appointments be made "accord-

ing to merit and fitness to be ascertained as far as possible by competitive examination." The court did not find it necessary to decide the question of the constitutionality of the by-law requiring separate eligibility lists for men and for women. Courts usually attempt to decide issues on other principles, by-passing constitutional questions wherever possible, because all laws and local regulations are *presumed* to be constitutional.

However, the practice of the board was declared arbitrary and capricious because the separate eligibility lists were prepared for use of different ratings of eligibility for each sex although educational requirements, duties and salaries were the same regardless of sex. Had the issue involved requirements of particular schools or varied educational training, depending on sex, the decision might have been different.

Povey et al. v. School Committee of Medford, 333 Mass. 70, 127 N. E. (2d) 925 (Massachusetts, 1955). [Fifteen taxpayers questioned the validity of the appointment of a principal.]

This case comes to us by appeal after the sustaining of demurrers and a decree dismissing the bill.

The material allegations of the bill are that the fifteen plaintiffs are residents and taxpayers in Medford, that the defendant Murphy is purporting to act as principal of the Hillside and Hervey schools; that the other defendants, except the city of Medford, are the members of the school committee; that the superintendent in accordance with his duty under rules of the committee recommended one Innis to be principal of these two schools, but that a majority of the committee voted to appoint Murphy, a brother-in-law of one of them, to the vacancy; that Murphy had not had the proper experience and was not qualified; that the majority of the committee acted in bad faith; that the plaintiffs bring the bill to enforce the duty owed by the defendants to the city and the taxpayers and in their behalf and in behalf of the school children, contending that the vote of the majority of the committee was contrary to law, in bad faith and invalid; and that doubt and controversy exist as to the rules of the committee requiring the recommendation of the superintendent, and as to the validity of the vote purporting to elect Murphy, and as to his contract as principal. . . .

The bill is not properly brought for a declaratory decree under G.L(Ter. Ed.) c. 231A, § 1. That section requires that an "actual controversy" must have "arisen," and we think it requires that the plaintiff or plaintiffs must be in some manner parties to the "controversy." The taxpayer plaintiffs have no interest of their own in the subject matter of the bill. Taxpayers of a municipality cannot make themselves parties to the appointment of every officer or employee of the municipality and thus require the appointing officers to account for their acts to such taxpayers as may volunteer to bring suit. We cannot believe that the Legislature intended that public officers

should be subject to harassment by taxpayers as to their official acts in this manner.

Since the bill states no case for declaratory or other relief, there was no error in sustaining the demurrers.

Case note. The judicial procedure in many states permits what is called a declaratory judgment; but to obtain a declaration from the court on the interpretation of a law in this kind of case, there must be an actual controversy. This means a controversy in which the parties have a legal interest. Taxpayers interested in the selection of a particular school employee do not have sufficient legal interest to permit them to obtain a declaratory judgment. The taxpayer-plaintiffs in this case alleged bad faith on the part of the board (called the school committee) but did not allege illegality of appointment. The board had appointed a relative of one of them—Massachusetts does not have an antinepotism law. The crux of the issue was that the board had appointed one other than the individual recommended by the superintendent. Rules of the local committee require the recommendation of the superintendent, but not the state law; therefore, the board could disregard its own rules.

The importance of this case is to show that taxpayers cannot judicially control a school board in its selection of teachers, unless it can be shown that the board violated state constitutional or statutory provisions. Taxpayers have insufficient legal interest.

Sources of Further Information

47 Am. Jur. "Schools" secs. 109-110, 114, 118.

78 C.J.S. "Schools and School Districts" secs. 159-168, 170-182, 509.

A.L.R. "Schools" Topic Nos. 31, 34-37.

American Digest System "Schools and School Districts" Key Nos. 127, 192-133.4.

National Education Association, National Commission on Teacher Education and Professional Standards, *A Manual on Certification Requirements for School Personnel in the United States.* Washington, D.C.: the Association. 1961 edition in press (issued every two years).

Work Sheet

For the state in which you are interested, find the statutes and state board regulations to answer the following questions regarding certification:

1. What are the personal qualifications for certification, aside from professional preparation?

2. How many kinds of certificates are granted and for what kinds of positions?

3. For how long are the different kinds of certificates valid?

4. How may certificates be renewed?

5. Does the state issue life certificates?

6. How may a certificate be exchanged for one of higher grade?

7. Are local certificates given in any school districts?

8. Is it necessary to hold a proper certificate at the time of employment, or is it sufficient if the certificate is obtained before service begins?

9. For what causes are certificates revocable?

To answer the following questions on employment practices, you may need to consult local school-board rules as well as state statutes and state board regulations:

1. Who recommends teachers in your district?

2. Who employs teachers?

3. What procedure must be followed in employing teachers?

4. Are eligibility lists used?

5. If so, what is the basis for the ranking of applicants on such lists?

Chapter 2.

CONTRACTS OF EMPLOYMENT AND TENURE

Editorial Comment

Teachers, and usually other professional school employees, are employed under term contracts or tenure laws. In practically every state, there is some legislation regarding the employment of teachers. Only in the absence of such legislation is the common law, per se, applicable. In many nontenure areas, legislation provides the length of contract by which teachers may be employed, the procedure to be followed, sometimes the provisions of the contract document, and often the causes to be considered justifiable reasons for dismissal before the end of the contract period. Under such provisions, the statute takes precedence over the contract document.

When dismissed before the end of a term contract, principles of contract law apply, unless superseded by statutory provisions. If dismissal violates the provisions of the statute (or the contract), the dismissal is a breach of contract on the part of the employer and the teacher is entitled to sue for damages; if the provisions of the statute (or the contract) provide for dismissal under specified circumstances, and the dismissal is consistent with those provisions, there has been no breach of contract.

Any contract for a specified length of time is a term contract. Common-law or due process of law redress for breach of contract does not protect a teacher from unwarranted "dismissal" at the end of a contract period; that is not a dismissal in the legal sense, being only failure to renew a term contract. Only by a tenure law is continuity of employment provided. Before tenure laws are discussed, a few general principles of contract law should be mentioned, because they would be applicable also in certain so-called tenure areas or in real tenure areas if the issue is not preempted by statutory provisions.

A contract is an agreement enforceable at law. The word "contract"

23

is used for the agreement as well as for the document which is evidence of the agreement. A contract usually need not be in writing to be enforceable, unless so prescribed by statute. Many school laws require written contracts for the employment of teachers, and in a few states the contract form is prescribed. In these states an agreement which is oral, or on a form other than the one required, is not enforceable.

A contract in the sense of an agreement is formed by an offer which is accepted. An offer is a proposal to enter into a contract. It must be certain and definite, stating the service sought and the salary to be paid. The offer becomes a binding contract when it is accepted. Acceptance, however, must be unequivocal and in compliance with the terms of the offer. A conditional acceptance is a rejection of the original offer; it is really a counteroffer. In general, acceptance may be by simple assent as well as by signing a document, but when teachers' contracts of employment must be in writing, the contract of employment is not completely made until the document is signed, and the acceptance of an offer is merely preliminary negotiation until it is put into writing.

Both parties to a contract must have legal capacity to enter into the agreement. Lack of certificate has been shown to make the teacher legally disabled; sometimes, also, the school board's legal capacity is challenged. Furthermore, some contracts are unenforceable because they were executed without due regard for proper procedure. These factors make the contract unenforceable regardless of the use of the proper form.

One essential of a contract is sufficient certainty in terms to enable a court to understand the intention of the parties. Ambiguous language is interpreted by a court against the person who uses it. Uncertainties are caused by failing to express one's intention or by expressing intention ambiguously. In the latter instance, the court will listen to testimony of oral conversations at the time of making the contract, in order to ascertain just what the parties really meant by the ambiguous language of the contract. However, when ambiguity is caused by failure to include any expression of an intention, the court will not hear such evidence. Oral testimony is excluded in such cases under what is called the "parol-evidence rule." When the terms of an agreement are in writing, those terms cannot be added to or varied from by oral testimony as to their unexpressed intention. It is essential that a contract include the exact intention of the parties in terms as clear as possible so that there is no necessity for altercation.

If a contract is defectively executed and therefore voidable, it may be turned into a binding agreement by ratification; if the contract is void, however, it cannot be ratified. Ratification of a defective and voidable contract may be accomplished by subsequent action by the board when it followed the proper procedure. Or, a voidable contract may be considered ratified if the board accepts partial performance. Cases in which ratification is an important element usually revolve around implied ratification. That is, although the contract was defectively executed and although the board did not subsequently take steps to cure the defects in its original procedure, it accepted services from the teacher under circumstances which cured the defects and made the contract enforceable as a whole. An important principle of law is that a contract which is void because of the legal disability of one of the parties cannot be ratified (even by subsequent action by the board); whereas, one which is voidable because of defective procedure can be ratified even by acceptance of partial performance. To illustrate: a teacher employed without a certificate has a void contract and if dismissed before the end of the contract period that teacher has no recourse. However, if a properly certificated teacher employed by a defective procedure is dismissed without cause before the end of the contract period after having taught for part of the contract period, the voidable contract is enforceable as a whole and that teacher can sue the board for salary for the balance of the contract period.

"Tenure" in its broad sense means the duration of employment, and a teacher employed by an annual or a five-year contract has tenure in this sense for a year or for five years, as the case may be. However, the word "tenure" has developed a technical meaning in school law which refers to indefinite or permanent employment from year to year under certain conditions. Tenure in this technical sense is provided by statute; there is no common law involved. The tenure status of teachers therefore depends upon the provisions of the particular tenure law under which they are employed.

Tenure laws are sometimes called continuing-contract laws; continuing-contract laws are sometimes called tenure legislation. Strictly speaking, however, there are two distinct kinds of statutes regardless of interchanged terminology. A true continuing-contract law is an annual contract, or a contract for a stated period, which is automatically renewed if the teacher is not notified of nonrenewal by a specified date. Ordinarily no reasons need be given with the notice of nonrenewal, nor is any hearing required. A tenure law, on the other hand, even if it is called a continuing-contract law, includes also cer-

tain provisions which mark it definitely as a tenure law. These features may be stated briefly to provide premanent status when the teacher cannot be dismissed, even at the end of a school year, except for stated causes after due notice and opportunity for self-defense.

Practically all tenure laws require the teacher newly appointed to pass through a probationary period before acquiring tenure status. The probationary period in various states is from one to five years, most commonly three. During the probationary period, annual contracts are customary and teachers on probation may be dismissed at the end of any school year. In other tenure laws, permission is given to dismiss a probationary teacher at any time during the probationary period, and in these states the probationary teacher may be dismissed even during a school year, the annual contract having been made with the statutory limitation. Ordinarily, it is not necessary to state a reason or conduct a hearing before dismissing probationary teachers.

In recent years, probationary teachers have been employed under spring-notification continuing-contract laws. Thus, throughout the probationary period these teachers are automatically reemployed each ensuing year unless notified by the specified date in the spring that they will not be reemployed.

At the end of the probationary period, teachers acquire tenure status, usually by nomination of the superintendent and appointment by the school board. This procedure has allowed some abuse if the board employs a disproportionate number of probationary teachers and, by dismissing them at the end of the probationary period, prevents the majority of probationary teachers from acquiring tenure status. Probationary teachers have been dismissed and then reemployed as probationary teachers. Some laws have sought to ameliorate this practice by stating that the teacher who serves beyond the probationary period automatically acquires tenure status, or that tenure is gained at the end of the probationary period without overt sanction by the board if the teacher has not been notified of dismissal before the end of the probationary period.

After a teacher acquires tenure status, dismissal is legal only for certain causes and after certain procedure. The causes for justifiable dismissal may be enumerated in the law, or the law may be more general, stating merely that tenure teachers may be dismissed "for reasonable and just cause." Other tenure laws combine an enumeration with the general term.

Before dismissal the tenure teacher is entitled to notice, with a statement of the charges, and a hearing before the school board in which

hearing the teacher may defend himself against the charges. There usually is provision for appeal from the school board's decision to dismiss, either to a higher school authority such as the state superintendent, or to the courts.

A number of issues arise over the school board's procedure in dismissing tenure teachers, regardless of the merit of the dismissal. If the school board does not follow the prescribed statutory procedure, its act in dismissing a teacher, no matter how deserved is the dismissal, may be void. Procedure in conducting the hearing is outlined in some laws with more particularity than in others. Regardless of statutory prescriptions, the hearing, to constitute due process, must contain certain essential features.

The teacher whose dismissal is under consideration must be given sufficient notice to prepare his self-defense before the hearing. He should be permitted to appear with counsel. The testimony of witnesses, for and against the teacher, should be taken only after the witnesses have been given an oath or affirmed that they will tell the truth. The right to subpoena witnesses should be allowed the teacher. The evidence heard in the hearing should be restricted to evidence bearing upon the charges of which the teacher has been apprised. Counsel for the teacher should have the right to present argument on the evidence and the law involved. A stenographic transcript of the hearing should be taken so that it will be available in case of an appeal.

Tenure laws, being an abrogation of the freedom of contract, a common-law privilege, are sometimes construed by the courts strictly, because they made a change in the common law. Other courts have said that tenure laws must be interpreted liberally in order to guarantee to the beneficiaries thereof the benefits provided by the law.

In the early days of tenure legislation, allegations were made frequently that the law was unconstitutional because it was class legislation, or because it denied the freedom of contract, or for some like reason. Such constitutional challenges were denied, and every tenure law but one has been upheld. That one was for a city in Oklahoma; it violated the constitutional provisions of the state regarding the expenditure of public funds.

A number of tenure laws are applicable to one city or county or those of a designated category. Other cities and counties have occasionally established local tenure by school board resolution. These local regulations are enforceable so long as not changed by a subsequent resolution of the school board, provided they do not violate

the general law of the state regarding the employment of teachers. The right of a local school board to take away tenure granted locally depends on the same distinction between contract- and legislative-type tenure laws enacted by state legislatures.

Tenure provisions, state or local, provide for teachers a legislative or a contract status, depending on how the law is written. If the teacher has a legislative status, his employment depends entirely on the legislative enactment and if the legislature changes the law, the status of the teacher changes. Thus a teacher on tenure may lose his tenure status if the tenure law is repealed, if it has established legislative status for him. However, if the teacher has a contract status under the tenure law, his employment, although depending partly on the statute, depends also upon the contractual relation created by the statute. Under such circumstances if the legislature changes the tenure law, it does not apply to those teachers who have already acquired tenure because the Federal Constitution forbids the impairment of the obligation of contracts. The change in a tenure law of this type applies only to teachers subsequently employed or those in a probationary status.

The distinction between a contract-type tenure law and a policy-stating legislative tenure law is not always clear. There are several laws which include a reservation of the right to amend or repeal, obviously creating only a legislative status in which no vested rights may accrue. In these states there could be no judicial determination that the law established a contractual status. However, most tenure laws do not contain this reservation, and the question is one which must be decided by the courts. In many states the issue has not come before the courts. Indiana has a judicially designated contract-type tenure law. Where the issue has arisen in other states, their tenure laws have been held to be policy-stating legislation.

A policy-stating tenure law is just as good as a contract-type tenure law, until the legislature changes the policy in a way as to show an intention to deprive tenure teachers of their rights acquired under the previous provisions. In Wisconsin the law was repealed; in several states it has been amended so as to repeal its application to certain kinds of teachers, usually rural or aged teachers.

In summation: under a term contract, a teacher can be dismissed ordinarily only for just cause during the school year, but has no "right" to renewal of the contract; under a spring-notification continuing-contract law (even if called a tenure law) a teacher can be dismissed during the school year only for just cause but also has an enforceable right to renewal of that contract unless notified of non-

renewal by the specified date; under a real tenure law (even if called a continuing-contract law) a tenure teacher cannot be dismissed either during the school year or at the end of the school year except for statutory causes after procedure prescribed by the tenure law.

Tenure laws protect teachers from unjust demotion or reduction in salary as well as dismissal. They do not, however, interfere with the school board's right to transfer teachers, since tenure does not guarantee continuance in the same position. It is usually held that a transfer is not violative of the tenure law unless the change is to a position of such difference in rank and prestige that arbitrariness on the part of the school board is obvious; e.g., a high-school teacher transferred to a small ungraded rural school. Reduction in salary with or without a transfer is usually prevented by tenure laws, regardless of whether they are contract- or legislative-type laws.

Statutory Material
Arkansas Statutes, subsec. 80-1304 (b) (continuing-contract law).

Every contract of employment hereafter made between a teacher and a board of school directors shall be renewed in writing on the same terms and for the same salary, unless increased or decreased by law, for the school year next succeeding the date of termination fixed therein, which renewal may be made by endorsement on the existing contract instrument; unless during the period of such contract or within ten (10) days after the termination of said school term, the teacher shall be notified by the school board in writing delivered in person or mailed to him or her at last and usual known address by registered mail that such contract will not be renewed for such succeeding year, or unless the teacher during the period of the contract or within ten (10) days after close of school shall deliver or mail by registered mail to such school board his or her written resignation as such teacher, or unless such contract is superseded by another contract between the parties. If a teacher quits or refuses to teach in accordance with his or her contract without just cause, she or he is hereby prohibited from teaching elsewhere, during the time for which he or she had been employed.

Statutory note. This is a continuing-contract law, not a tenure law. So long as notice of nonreemployment is given by the specified date, no reason therefor need be given. Statutes similar to this one exist in about five states for all teachers and in some others for probationary teachers.

General Statutes of Connecticut, sec. 10-151.

(a) Any board of education may authorize the superintendent or supervising agent to employ teachers. Any superintendent or supervising agent not authorized to employ teachers shall submit to the board of education nominations for teachers for each of the schools in the town or towns in his

jurisdiction and, from the persons so nominated, teachers may be employed. Such board shall accept or reject such nominations within one month from their submission. If such board rejects such nominations, the superintendent or supervising agent shall submit to such board other nominations and such board may employ teachers from the persons so nominated and shall accept or reject such nominations within one month from their submission. The contract of employment of a teacher shall be in writing and may be terminated at any time for any of the reasons enumerated in subdivisions (1) to (6), inclusive, of subsection (b) of this section, but otherwise it shall be renewed for a second, third or fourth year unless such teacher has been notified in writing prior to March first in one school year that such contract will not be renewed for the following year. Such teacher may, upon written request filed with the board of education within ten days after the receipt of such notice, be entitled to a hearing before the board to be held within fifteen days of such request and at such hearing the reason or reasons for the nonrenewal of the contract shall be made known. The teacher shall have the right to appear with counsel of his choice at such hearing. (b) Beginning with and subsequent to the fourth year of continuous employment of a teacher by a board of education, the contract of employment of a teacher shall be renewed from year to year, except that it may be terminated at any time for one or more of the following reasons: (1) Inefficiency or incompetence; (2) insubordination against reasonable rules of the board of education; (3) moral misconduct; (4) disability, as shown by competent medical evidence; (5) elimination of the position to which the teacher was appointed, if no other position exists to which he may be appointed if qualified; or (6) other due and sufficient cause; provided, prior to terminating a contract, a board of education shall give the teacher concerned a written notice that termination of his contract is under consideration and, upon written request filed by such teacher with such board within five days after receipt of such notice, shall within the next succeeding five days give such teacher a statement in writing of its reasons therefor. Within twenty days after receipt from a board of education of written notice that contract termination is under consideration, the teacher concerned may file with such board a written request for a hearing, which such board shall hold within fifteen days after receipt of such request. Such hearing shall be public if the teacher so requests or the board so designates. The teacher concerned shall have the right to appear with counsel of his choice at such hearing, whether public or private. A board of education shall give the teacher concerned its written decision within fifteen days after such hearing. Nothing herein contained shall deprive a board of education of the power to suspend a teacher from duty immediately when serious misconduct is charged without prejudice to the rights of the teacher as otherwise provided in this section. (c) For the purposes of this section, the term "teacher" shall include each employee of a board of education, below the rank of superintendent or supervising agent, who holds a regular certificate issued by the state board of education. (d) The provisions of any special act regarding the dismissal or employment of teachers shall prevail over the provisions of this section in the event of conflict.

Statutory note. Originally, this Connecticut law was a spring-notification type continuing-contract law; it was amended to include tenure features. Therefore, it illustrates a tenure-type continuing-contract law. Although a tenure law in its technical sense, it is less detailed than the Pennsylvania tenure law which follows. A tenure law should not be evaluated solely on the basis of the amount of detail it contains, provided essentials are contained in it. In fact, some tenure laws contain unnecessary detail; *e.g.*, judicial procedure which is included in the general laws of the state. On the other hand, experience in a state may suggest that inclusion of detail is desirable.

Purdon's Pennsylvania Statutes Annotated, Title 24, § 11-1121 to 11-1132.

Sec. 11—1121. Contracts; execution; form

In all school districts, all contracts with professional employes shall be in writing, in duplicate, and shall be executed on behalf of the board of school directors by the president and secretary and signed by the professional employe.

Each board of school directors in all school districts shall hereafter enter into contracts, in writing, with each professional employe who has satisfactorily completed two (2) years of service in any school district of this Commonwealth. Said contracts shall contain only the following:

"IT IS AGREED by and between .... Professional Employe, and the Board of Directors (or Board of Public Education) of the school district of ...., Pennsylvania, that said professional employe shall, under the authority of the said board and its successors, and subject to the supervision and authority of the properly authorized superintendent of schools or supervising principal, serve as a professional employe in the said school district for a term of .... months, for an annual compensation of $................, payable monthly or semi-monthly during the school term or year, less the contribution required by law to be paid to the Public School Employes' Retirement Fund, and less other proper deductions for loss of time.

"This contract is subject to the provisions of the 'Public School Code of 1949' and the amendments thereto.

"AND IT IS FURTHER AGREED by the parties hereto that none of the provisions of this act may be waived either orally or in writing, and that this contract shall continue in force year after year, with the right of the board of school directors (or board of public education) to increase the compensation over the compensation herein stated, from time to time, as may be provided under the provisions and proper operation of the established salary schedule, if any, for the school district, subject to the provisions of law, without invalidating any other provision of this contract, unless terminated by the professional employe by written resignation presented sixty (60) days before resignation becomes effective, or by the board of school directors (or board of public education) by official written notice presented to the professional employe: Provided, That the said notice

shall designate the cause for the termination and shall state that an opportunity to be heard shall be granted if the said professional employe, within ten (10) days after receipt of the termination notice, presents a written request for such hearing."

Sec. 11—1122. Causes for termination of contract

The only valid causes for termination of a contract heretofore or hereafter entered into with a professional employe shall be immorality, incompetency, intemperance, cruelty, persistent negligence, mental derangement, advocation of or participating in un-American or subversive doctrines, persistent and wilful violation of the school laws of this Commonwealth on the part of the professional employe: Provided, That boards of school directors may terminate the service of any professional employe who has attained to the age of sixty-two, except a professional employe who is a member of the old age and survivors' insurance system pursuant to the provisions of the act, approved the first day of June, one thousand nine hundred fifty-six (Pamphlet Laws 1973). In such case the board may terminate the service of any such professional employe at the age at which the employe becomes eligible to receive benefits under the Federal Social Security Act: Provided, That the services of such employe shall not be terminated before age sixty-two.

Nothing within the foregoing enumeration of causes, shall be interpreted to conflict with the retirement of professional employes upon proper evidence of disability, or the election by professional employes to retire during the period of voluntary retirement, or the authority of the board of school directors to require professional employes to retire during said period of voluntary retirement, or the compulsion on the part of professional employes to retire at the attainment of age seventy.

Sec. 11—1123. Rating system

In determining whether a professional employe shall be dismissed for incompetency, and in rating the services of a temporary professional employe, the professional employe or temporary professional employe shall be rated by an approved rating system which shall give due consideration to personality, preparation, technique, and pupil reaction, in accordance with standards and regulations for such scoring as defined by rating cards to be prepared by the Department of Public Instruction, and to be revised, from time to time, by the Department of Public Instruction with the cooperation and advice of a committee appointed by the Superintendent of Public Instruction, including representation from county and district superintendents of schools, classroom teachers, school directors, school supervisors, and such other groups or interests as the Superintendent of Public Intruction may deem appropriate. Rating shall be done by or under the supervision of the county or district superintendent of schools or, if so directed by him, the same may be done by an associate superintendent, an assistant superintendent, a supervising principal, a supervisor, or a principal, who has supervision over the work of the professional employe or temporary professional employe who is being rated: Provided, That no unsatisfactory rating shall be valid unless approved by the county or district superintendent.

Sec. 11—1124. Causes for suspension

Any board of school directors may suspend the necessary number of professional employes, for any of the causes hereinafter enumerated:

(1) Substantial decrease in pupil enrollment in the school district;

(2) Curtailment or alteration of the educational program on recommendation of the superintendent, concurred in by the board of school directors, approved by the Department of Public Instruction, as a result of substantial decline in class or course enrollments or to conform with standards of organization or educational activities required by law or recommended by the Department of Public Instruction;

(3) Consolidation of schools, whether within a single district, through a merger of districts, or as a result of joint board agreements, when such consolidation makes it unnecessary to retain the full staff of professional employes.

Sec. 11—1125. Suspensions and reinstatements; how made

(a) Whenever a board of school directors decreases the size of the staff of professional employes, the suspensions to be made shall be determined by the county superintendent of schools or the district superintendent, as the case may be, on the basis of efficiency rank determined by ratings made in accordance with standards and regulations, determined by rating cards prepared by the Department of Public Instruction, as required by section one thousand one hundred twenty-three of this act. It shall be the duty of boards of school directors to cause to be established a permanent record system, containing ratings for each professional employe employed within the district. Copies of all ratings for the year shall be transmitted to the professional employe upon his or her request, or, if any rating during the year is unsatisfactory, a copy of same shall be transmitted to the professional employe concerned. No professional employe shall be dismissed under this act unless such rating records have been kept on file by the board of school directors: Provided, That boards of school directors in districts under supervision of the county superintendent may establish a filing system for rating cards in the office of the county superintendent of schools.

(b) In cases in which suspensions are to be made, professional employes shall be retained on the basis of seniority rights, acquired within the school district of current employment, where no differences in ratings are found. Seniority rights shall also prevail where there is no substantial difference in rating. In cases where there are substantial differences in rating of those under consideration for suspension, seniority shall be given consideration in accordance with principles and standards of weighting incorporated in the rating cards.

(c) No suspended employe shall be prevented from engaging in other occupation during the period of such suspension. Suspended professional employes shall be reinstated in the inverse order of their suspension. No new appointment shall be made while there are suspended professional employes available, who are properly certified to fill such vacancies.

Sec. 11—1126. Public hearings; exceptions

All hearings, under the provisions of this article or any other provision

of the school laws pertaining to the dismissal or the termination of contracts of professional employes, shall be public, unless otherwise requested by the party against whom the complaint is made.

Sec. 11—1127. Procedure on dismissals; charges; notice; hearing

Before any professional employe having attained a status of permanent tenure is dismissed by the board of school directors, such board of school directors shall furnish such professional employe with a detailed written statement of the charges upon which his or her proposed dismissal is based and shall conduct a hearing. A written notice signed by the president and attested by the secretary of the board of school directors shall be forwarded by registered mail to the professional employe setting forth the time and place when and where such professional employe will be given an opportunity to be heard either in person or by counsel, or both, before the board of school directors and setting forth a detailed statement of the charges. Such hearing shall not be sooner than ten (10) days nor later than fifteen (15) days after such written notice. At such hearing all testimony offered, including that of complainants and their witnesses, as well as that of the accused professional employe and his or her witnesses, shall be recorded by a competent disinterested public stenographer whose services shall be furnished by the school district at its expense. Any such hearing may be postponed, continued or adjourned.

Sec. 11—1128. Subpoenas; testimony

The board shall have power to issue subpoenas requiring the attendance of witnesses at any hearing and shall do so at the request of the party against whom a complaint is made. If any person shall refuse to appear and testify in answer to any subpoena issued by the board, any party interested may petition the court of common pleas of the county setting forth the facts, which court shall thereupon issue its subpoena commanding such person to appear before it, there to testify as to the matters being inquired into. Any person refusing to testify before the court shall be held for contempt. All testimony at any hearing shall be taken under oath, and any member of the board of school directors shall have power to administer oaths to such witnesses.

Sec. 11—1129. Vote required for dismissals

After fully hearing the charges or complaints and hearing all witnesses produced by the board and the person against whom the charges are pending, and after full, impartial and unbiased consideration thereof, the board of school directors shall by a two-thirds vote of all the members thereof, to be recorded by roll call, determine whether such charges or complaints have been sustained and whether the evidence substantiates such charges and complaints, and if so determined shall discharge such professional employe. If less than two-thirds of all of the members of the board vote in favor of discharge, the professional employe shall be retained and the complaint shall be dismissed.

No member of any board of school directors shall vote on any roll call if he is related as father, mother, brother, sister, husband, wife, son, daughter, stepson, stepdaughter, grandchild, nephew, niece, first cousin, sister-in-law, brother-in-law, uncle or aunt to the professional employe involved or to any of the parties instituting the complaint.

Sec. 11—1130. Notice of discharge; procedure on decision favorable to employe

A written notice of any decision of the board of school directors discharging a professional employe, shall be sent by registered mail to such professional employe at his or her last known address within ten (10) days after such hearing is actually concluded.

In all cases where the final decision is in favor of the professional employe, the charges made shall be physically expunged from the records of the board of school directors, but a complete official transcript of the records of the hearing shall be delivered to the one against whom the charges were made. In all such cases there shall be no abatement of salary or compensation.

Sec. 11-1131. Appeals to superintendent of public instruction

In case the professional employe concerned considers himself [enrolled bill reads "him"] or herself aggrieved by the action of the board of school directors, an appeal by petition, setting forth the grounds for such appeal, may be taken to the Superintendent of Public Instruction at Harrisburg. Such appeal shall be filed within thirty (30) days after receipt by registered mail of the written notice of the decision of the board. A copy of such appeal shall be served by registered mail on the secretary of the school board.

The Superintendent of Public Instruction shall fix a day and time for hearing, which shall not be sooner than ten (10) days nor more than thirty (30) days after presentation of such petition, and shall give written notice to all parties interested.

The Superintendent of Public Instruction shall review the official transcript of the record of the hearing before the board, and may hear and consider such additional testimony as he may deem advisable to enable him to make a proper order. At said hearing the litigants shall have the right to be heard in person or by counsel or both.

After hearing and argument and reviewing all the testimony filed or taken before him, the Superintendent of Public Instruction shall enter such order, either affirming or reversing the action of the board of school directors, as to him appears just and proper.

Sec. 11-1132. Appeals to court

(a) The ruling or decision of the Superintendent of Public Instruction shall be final, unless, within thirty (30) days after receipt by registered mail of written notice of the decision or order of the Superintendent of Public Instruction, an appeal, which may be taken by either party, is taken therefrom to the court of common pleas of the county in which the district is located, except in Allegheny County where the appeal shall be to County Court of Allegheny. A copy of such appeal shall be filed, in writing, in the office of the prothonotary, and a copy shall be served on the Superintendent of Public Instruction, either by filing it in the office of the Superintendent of Public Instruction or by delivering the same to the Superintendent of Public Instruction.

(b) When appeal is taken from the decision of the Superintendent of Public Instruction to the court of common pleas of the county in which the

district is located or to County Court of Allegheny County, the judge of the court to whom such petition is presented shall fix a date for hearing by the court, which shall be not sooner than ten (10) days nor more than twenty (20) days after the presentation of such petition. If the professional employe aggrieved shall so request in his petition, such hearing shall be de novo. Upon the hearing of said petition, the court shall make whatever order it considers just, either affirming or reversing the action of the Superintendent of Public Instruction, and stating plainly whether the professional employe is to be discharged or is to be retained.

Statutory note. The Pennsylvania tenure law has been quoted at length to show the detail that some such laws contain. This state is unusual also in that the tenure law contains the contract form. Furthermore, Pennsylvania has gone farther than most states in rating probationary teachers before granting them tenure status.

Laws of Florida, 1947. Chapter 24745, sec. 9.
[Applicable to Orange County only.]

A teacher shall lose his or her status as a "contract teacher" (and in that event shall not be entitled to have any provision for reemployment in her contract of employment) under any of the following circumstances:

(a) During each five-year period failure to earn six semester hours of college credit or what may be defined by the Board of Public Instruction of Orange County, Florida, by regulation in advance of such failure as the equivalent of such six semester hours of college credit. So far as such credit is college credit, same shall be earned in a recognized institution of higher learning approved by the State Superintendent of Public Instruction of Florida. The first period shall extend from January 1, 1948, through December 31, 1952, and these five-year periods shall follow in successive calendar sequence thereafter;

(b) Failure to comply with any other rules and regulations regarding professional advancement adopted, in advance of such failure, by the Board of Public Instruction of Orange County; the County Board of Public Instruction of Orange County shall determine all questions regarding compliance with this section; and its determination shall be final. A teacher who has lost his or her status as a "contract teacher" under this Section or under Section 5 hereof shall fulfill anew the requirements as set forth in Section 2 of this Act [having to do with probationary period] before being reinstated as a "contract teacher" under this Act.

Statutory note. Many teachers are required to meet professional growth standards to exchange a certificate for one of a higher grade, to move to a higher step on the salary schedule, or to acquire tenure status. No statewide tenure law includes professional growth requirements for tenure teachers. The above is the only law under which a teacher may lose tenure status for failure to fulfill professional growth requirements.

TEACHER'S CONTRACT

STATE OF MARYLAND,

COUNTY OF ....

IT IS HEREBY AGREED by and between the COUNTY BOARD OF EDUCATION of ....
.... County and ....
that the said teacher shall be and is hereby employed to teach in the public schools of the said County as
...., subject to
assignment by the County Superintendent or transfer to some other teaching position within the County, provided
that if the transfer be made during the school year or after the opening of the school *for any year*, the salary shall
not be reduced for the *remainder of the year*. The salary of said teacher shall be fixed by the County Board of
Education, which salary shall be not less than the minimum salary provided by law.

AND IT IS FURTHER AGREED that the teacher named herein shall become a member of the Maryland
Teachers' Retirement System as of date on which h......... teaching service begins.

AND IT IS FURTHER AGREED that the said teacher will not vacate the position to which assigned during
any school year, except in case of emergency, of which the County Board of Education shall judge.

AND IT IS FURTHER AGREED that either of the parties to this contract may terminate it at the end of the
first or second school year by giving thirty days' notice in writing to the other during the month of June or July.

AND IT IS FURTHER AGREED that if the teacher named herein wishes to vacate his or her position after
the second year, thirty days' notice in writing shall be given the County Board of Education during the month of
June or July, except in case of emergency, of which the County Board of Education shall judge.

If any of the conditions of this contract shall be violated by the teacher named herein, salary already accrued
will be forfeited, in the discretion of the County Board of Education.

This contract shall continue from year to year, subject to the aforegoing conditions, provided that if the teacher, on recommendation of the County Superintendent, is suspended by the County Board of Education in accordance
with the provisions of Sections 64 and 102 of Article 77 of the Annotated Code of Maryland, 1957 Edition, said
teacher shall have the right of appeal to the State Superintendent of Schools, if the decision of said board is not
unanimous.

This contract is made in accordance with the provisions of the school law, and is subject to Sections 64, 99, and
102 of Article 77 of the Annotated Code of Maryland, and any amendments thereto, and will be filed among the records of the County Board of Education.

The said teacher on his or her part hereby accepts said appointment, to take effect on the ....
.... day of .... 19...............

Date of signing this contract .... 19...............
WITNESS OUR HANDS:

(SEAL)

....
President, County Board of Education

....
Secretary, County Board of Education

....
Teacher

OATH OF OFFICE

I, ..., having been appointed a teacher in the public schools of
.... County, State of Maryland, do swear (or affirm) that I will obey
the school law of the State of Maryland and all rules and regulations governing my position as teacher, passed in
pursuance thereof by the proper authority; that I will, to the best of my skill and judgment, diligently and faith-
fully, without partiality or prejudice, discharge the duties of a teacher in the public schools of said county, including attendance on teachers' institutes and associations when legally called thereto and will honestly and correctly
make all reports as required by law or the school authorities of said county.

....
Teacher

STATE OF MARYLAND .... County, to wit:

Sworn (or affirmed) before the subscriber ....

by ...., teacher, who in my presence has thereto

affixed h............ signature this ... . day of ...., 19...............

NOTARIAL SEAL

....
Signature

THOS. G. PULLEN, JR.
STATE SUPERINTENDENT OF SCHOOLS

MARYLAND STATE DEPARTMENT OF EDUCATION

Baltimore 1

The sections of the law referred to in the body of the prescribed form for teacher's contract, as printed on the other side of this sheet, are given below. The form of contract was adopted by the State Board of Education, June 6, 1918, under the authority of Section 21 (Annotated Code of Maryland, 1957 edition) of the school law.

THOS. G. PULLEN, JR.

State Superintendent of Schools

Annotated Code of Maryland, 1957 edition, Article 77, Sec. 99

99. No person shall be employed as county superintendent, assistant superintendent, supervisor, principal or teacher unless such person shall hold a certificate issued by the superintendent of public education and for the grade required for the position, but any county of the State may require as a condition of employment a higher standard for a certificate of a similar kind and grade than is required by the State. Provided that all teachers' certificates and diplomas in force on April 18, 1916, shall continue in force for the full time for which they were issued or are valid, and shall remain valid for the grade and position for which issued. Provided, that no renewal or extension of such certificates shall be granted under this section by the State superintendent of schools, nor shall the renewal or extension of any certificate by a county superintendent expiring between the time this section goes into effect and September the thirtieth, 1916, be for more than one year. Provided also that no certificate issued by a county superintendent of schools between April 18, 1916, and September thirtieth, 1916, shall be valid for more than one year. Provided further that no certificate heretofore issued shall be valid after April 18, 1916, for appointment to the position of county superintendent, assistant superintendent, supervisor, high school principal or elementary school principal in elementary schools having three or more teachers, including the principal, except in case of persons holding the foregoing positions on April 18, 1916, and then valid only for the particular position they are then holding and in the particular county.

Annotated Code of Maryland, 1957 edition, Article 77, Sec. 110

110. (Membership.) The membership of this retirement system shall be composed as follows: (1) All persons who shall become teachers after the date as of which the retirement system is established, **(June 1, 1927) (For exceptions see remainder of this section.)**

Annotated Code of Maryland, 1957 edition, Article 77, Sec. 102

102. Any county board of education may, on the recommendation of the county superintendent, suspend any teacher, principal, supervisor, or assistant superintendent for immorality, dishonesty, intemperance, insubordination, incompetency, or wilful neglect of duty, and may recommend to the state superintendent of schools the revocation of the certificate of such person, stating in writing the grounds for such recommendations, and giving an opportunity, upon not less than ten days' notice, to be heard in defense, in person or by counsel, and the state superintendent of schools may order such investigations as he may deem necessary. If he approves the recommendation, the teacher's certificate shall be revoked and the teacher shall be dropped from the service.

Annotated Code of Maryland, 1957 edition, Article 77, Sec. 64

64. The county board of education shall appoint, on the written recommendation of the county superintendent, all principals and assistant teachers, and fix their salaries, subject to the provisions of Chapter 8 of this Article. The county board may suspend or dismiss without appeal any teacher so appointed, on the written recommendation of the county superintendent, for immorality, misconduct in office, insubordination, incompetency, or wilful neglect of duty, provided that the charges be stated in writing, and that the teacher be given an opportunity to be heard by the board upon not less than ten days' notice; provided further that in all cases when the board is not unanimous in its decision to suspend or dismiss, the right of appeal shall lie to the state superintendent of schools.

By-law 14

All contracts with teachers, both principals and assistants, employed after June 1, 1918, shall be in writing and on one of two contract blanks furnished by the State Board of Education. For teachers who hold non-emergency certificates the blank entitled "Teacher's Contract," the form for which follows, shall be used; for teachers who hold emergency certificates, the blank entitled "Emergency Teacher's Contract," the form for which also follows, shall be used. The contract shall be signed by the teacher, and the president and the secretary of the county board of education, and when so signed shall be filed by the secretary in the office of the board; provided teachers employed prior to June 1, 1918, and continuing in the service, shall have the contract herein prescribed when they so desire. The following shall be the forms of contract and, under the foregoing conditions, no others shall be recognized:

(Only the non-emergency "Teacher's Contract" is printed on the reverse side of this page.)

(Over)

Contract note. The Maryland contract is given to teachers when initially employed; note that it is an indefinite contract, subject to termination at the end of the first or the second year. This, in other words, makes the probationary period two years.

Like most contracts for the employment of teachers, the Maryland contract includes a loyalty oath. On the reverse side of the contract is the verbatim language of the statutes to which the teachers agree. In most contracts there is a general reference to the school laws of the state, or, at most, reference to some by citation. The teacher, then, is presumed to know these laws or look them up.

The Maryland contract contains a provision for forfeiture of accrued salary in the event that the teacher does not fulfill the contract. Similar penalties will be discussed in Chapter 4 on Resignation and Abandonment of Contract.

The contract form which must be used is included in the Pennsylvania tenure law. In many other states, the employment contract form is state-adopted by the state board of education and no other can be used. Other state departments have recommended forms which local school boards may use if they wish, but they have the option of preparing another for local use. Though some teachers are employed without use of a contract form, the policy is unwise.

Case Material

Thomas v. Bagwell et al., 123 Colo. 169, 226 P. (2d) 563 (Colorado, 1950). [Preliminary negotiations not resulting in contract of employment.]

Frank E. Thomas brought an action against "Lavere Bagwell, J. D. Haynie, and H. B. Silvers, as the Board of Directors of Manassa School District No. 30 in the County of Conejos and State of Colorado" to obtain a mandatory injunction and other relief. Trial was had to the court, at the conclusion of which judgment was entered for defendants. Plaintiff seeks a review by writ of error. . . .

Plaintiff testified that in March 1947, he wrote each member of the school board, advising that he was available for appointment as a teacher in said school district for the school year 1947-48, and until September 8, 1947, had no contract of employment. On September 7, 1947, he was notified by his daughter or son-in-law that Mr. Haynie wanted him to appear on Monday morning, September 8, 1947, to commence his duties as a teacher. On September 8, 1947, plaintiff appeared at the school house and found everything in a state of confusion and on that evening had a conversation with Mr. Haynie and Mr. Bagwell, during which he was advised

that he was to be employed commencing a week from that day in event another teacher did not desire the position, and that his salary was to be $400 in excess of that paid other teachers, which would make him a salary of $2,050 for the school year. He further testified that the other teacher had not reported for duty; he demanded that duties be assigned to him, and he learned that there had been some rearrangement of classes and that there was no available place for him. The minutes of board meeting held on September 3, 1947 were admitted in evidence and contained the following with reference to plaintiff's employment: "Due to a shortage of teachers it was proposed to contact Frank Thomas as possibly available. H. B. Silvers voted against this saying it would disrupt our system." No subsequent formal meeting of the board of directors was held at which plaintiff's employment was discussed.

Director Bagwell, called as a witness for cross examination under the statute and subsequently on direct examination, testified that Thomas' application had never been considered by the board of directors and that there had never been an agreement between him and director Haynie for plaintiff's employment. This witness further testified that on September 8, 1947 he and Mr. Haynie had a conversation with plaintiff in which plaintiff was told that another teacher had been employed but that if the other teacher failed to report for duty, then he and Mr. Haynie would see plaintiff if they wanted his services. This witness testified that neither he and Mr. Haynie promised plaintiff an appointment in event the other teacher did not report for duty, and also testified that there was no discussion whatever as to salary. . . .

The only point specified as error is that the court committed an error in law in determining that the evidence did not disclose a contract of employment. . . .

Here was a conflict in the evidence with sufficient competent evidence to support the court in its findings, and its findings and judgment will not be disturbed. . . .

Case note. Appeal was taken because the lower court had held that the evidence was insufficient to disclose a contract. The appellate court agreed. The teacher thought he was employed but his conversations with members of the board constituted preliminary negotiations only. No formal board action had been taken.

This case illustrates the informality sometimes used in the selection of teachers in small towns. On the other hand, however, it is possible that in large cities preliminary interviews with school officers may mislead applicants into thinking that they have been employed. The case is a warning to watch out for the distinction between preliminary negotiations and employment.

Kuehn v. School District No. 70, Goodhue County, 221 Minn. 443, 22 N.W. (2d) 220 (Minnesota, 1946). [Teacher sought to collect balance of contract salary for remainder of term after dismissal.]

This is an appeal from a judgment in a case involving the legality of the discharge of a nontenure school teacher. The school board of School District No. 70, Goodhue County, engaged plaintiff to teach during the 1943-44 session of school at a salary of $100 a month. She assumed her duties in the fall of 1943 and taught until April 4, 1944, when she received the following notice:

"April 4, 1944.

"Miss Kuehn:

"We the school board, hereby give you notice that you have by all means, not lived up to your contract, as you have agreed to [sic].

"You have been told at different times that your teaching school was not satisfactory.

"You have not followed your rules and school regulations according to laws.

"You have not put in your school classes, you have left out classes days and days.

"You have not put in full hours at school which is required of law for teachers to do.

"Therefore we expel you as teacher of district 70.

"Yours truly,
"School Board.
"O. J. Heydmann
"John Brunckhorst
"Albert Tiedemann

"P.S. We hereby pay you in full."

No hearing was granted plaintiff on the charges against her. Upon receipt of the above notice, she informed the board that she was ready, willing and able to perform her contract. Her offer was not accepted.

She commenced this action for the balance due on the contract upon the theory that the action of the school board had been arbitrary and unwarranted. The case was tried before a jury. The court instructed the jury that if it found that the action of the board had been arbitrary and capricious or in bad faith it should find for plaintiff. The jury found for plaintiff and defendant moved for a new trial. This was denied solely on the ground that, since in dismissing a teacher the board acted in a quasi-judicial capacity, plaintiff was entitled to a notice and hearing before dismissal and that the action of the board in not proceeding in this manner was lacking due process of law as arbitrary and capricious. The court did not pass on the sufficiency of the evidence or the credibility of plaintiff's testimony, since the denial of a hearing was conclusive that the board's action was arbitrary.

Defendant has assigned as error this ruling by the court.

Defendant has the statutory power to discharge "for cause." Minn. St. 1941, sec. 125.06. . . .

The statutes do not provide a procedure for the removal of a nontenure teacher "for cause." However, even though no method of procedure is set out in the statutes for the guidance of the school board, a teacher is, never-

theless, entitled to notice of charges made against him and a fair hearing before an impartial board.

Case note. This case was the first of this kind. There has been only one other, at least in a court of record. In the absence of legislation a school board has been held to have power to dismiss a teacher before the end of the contract without a hearing, provided only that there is justifiable cause for dismissal. The justification is usually part of the evidence in a breach-of-contract action by the dismissed teacher. Here, the court did not go into the causes for dismissal but decided in favor of the teacher on procedural grounds. Due process of law is a requirement of the Federal Constitution. The Fifth Amendment reads "No person shall be . . . deprived of life, liberty, or property, without due process of law. . . ."

Eastman v. School District No. 1 of Lewis and Clark County, 120 Mont. 63, 180 P. (2d) 472 (Montana, 1947). [Teacher employed under continuing-contract law sought to compel board to continue her employment.]

The following facts material to the determination of the case are established by the evidence: Miss Eastman, who will be hereafter designated as the plaintiff, is a school teacher, the holder of a Bachelor of Arts degree and a secondary life certificate authorizing her to teach in Grades VI to XII in any school in the State of Montana. Plaintiff first started teaching in School District No. 1 of Lewis and Clark county in the year 1938. She continued to teach in said position continuously up to the school year of 1944-45 under successive contracts of employment with the trustees of the school district. On April 25, 1945, plaintiff received from the defendant school board a letter written on the letterhead of said board which, omitting only the names of the trustees which were printed on the letterhead, reads as follows:

"Helena, Montana
"April 25, 1945

"Miss Violet M. Eastman
"229 6th Avenue
"Helena, Montana

"Dear Miss Eastman:

"The School Board of District #1 at a meeting held last night, Tuesday, April 24th, 1945, decided not to renew your contract for the 1945-46 school year.

"Sincerely yours,

"s/J. F. McBride
"J. F. McBride
"Secretary."

The above letter was sent to the plaintiff by the secretary of the school board pursuant to the following action of the trustees of said school district, as appears from the minutes of said board of April 24, 1945. . . .

First, did the notice of April 25, 1945, which was sent to plaintiff by the defendant school board substantially comply with the requirements of Section 1075, Revised Codes of Montana, 1935? . . .

It would almost seem that the very asking of the question is sufficient to indicate its answer without reference to decided cases involving similar facts. Section 1015 reads in part as follows: "Subdivision 2. . . . no teacher shall be employed except under resolution agreed to by a majority of the board of trustees at a special or regular meeting. . . . All contracts of employment of teachers, authorized by proper resolution of a board of trustees, shall be in writing and executed in duplicate by the chairman and clerk of the board, for the district, and by the teacher." Under this statute no person can be employed to teach in the public schools without a contract with the board of school trustees. The so-called teachers' tenure act (sec. 1075, Rev. Codes) which is operative after the third consecutive year of a teacher's employment does not do away with the necessity of having a contract as required by Section 1015. The only effect of said Section 1075 is to renew the teacher's existing contract for another year by operation of law, after her election for the third consecutive year unless the notice specified in said section is given. . . .

Our conclusions relative to the construction to be given Section 1075 find further support in the fact that while said section is commonly referred to as a "teachers' tenure Act" it is not in fact a complete teachers' tenure law but only partially covers the matter of retention or discharge of teachers. The act makes no provision for any showing of cause or for a hearing before a teacher can be discharged. . . .

Dissenting opinions: (1) The powers of boards of trustees and the rights, tenure, and status of teachers in the public schools of this state are fixed, limited and determined by the provisions of the School Code. . . . The contract of a nontenure teacher is for the period of one year or less. It *expires* annually. It must be renewed each year or the nontenure teacher loses her employment. The board of school trustees is empowered to terminate such contract before its expiration only for the causes and in the manner contemplated by Section 1085, Revised Codes of Montana of 1935. . . . *After* the election of any teacher for the third consecutive year in any public school district in the state, such teacher so elected thereby acquires the status and rights of a tenure teacher. Sec. 1075, Rev. Codes. Such teacher's contract, by operation of law, becomes a continuing contract. *It does not expire. It requires no renewal.* It can be terminated by the board of school trustees only for the causes and in the manner contemplated by Sections 1075 and 1085, Revised Codes. . . . The unexpired contract of a teacher in the public schools may be terminated by the board of school trustees for cause only after a hearing. . . .

(2) The legislature enacted a tenure law. They called it a tenure law. In construing such law we must look to the purpose sought to be achieved by

the legislature and we must construe the law in order to protect the individuals for whose benefit the law was enacted.

Keeping in mind the purpose of the Act, the provision in Section 1075, Revised Codes of Montana 1935, that the "board of trustees shall by majority vote of its members on or before the first day of May give notice in writing to said teacher or principal that he has been reelected or that his services will not be required for the ensuing year"; can only mean that no teacher will be needed to teach in the district the following year. . . .

If the phrase "his services will not be required" is construed to mean that the board may refuse to rehire the teacher for trivial or undisclosed reasons and emphasis is placed upon the word "his" without regard to the reason for the Act or the other portions of the school law, then the Act is nullified, the will of the legislature ignored and the persons for whose benefit the legislation enacted are left in a worse position than they would have been had there been no legislation at all. . . .

. . . the plain intention of the legislature in enacting Section 1075 was to provide for a continuing contract for an indefinite period for teachers, who had demonstrated their efficiency and qualifications after a three-year probationary period. Such teacher can only be dismissed under the provisions of Section 1085 and after a hearing before the board. . . .

Case note. At this time, Montana's was the only state continuing-contract law requiring a probationary period. That was its only similarity with real tenure laws at the time of this case. The majority opinion of the court is in line with the prevailing view that continuing-contract laws provide only that the annual contract is automatically renewed if no notice of nonrenewal is sent by the specified date. Tenure provisions regarding statement of reasons and a hearing before dismissal are not included in this type of continuing-contract law. Actually there was no "dismissal" as the contract for the year had been completely performed, and termination of employment was merely the nonrenewal of the contract. After this case was decided, the Montana law was amended so as to include real tenure provisions.

Contrast the reasoning of the majority opinion in this case with the reasoning in the Kuehn case (see page 41). There, due process was said to require a hearing before dismissal during the term of contract. If a continuing-contract law were construed to provide an indefinite contract from year to year, due process might be called upon to prevent termination of employment at the end of any school year without a hearing. To date, however, no court has so interpreted a continuing-contract law.

Hovland v. School District No. 52, 128 Mont. 507, 278 P. (2d) 211 (Montana, 1954). [Dismissal of teacher for noncooperation with superintendent.]

This is an action by plaintiff, Gladys Hovland, a teacher in the Absarokee high school, against school district No. 52 of Stillwater County, Montana, for salary lost by her alleged wrongful discharge in violation of her teacher's contract by the school board of such school district, after unsuccessful appeals to the county superintendent of schools and the superintendent of public instruction. A jury which tried the issues returned a verdict in her favor in the amount of $2,053.34. From a judgment rendered on such verdict, the defendant school district appealed.

The teacher's contract between plaintiff and defendant dated August 28, 1948, in part provides:

> "(1) That the teacher is hereby employed to teach, as and where assigned, in the schools of the District for and during the school year beginning on or about the 7th day of September, 1948, and thereafter continuing for a period of not less than one hundred and seventy-five nor more than one hundred and eighty-five teaching days;
> "(2) That this contract and the rights and the obligations of the parties thereunder shall be governed by the laws of the State of Montana, and by the rules and regulations adopted by the Board of Trustees of the District, which are made a part hereof by reference. . . ."

Plaintiff was discharged on November 15, 1948.

The trial judge, without objection, properly gave the jury instruction No. 10, which is as follows:

> "You are instructed that our statutes [R.C.M. 1947, §75-2411] give a school board the right and power to discharge a teacher for only the following causes:
> "(1) Immorality, (2) Incompetence, (3) Unfitness, (4) Violation of rules.
> "And, therefore, if you find from a preponderance of the evidence that the school board dismissed the plaintiff on any ground than those listed above, then you must find that the school board breached its contract with the plaintiff."

The "rules," a violation of which gives the school board the right and power to discharge, are the rules referred to in the teacher's contract, viz., "rules and regulations adopted by the Board of Trustees of the District, which are made a part hereof by reference."

The defendant school board attempted to justify the discharge of plaintiff upon but one ground set out in instruction No. 10, a violation of a rule or rules, not of the school board, but of the superintendent of the high school, and it was neither alleged nor proven that such rules of the superintendent were part of "the rules and regulations adopted by the Board of Trustees of the District, which are made a part" of the teacher's contract.

The answer of the defendant and the evidence adduced thereunder show that plaintiff was discharged because of "written charges against plaintiff to the board of trustees of said defendant school district" made by Virgil T. Carmichael, school superintendent. These charges were made in a letter

dated November 8, 1948, addressed to the school trustees of school district No. 52. In part it states:

> "Dear Trustees: I recommend that you discharge Mrs. Gladys M. Hovland from the position of teacher in Absarokee High School for lack of cooperation with the Superintendent of the Absarokee Schools.
>
> "Following are some instances of lack of cooperation. From the first day of school she began complaining about the way the high school was run and has never failed to complain about many things. She just started in to complain the first day about taking her turn staying at noon hour one week each month as requested by the superintendent. Since which time she has complained about something at most teachers' meetings. . . ."

The letter which takes up five pages of the transcript, continues throughout in much the same vein.

The testimony of school trustee Campbell, the only school trustee to testify, shows that plaintiff was discharged because of "noncooperation charged by V. T. Carmichael." . . .

A reading of the entire record leads to but one conclusion and that is: Plaintiff was discharged solely for alleged lack of cooperation or noncooperation with the superintendent of schools, in failing to obey certain rules he laid down.

Since the teacher's contract did not provide that plaintiff could be discharged for failure to cooperate with such superintendent of schools, and it was not shown by the rules and regulations adopted by the Board of Trustees of the District, which "were made a part" of the teacher's contract, that failure to so cooperate constituted a ground for such discharge, the school board's act in discharging plaintiff was an arbitrary one and constituted a violation of said teacher's contract.

Under the evidence and the instructions of the court, the jury properly brought in its verdict in favor of the plaintiff.

For the reasons stated the judgment of the district court is affirmed.

Concurring opinion: No public school official or board is above the laws of this state. None is clothed with arbitrary power. All are answerable to the people and their laws. The dismissal of the teacher, Gladys Hovland, was in violation of her express contract with the district. It was brought about by the arbitrary action of the school superintendent. . . .

Neither the trustees nor the school superintendent may capriciously exercise arbitrary powers of dismissal in violation of a teacher's contract rights.

Case note. This case shows poor judgment on the part of the superintendent and board. The dismissal likely would have been upheld if the charge had been incompetence or unfitness since these terms are broadly interpreted. An alternative would have been for the superintendent to present his list of rules to the board for adoption as board

rules, after which the charge of violation of rules could have been sustained.

Many school administrators object to tenure laws on the ground that they prevent the dismissal of undesirable teachers. Usually, such opinions are based on isolated instances such as in this case where proper foundation for the dismissal had not been laid.

Travis v. Teter et al., 370 Pa. 326, 87 A. (2d) 177 (Pennsylvania, 1952). [Rating of probationary teachers prerequisite to acquisition of tenure status.]

The facts were as follows: Appellant was employed as a temporary teacher (without tenure status) in the Lehman Township Schools during the school years 1947-1948 and 1948-1949. Appellant, during the period from 1947 to 1949, received three intermediate satisfactory ratings. On June 29, 1949, appellant received from the county superintendent an *unsatisfactory* rating, covering the entire two year period. As a result of this unsatisfactory rating, appellant was not offered a contract of employment as a professional permanent teacher by the School District of Lehman Township, and this is probably the main reason for her suit.

Appellant's position is that the unsatisfactory rating is void (1) because the county superintendent did not exercise his own judgment in giving the rating; (2) because the supervising principal participated in the rating; (3) because the rating was given on June 29, 1949, several weeks after the expiration of the school term; and (4) because the county superintendent failed to hold a hearing on appellant's rating and consequently she was deprived of due process.

Plaintiff's first and second contentions will be considered together. The duty of the county superintendent with respect to rating a temporary teacher is set forth in the Act of May 18, 1911, as follows: "It shall be the duty of the county superintendent of schools . . . to notify each temporary professional employe, at least twice each year during the period of his or her employment, of the professional quality, professional progress, and rating of his or her services. . . ."

The rating made by Mr. Teter, the county superintendent of schools, required a consideration of four major factors: I. Personality; II. Preparation; III. Technique; and IV. Pupil Reaction. These four headings were subdivided into 27 parts pertaining to specific characteristics and qualifications. Mr. Teter had been a teacher for 31 years and had served as assistant superintendent of schools for 10 years and superintendent for several years. He did not know plaintiff personally, although he and her husband were members of the same Kiwanis Club. Mr. Teter, in spite of many complaints concerning plaintiff's teaching, her personality, her preparation, and pupil reaction, gave her a satisfactory rating in the first three quarters of her two year term. This was mainly because the criticisms were verbal and were not accompanied by an anecdotal written record or report, and in the hope that she would improve, or would not continue teaching after her two year contract.

In spite of appellant's argument to the contrary, it seems hardly necessary to point out that three satisfactory ratings do not of themselves entitle a teacher to four satisfactory ratings; and four, not three, were required for this plaintiff to become entitled to the tenure status of a permanent teacher. In a four lap race the leader at the end of the third lap is often not the winner and sometimes does not even finish.

Mr. Teter rated plaintiff as *unsatisfactory* for the two year period. His rating was based on adverse reports which he had received from time to time from various persons as to plaintiff's performance as a teacher, including a number of reports from the assistant county superintendent, and from the supervising principal, and from the succeeding supervising principal; also discussions with the president and with the secretary of the school board, and on at least two occasions with the father of one of the pupils, who in turn had discussed the plaintiff's qualifications with the parents of other pupils; as well as on the adverse written anecdotal report of the supervising principal. All of these persons considered plaintiff unsatisfactory and their comments and criticisms were adverse. The anecdotal record which was prepared by the supervising principal who was directly in charge of plaintiff contained a rating adverse to the plaintiff with respect to her personality, her emotional stability, her professional relationships, her judgment, her preparation, her professional attitudes, her civic responsibility, her dependability, her classroom generalship, her ability to compromise, and the reaction of her pupils. The county superintendent's testimony was corroborated by five witnesses and it is easy to understand why he finally gave plaintiff an "unsatisfactory" rating.

There was no averment or proof of fraud or that the rating was arbitrary or capricious. Appellant objects to this rating, mainly (a) because the supervising principal participated in the rating; (b) because the assistant county superintendent said that one of her classes was well conducted or good; and (c) because the county superintendent did not exercise his own judgment in giving her the rating since he relied solely upon the recommendation of the supervising principal, as is evident from a letter he wrote plaintiff dated June 30, 1949, advising her that the supervising principal had recommended an unsatisfactory rating and that it has been the policy of the county school office to accept the recommendation of supervising principals in the rating of teachers. We do not give to any of these contentions the force and effect which appellant does.

Most executives and public officials, in formulating decisions, must, of necessity, frequently rely (in part at least) upon information received from and recommendations made by subordinates. The Act of 1911 (as amended), supra, does not require, and a reasonable construction thereof makes clear that it does not contemplate that the county superintendent rate all of the 1335 teachers within the county on the basis of his own personal knowledge of them, and without any consideration of recommendations made by the supervising principal, who was in the best possible position to know the teaching capabilities and other essential qualifications of the teachers under his immediate supervision.

Appellant's next contention that the rating is void because made after the termination of the school term is likewise without merit. This rating was

made on June 29, 1949, three weeks after the last examination. The School Code states that the county superintendent must "notify each temporary professional employe, at least twice each year *during the period of his or her employment,* of the . . . rating. . . ." Plaintiff's contract was dated September 14, effective September 1, 1948, and provided, inter alia, "I. That said Temporary Professional Employe shall under the authority of said board [of school directors] . . . and subject to the supervision and authority of the . . . Supervising Principal teach in the said school district for a term of nine months [ending June 1; before the end of the examinations or the school term] for an annual compensation of $2,250 Dollars. . . . II. That if said Temporary Professional Employe shall have served the above named School District *for a period of two years* and shall have received a satisfactory rating during the last four months of the second year from the County Superintendent or District Superintendent, the above employe thereafter shall be considered a professional employe. . . . IV. That this contract shall continue in effect until the expiration of two years of satisfactory service rendered to the School District above named by the said Temporary Professional Employe. . . ."

It is not clear when the two year period of plaintiff's employment expired, but it is certain that both the statute and the contract should receive a reasonable construction. It is reasonable to assume that the legislature and the contracting parties knew that a wise and fair appraisal of performance and a *rating* can best be made after the teacher's entire probationary period has ended, and not during or prior to the last few days of an examination period; and therefore must have intended to give the county superintendent a reasonable period after the end of the last examination to determine whether the rating should be satisfactory or unsatisfactory. The unreasonableness of plaintiff's construction is apparent when we consider that if conditions had been reversed and the county superintendent had given her a satisfactory rating one day after June 1, or one day after the examinations, her rating could have been challenged and voided. It is easy to guess what her attitude and contention would have been in such a case.

The plaintiff next contends that even though she did not request a hearing by the superintendent, the denial of a hearing to enable her to obtain tenure status by qualifying as a permanent professional teacher, was a violation of due process. There was no provision in this statute authorizing or providing for a hearing for a temporary teacher *who desired to attain permanent status,* and in the absence thereof, plaintiff had no property or other vested right in or to the position or status of a permanent teacher. Moreover, no liability or penalty was imposed upon her by the action of the county superintendent. It is clear, therefore, that the superintendent's failure to hold a hearing for the purpose of giving plaintiff a rating as a permanent teacher was not a violation of the due process clause of the Fourteenth Amendment of the Constitution of the United States nor of Article I, Section 9 of the Constitution of Pennsylvania.

Dissenting opinion: . . . If the teacher's work was unsatisfactory for the fourth term and that of itself disqualified her for the permanent position, the decision of the county superintendent would be understandable and

acceptable, but it does not comport with logic to say that the fourth term unsatisfactory rating rendered the *previous* three satisfactory terms unsatisfactory.

A baseball batter may strike out in the last inning, but this does not wipe out the runs he knocked in during the previous innings.

It would appear to me that Dorothy S. Travis, the school teacher in this case, was lulled into a sense of false security by the first three approval ratings. She could not have been competent and satisfactory for eighteen months and then become so incompetent as to vitiate even what went before. In accordance with all standards of fairness, a duty devolved upon the school authorities to instruct the teacher on her failings in the first, second and third terms, if any there were, and that duty was not met by waiting until the end of her provisional incumbency when opportunity to correct deficiencies no longer existed.

Case note. A superintendent may accept recommendations of principals and adopt same as his own judgment in rating teachers. Furthermore, the court held that a reasonable interpretation of the rating requirement permitted the final rating to be made after the end of the last school term in the probationary period. Under laws which provide continuing contracts for probationary teachers, lack of notice of nonreemployment by the end of the school year (or by an earlier designated date) would result in the teacher's acquiring tenure automatically.

Nyboe v. Allen et al., 10 Misc. (2d) 895, 175 N.Y.S. (2d) 334 (New York, 1958) *aff'd* (memorandum opinion) 7 A. D. (2d) 822, 181 N.Y.S. (2d) 132 (1958). [Prerequisites to acquisition of tenure status.]

In this proceeding instituted pursuant to the provisions of article 78 of the Civil Practice Act petitioner seeks to review and annul respondent Commissioner's determination which dismissed her appeal from the respondent Board of Education's action in terminating her employment as a teacher of instrumental music in a union free school district under its supervision at the expiration of the term specified in her employment contract. Her reinstatement with back pay is also sought. Concededly, the problem which the proceeding poses concerns the interpretation of the tenure provisions of section 3013 of the Education Law and presents no issues of fact.

Petitioner's employment commenced in 1948 under a one-year contract with the Board as a teacher of instrumental music for two days each week. The contract was regularly renewed for a similar term, with appropriate increments in salary, until 1952 when she became employed on a three day per week basis. In April, 1956 petitioner's employment was terminated by the Board of Education effective June 30, 1956 for the stated reason that it had decided to discontinue the course of instruction in instrumental music. On June 5, 1956, the Board restored the course to its curriculum, increased it to a full time program for the ensuing school year, declined to continue

petitioner as a full time teacher therein and appointed another to the position.

The petitioner contends that her employment by the Board under eight successive written contracts of one year each for the consecutive school years beginning in 1948 and ending in 1956 equated the maximum probationary period prescribed by the statute and thereafter by acquiescence of the Board entitled her to the benefits of permanent tenure in the full time position from which she could be removed only for cause. She argues that the Commissioner's contrary interpretation of the statute is arbitrary in a legal sense. . . .

Probationary tenure is granted and permanent tenure assured only to those persons who obtain their positions in the school system in the manner prescribed by the Education Law, § 3012; § 3013, subds. 1,2. In those school districts where, as here, the tenure provisions of the statute are applicable, an appointment by a majority vote of the governing body upon appropriate recommendation of the supervisory authority is necessary for the attainment of both probationary and permanent status. In this instance the required basic statutory conditions were not met by the execution of successive employment contracts of yearly duration. Carter v. Kalamejski, 255 App. Div. 694, 8 N.Y.S. 2d 926, affirmed 280 N.Y. 803, 21 N.E. 2d 692. Nor is the doctrine of tenure by estoppel available to the petitioner. This is applicable only in cases in which a probationary appointment has been made in compliance with the statutory procedure which has ripened into permanent tenure by continuing employment thereafter with the acquiescence of the Board and the district superintendent of schools. See Matter of Armlin, 73 State Dept. Rep. 32; Monan v. Board of Education, City of Buffalo, 280 App. Div. 14, 111 N.Y.S. 2d 797. This obviously was not the case here. It follows that the petitioner's employment terminated on the date on which her last contract with the Board expired. . . .

The determination of the respondent Commissioner was neither factually nor legally arbitrary and hence is not subject to review in the courts, Education Law, § 310.

Accordingly, the petition is dismissed on the merits, without costs.

Appellant was not obliged to appeal to the Commissioner of Education and could have brought her controversy to the Courts, but having elected to do so she is bound in our judgment by the decision of the Commissioner unless his decision was so arbitrary and capricious that it cannot be sustained, and we do not find it to be so. Under Section 310 of the Education Law the Commissioner's decision on a controversy wholly within the Educational System of the State is ordinarily final and conclusive. There is a long line of authorities to this effect. . . .

Case note. This is one of the courts which holds that tenure, being in derogation of common-law rights of contract, should be strictly construed. On the other hand, there was ample basis for the court's reasoning since Nyboe had not been employed as a regular probationary teacher through the procedure fixed by law. Yet, the tenure law did not prevent the board from employing a part-time teacher

on annual contracts without following the procedure it would have been required to follow had the appointment been to a regular position. If Nyboe had been appointed as a regular probationary teacher, the board would have been estopped from denying her tenure status.

This case might have been decided otherwise under other tenure laws, especially if the teacher had been employed as a full-time teacher. Courts have said that a board has no right to employ a teacher initially in any status except as a probationary teacher, even though the contract did not designate the teacher a probationary teacher. To permit a contrary practice, say the courts, would nullify the tenure laws by preventing teachers so employed from eventually acquiring tenure status.

Note also that New York law permits aggrieved teachers to appeal to the State Commissioner of Education or to the courts; that after electing to appeal to the Commissioner the courts will not interfere.

Phelps v. Board of Education of West New York, 300 U.S. 319 (1937). [Teacher sought to have set aside school-board resolution reducing all salaries of its employees and the enabling legislation declared unconstitutional because it impaired the obligation of the contract created by the tenure law of New Jersey.]

An act of February 4, 1933 [of the New Jersey legislature], premising that existing economic conditions require that boards of education be enabled to fix and determine the amount of salary to be paid to persons holding positions in the respective school districts, authorizes each board to fix and determine salaries to be paid officers and employes for the period July 1, 1933, to July 1, 1934, "notwithstanding any such person be under tenure." . . . June 23, 1933, the board adopted a resolution reducing salaries for the school year July 1, 1933, to July 1, 1934, by a percentage of the existing salaries graded upward in steps as the salaries increased in amount. . . .

The position of the appellants is that by virtue of the Act of 1909 three years of service under contract confer upon an employe of a school district a contractual status indefinite in duration which the legislature is powerless to alter or to authorize the board of education to alter. The [state] Supreme Court holds that the Act of 1909 "established a legislative status for teachers, but we fail to see that it established a contractual one that the legislature may not modify. . . . The status of tenure teachers, while in one sense perhaps contractual, is in essence dependent on a statute, like that of the incumbent of a statutory office, which the legislature at will may abolish, or whose emoluments it may change."

This court is not bound by the decision of a state court as to the existence and terms of a contract, the obligation of which is asserted to be impaired, but where a statute is claimed to create a contractual right we give weight to the construction of the statute by the courts of the state. Here those courts have concurred in holding that the Act of 1909 did not amount to a

legislative contract with the teachers of the state and did not become a term of the contracts entered into with employes by boards of education. Unless these views are palpably erroneous we should accept them.

It appears from a stipulation of facts submitted in lieu of evidence that after a teacher has served in a school district under yearly contracts for three years it has not been customary to enter into further formal contracts with such teacher. From time to time, however, promotions were granted and salary raised for the ensuing year by action of the board. In the case of many of the appellants there have been several such increases in salary.

Although after the expiration of the first three years of service the employe continued in his then position and at his then compensation unless and until promoted or given an increase in salary for a succeeding year, we find nothing in the record to indicate that the board was bound by contract with the teacher for more than the current year. The employe assumed no binding obligation to remain in service beyond that term. Although the Act of 1909 prohibited the board, a creature of the state, from reducing the teacher's salary or discharging him without cause, we agree with the courts below that this was but a regulation of the conduct of the board and not a term of continuing contract of indefinite duration with the individual teacher. . . .

Case note. The United States Supreme Court in this case established the status of New Jersey teachers under their tenure law, as a legislative status. The Court was aided by a number of factors: the law was called "Tenure of Office Act" suggesting that teachers were public officers as distinguished from employees under contract; the board did not execute contracts with tenure teachers; the tenure law did not expressly require contracts or establish for tenure teachers a contractual relation with the board. Compare this case with the following one from Indiana. Although the issue here was reduction of salary, and thus different from the issue in the Indiana case which follows, the essential difference is in the type of protection the two laws provide teachers in New Jersey and in Indiana, respectively.

Indiana ex rel. Anderson v. Brand, 303 U.S. 95 (1938). [Dismissed teacher sought writ of mandamus to compel school trustee to continue her employment on ground that she was a tenure teacher, although the legislature had repealed the tenure law as it applied to township schools where Anderson was formerly employed.]

Her complaint alleged that as a duly licensed teacher she entered into a contract in September, 1924, to teach in the township schools, and pursuant to successive contracts, taught continuously to and including the school year 1932-33; that her contracts for the school year 1931-32 and 1932-33 contained this clause: "It is further agreed by the contracting parties that all of the provisions of the Teachers' Tenure Law, approved March 8, 1927, shall be in full force and effect in this contract"; and that by force of that

Act she had a contract, indefinite in duration, which could be cancelled by the respondent only in the manner and for the causes specified in the Act. . . .

The respondent demurred on the grounds that . . . (2) the Teachers' Tenure Law had been repealed in respect of teachers in township schools. The demurrer was sustained and the petitioner appealed to the State Supreme Court which affirmed the judgment. The court . . . held that the repeal did not deprive the petitioner of a vested property right and did not impair her contract within the meaning of the Constitution. . . .

The court below holds that in Indiana teachers' contracts are made for but one year; that there is no contractual right to be continued as a teacher from year to year; that the law grants a privilege to one who has taught five years and signed a new contract to continue in employment under given conditions; that the statute is directed merely to the exercise of their powers by the school authorities and the policy therein expressed may be altered at the will of the legislature; that in enacting laws for the government of public schools the legislature exercises a function of sovereignty and the power to control public policy in respect of their management and operation cannot be contracted away by one legislature so as to create a permanent public policy unchangeable by succeeding legislatures. . . .

On such a question, one primarily of state law, we accord respectful consideration and great weight to the views of the State's highest court but, in order that the constitutional mandate may not become a dead letter, we are bound to decide for ourselves whether a contract was made, what are its terms and conditions, and whether the State has, by later legislation, impaired its obligation. This involves an appraisal of the statutes of the State and the decisions of its courts.

The courts of Indiana have long recognized that the employment of school teachers was contractual and have afforded relief in actions upon teachers' contracts. An Act adopted in 1899 required all contracts between teachers and school corporations to be in writing, signed by the parties to be charged, and to be made a matter of public record. . . .

In 1927 the State adopted the Teachers' Tenure Act under which the present controversy arises. . . . By an amendatory Act of 1933 township school corporations were omitted from the provisions of the Act of 1927. The court below construed this Act as repealing the Act of 1927 so far as township schools and teachers are concerned and as leaving the respondent free to terminate the petitioner's employment. But we are of opinion that the petitioner had a valid contract with the respondent, the obligation of which would be impaired by the termination of her employment.

Where the claim is that the State's policy embodied in a statute is to bind its instrumentalities by contract, the cardinal inquiry is as to the terms of the statute supposed to create such a contract. . . .

The title of the Act is couched in terms of contract. It speaks of the making and canceling of indefinite contracts. In the body the word "contract" appears ten times in Section 1, defining the relationship; 11 times in Section 2, relating to the termination of the employment by the employer, and four times in Section 4, stating the conditions of termination by the teacher.

The tenor of the Act indicates that the word "contracts" was not used inadvertently or in other than its usual legal meaning. By Section 6 it is expressly provided that the Act is a supplement to that of March 7, 1921, *supra*, requiring teachers' employment contracts to be in writing. By Section 1 it is provided that the written contract of a permanent teacher "shall be deemed to continue in effect for an indefinite period and shall be known as an indefinite contract." Such an indefinite contract is to remain in force unless succeeded by a new contract signed by both parties or cancelled as provided in Section 2. No more apt language could be employed to define a contractual relationship. . . . Examination of the entire Act convinces us that the teacher was by it assured of the possession of a binding and enforceable contract against school districts.

Until its decision in the present case the Supreme Court of the State had uniformly held that the teacher's right to continued employment by virtue of the indefinite contract created pursuant to the Act was contractual. . . .

We think the decision in this case runs counter to the policy evinced by the Act of 1927, to its explicit mandate and to earlier decisions construing its provisions. . . .

Dissenting opinion: In my opinion this reversal unconstitutionally limits the right of Indiana to control Indiana's public school system. . . . I cannot agree that the constitutional prohibition against impairment of contracts was intended to—or does—transfer in part the determination of the educational policy of Indiana from the legislature of that State to this Court.

Indiana, in harmony with our national tradition, seeks to work out a school system, offering education to all, as "essential to the preservation of free government." That great function of an advancing society has heretofore been exercised by the states. I find no constitutional authority for this Court to appropriate that power. Indiana's highest court has said that the *State did not*, and has strongly indicated that the *legislature could not*, make contracts with a *few citizens*, that would take away from *all the citizens*, the continuing power to alter the educational policy for the best interests of Indiana school children. . . .

Case note. The decision of the United States Supreme Court in this case is not contradictory to its decision in the previous case from New Jersey. The language of the two tenure laws is different, necessitating a different interpretation. Furthermore, the traditional status of teachers in the two states was different.

A legislative contract cannot be impaired by subsequent legislation any more than a private contract. The Federal Constitution prohibits the enactment of any law impairing the obligation of contracts.

This Indiana case teaches at least two lessons: (1) Those who say that one legislature cannot tie the hands of future legislatures are not always correct. There is a presumption that a tenure law is, like New Jersey's, legislative policy only and that it does not create a contractual status. But, that presumption may be overcome by legislative language

showing the intent of the legislature, as in this case. (2) Those who would establish a contractual-type tenure law could model it on the one held to be so by the Supreme Court of the United States.

Sources of Further Information

47 Am. Jur. "Schools" secs. 115-119, 125-145.
78 C.J.S. "Schools and School Districts" secs. 183-217, 510.
A.L.R. "Schools" Topic Nos. 32-33, 42-44.
American Digest System "Schools and School Districts" Key Nos. 133.5-138, 140-142.

Work Sheet

1. Are teachers' contracts required to be in writing in your state?
2. Is the contract form prescribed by the state department?
3. Is the school board required to employ teachers in a formal board meeting?
4. Of what duration are teachers' contracts: one, two, three, five years, or indefinite?
5. Is there any date on which teachers must be notified of non-renewal of the contract for the ensuing school year?
6. Is there any date before which employment of teachers would be unenforceable?

If there is a tenure law applicable in the district of your employment, study its provisions and answer the following questions. If you are not teaching under a tenure law, answer the questions on the basis of proposed legislation, if any. If no legislation is under consideration, answer the questions from the point of view of best policies.

1. Are administrators included as well as classroom teachers?
2. How long is the probationary period?
3. Is the probationary period the same length for all teachers regardless of experience?
4. Is substitute service counted toward the probationary requirement?
5. Are probationary teachers employed on a continuing-contract basis?
6. What are the causes for dismissal stated in the law as being justifiable?
7. What provisions are contained in the law to ensure a fair hearing to tenure teachers before dismissal?
8. Does the tenure law protect tenure teachers from unfair demotions and reduction in salary, as well as from unjust dismissals?

Chapter 3.

LOYALTY REQUIREMENTS

Editorial Comment

It was mentioned in Chapter 1 on Certification and Appointment that a loyalty oath is often required of applicants for certificates. The Maryland contract of employment reproduced in Chapter 2 on Contracts of Employment and Tenure illustrates the loyalty oath typically prerequisite to employment. Signing a loyalty oath is a requirement for certification and/or employment in about three-fourths of the states, statewide, and in many local districts of other states. However, what the teachers are required to swear to in some states is more extensive than support of the Constitution of the United States (and of the particular state); in a few they must promise to teach specific aspects of patriotism and/or promise not to teach specific theories of government contrary to our own. In many states teachers are required to swear that they will not advocate the overthrow of our government by violent methods, but, even without such a prescription specifically applicable to teachers, they, like other citizens, are forbidden to do this in anarchy and sedition laws of general application on the statute books of practically all states. Another frequent requirement of teachers is that they refrain from membership in subversive groups, and in several states teachers are required to testify when called before investigating agencies.

Loyalty requirements have been challenged as unconstitutional on the grounds that they violate the First, Fifth, and Fourteenth Amendments to the Federal Constitution because they abridge the rights of freedom of speech, press, and assembly, or because they deny due process of law; other grounds have been that such laws are bills of attainder or ex post facto laws forbidden by the Constitution. The courts have almost universally upheld these loyalty requirements against all challenges. Several cases have gone to the Supreme Court of the United States. In fact, the Court had laid down the principles in nonschool cases involving loyalty requirements imposed on other

59

categories of public employees before it had to consider any school case.

The principles are the same no matter whether the individual concerned is a teacher or a nonteaching public employee. One of the principles is that no one has a "right" to public employment; if he accepts public employment he must be willing to accept requirements set down for the public good. The state may fix reasonable methods for screening out disloyal employees and the loyalty oath requirement is a reasonable method for accomplishing that objective. However, it is a denial of due process of law if the loyalty requirement penalizes one who innocently joined a group and withdrew upon acquiring the knowledge that it was subversive.

When the law requires teachers to testify before an investigating agency, the question arises as to one's right to refuse to testify on the basis of the Fifth Amendment. The Fifth Amendment states that "no person . . . shall be compelled in any criminal case to be a witness against himself." This protection against self-incrimination has long been interpreted to apply to any investigation if the witness believes that his testimony may provide evidence by which his guilt may be established in a subsequent criminal case. Critics of court decisions upholding an individual's right to plead the Fifth Amendment say that the courts are protecting disloyal persons. When that person is a teacher, the critics are even more vociferous, because they say it prevents a school board from ridding the schools of teachers who may inculcate Communistic doctrines in the minds of their youthful students. However, the courts say that a person may plead the Fifth Amendment under some circumstances when he is not guilty. On the other hand, it has been proved that disloyal teachers can be dismissed on other grounds so as to avoid the constitutional question. In the long run, it should be recognized that a teacher has the constitutional right to plead the Fifth Amendment but he has no constitutional right to be a teacher.

Statutory Material

Deering's Education Code of California, secs. 12951-12958.

Sec. 12951. Legislative findings. The Legislature of the State of California finds that:

(a) There exists a world-wide revolutionary movement to establish a totalitarian dictatorship based upon force and power rather than upon law.

(b) This world-wide revolutionary movement is predicated upon and it is designed and intended to carry into execution the basic precepts of communism as expounded by Marx, Lenin, and Stalin.

(c) Pursuant to the objectives of the world communism movement, in numerous foreign countries the legally constituted governments have been overthrown and totalitarian dictatorships established therein against the will of the people, and the establishment of similar dictatorships in other countries is imminently threatening. The successful establishment of totalitarian dictatorships has consistently been aided, accompanied, or accomplished by repeated acts of treachery, deceit, teaching of false doctrines, teaching untruth, together with organized confusion, insubordination, and disloyalty, fostered, directed, instigated, or employed by communist organizations and their members in such countries.

(d) Within the boundaries of the State of California there are active disciplined communist organizations presently functioning for the primary purpose of advancing the objectives of the world communism movement, which organizations promulgate, advocate, and adhere to the precepts and the principles and doctrines of the world communism movement. These communist organizations are characterized by identification of their programs, policies, and objectives with those of the world communism movement, and they regularly and consistently cooperate with and endeavor to carry into execution programs, policies, and objectives substantially identical to programs, policies, and objectives of such world communism movement.

(e) One of the objectives of the world communism movement is to place its members in local government positions and in the Public School System. If this objective is successful, propaganda can be disseminated by the members of these organizations among public school pupils by those members who would have the opportunity to teach them and to whom, as teachers, they would look for guidance, authority, and leadership. The members of such groups would use their positions to advocate and teach their doctrines and teach the prescribed Communist Party line group dogma or doctrine without regard to truth or free inquiry. This type of propaganda is sufficiently subtle to escape detection in the classroom.

There is a clear and present danger, which the Legislature of the State of California finds is great and imminent, that in order to advance the program, policies and objectives of the world communism movement, communist organizations in the State of California and their members will engage in concerted effort to hamper, restrict, interfere with, impede, or nullify the efforts of the governing boards of school districts to comply with and enforce Section 8455 of the Education Code of the State of California which prohibits the advocacy or teaching of communism with the intent to indoctrinate any pupil with or inculcate a preference in the mind of any pupil for communism for the purpose of undermining the patriotism for and the belief in the Government of the United States and of the State of California in the minds of the pupils of the Public School System.

The Legislature specifically finds that the requirement that all persons (certificated or noncertificated) now employed by the school districts of this State, or hereafter making application for employment by any of such districts, shall declare under oath that they are not knowingly

members of the Communist Party, is a reasonable measure to meet the clear and present danger hereinabove found.

The Legislature further specifically finds that an indirect or evasive answer to a question relating to any of the matters specified in Section 12955 or 12956, or an answer which neither affirms nor denies shall, for the purposes of this act and chapter, be considered as a failure and refusal to answer, regardless of the ground or explanation given for any such answer.

Sec. 12952. Oath of employees. No person who is knowingly a member of the Communist Party shall after September 9, 1953, be employed by, or, except as provided in Section 12953, retained in the employment of, any school district. Prior to the first day of service as an employee of any school district, the applicant shall state under oath whether or not he is knowingly a member of the Communist Party. If the applicant states that he is knowingly a member of the Communist Party, he shall not become an employee of any school district.

Sec. 12953. Verified statement of nonmembership. Any employee of any school district who on September 9, 1953, is or since October 3, 1945, was knowingly a member of the Communist Party, and who has not previously filed the statement required by this section, shall within ninety (90) days of the effective date of the amendment of this section made at the 1955 Regular Session of the Legislature, file with the governing board of the school district employing him a verified statement that he is no longer a member of the Communist Party and that such membership has been terminated in good faith. Any such employee who fails to file such a statement within the time specified shall be guilty of insubordination and guilty of violating this section and shall be suspended and dismissed from his employment in the manner provided by law.

Sec. 12954. Suspension and dismissal. Any employee of any school district who after September 9, 1953, knowingly becomes a member of the Communist Party shall be guilty of insubordination and guilty of violating this section and shall be suspended and dismissed from his employment in the manner provided by law.

Sec. 12955. Appearance before Legislative Committees. It shall be the duty of any employee of any school district who may be subpoenaed by a United States Congressional Un-American Activities Committee or a subcommittee thereof or a California Legislative Un-American Activities Committee or a subcommittee thereof or any other committee or subcommittee of the United States Congress or the California legislature or of either house of either thereof to appear before said committee or subcommittee and specifically to answer under oath a question or questions propounded by any member or counsel of the committee or subcommittee relating to:

(a) Present personal advocacy by the employee of the forceful or violent overthrow of the Government of the United States or any state or political subdivision.

(b) Present knowing membership in any organization which, to the knowledge of such employee, advocates the forceful or violent overthrow

of the Government of the United States or of any state or political sub-division.

(c) Past knowing membership at any time since October 3, 1945, in any organization which, to the knowledge of such employee, during the time of the employee's membership advocated the forceful or violent over-throw of the Government of the United States or of any state or political subdivision.

(d) Past knowing membership of such employee in the Communist Party at any time since October 3, 1945.

(e) Present knowing membership of such employee in the Communist Party.

(f) Present personal advocacy by the employee of the support of a foreign government against the United States in the event of hostilities.

Any employee who fails or refuses to answer under oath on any ground whatsoever any such question propounded by any member or counsel of any such committee or subcommittee shall be guilty of insubordination and guilty of violating this section and shall be suspended and dismissed from his employment in the manner provided by law.

Sec. 12956. Appearance before governing boards. It shall be the duty of any employee of any school district who is ordered to appear before the governing board of the employing school district to appear and specifically to answer under oath a question or questions propounded by a member or counsel of the governing board or by the superintendent of schools relating to any of the matters specified in Section 12955.

Any employee who fails or refuses to appear or to answer under oath on any ground whatsoever any such question propounded by a member or counsel of the governing board or by the superintendent of schools shall be guilty of insubordination and guilty of violating this section and shall be suspended and dismissed from his employment in the manner provided by law.

Sec. 12957. Cause for suspension and dismissal. It shall be sufficient cause for the suspension and dismissal, in the manner provided by law, of any employee of a school district when such employee is knowingly a member of the Communist Party.

Sec. 12958. Unprofessional conduct of certificated employees. Any certificated employee of a school district who violates any of the provisions of Sections 12952 to 12957, inclusive, of this code shall be guilty of unprofessional conduct and shall be suspended and dismissed in the manner provided by law.

Statutory note. The matter of "scienter" (see glossary, Appendix B) is very definite in this law. In another California law scienter was not specifically required; however, the Court upheld it because scienter was implied. See *Garner et al. v. Board of Public Works of Los Angeles,* 341 U. S. 716 (1951). On the other hand, the Oklahoma loyalty requirement was declared unconstitutional by the Court because it contained no scienter clause and the state supreme court had not in-

terpreted the law as requiring scienter. See *Wieman et al. v. Updegraff et al.*, 344 U. S. 183 (1952).

Case Material

Adler et al. v. Board of Education, 342 U. S. 485 (1952). [Constitutionality of New York's teacher loyalty law.]

Appellants brought a declaratory judgment action in the Supreme Court of New York, Kings County, praying that § 12-a of the Civil Service Law, as implemented by the so-called Feinberg Law, be declared unconstitutional, and that action by the Board of Education of the City of New York thereunder be enjoined.

Section 3022 of the Education Law, added by the Feinberg Law, provides that the Board of Regents, which has charge of the public school system in the State of New York, shall, after full notice and hearing, make a listing of organizations which it finds advocate, advise, teach, or embrace the doctrine that the government should be overthrown by force or violence or any other unlawful means, and that such listing may be amended and revised from time to time.

It will be observed that the listings are made only after full notice and hearing. In addition, the Court of Appeals construed the statute in conjunction with Article 78 of the New York Civil Practice Act, Gilbert-Bliss' N. Y. Civ. Prac., Vol. 6B, so as to provide listed organizations a right of review.

The Board of Regents is further authorized to provide in rules and regulations, and has so provided, that membership in any listed organization, after notice and hearing, "shall constitute prima facie evidence for disqualification for appointment to or retention in any office or position in the school system"; but before one who is an employee or seeks employment is severed from or denied employment, he likewise must be given a full hearing with the privilege of being represented by counsel and the right to judicial review. It is § 12-a of the Civil Service Law, as implemented by the Feinberg Law as above indicated, that is under attack here.

It is first argued that the Feinberg Law and the rules promulgated thereunder constitute an abridgment of the freedom of speech and assembly of persons employed or seeking employment in the public schools of the State of New York.

It is clear that such persons have the right under our law to assemble, speak, think and believe as they will. *Communications Assn.* v. *Douds*, 339 U. S. 382. It is equally clear that they have no right to work for the State in the school system on their own terms. *United Public Workers* v. *Mitchell*, 330 U. S. 75. They may work for the school system upon the reasonable terms laid down by the proper authorities of New York. If they do not choose to work on such terms, they are at liberty to retain their beliefs and associations and go elsewhere. Has the State thus deprived them of any right to free speech or assembly? We think not. Such persons are or may be denied, under the statutes in question, the privilege

of working for the school system of the State of New York because, first, of their advocacy of the overthrow of the government by force or violence, or, secondly, by unexplained membership in an organization found by the school authorities, after notice and hearing, to teach and advocate the overthrow of the government by force or violence, and known by such persons to have such purpose.

If, under the procedure set up in the New York law, a person is found to be unfit and is disqualified from employment in the public school system because of membership in a listed organization, he is not thereby denied the right of free speech and assembly. His freedom of choice between membership in the organization and employment in the school system might be limited, but not his freedom of speech or assembly, except in the remote sense that limitation is inherent in every choice. Certainly such limitation is not one the state may not make in the exercise of its police power to protect the schools from pollution and thereby to defend its own existence.

It is next argued by appellants that the provision in § 3022 directing the Board of Regents to provide in rules and regulations that membership in any organization listed by the Board after notice and hearing, with provision for review in accordance with the statute, shall constitute prima facie evidence of disqualification, denies due process, because the fact found bears no relation to the fact presumed. In other words, from the fact found that the organization was one that advocated the overthrow of government by unlawful means and that the person employed or to be employed was a member of the organization and knew of its purpose, to presume that such member is disqualified for employment is so unreasonable as to be a denial of due process of law. We do not agree.

Membership in a listed organization found to be within the statute and known by the member to be within the statute is a legislative finding that the member by his membership supports the thing the organization stands for, namely, the overthrow of government by unlawful means. We cannot say that such a finding is contrary to fact or that "generality of experience" points to a different conclusion. Disqualification follows therefore as a reasonable presumption from such membership and support. Nor is there here a problem of procedural due process. The presumption is not conclusive but arises only in a hearing where the person against whom it may arise has full opportunity to rebut it.

Where, as here, the relation between the fact found and the presumption is clear and direct and is not conclusive, the requirements of due process are satisfied.

We find no constitutional infirmity in § 12-a of the Civil Service Law of New York or in the Feinberg Law which implemented it, and the judgment is

Affirmed.

Case note. The Feinberg Law was upheld primarily because the organizations listed as subversive had received notice, were given a hearing as to their suspected subversive nature, and were entitled to review. Those who continue to be members after an organization has

been listed have chosen between withdrawal from membership and public employment. Their right of membership is not denied; merely their right to employment as teachers if they do not withdraw. This is not a denial of due process, especially since the individual concerned is given notice and hearing before dismissal.

Slochower v. Board of Higher Education, 350 U. S. 551 (1956). [Dismissal of teachers for refusal to answer questions as to loyalty.]

The appeal brings into question the constitutionality of § 903 of the Charter of the City of New York. That section provides that whenever an employee of the city utilizes the privilege against self-incrimination to avoid answering a question relating to his offical conduct, "his term or tenure of office or employment shall terminate and such office or employment shall be vacant, and he shall not be eligible to election or appointment to any office or employment under the city or any agency." Appellant Slochower invoked the privilege against self-incrimination under the Fifth Amendment before an investigating committee of the United States Senate, and was summarily discharged from his position as associate professor at Brooklyn College, an institution maintained by the City of New York. He now claims that the charter provision, as applied to him, violates both the Due Process and Privileges and Immunities Clauses of the Fourteenth Amendment. . . .

Professor Slochower, when called to testify, stated that he was not a member of Communist Party, and indicated complete willingness to answer all questions about his associations or political beliefs since 1941. But he refused to answer questions concerning his membership during 1940 and 1941 on the ground that his answers might tend to incriminate him. The Chairman of the Senate Subcommittee accepted Slochower's claim as a valid assertion of an admitted constitutional right. . . .

Shorty after testifying before the Internal Security Subcommittee, Slochower was notified that he was suspended from his position at the College; three days later his position was declared vacant "pursuant to the provisions of Section 903 of the New York City Charter." . . . It appears that neither the Subcommittee nor Slochower was aware that his claim of privilege would *ipso facto* result in his discharge, and would bar him permanently from holding any position either in the city colleges or in the city government. . . .

Slochower argues that § 903 abridges a privilege or immunity of a citizen of the United States since it in effect imposes a penalty on the exercise of a federally guaranteed right in a federal proceeding. It also violates due process, he argues, because the mere claim of privilege under the Fifth Amendment does not provide a reasonable basis for the State to terminate his employment. Appellee insists that no question of "privileges or immunities" was raised or passed on below, and therefore directs its argument solely to the proposition that § 903 does not operate in an arbitrary or capricious manner. We do not decide whether a claim under the "privileges or immunities" clause was considered below,

since we conclude the summary dismissal of appellant in the circumstances of this case violates due process of law.

The problem of balancing the State's interest in the loyalty of those in its service with the traditional safeguards of individual rights is a continuing one. To state that a person does not have a constitutional right to government employment is only to say that he must comply with reasonable, lawful, and nondiscriminatory terms laid down by the proper authorities. Adler v. Board of Education, 342 U. S. 485, upheld the New York Feinberg Law which authorized the public school authorities to dismiss employees who, after notice and hearing, were found to advocate the overthrow of the Government by unlawful means, or who were unable to explain satisfactorily membership in certain organizations found to have that aim. Likewise Garner v. Los Angeles Board, 341 U. S. 716, 720, upheld the right of the city to inquire of its employees as to "matters that may prove relevant to their fitness and suitability for the public service," including their membership, past and present, in the Communist Party or the Communist Political Association. There it was held that the city had power to discharge employees who refused to file an affidavit disclosing such information to the school authorities.

But in each of these cases it was emphasized that the State must conform to the requirements of due process. In Wieman v. Updegraff, 344 U. S. 183, we struck down a so-called "loyalty oath" because it based employability solely on the fact of membership in certain organizations. We pointed out that membership itself may be innocent and held that the classification of innocent and guilty together was arbitrary. This case rests squarely on the proposition that "constitutional protection does extend to the public servant whose exclusion pursuant to a statute is patently arbitrary or discriminatory." 344 U. S., at 192.

Here the Board, in support of its position, contends that only two possible inferences flow from appellant's claim of self-incrimination: (1) that the answering of the question would tend to prove him guilty of a crime in some way connected with his official conduct; or (2) that in order to avoid answering the question he falsely invoked the privilege by stating that the answer would tend to incriminate him, and thus committed perjury. Either inference, it insists, is sufficient to justify the termination of his employment. . . .

At the outset we must condemn the practice of imputing a sinister meaning to the exercise of a person's constitutional right under the Fifth Amendment. The right of an accused person to refuse to testify, which had been in England merely a rule of evidence, was so important to our forefathers that they raised it to the dignity of a constitutional enactment, and it has been recognized as "one of the most valuable prerogatives of the citizen." . . . The privilege against self-incrimination would be reduced to a hollow mockery if its exercise could be taken as equivalent either to a confession of guilt or a conclusive presumption of perjury. As we pointed out in Ullmann [350 U.S. 422], a witness may have a reasonable fear of prosecution and yet be innocent of any wrongdoing. . . .

With this in mind, we consider the application of § 903. As interpreted and applied by the state courts it operates to discharge every city em-

ployee who invoked the Fifth Amendment. In practical effect the questions asked are taken as confessed and made the basis of the discharge. No consideration is given to such factors as the subject matter of the questions, remoteness of the period to which they are directed, or justification for exercise of the privilege. It matters not whether the plea resulted from mistake, inadvertence or legal advice conscientiously given, whether wisely or unwisely. The heavy hand of the statute falls alike on all who exercise their constitutional privilege, the full enjoyment of which every person is entitled to receive. . . .

It is one thing for the city authorities themselves to inquire into Slochower's fitness but quite another for his discharge to be based entirely on events occurring before a federal committee whose inquiry was announced as not directly at "the property, affairs, or government of the city, or . . . official conduct of city employees." In this respect the present case differs materially from Garner, where the city was attempting to elicit information necessary to determine the qualifications of its employees. Here, the Board had possessed the pertinent information for 12 years, and the questions which Professor Slochower refused to answer were admittedly asked for a purpose wholly unrelated to his college functions. On such a record the Board cannot claim that its action was part of a bona fide attempt to gain needed and relevant information.

Without attacking Professor Slochower's qualification for his position in any manner, and apparently with full knowledge of the testimony he had given some 12 years before at the state committee hearing, the Board seized upon his claim of privilege before the federal committee and converted it through the use of § 903 into a conclusive presumption of guilt. Since no inference of guilt was possible from the claim before the federal committee, the discharge falls of its own weight as wholly without support. . . .

This is not to say that Slochower has a constitutional right to be an associate professor of German at Brooklyn College. The State has broad powers in the selection and discharge of its employees, and it may be that proper inquiry would show Slochower's continued employment to be inconsistent with a real interest of the State. But there has been no such inquiry here. We hold that the summary dismissal of appellant violates due process of law.

The judgment is reversed and the cause is remanded for further proceedings not inconsistent with this opinion.

Dissenting opinions: (1) . . . Cities, like other employers, may reasonably conclude that a refusal to furnish appropriate information is enough to justify discharge. Legally authorized bodies have a right to demand that citizens furnish facts pertinent to official inquiries. The duty to respond may be refused for personal protection against prosecution only, but such avoidance of public duty to furnish information can properly be considered to stamp the employee as a person unfit to hold certain official positions. Such a conclusion is reinforced when the claimant for protection has the role of instructor to youth. The fact that the witness has a right to plead the privilege against self-incrimination protects him against prosecution but not against the loss of his job. . . .

Numerous employees had refused to testify as to criminal acts on the ground of self-incrimination. New York decided it did not want that kind of public employees. We think New York had that right. . . .

(2) . . . the Court has misconceived the nature of § 903 as construed and applied by the New York Court of Appeals, and has unduly circumscribed the power of the State to ensure the qualifications of its teachers. . . .

Since § 903 is inoperative if even incriminating answers are given, it is apparent that it is the exercise of the privilege itself which is the basis for the discharge, quite apart from any inference of guilt. . . . The question this case presents, therefore, is not whether any inferences can constitutionally be drawn from a claim of privilege, but whether a State violates due process when it makes a claim of privilege grounds for discharge. . . .

This Court has already held, however, that a State may properly make knowing membership in an organization dedicated to the overthrow of the Government by force a ground for disqualification from public school teaching. . . . A requirement that public school teachers shall furnish information as to their past or present membership in the Communist Party is a relevant step in the implementation of such a state policy, and a teacher may be discharged for refusing to comply with that requirement. . . .

Case note. The point in this case is that the teachers who pleaded the Fifth Amendment were *summarily* dismissed, their refusal to testify being interpreted as a confession of guilt. This is a denial of due process. The dissenting justices felt that the majority had unduly interfered with New York's right to eliminate disloyal teachers from its schools; they said that, since a state may make membership in a subversive organization a ground for dismissal, a requirement that teachers must furnish information as to their membership in such organizations is "a relevant step in the implementation of such a state policy."

The Slochower case caused considerable agitation among school people who felt that it prevented them from investigating the loyalty of teachers because they could plead the Fifth Amendment. However, the Beilan case which follows points out an acceptable procedure in such circumstances.

Beilan v. Board of Public Education, 357 U. S. 399 (1958). [Dismissal of teacher on grounds of incompetency after his refusal to answer questions as to loyalty.]

The question before us is whether the Board of Public Education for the School District of Philadelphia, Pennsylvania, violated the Due Process Clause of the Fourteenth Amendment to the Constitution of the United States when the Board, purporting to act under the Pennsylvania Public School Code, discharged a public school teacher on the ground of "incompetency," evidenced by the teacher's refusal of his Superintendent's

request to confirm or refute information as to the teacher's loyalty and his activities in certain allegedly subversive organizations. For the reasons hereafter stated, we hold that it did not.

On June 25, 1952, Herman A. Beilan, the petitioner, who had been a teacher for about 22 years in the Philadelphia Public School System, presented himself at his Superintendent's office in response to the latter's request. The Superintendent said he had information which reflected adversely on petitioner's loyalty and he wanted to determine its truth or falsity. In response to petitioner's suggestion that the Superintendent do the questioning, the latter said he would ask one question and petitioner could then determine whether he would answer it and others of that type. The Superintendent, accordingly, asked petitioner whether or not he had been the Press Director of the Professional Section of the Communist Political Association in 1944. Petitioner asked permission to consult counsel before answering and the Superintendent granted his request.

On October 14, 1952, in response to a similar request, petitioner again presented himself at the Superintendent's office. Petitioner stated that he had consulted counsel and that he declined to answer the question as to his activities in 1944. He announced he would also decline to answer any other "questions similar to it," "questions of this type," or "questions about political and religious beliefs. . . ." The Superintendent warned petitioner that this "was a very serious and a very important matter and that failure to answer the questions might lead to his dismissal." The Superintendent made it clear that he was investigating "a real question of fitness for [petitioner] to be a teacher or to continue in the teaching work." These interviews were given no publicity and were attended only by petitioner, his Superintendent and the Assistant Solicitor of the Board.

On November 25, 1953, the Board instituted dismissal proceedings against petitioner under § 1127 of the Pennsylvania Public School Code of 1949. The only specification which we need consider charged that petitioner's refusal to answer his Superintendent's questions constituted "incompetency" under § 1122 of that Code. The Board conducted a formal hearing on the charge. Petitioner was present with counsel but did not testify. Counsel for each side agreed that petitioner's loyalty was not in issue, and that evidence as to his disloyalty would be irrelevant. On January 9, 1954, the Board found that the charge of incompetency had been sustained and, by a vote of fourteen to one, discharged petitioner from his employment as a teacher. . . .

The only question before us is whether the Federal Constitution prohibits petitioner's discharge for statutory "incompetency" based on his refusal to answer the Superintendent's questions.

By engaging in teaching in the public schools, petitioner did not give up his right to freedom of belief, speech or association. He did, however, undertake obligations of frankness, candor and cooperation in answering inquiries made of him by his employing Board examining into his fitness to serve it as a public school teacher. . . .

The question asked of petitioner by his Superintendent was relevant to the issue of petitioner's fitness and suitability to serve as a teacher. Peti-

tioner is not in a position to challenge his dismissal merely because of the remoteness in time of the 1944 activities. It was apparent from the circumstances of the two interviews that the Superintendent had other questions to ask. Petitioner's refusal to answer was not based on the remoteness of his 1944 activities. He made it clear that he would not answer any question of the same type as the one asked. Petitioner blocked from the beginning any inquiry into his Communist activities, however relevant to his present loyalty. The Board based its dismissal upon petitioner's refusal to answer any inquiry about his relevant activities—not upon those activities themselves. It took care to charge petitioner with incompetency, and not with disloyalty. It found him insubordinate and lacking in frankness and candor—it made no finding as to his loyalty.

We find no requirement in the Federal Constitution that a teacher's classroom conduct be the sole basis for determining his fitness. Fitness for teaching depends on a broad range of factors. The Pennsylvania tenure provision specifies several disqualifying grounds, including immorality, intemperance, cruelty, mental derangement and persistent and willful violation of the school laws, as well as "incompetency." However, the Pennsylvania statute, unlike those of many other States, contains no catch-all phrase, such as "conduct unbecoming a teacher," to cover disqualifying conduct not included within the more specific provisions. Consequently, the Pennsylvania courts have given "incompetency" a broad interpretation.

Our recent decisions in Slochower v. Board of Higher Education, 350 U.S. 551, 76 S.Ct. 637, 100 L.Ed. 692, and Konigsberg v. State Bar of California, 353 U.S. 252, 77 S.Ct. 722, 1 L.Ed.2d 810, are distinguishable. In each we envisioned and distinguished the situation now before us. In the Slochower case, 350 U.S. at page 558, 76 S.Ct. at page 641, the Court said:

"It is one thing for the city authorities themselves to inquire into Slochower's fitness, but quite another for his discharge to be based entirely on events occurring before a federal committee whose inquiry was announced as not directed at 'the property, affairs, or government of the city, or . . . official conduct of city employees.' In this respect the present case differs materially from Garner [Garner v. Board of Public Works, 341 U.S. 716, 71 S.Ct. 909, 95 L.Ed. 1317], where the city was attempting to elicit information necessary to determine the qualifications of its employees. Here, the Board had possessed the pertinent information for 12 years, and the questions which Professor Slochower refused to answer were admittedly asked for a purpose wholly unrelated to his college functions. On such a record the Board cannot claim that its action was part of a bona fide attempt to gain needed and relevant information."

In the Konigsberg case, supra, 353 U.S. at pages 259-261, 77 S.Ct. at pages 726-727, this Court stressed the fact that the action of the State was not based on the mere refusal to answer relevant questions—rather, it was based on inferences impermissibly drawn from the refusal. In the instant case, no inferences at all were drawn from petitioner's refusal to answer. The Pennsylvania Supreme Court merely equated refusal to answer the employing Board's relevant questions with statutory "incompetency."

Inasmuch as petitioner's dismissal did not violate the Federal Constitution, the judgment of the Supreme Court of Pennsylvania is affirmed.

Case note. Distinguish between the facts of the Slochower and the Beilan cases. In the Slochower case the teacher's connection with the Communist Party had been known for twelve years because he had testified openly before a state investigating committee at that time. It was not until he refused to testify before a federal subcommitee as to his past association with Communists that he was dismissed. Also, he was not given notice and a hearing before his dismissal. Beilan, on the other hand, was questioned by the school superintendent who was seeking information as to the truth or falsity of rumors as to Beilan's disloyalty. At the time of his refusal he was warned of possible dismissal and later he was given a hearing before dismissal on charges of incompetency. Therefore, he was not denied due process of law. Furthermore, his loyalty was not in question at this time; only his refusal to answer the questions of his superior in the school system— those questions having to do with his fitness as a teacher. Incompetency in tenure laws is broadly interpreted. Although Pennsylvania has a loyalty act, the board of education proceeded under the tenure law. Its action was upheld.

Sources of Further Information

11 Am. Jur. "Constitutional Law" sec. 347; 9 Am. Jur. "Oath" sec. 7; 47 Am. Jur. "Schools" secs. 9, 109, 189.

16A C.J.S. "Constitutional Law" secs. 472, 600; 67 C.J.S. "Officers" sec. 62.

A.L.R. "Schools" Topic Nos. 34 and 43. See especially, 18 A.L.R. (2d) 268, 19 A.L.R. (2d) 388, and 27 A.L.R. (2d) 487.

American Digest System "Constitutional Law" Key Nos. 82, 90, 91, 277(2); "Municipal Corporations" Key No. 217(3); "Office" Key Nos. 18, 36(1); "Schools and School Systems" Key Nos. 55, 59, 127, 133, 133.1, 138, 144.3; "Statutes" Key No. 47.

Work Sheet

1. Do teachers in your state sign a loyalty oath on their applications for certificates? On their contracts of employment?

2. To what do teachers swear to demonstrate their loyalty?

3. Is membership in a subversive group or the Communist Party forbidden?

4. If so, what is the penalty?

5. Does your state have a law requiring teachers to testify before investigating agencies?

6. If so, does it contain or imply scienter?

Chapter 4.

RESIGNATION AND
ABANDONMENT OF CONTRACT

Editorial Comment

Closely allied to the dismissal of teachers, regulated by tenure laws or principles of contract law, is the problem of the resignation of teachers. If the school board is required to give teachers due notice before dismissal, teachers should give notice to the school board of their intention to quit the job and should not leave at a moment's notice. If a teacher feels free to sue for breach of contract when the board refuses to permit him to complete the term of a contract, he should consider that it is also breach of contract on his part when he leaves the service before the end of his contract term. Rarely, if ever, has a school board sued a teacher for breach of contract. This one-way procedure is not a matter of legal rights, but mere expediency. Damages from the school board are measurable by the contract salary of the teacher; if the school board sued a teacher, however, there would be difficulty in measuring the damages the school district sustained. Some teachers are harder to replace than others, and much depends upon the current labor market.

Because school boards had no practical redress at law when teachers abandoned their contracts, they included in some contracts of employment a penalty clause to the effect that if the teacher did not complete the contract he would be required to pay to the school district a stated sum as damages. Many contracts provide for the withholding of the salary due, or a stated sum, if the teacher quits before the end of the school term for which he is employed.

No cases have come before the courts recently on this question, but by analogy with contract law in general, the penalty clause is of doubtful legality. If construed by the court as a penalty, it is illegal; if construed as liquidated damages, it may be valid. Technically, to be considered liquidated damages the amount the teacher must forfeit is

related to the amount of injury suffered by the abandoned school board. Without making any distinction between penalties and liquidated damages, several states have proscribed penalty clauses, but permit the deserted employer to request revocation of certificate.

Some tenure laws prescribe the length of notice required of a teacher before his resignation is to become effective. Some states and local school board regulations have such provisions quite apart from tenure laws, or even in the absence of a tenure law. Most contracts of teachers include a provision regarding the teacher's resignation, either requiring a specified length of notice, or prohibiting resignations at certain critical dates when notice that a teacher will not fulfill his contract would work a particular hardship upon the school system.

If a teacher resigns and the resignation is accepted, the teacher cannot thereafter change his mind and claim the position. If another teacher is employed to take his place, the replacement teacher is entitled to the position. On the other hand, a teacher may rescind his resignation if he does so before the board has acted upon it. This is the general rule. However, some courts have held that a resignation can be rescinded if notice of withdrawal is made before its effective date, even though, in the meantime, the employer has accepted it for its effective date in the future.

If the board accepts a resignation and the teacher is released by mutual consent, there is no breach of contract on the part of the teacher. Any contract may be terminated by mutual consent, precluding any claims on either side thereafter.

When a group of teachers go on strike, they are abandoning their contracts. It is generally conceded that teachers, like other public employees, have no right to strike. Several states have enacted antistrike laws, providing penalties for those who strike against the government. If employed by a term contract, striking teachers have breached their contracts; if in tenure status, they have, theoretically at least, abandoned their tenure status. A school board could require teachers who had tenure status prior to the strike to fulfill the probationary period anew. Opinions of state and municipal attorneys are almost unanimous in holding that government employees cannot legally strike. Labor laws providing the right to strike are almost unanimously interpreted as not including public employees, even if the statute is silent with regard to them. On the other hand, the legislature could, if it wished, grant the right to strike to public employees. So far as is known, no legislature has done so.

Statutory Material

New Jersey Statutes Annotated, sec. 18:13-12.

A teacher employed by a board of education, who shall, without the consent of the board, leave the school before the expiration of the term of his employment, shall be deemed guilty of unprofessional conduct. The commissioner may, upon receiving notice of that fact, suspend the certificate of the teacher for a period not exceeding one year.

Statutory note. This statute is not unusual. In some other states the penalty is ineligibility for employment anywhere in the state for the remainder of the contract period. Imposition of these penalties, however, is not automatic; it depends upon action taken by the abandoned school board. When the school board notifies the state department of education that a teacher has abandoned his contract, some laws give the state superintendent discretionary power to impose the penalty while other laws make it mandatory for him to do so upon notice from the local school board. Discretionary power is the better provision because it gives the teacher an opportunity to explain extenuating circumstances.

New York Civil Service Law, sec. 108.

1. As used in this section the word "strike" shall mean the failure to report for duty, the wilful absence from one's position, the stoppage of work, or the abstinence in whole or in part from the full, faithful and proper performance of the duties of employment, for the purpose of inducing, influencing or coercing a change in the conditions or compensation, or the rights, privileges or obligations of employment; provided, however, that nothing contained in this section shall be construed to limit, impair or affect the right of any public employee to the expression or communication of a view, grievance, complaint or opinion on any matter related to the conditions or compensation of public employment or their betterment, so long as the same is not designed to and does not interfere with the full, faithful and proper performance of the duties of employment.

2. No person holding a position by appointment or employment in the government of the State of New York, or in the government of the several cities, counties, towns or villages thereof, or any other political or civil division of the state, or of a municipality, or in the public school service, or in any public or special district, or in the service of any authority, commission, or board, or in any other branch of the public service, hereinafter called "public employee," shall strike.

3. No person exercising any authority, supervision or direction over any public employee shall have the power to authorize, approve or consent to a strike by one or more public employees, and such person shall not authorize, approve or consent to such strike.

4. Notwithstanding any other provision of law, any public employee who violates the provisions of this section shall thereby abandon and ter-

minate his appointment or employment and shall no longer hold such position, or be entitled to any of the rights or emoluments thereof, except if appointed or reappointed as hereinafter provided.

5. Notwithstanding any other provision of law, a person violating the provisions of this section may subsequent to such violation be appointed or reappointed, employed or re-employed as a public employee, but only upon the following conditions:

(a) His compensation shall in no event exceed that received by him immediately prior to the time of such violation;

(b) The compensation of such person shall not be increased until after the expiration of three years from such appointment or reappointment, employment or re-employment; and

(c) Such person shall be on probation for a period of five years following such appointment or reappointment, employment or re-employment, during which period he shall serve without tenure and at the pleasure of the appointing officer or body.

6. Notwithstanding the provisions of any other law, any person holding such a position who, without the lawful approval of his superior, fails to report for duty or otherwise absents himself from his position, or abstains in whole or in part from the full, faithful and proper performance of his position shall be deemed on strike; provided, however, that such person, upon request, shall be entitled, as hereinafter provided, to establish that he did not violate the provisions of this section. Such request must be filed in writing with the officer or body having power to remove such employee, within ten days after regular compensation of such employee has ceased. In the event of such request, such officer or body shall within ten days commence a proceeding for the determination of whether the provisions of this section have been violated by such public employee, in accordance with the law and regulations appropriate to a proceeding to remove such public employee. Such proceedings shall be undertaken without unnecessary delay.

Statutory note. This law is probably the most severe in the United States. It spells out all the penalties which, in other states, might be imposed under common-law principles of contract—and more. A teacher who has gone on strike not only must fulfill a new probationary period but one longer than is required of teachers upon initial employment, and he cannot benefit by increased compensation as a result of the strike. In fact, he cannot be eligible for increases he would have received normally until a three-year period has elapsed. Probably because the penalties in New York are so severe, the law provides for opportunity to prove nonviolation of the antistrike provisions; in other words, a hearing must be given upon request of any teacher. Notice, also, that New York school boards and their officers are denied the right to consent to a strike by their employees.

Case Material

French v. Board of Education of Unified School District of San Diego,
54 Cal. App. (2d) 148, 128 P. (2d) 722 (California, 1942). [Teacher,
claiming to be permanent, applied for mandamus to compel the board
to recognize her as a permanent teacher and pay salary for time she
was not assigned to a position.]

In 1934, the appellant was and for some years had been a teacher in
respondent district with permanent tenure. She and her husband were living
in San Diego but during the preceding school year her husband had been
employed as a teacher at Lakeside, some 21 miles from San Diego. During
the summer of 1934, appellant and her husband approached the respondent
with the request that the husband be given work as a probationary teacher
in respondent district. They were informed that it was the policy of the
respondent board not to give initial employment as teachers to a husband
and wife at the same time. After some discussion, an understanding was
arrived at between the parties for the purpose of enabling the husband to
substitute himself for the appellant as the member of the family having
permanent status in said district. To this end, and in order to maintain her
permanent status until her husband acquired tenure, it was understood and
agreed that the husband would be employed on the condition that the
appellant would take annual leaves of absence during his probationary
period, and that she would resign her position as a permanent teacher if
and when he acquired tenure. Incidentally, it appears that the appellant
was suffering from tuberculosis for several years from and after 1934, al-
thought she testified that she did not know that she had this disease until
December of that year.

Pursuant to this agreement, the terms of which were set forth in letters
exchanged between the parties, the husband taught in this district the next
three years, and each year the appellant was granted a leave of absence
upon her written application in which she mentioned the understanding.
For some reason which does not appear in the record the husband was not
re-employed for the school year 1937-38. During that year the appellant
was assigned to a half-time teaching position upon her written request in
which she said: "My physician says that it must be in the morning as he
would like me to rest in the afternoons." Beginning with the next year,
however, the understanding previously arrived at was reinstated by mutual
consent and the appellant took annual leaves of absence and her husband
was employed as a probationary teacher for the three school years between July, 1938 and June, 1941.

In March, 1941, the respondent's superintendent wrote to the appellant
notifying her that her leave of absence would soon expire and requesting
information as to whether or not she was planning to teach the next year.
She called on the superintendent and was told by him that she would have
to resign because her husband was on the list to be made permanent and
that if she did not resign he would not hire her husband. She replied that
she did not want to resign and was told that she could either go back to
teaching or that she could resign and that her husband would be em-

ployed. Some days later, after further discussions with her and with her husband, she sent in her written resignation to take effect "at such time as my husband is made permanent" and in which she also said: "I am resigning because my husband would not become permanent unless I resign." This was accompanied by a letter to the respondent board in which she stated that she was tendering her resignation as a teacher; that she was resigning "to insure my husband's permanent status, upon request of the superintendent"; that "I wish my resignation to become effective at such time as my husband is made permanent"; and that "I do not want to sever relationships with the schools and I hope the board will reconsider my reemployment as a teacher."

After discussing this resignation the board instructed one of its members to talk the matter over with Mr. and Mrs. French and her father. This he did and at this conversation this board member asked the appellant if she really intended to resign and if there were any strings attached to the resignation. She replied that she wanted to resign, that she wanted to be sure that her husband would get tenure, and that she intended to stop teaching at any rate upon her husband's getting tenure. When the board member asked her why she sent the resignation in in that form she replied: "I wanted to be sure my husband will have permanent status." After some further discussion along this line she expressed a desire to occasionally do some work if called upon and this board member told her that he did not see why this could not be done after a time although, as he testified, he made no promises to her.

Her written resignation was dated April 28, 1941, and it was accepted by the respondent at a board meeting on May 6, 1941, and at the same meeting the appellant's husband was employed for the next year and he began his work in September, 1941, thus attaining permanent status. On September 10, 1941, the appellant wrote to the respondent stating that she was in good health and requesting an assignment to teach, naming her preference as to schools. She was not assigned as such teacher and this proceeding followed. . . .

The first point specifically presented is that "the resignation was invalid as against public policy." It is first argued that appellant's resignation was based wholly upon the consideration that her husband be employed as a teacher; that the qualifications of the appellant or of her husband played no part in the matter; that teachers are supposed to be selected wholly upon their qualifications; and that the respondent board acted contrary to our educational ideals and violated its duty to the public in thus making a "deal" for the employment of a teacher without regard to his qualifications. It in no way appears that the husband's qualifications were not considered, and it was arranged so that the appellant could retain her status until he proved that his qualifications justified his being retained long enough for him to acquire tenure. . . . The real question in this case is not one of public policy in the sense contended for, but is as to whether or not the appellant's resignation was given as a result of an unlawful coercion or compulsion. . . .

There was no compulsion here in either a legal or equitable sense. The appellant was free to make her own choice, which she did. She fully understood the matter from the beginning and not only chose at that time, but

probably then intended to follow it to completion, the course which she pursued to the desired final conclusion. . . . It clearly appears that she very much preferred to secure tenure for her husband, rather than keep it for herself, if only one of them was to be allowed to have tenure. . . . It is not claimed that anything was at any time misrepresented to her. With full knowledge she exercised a free choice between two situations either of which, but only one of which, was available to her. The only element of compulsion assigned to respondent is its refusal to do something it was under no obligation to do unless she did something which she had agreed to do. Even in this regard the appellant was given the opportunity to abandon the agreement . . . she voluntarily chose the benefit and course which she at all times had most desired, and no coercion or compulsion appears.

Case note. An agreement coerced by misrepresentation or entered into under duress can be avoided. Had the teacher's resignation been proved to have been made under duress, she could have rescinded it. There was no compulsion of an illegal nature in these circumstances, however, and the teacher, by seeking reemployment after her husband had acquired tenure, tried to break the agreement when it was too late for the board to avoid the husband's tenure employment.

Cuba Consolidated School District No. 1 v. Fox et al., Mo. App.__, 79 S.W. (2d) 772 (Missouri, 1935). [School board petitioned court to stop teachers from entering school building, from interfering with conduct of school, and from inciting rebellion among students.]

The petition is based upon the following statement of facts:

That on April 22, 1933, appellant school district had employed teachers in the school for the ensuing year, omitting to employ the five defendants, who were then teaching under contract until some time in May, 1933.

That on Sunday, the 23d, the president of appellant school board interviewed five other teachers, who had been employed on the previous day, to teach the ensuing year, in the places and instead of respondents, and had arranged with the five newly employed teachers to be in Cuba the following Monday morning.

That on Sunday, April 23d, the five respondents with perhaps another one or two of the teachers, held two meetings, one in the afternoon and one in the evening, discussing the fact that they had not been re-employed for the coming year. Defendants finally concluded in these conferences that they would go to the school building on Monday morning, as usual, teach their first hour classes, and then leave with the purpose, as they said, to go to Jefferson City and interview the state superintendent concerning the situation. On Monday morning, April 24, 1933, each of the defendants went to the school building and proceeded with his or her first class for that day, with the exception of respondent Fox, principal of the high school, who consumed the full class period in making a statement to the students to the effect that he had been unfairly treated by the board of directors and the superintendent of the school; that he was leaving and

that no doubt other teachers would be employed in the places of defendants; that the school would perhaps continue as usual. The other respondents also told their classes that they were leaving, and no doubt other teachers would be employed in their places.

None of the defendants advised the superintendent or the board of directors of their intention to leave, or when, if ever, they expected to return to their duties as teachers.

At the close of the first class period on Monday morning, the five respondents, as they had agreed, left the school building and absented themselves for the remainder of that day.

The five teachers who had been requested by the board on Sunday, to be in town on Monday, and who had been employed on Saturday evening before, as teachers for the ensuing year, in the places of the five respondents, came to the school building on Monday, and by order of the board assumed their duties as teachers in the places of the defendants, and continued to teach in their places during the day, on Monday, after the first class period.

After the five respondents left the school building, at the close of the first period, on Monday, the student body became boisterous and unruly, and refused to obey the orders of the superintendent; formed a parade, and marched about the town shouting, "We want our teachers back."

On Monday evening the board met and employed for the balance of the year the five teachers who had taken the places of the five defendants.

On Tuesday morning the substitute teachers were again in the school building to assume their duties as teachers, and the five defendants also reappeared in the school building, and attempted to continue as teachers.

The board of directors again went to the school building on Tuesday morning, found the defendants also there, and after having been advised by one of them, as spokesman for the five, that they intended to continue as teachers for the balance of the year, the superintendent dismissed the school for that day.

Thereupon the petition for injunction herein was filed, and a temporary writ in vacation issued by the judge of the circuit court.

On the next day, the defendants again appeared at the school building for the avowed purpose of continuing as teachers, notwithstanding the fact that the five newly employed teachers were also present for the purpose of replacing them.

Thereupon the sheriff of the county served the defendants with the temporary writ. . . .

The evidence further was that the class bells did not ring on Tuesday morning, and while the student body was assembled in the study hall defendant Fox, formerly the high school principal, without consulting the superintendent, asked the student body if they wanted to pass to their classes, upon which the superintendent of the school advised the pupils that no classes would pass, meaning that they would not assemble on that day, and the school was thereupon by the superintendent dismissed. . . .

[The trial court dismissed the petition and dissolved the injunction.]

Upon the evidence, showing the defendant's conduct in refusing to continue the school, after the first hour, on Monday, it is our opinion that

when the teachers (defendants) walked out on that day and remained away from their plain duty, without the consent and against the will of the school board, they breached their contract with the appellant district.

The plain provisions of Section 9210, R.S. 1929 (Mo. St. Ann. sec. 9210, p. 7083) are that: "Neither party shall suspend or dismiss a school under said contract without the consent of the other party."

From the foregoing section of the statutes it appears clear to us that the teachers had no authority or legal right to dismiss the school or willfully absent themselves from their plain statutory duty, without consent of the board of directors previously obtained.

Section 9210, R.S. 1929 (Mo. St. Ann. sec. 9210, p. 7083), contains the additional provision: "The contract required in the preceding section shall be construed under the general law of contracts, each party thereto being equally bound. . . ."

. . . it is our opinion that plaintiff was entitled to equitable relief in the form of a decree, personally enjoining defendants from entering upon the premises of the school building or plaintiff district and interfering with the peaceable and harmonious conduct of the general school program and class recitations of said school, during school hours. . . .

The evidence does not disclose whether the respondents were considering the question of resigning as teachers, because of not being retained, or because the district had not paid them for some time previous, neither of which, however vexatious, were legal reasons for quitting at the time. The fact of the walkout of the teachers on Monday morning, with no information furnished to the board as to when, if at all, they might be expected to return, was a situation for which the board could reasonably be expected to make speedy preparation to provide for and be ready to meet. This the school board did. . . . The board in this, we think, did what any faithful representative should have done, as representatives of any business either private or public. . . .

Therefore, the judgment of the trial court should be, and is, reversed outright.

Case note. There are implications in this decision bearing upon teachers' right to strike; in fact, the circumstances in this case might be called a one-day strike of the five teachers. These teachers were employed on annual contracts, but it has been the consensus of legal opinion that even tenure teachers, theoretically if not practically, lose their status if they go on strike. There is a difference, however, in that a teacher who unlawfully absents himself from his duties during the term of a contract may be considered to have breached the contract and may therefore be replaced immediately; a tenure teacher would be entitled to notice and hearing under the tenure law before any other teacher could take his place except on a day-to-day substitute basis.

On the other hand, in the instant case it might be argued that the school board had breached the contract in not paying the teachers

according to contract terms. However, this argument was apparently not placed before the court; at least, no mention of it was made by the court in its opinion.

City of Manchester v. Manchester Teachers Guild et al., 100 N.H. 507, 131 A. (2d) 59 (New Hampshire, 1957). [Right of teachers to strike.]

The only issue involved on this appeal is the correctness of the ruling made by the Trial Court that public school teachers do not have the right to strike against the city and that such a strike is illegal and subject to injunction.

This strike was found by the Court to have been conducted in a completely peaceful manner, without violence, picket lines, disturbances or damage to person or property. Its purpose was to obtain salary increases. The Court's ruling that the existence of individual annual teaching contracts with each teacher was not material to its decision has not been challenged by any of the parties. The law appears to be settled however, that if such contracts were of employment for a term subsisting at the time of the strike, the strike would be illegal. . . . Apart from any contracts for a stated term however, and if this strike had occurred in the course of negotiations between a private employer and his employees it would not have been subject to injunction because of its lawful purpose and the reasonableness of its execution. . . .

If this strike was properly enjoined it must be because public policy renders illegal strikes by school teachers in public employment. Although that question has not been decided heretofore by this court other jurisdictions have held that public employees have no right to strike against the government be it federal, state, or a political subdivision thereof. . . .

It would serve no useful purpose to detail the many reasons which support this policy. Absence of the profit motive on the part of the public employer and the necessity that there be no interruption in the operation of public functions because of the serious consequences which would ensue are some of them. However like the common law doctrine of the State's immunity from liability for any negligence of its agents or servants while engaged in a governmental function, *Cushman v. Grafton County,* 97 N.H. 32, 79 A. 2d 630, as well as its immunity from suit, *Moore v. Dailey,* 97 N.H. 278, 86 A. 2d 342: *D'Amours v. Hills,* 96 N.H. 498, 79 A. 2d 348, the underlying basis for the policy against strikes by public employees is the doctrine that governmental functions may not be impeded. . . .

"In the American system, sovereignty is inherent in the people. They can delegate it to a government which they create and operate by law. . . . The government so created and empowered must employ people to carry on its task. Those people are agents of the government. They exercise some part of the sovereignty entrusted to it. They occupy a status entirely different from those who carry on a private enterprise. They serve the public welfare and not a private purpose. To say that they can strike is the equivalent of saying that they can deny the authority of government and

contravene the public welfare." . . . This doctrine does not violate any constitutional rights of public employees. . . .

In the light of the increase in public employment, the disparity existing in many cases in the salary of public employees as compared to similar positions in private employment, and the enactment in recent years of legislation guaranteeing the right of private employees to bargain collectively and to strike, it may seem anomalous and unfair to some that government should deny these same rights to its employees working in similar employment, 36 Va. L. Rev. 258, 259. However any modification in the common law doctrine that the sovereignty of the state should not be hampered by strikes by public employees involves a change in public policy. It has been the consistent opinion of this court that such a change is for the Legislature to determine rather than being within the province of the court. . . .

The only enactment by the Legislature on this subject is Laws 1955, c. 255 which amended RSA 31:3 by adding to the powers of towns and cities the power to "recognize unions of employees and make and enter into collective bargaining contracts with such unions." . . . This legislation removed the doubt previously existing as to the power of municipalities and other public bodies to enter into a contract with a labor union, it having been argued that to do so would constitute an abdication of the continuing legislative discretion which these bodies should exercise. . . .

There had been introduced in the 1951 session of the Legislature a bill to the same effect which was not enacted into law. It had a provision, however, that contracts entered into between public officials and their employees shall be void unless they contained a provision that every employee covered by the contract, "shall be conclusively deemed to have agreed not to engage directly or indirectly, in any strike." Defendants argue that the absence of such a prohibition in Laws 1955, c. 255, is conclusive evidence that the Legislature not only recognized the right of municipal employees to strike but did not wish to curtail it.

Defendants further argue that the right to strike is a necessary concomitant to the right to bargain collectively and that by granting the latter the Legislature necessarily intended to also grant to public employees the right to strike. . . .

In legislation affecting rights of the sovereign the intent of the Legislature to abrogate an immunity must be expressed "in 'explicit language' . . . or at least by implication of such reasonable clarity that the courts need not strain the words of the statute to reach such a conclusion." . . . We do not see in Laws 1955, c. 255 such a clear expression of legislative intent to abrogate the right of the sovereign to be free from strikes by public employees. Furthermore said statute provides for collective bargaining contracts with unions of employees and no such contract is involved in this case.

There is no doubt that the Legislature is free to provide by statute that public employees may enforce their right to collective bargaining by arbitration or strike. . . .

Absent such legislation the collective action of the school teachers in refusing to work for the city in order to obtain salary increases even though

executed in a reasonable manner was subordinate to the right enjoyed by the city against a strike by its employees. It was therefore illegal and properly enjoined. . . . The injunction restrained the concerted action of the defendants and did not in any way impose on any individual an obligation to work against his will. . . .

Case note. This case illustrates a situation which occurs occasionally when the court must decide the issue in a way contrary to its belief as to the justice of a contrary decision. Even though the court felt that it was unfair to deny government employees the same rights as enjoyed by private employees, it concluded that those rights did not exist unless granted by the legislature. Frequently, courts will say "It is not for the courts to change the common law; it is for the legislature, if it wishes," or words to that effect.

In New Hampshire teachers have the statutory right to bargain collectively with the local school boards, but that statutory right does not include the right to strike. In other words, though collective bargaining in private employment includes the right to strike, it does so because of affirmative labor laws and, as the court here held, collective bargaining can be carried on without the right to strike.

Sources of Further Information

47 Am. Jur. "Schools" sec. 138; "Declaratory Judgment" sec. 76n.
78 C. J. S. "Schools and School Districts" sec. 206.

American Digest System "Schools and School Districts" Key No. 139; "Constitutional Law" Key Nos. 81, 121 (1, 2), 238 (1), 277 (2); "Labor Relations" Key Nos. 284, 342, 415, 480.

Rhyne, Charles S. *Labor Unions and Municipal Employe Law.* Washington, D. C.: National Institute of Municipal Law Officers. 1946. 583 p.

Work Sheet

1. Does your contract form contain any provision penalizing you for terminating service before the expiration of the contract?
2. How much notice is required before a resignation takes effect?
3. Are there specific times of year when the board has a right to refuse to accept resignations?
4. Are teachers and other school employees permitted or prohibited by statute from striking in your state?
5. If prohibited, what is the statutory penalty?
6. Have there been any cases in your state in which teachers' rights to strike have been explored by the courts? If so, what have the courts decided?

Chapter 5.

COLLECTIVE BARGAINING

Editorial Comment

Private employees have the right to bargain collectively through their unions representing them in negotiations with their employers for better working conditions. The procedure to be followed by employers and unions is set down in labor laws. Most state labor laws are similar to the National Labor Relations Act which provides that (1) the employer must respond to the request of a union for a conference when assured that the majority of the employees are represented by the union requesting the conference; (2) the employer must deal with those union representatives and not with individual employees or minority groups; (3) the employer must negotiate all particulars within the subject of the controversy; (4) although the employer is not required to agree to any specific demands of the union representatives, he must make counterproposals and bargain in good faith in the attempt to reach a conclusion acceptable to employer and employees; (5) after agreement has been reached, it must be put into a written document which constitutes a contract for a definite period of time. The National Labor Relations Act and most state labor laws explicitly exclude public employees; the few state labor laws which are silent as to their application to public employees are almost universally held by the attorneys general of those states to exclude public employees. Special grievance procedures have been adopted in one or two states for public employees, but, so far as is known, New Hampshire is the only state with affirmative legislation authorizing towns to bargain collectively with school employees.

There are a number of reasons why collective bargaining, as practiced in private employment, is not considered legal in public employment. Many of the issues on which private employees bargain with their employers are not subject to bargaining in public employment because those matters are fixed by statute. Also, it is said that to permit public employees to bargain collectively would be for the school board to

abdicate from its statutory authority to settle such matters unilaterally. Furthermore, the closed or union shop and the right to strike are considered a part of collective bargaining in private employment and there are those who cannot see collective bargaining procedure when public employees have no right to strike and when the closed or union shop is illegal in public employment. There have been few cases where school employees have been upheld in their right to bargain collectively; almost always either the closed or union shop or the right to strike was also involved; and, therefore, the courts in these cases have denied the validity of the bargain but primarily because it contained either or both of these two undesirable features. A closed or union shop is illegal in public employment because it restricts the employer from selection of employees other than persons who are members of the union, and thus violates statutes which give employers the authority to select their employees.

It would seem that, if the right to strike is denied in the bargain and if the bargain guarantees an open shop, public employees could legally bargain collectively. As a matter of fact, committees of teachers frequently appear before school boards seeking better working conditions although no one ever considers that this practice is a form of collective bargaining because the board may listen or not as it wishes, accept or reject the proposals of the teachers' representatives; and, if the board does accept the proposal it is still a unilateral action taken by the board not necessarily because the matter was proposed by the teachers.

Statutory Material

Revised Laws of New Hampshire. Chapter 51, sec. 3.

Town may purchase and hold real and personal estate for the public uses of the inhabitants, and may sell and convey the same; may recognize unions of employees and make and enter into collective bargaining contracts with such unions; and may make any contracts which may be necessary and convenient for the transaction of the public business of the town.

Statutory note. Though teachers and other school employees have bargained collectively in a few localities of other states, *e.g.*, Connecticut and Montana, they seldom have statutory right to do so. The enabling legislation in New Hampshire is very general. The scope of the activity it authorized had to be determined by the court in the Manchester case (included in the preceding chapter of this text).

Case Material

Chapin v. Board of Education of the City of Peoria, Circuit Court of Illinois, Peoria, Illinois. No. 21255. December 9, 1939. [Right of school employees to bargain.]

The matter presented for determination is the motion of the Board of Education of City of Peoria and certain members of said Board as individuals to dismiss the complaint filed by certain taxpayers which seeks to restrain the Board of Education from entering into or carrying out the terms of a certain agreement between said board and the school employes, Firemen and Oilers Local 8-A, American Federation of Labor.

Among other things, the agreement provides that all people who work for the board in the capacity of janitors, firemen, engineers, ground keepers and janitresses shall be and remain members in good standing in said local. In addition to the foregoing, the agreement makes provisions as to wages, which are to remain same as those previously paid, deals with overtime activities in school buildings, the hours of employment and other matters pertinent to the maintenance of the school buildings and the discharge of duties in connection therewith.

It is elementary that the courts cannot be called upon to usurp the functions of a board of education. The board, in its discretion, has ample authority, and the duty devolves upon it, to prescribe rules and regulations of the nature of those contained in the contract in question and which are complained of in the bill of complaint. Many of the provisions of the contract are clearly within the discretionary power of the board.

However, the question of the legal authority of the board to enter into a contract by the terms of which employment will be given exclusively to the members of a certain organization is entirely another question.

The solution of this legal problem requires an analysis of the legal status of a board of education. It has been declared by the courts of our State to be a corporation or quasi-corporation created by the State to aid in the administration of our state government. It is charged with duties purely governmental in character. It is an agency of the State and has existence for the sole purpose of performing certain duties necessary to the maintenance of a school system within the jurisdiction of the particular school board. It receives its funds from the taxpayers and occupies the position of a trustee of the moneys so received. The owners of those funds are the taxpayers, and the board is bound to expend the money so held for the benefit of the real owners, namely, the taxpayers.

The owner of a private business or industry may enter into a contract of employment whereby he agrees to employ only members of a certain organization. The money so expended belongs to him, and so long as it is expended for lawful purposes he has a right to spend it as he sees fit. In fact, in private industry, the so-called closed shop is more the general rule than it is the exception, and through the agencies of union organization much has been accomplished to bring about better wages and working conditions for their membership. The courts have held labor unions to be lawful organizations. However, for a governmental agency such as a

board of education, which is representative of all the taxpayers, to enter into a contract as is involved in this case has been held to be a discrimination between different classes of citizens and to be illegal and void.

The Supreme Court of Illinois, in *Adams v. Brennan*, 177 Illinois, page 194, which was a case involving the same questions and is controlling in the decision of the case at bar, said: "No question concerning the merits of labor or trades unions is in any way involved in this case. The right of organization for mutual benefit in all lawful ways is not denied. The question is whether the board of education has a right to enter into a combination with such an organization for the expenditure of the taxpayers' money for the benefit of members of the organization, and to exclude any portion of the citizens following lawful trades and occupations from the right to labor. It has no such right."

It has also been decided by the Illinois Supreme Court in *Fiske v. People*, 188 Illinois, page 206, and *Holder v. City of Alton*, 179 Illinois, page 318, that cities, which are also corporations of a public nature, cannot legally adopt ordinances providing that certain public works be done only by members of a certain organization because it amounts to a discrimination between different classes of citizens.

It would not be contended that the legislature of our State could pass a law providing that certain work required by the State or by a board of education should be done only by members of a particular organization. Such a law would be unconstitutional and void on the ground of discrimination. So, a school board, an agency and creature of the State, which could have no more authority in this regard than the State itself, cannot enter into a contract of the nature of the one involved in this case except under the penalty of it being illegal and void for the same reason. It may be true that without any contract the board can employ members of the local in question to the exclusion of non-members. It may be within its discretion to do so. The board cannot, however, by contract, foreclose the possibility of a non-member securing employment. The law finds no fault with a school board employing union labor or with its employes belonging to labor unions, but it does not permit the board to bind itself by contract to employ only those who belong to a particular association or organization. In that respect the contract is illegal and funds expended under and by virtue of such a contract would necessarily amount to an illegal expenditure of public funds, and a taxpayer may maintain a suit for injunction.

For the foregoing reasons this court concludes that it is the settled law of this State that public or municipal corporations, as school boards and cities, although free to employ whom they will, cannot by contract, rules or ordinances provide that public work can be performed only by members of certain organizations. This is true whether the organizations in question be trades unions, societies, associations or any other particular groups of individuals.

The motion to dismiss the complaint is denied.

Case note. Though this case concerned employees of the school board other than teachers, the decision would have been the same had the employees been teachers. The agreement was declared illegal be-

cause it contained a closed-shop provision. Furthermore, the court by dictum said that the legislature could not grant unions closed-shop rights in public employment because to do so would be unconstitutionally discriminatory. Since no legislature has attempted to enact such a law, this point has never been litigated.

Norwalk Teachers' Association v. Board of Education of City of Norwalk, 138 Conn. 269, 83 A. (2d) 482 (Connecticut, 1951). [Collective bargaining rights of a teachers' association.]

This is a suit between the Norwalk Teachers' Association as plaintiff and the Norwalk board of education as defendant for a declaratory judgment, reserved on the admitted allegations of the complaint for the advice of this court.

The complaint may be summarized as follows: The plaintiff is a voluntary association and an independent labor union to which all but two of the teaching personnel of approximately 300 in the Norwalk school system belong. In April, 1946, there was a dispute between the parties over salary rates. The board of estimate and taxation was also involved. After long negotiations, 230 members of the association rejected the individual contracts of employment tendered them and refused to return to their teaching duties. After further negotiations, in which the governor and the state board of education took part, a contract was entered into between the plaintiff and the defendant, and the teachers returned to their duties. The contracts subject to conditions precedent therein set forth, recognized the plaintiff as the bargaining agent for all of its members, defined working conditions and set up a grievance procedure and salary schedule. Similar contracts were entered into for the succeeding school years, including 1950-1951. From September, 1946, to the present and particularly with reference to the contract for 1950-1951, much doubt and uncertainty have arisen concerning the rights and duties of the respective parties, the interpretation of the contract and the construction of the state statutes relating to schools, education and boards of education. "In addition," the complaint states, "there has been the possibility of strikes, work stoppage or collective refusals to return to work by the teachers through their organization and the possibility of discharges or suspensions by the defendant by reason of difficult personnel relations, all of which tends to disharmony in the operation of the school system and to the ever present possibility that either, or both, the parties may be unwittingly violating statutes by reason of mistaken or erroneous interpretation thereon." The parties agreed that the contract for the school year 1949-1950 would govern their relations for the school year 1950-1951, that they would join in this action, and "that whatever contractual obligations exist will be forthwith modified so soon as they shall have received from the Court judgments and orders declaring their respective rights, privileges, duties and immunities." The specific points of dispute are stated in the questions reserved, printed in the footnote.

[The following is the footnote to which the preceding sentence refers.]

The plaintiff claimed a declaratory judgment answering and adjudicating the following questions:

"(a) Is it permitted to the plaintiff under our laws to organize itself as a labor union for the purpose of demanding and receiving recognition and collective bargaining?

"(b) Is it permitted to the plaintiff organized as a labor union to demand recognition as such and collective bargaining?

"(c) Is it permissible under Connecticut law for the defendant to recognize the plaintiff for the purpose of collective bargaining?

"(d) Is collective bargaining to establish salaries and working conditions permissible between the plaintiff and the defendant?

"(e) May the plaintiff engage in concerted action such as strike, work stoppage, or collective refusal to enter upon duties?

"(f) Is arbitration a permissible method under Connecticut law to settle or adjust disputes between the plaintiff and the defendant?

"(g) Is mediation a permissible method under Connecticut law to settle or adjust disputes between the plaintiff and the defendant?

"(h) If the answer to the previous question is yes, are the State's established administrative facilities, such as the State Board of Mediation and Arbitration and the State Labor Relations Board, available, as they are available in industrial disputes, to the plaintiff and the defendant?

"(i) Does the continuing contract law, so-called, create a status of employment within which the plaintiff may claim employment subject to the right to bargain salaries and working conditions?

"(j) Has the plaintiff the right to establish rules, working conditions and grievance resolution procedures by collective bargaining?"

[End of footnote.]

. . . Question (e) will be considered first.

Under our system, the government is established by and run for all of the people, not for the benefit of any person or group. The profit motive, inherent in the principle of free enterprise, is absent. It should be the aim of every employee of the government to do his or her part to make it function as efficiently and economically as possible. The drastic remedy of the organized strike to enforce the demands of unions of government employees is in direct contravention of this principle. It has been so regarded by the heads of the executive departments of the states and the nation. . . .

Few cases involving the right of unions of government employees to strike to enforce their demands have reached courts of last resort. That right has usually been tested by an application for an injunction forbidding the strike. The right of the governmental body to this relief has been uniformly upheld. It has been put on various grounds: public policy; interference with governmental function; illegal discrimination against the right of any citizen to apply for government employment (where the union sought a closed shop). . . .

In the American system, sovereignty is inherent in the people. They can delegate it to a government which they create and operate by law. They can give to that government the power and authority to perform certain duties and furnish certain services. The government so created and empowered must employ people to carry on its task. Those people are agents of the government. They exercise some part of the sovereignty entrusted to it. They occupy a status entirely different from those who carry on a private enterprise. They serve the public welfare and not a private purpose. To say that they can strike is the equivalent of saying that they can deny the authority of government and contravene the public welfare. The answer to question (e) is "No."

Questions (a) and (b) relate to the right of the plaintiff to organize itself as a labor union and to demand recognition and collective bargaining. The right to organize is sometimes accorded by statute or ordinance. . . . The right to organize has also been forbidden by statute or regulation. . . . In Connecticut the statutes are silent on the subject. Union organization in industry is now the rule rather than the exception. In the absence of prohibitory statute or regulation, no good reason appears why public employees should not organize as a labor union. . . . It is the second part of the question (a) that causes difficulty. The question reads: "Is it permitted to the plaintiff under our laws to organize itself as a labor union for the purpose of demanding and receiving recognition and collective bargaining?" The question is phrased in a very peremptory form. The common method of enforcing recognition and collective bargaining is the strike. It appears that this method has already been used by the plaintiff and that the threat of its use again is one of the reasons for the present suit. As has been said, the strike is not a permissible method of enforcing the plaintiff's demands. The answer to questions (a) and (b) is a qualified "Yes." There is no objection to the organization of the plaintiff as a labor union, but if its organization is for the purpose of "demanding" recognition and collective bargaining the demands must be kept within legal bounds. What we have said does not mean that the plaintiff has the right to organize for all of the purposes for which employees in private enterprise may unite, as those are defined in § 7391 of the General Statutes. Nor does it mean that, having organized, it is necessarily protected against unfair labor practices as specified in § 7392 or that it shall be the exclusive bargaining agent for all employees of the unit, as provided in § 7393. It means nothing more than that the plaintiff may organize and bargain collectively for the pay and working conditions which it may be in the power of the board of education to grant.

Questions (c) and (d) in effect ask whether collective bargaining between the plaintiff and the defendant is permissible. The statutes and private acts give broad powers to the defendant with reference to educational matters and school management in Norwalk. If it chooses to negotiate with the plaintiff with regard to the employment, salaries, grievance procedure and working conditions of its members, there is no statute, public or private, which forbids such negotiations. It is a matter of common knowledge that this is the method pursued in most school systems large enough to support a teachers' association in some form. It would seem to make no difference theoretically whether the negotiations are with a committee

of the whole association or with individuals or small related groups, so long as any agreement made with the committee is confined to members of the association. If the strike threat is absent and the defendant prefers to handle the matter through negotiation with the plaintiff, no reason exists why it should not do so. The claim of the defendant that this would be an illegal delegation of authority is without merit. The authority is and remains in the board. This statement is not to be construed as approval of the existing contracts attached to the complaint. Their validity is not in issue.

As in the case of questions (a) and (b), (c) and (d) are in too general a form to permit a categorical answer. The qualified "Yes" which we give to them should not be construed as authority to negotiate a contract which involves the surrender of the board's legal discretion, is contrary to law or is otherwise ultra vires. For example, an agreement by the board to hire only union members would clearly be an illegal discrimination. . . .

Question (f) reads, "Is arbitration a permissible method under Connecticut law to settle or adjust disputes between the plaintiff and the defendant?" If it is borne in mind that arbitration is the result of mutual agreement, there is no reason to deny the power of the defendant to enter voluntarily into a contract to arbitrate a specific dispute. On a proposal for a submission, the defendant would have the opportunity of deciding whether it would arbitrate as to any question within its power. . . . Agreement to submit all disputes to arbitration, commonly found in ordinary union contracts, are in a different category. If the defendant entered into a general agreement of that kind, it might find itself committed to surrender the broad discretion and responsibility reposed in it by law. For example, it could not commit to an arbitrator the decision of a proceeding to discharge a teacher for cause. So, the matter of certification of teachers is committeed to the state board of education. . . . The best answer we can give to question (f) is, "Yes, arbitration may be a permissable method as to certain specific, arbitrable disputes."

From what has been said, it is obvious that within the same limitations, mediation to settle or adjust disputes is not only permissible but desirable. The answer to question (g) is "Yes." The state board of mediation and arbitration and the state labor relations board, however, are set up to handle disputes in private industry and are not available to the plaintiff and defendant for reasons given in the opinion of the attorney general dated July 6, 1948.

The answer to question (h) is "No."

General Statutes, Sup. 1949, § 160a, provides in part: "The contract of employment of a teacher shall be renewed for the following school year unless such teacher has been notified in writing prior to March first of that year that such contract will not be renewed." Question (i) asks whether this law creates "a status of employment within which the plaintiff may claim employment subject to the right to bargain salaries and working conditions?" The meaning of this is not clear and the briefs do not clarify it. It is the type of question that should be related to a specific state of facts. It cannot be answered in vacuo.

As to question (j), the plaintiff has no right to establish rules. As stated above, the right is and remains in the board.

Case note. This case is one of the most liberal and most detailed as to rights of public-school employees. The court denied them the right to strike and held that a closed-shop agreement would be illegal. However, school employees were said to have the right to organize into unions or associations, in the absence of a statutory prohibition, and that these associations may legally bargain collectively with their school boards. On the other hand, the employees cannot *demand* the board to bargain with them or to accede to their proposals. Nor can the board agree to arbitrate all disputes because it would thereby surrender part of its statutory power in discretionary matters.

The court was more liberal than the typical state attorney general who has opined that public employers have no right to enter into collective bargaining agreements with their employees, even if they wish to on matters not prescribed by statute. Two suggestions may be made: that most state attorneys general have been influenced by the difficulty of separating closed shop and right to strike from collective bargaining, and that the Connecticut court in this case took a position which is forward-looking toward what may become generally acceptable practice in the future.

Benson et al. v. School District No. 1 of Silver Bow County,—— Mont.——, 344 P. (2d) 117 (Montana, 1959). [Validity of collective bargaining agreement of teachers' union.]

Plaintiffs brought this proceeding in mandamus and for a declaratory judgment to compel the defendant School District to enter into contracts with them and to require the issuance of salary warrants for the payment of the salary schedule designated under what is known as the "Master Agreement" made and entered into between the School District and the Teachers' Union. They also prayed for a declaratory judgment, declaring that the defendants have no authority to discriminate against plaintiffs or any other teachers who do not become members of the Butte Teachers' Union, and that the provisions of the Master Agreement providing for union security be declared null and void and of no effect. . . .

Plaintiffs are school teachers of defendant School District. They obtained a judgment in their favor upon the pleadings, and defendants and certain interveners appealed.

Since the judgment was entered on the pleadings it becomes necessary to consider the state of the pleadings. The complaint alleges that the plaintiffs are school teachers in School District No. 1 of Silver Bow County; that the defendants are the trustees of that School District; that on the 2nd day of April 1956, the defendant School District approved what is called a Master Agreement which among other things contained the following provisions

that "The single salary principle of equal salary for equal training and experience shall prevail."

It established a salary schedule for the plaintiffs of $5,100 per year for four of them and $4,900 for the other four. The Master Agreement then contained these clauses:

"(a) All members now employed by the Board, who are not members of the Union, must become members of the Union on or before the 4th day of September, 1956, and shall maintain their membership in the Union in good standing as defined by the constitution and by-laws of the Union during the term of their employment.

"(b) All teachers now employed by the Board, who are now members of the Union, shall maintain their membership in the Union in good standing as defined by the constitution and by-laws of the Union during the term of their employment.

"(c) All new teachers or former teachers employed by the Board shall become members of the Union within thirty (30) days after date of their employment and shall maintain their membership in good standing as defined in the constitution and by-laws of the Union during the term of their employment.

"The provisions of this Union Security Clause shall be adopted as a Board Rule and shall be a condition of all contracts issued to any teacher covered by this agreement.

"Any teacher who fails to sign a contract which includes the provisions of this Union Security Clause and who fails to comply with the provisions of this Union Security Clause shall be discharged on the written request of the Union, except that any such teacher who now has tenure under the laws of the State of Montana shall not be discharged but shall receive none of the benefits nor salary increases negotiated by the Union and shall be employed, without contract, from year to year on the same terms and conditions as such teacher was employed at during the year 1955-1956."

The complaint alleges that the plaintiffs are not members of the Butte Teachers' Union Local 332, and that they all signed and returned the contracts to the trustees of the district, but deleted therefrom the provisions that required them to become members of Butte Teachers' Union; that each of the plaintiffs was then advised by letter that their salaries would be at the rates enjoyed by them prior to the making of this contract, which was $300 per year less than the contract price stated in the Master Agreement. This letter after referring to the salary at which they would be retained contained a clause that should the teachers thereafter sign the Master Agreement they should then receive the higher salary from the date of so signing. The complaint alleges that it is above and beyond the powers of the defendant Board of Trustees to compel the plaintiffs to join or belong to the Butte Teachers' Union in order to qualify for and receive the wages, salary and compensation fixed by the Board.

It alleges the failure and refusal of the defendant Trustees to issue to the plaintiffs warrants for the payment of their increased salary though demand therefor has been made. It is alleged that the defendant Board of Trustees did issue to plaintiffs warrants for the lesser salary. It is alleged that plaintiffs

entered upon their duties as teachers and have continued to perform those duties as teachers for the School District.

Hence we come to the question whether the Union Security Clause in the contract is void and illegal as contended by plaintiffs. We hold that it is.

It is not competent for the school trustees to require union membership as a condition to receiving the increased salary. So far as this case is concerned it is sufficient to say that the Legislature has not given the school board authority to make the discrimination sought to be imposed here.

We do not pass upon the point whether it would be competent for the Legislature to place such authority in the school trustees. There is respectable authority holding that such action by the Legislature would be unconstitutional. Thus in the note in 31 A.L.R.2d §19, p. 1170, it is said: "Constitutional and statutory provisions granting the right of private industry to bargain collectively do not confer such rights on public employers and employees."

For the purpose of this case it is sufficient to say that the School Trustees have no authority or power to discriminate between the teachers employed by it as to the amount of salary paid to each because of their membership or lack of membership in a labor union. The School Trustees have no authority to invade that field. As well might it be argued that the Board of School Trustees might provide that the increased salary shall not be allowed to those who do not affiliate with a certain lodge, service club, church or political party.

It is our view that the trial court was right in its ruling, that the clause complained of here and which was deleted by the teachers is void and illegal, and that the writ of mandamus issued by the trial court should in all respects be affirmed unless there is merit in defendants' contention as to attorneys' fees.

Case note. The union's agreement provided that nontenure teachers should be dismissed by the board, on request of the union. This provision invaded the board's discretionary powers. Teachers who had acquired tenure status could not be dismissed for nonunion membership because that was not one of the statutory causes for dismissal of tenure teachers; therefore, the agreement provided that tenure teachers who did not belong to the union would be denied salary increases. The court held that the closed (actually, here it was union rather than closed) shop is illegal. The board could not discriminate against nonunion members as to their salaries. A dissenting opinion said that the nonunion tenure teachers were given all they were guaranteed under the tenure law—retention in their positions.

The agreement in question in this case contained some other provisions which were not before the court. For example, the board agreed not to employ married women teachers, unless they were already on tenure in which event they also would be denied salary increases. This case was taken by eight tenure teachers none of whom, apparently,

was a married woman; at least, that provision of the agreement was
not discussed by the court and could not have been unless one of
these eight teachers brought up the issue of discrimination because
of marriage.

Sources of Further Information

31 Am. Jur. "Labor" sec. 87.
63 C.J.S. "Municipal Corporations" sec. 980; 73 C.J.S. "Public Ad-
ministrative Bodies and Procedures" sec. 33.
American Digest System "Labor Relations" Key Nos. 52, 88, 1248.
Rhyne, Charles S. *Labor Unions and Municipal Employe Law.*
Washington, D. C.: National Institute of Municipal Law Officers.
1946. 583 p.
National Education Association, Research Division, *Professional
Negotiations with School Boards.* Washington, D. C.: the Association,
October 1961. 79 p. (offset). [The October publication is a prelimi-
nary edition constituting "A Legal Analysis and Review." Prepared by
the NEA Research Division for the NEA Board of Directors.]

Work Sheet

Review some grievance among the teachers in your school system and
determine if an adjustment could have been achieved by collective
bargaining procedures; outline the procedure you think would best
accomplish the desired result.

Chapter 6.

SALARIES

Editorial Comment

Salary is the issue most commonly sought to be settled by collective bargaining, and dissatisfaction with salaries is most often the controversy resulting in teachers' strikes. It is a logical sequence, therefore, at this point to examine the law on teachers' salaries.

The salary a teacher is to be paid usually is and certainly should always be named in the employment contract. Many cities, especially the larger ones, have adopted salary schedules in which teachers are classified and salary is stated for each class with increments of specified amounts due at stated times. Salary schedules are usually matters of local regulation but some are statewide statutes.

State laws sometimes require that local school boards adopt salary schedules, but place no restrictions as to the nature of the schedule upon local boards. In two-thirds of the states, minimum salary standards are set, either through a stated sum which must be paid to teachers with a stated amount of preparation, or a single minimum salary for all teachers, or a minimum salary which the district must pay in order to get its portion of state-aid funds. In some other states the state-aid plans influence the amounts paid in teachers' salaries but do not set a minimum amount for individual salaries.

In about one-third of the states, there are laws prohibiting discrimination in salaries because of sex; in several, there is a prohibition against discrimination on the basis of marital status.

When state minimum salary laws were first enacted, there was some thought that such a law interfered with the freedom of contract and would therefore be unconstitutional, but the law was upheld in Iowa many years ago, and rarely have the courts since then been called upon to consider the question.

In times of economic stress, the burning question has been the right of the board to modify or abolish its salary schedule, as opposed to the view that the teachers have a vested right in the increments set

up on the schedule. The general principle is that a salary schedule does not create vested rights for the future. If a board makes the downward modification before contracts for the ensuing school year are issued (or before the ensuing school year begins in the event that written contracts are not issued annually), such modification is legal. However, after contracts for the ensuing school year have been issued (or after the ensuing school year has begun in the event that contracts are not issued annually), such modification is an impairment of an accrued right of the teachers.

In past years there has been considerable litigation on the necessity of paying teachers of like training and experience equal salaries regardless of race. Several cases have held that the Fourteenth Amendment to the Federal Constitution requires that no race discrimination be made.

Statutory Material

Deering's California Education Code, sec. 13525.

The governing board of each school district shall pay to each person employed in a day school of the district for full time in a position requiring certification qualifications and serving under other than an emergency or provisional credential an annual salary of not less than four thousand two hundred dollars ($4,200) prior to July 1, 1960, and four thousand five hundred dollars ($4,500) on and after July 1, 1960.

The governing board of each school district shall pay to each person employed for less than full time in a position requiring certification qualifications and serving under other than an emergency or provisional credential an annual salary of not less than an amount which bears the same ratio to four thousand two hundred dollars ($4,200) prior to July 1, 1960, and to four thousand five hundred dollars ($4,500) on and after July 1, 1960, as the time required of the person bears to the time required of a person employed full time.

"Full time" means not less than the minimum school day for each day the schools of the district are maintained during the school year.

The provisions of this section shall not be construed as applying to substitute employees of a school district.

Massachusetts General Laws Annotated. Chapter 71, sec. 40.

The compensation of every teacher employed in any public day school in the commonwealth, except persons in training and those employed as temporary substitutes, shall be at a rate of not less than four thousand dollars for the school year. Women teachers employed in the same grades and doing the same type of work with the same preparation and training as men teachers shall be paid at the same rate as men teachers. Such equal pay shall not be effected by reducing the pay of men teachers. The provisions of this

section relative to equal pay for men and women teachers shall be in force in any city or town which accepts or has accepted provisions relative to equal pay for men and women teachers in any manner from time to time as provided by law.

Statutory note. California has for many years been in the forefront among states having minimum salary laws and, as may be seen, Massachusetts is now not far behind. Some states have set the minimum salary at low figures, such as $1,200 or even lower, in laws long since unrealistic. Some teachers object to minimum salary laws on the ground that salaries paid may be the minimum payable; however, practice does not bear out this fear.

Case Material

Alston et al. v. School Board of Norfolk, 112 F. (2d) 992 (C.C.A. 4th, 1940) (Virginia) *cert. den.* 311 U.S. 693 (1940). [Negro teachers challenged board's policy of paying them less than white teachers.]

The purpose of the suit is to obtain a declaratory judgment, to the effect that the policy of defendants in maintaining a salary schedule which fixes the salaries of Negro teachers at a lower rate than that paid to white teachers of equal qualifications and experience, and performing the same duties and services, on the sole basis of race and color, is violative of the due process and equal protection clauses of the Fourteenth Amendment, and also to obtain an injunction restraining defendants from making any distinction on the ground of race or color in fixing the salaries of public-school teachers in Norfolk.

The suit was dismissed by the court below on the ground that Alston and the School Board were the only necessary parties to the cause and that Alston had waived such constitutional rights as he was seeking to enforce by having entered into a written contract with the School Board to teach for a year at the price fixed in the contract. On appeal . . . three questions arise: (1) whether upon the face of the complaint an unconstitutional discrimination is shown in the fixing of school teachers' salaries by the defendants; (2) whether rights of plaintiffs are infringed by such discrimination; and (3) whether plaintiffs have waived their right to complain of the discrimination by entering into contracts with the School Board for the current year.

On the first question, there can be no doubt but that the fixing of salary schedules for the teachers is action by the state which is subject to the limitations prescribed by the Fourteenth Amendment. . . . While provision is made in the law for separate schools for white and colored persons, the positive duty is enjoined of maintaining these separate schools under the same general regulations as to management, usefulness and efficiency. Va. Code, sec. 680. All teachers are required to hold teaching certificates in accordance with the rules of certification of the State Board of Education. Va. Code, Ch. 33, sec. 660 and Ch. 35, sec. 786. White and Negro teachers

must meet the same requirements to receive teachers' certificates from the Board of Education and upon qualifying are issued identical certificates. . . .

Defendants over a long period of years have consistently pursued and maintained and are now pursuing and maintaining the policy, custom, and usage of paying Negro teachers and principals in the public schools in Norfolk less salary than white teachers and principals in said public-school system possessing the same professional qualifications, certificates and experience, exercising the same duties and performing the same services as Negro teachers and principals. Such discrimination is being practiced against the plaintiffs and all other Negro teachers and principals in Norfolk, Virginia, and is based solely upon their race or color

The plaintiff Alston and all of the members of the plaintiff association and all other Negro teachers and principals in the public schools in the City of Norfolk are teachers by profession and are specially trained for their calling. By rules, regulations, practice, usage and custom of the Commonwealth acting by and through the defendants as its agents and agencies, the plaintiff Alston and all of the members of the plaintiff association and all other Negro teachers and principals in the City of Norfolk are being denied the equal protection of the laws in that solely by reason of their race and color they are being denied compensation from public funds for their services as teachers equal to the compensation provided from public funds for and being paid to white teachers with equal qualifications and experience for equivalent services pursuant to rules, regulations, custom and practice of the Commonwealth acting by and through its agents and agencies, the School Board of the City of Norfolk and the Superintendent of Schools. . . .

That an unconstitutional discrimination is set forth in these paragraphs hardly admits of argument. The allegation is that the state, in paying for public services of the same kind and character to men and women equally qualified according to standards which the state itself prescribes, arbitrarily pays less to Negroes than to white persons. This is as clear a discrimination on the ground of race as could well be imagined and falls squarely within the inhibition of both the due process and the equal protection clauses of the Fourteenth Amendment. . . .

We come, then, to the second question, *i.e.*, do plaintiffs as Negro teachers holding certificates qualifying them to teach in the public schools of Norfolk have rights which are infringed by the discrimination of which they complain? The answer to this must be in the affirmative. As teachers holding certificates from the state, plaintiffs have acquired a professional status. It is true that they are not entitled by reason of that fact alone to contracts to teach in the public schools of the state; for whether any particular one of them shall be employed to teach is a matter resting in the sound discretion of the school authorities; but they are entitled to have the compensation for positions for which they may apply, and which will unquestionably be awarded to some of them, fixed without unconstitutional discrimination on account of race. . . .

Nor do we think that the fact that plaintiffs have entered into contracts with the school board for the current year at the rate fixed by the discriminatory practice precludes them from asking relief. What the effect

of such contracts may be on right to compensation for the current year, we need not decide, since plaintiffs are not insisting upon additional compensation for the current year and their prayer for relief asks a broad declaration of rights and injunctive relief for the future. As qualified teachers holding certificates, they have rights as above indicated which are not confined to the contract for the current year, *i.e.*, the right to apply for positions in the future and to have the Board award the positions without unconstitutional discrimination as to the rate of pay.

The defendants take the position that no one but a teacher holding a contract with the Board has any such interest in the rate of pay as would give him standing to sue concerning it, and that he cannot sue because he has waived the unconstitutional discrimination by entering into the contract. If this were sound, there would be no practical means of redress for teachers subjected to the unconstitutional discrimination. But it is not sound. . . . "It is inconceivable that guarantees embedded in the Constitution of the United States may thus be manipulated out of existence." [The court also held that the teachers association was a proper party to the suit, since it was brought as a class suit for the members of the association.]

Case note. Many states have civil-rights laws which would prevent this sort of discrimination, and the state laws receive more local publicity than the provisions of the Federal Constitution which may be applied to a situation by interpretation. However, with or without a state law on the subject, the Federal Constitution protects its citizens from discriminations on account of race, color, or creed.

Murphy v. School Committee of Lawrence, 321 Mass. 478, 73 N. E. (2d) 835 (Massachusetts, 1947). [Application of an equal pay law.]

This is a bill for a declaratory judgment as to the rights of the plaintiff under G.L. (Ter.Ed.) c. 71, § 40, . . .

The statute, sometimes called the teachers' equal pay law, contains this provision: "Women teachers employed in the same grades and doing the same type of work with the same preparation and training as men teachers shall be paid at the same rate as men teachers." The city of Lawrence has accepted this statute. The plaintiff is employed in the public schools of Lawrence as a supervisor of arithmetic. It is her contention that she is entitled to the same pay as that received by one Durgin, a man teacher who is employed in the public schools of Lawrence as a supervisor of manual training and whose pay is higher than that of the plaintiff. The school committee has decided against her contention. Detailed findings of fact were made by the trial judge. He ruled upon the findings that the plaintiff was not entitled to the benefit of the statute and entered a decree accordingly. The plaintiff appeals. The evidence is reported.

The findings, amply supported by the evidence, show that the work of the plaintiff is in the fourth, fifth, and sixth grades, while the work of Durgin is in the sixth, seventh, and eighth grades, and that, although both the plaintiff and Durgin are called supervisors, the type of work performed

by them differs substantially in that the plaintiff supervises the teaching of arithmetic to both girls and boys, while Durgin supervises the teaching of woodworking to boys only and in addition performs other duties, not similar to any performed by the plaintiff, in ordering and distributing supplies and in keeping the time of other teachers. Supervision is the only common element in the work of the two teachers, and it is obvious that supervision of the work in manual training must differ substantially from supervision of the teaching of arithmetic. There are also great differences in the preparation and training of the two teachers. The plaintiff has had extensive education and experience on the scholastic side of teaching. Durgin's preparation and training consisted principally of experience as a journeyman carpenter, with the addition of a short normal school course in the teaching of manual training.

This case does not call for a careful definition of the words "the same" used four times in the statute. Neither do we determine to what extent, if at all, the court must give weight to the judgment of the school committee as to whether the "grades," "type of work," and "preparation and training" are "the same." It is clear that, in this case, none of the three requirements of the statute is met.

The question is not whether these teachers ought to receive the same pay. That question involves many considerations which are to be weighed by the school committee. The question for us is simply whether the plaintiff has proved a case establishing rights within the statute. The trial judge correctly ruled that she has not.

Decree affirmed.

Case note. It is not always easy for a court to determine what are like services in a school system. Here, a supervisor of arithmetic and a supervisor of manual training were said to engage in different work, the only common element being supervision. California is another one of the states with an equal pay law and the courts, there, have given broad meaning to it; *e.g.*, in *Chambers v. Davis et al.*, 131 Cal. App. 500, 22 P. (2d) 27 (California, 1933) the court required the board to pay a woman physical education teacher the same as it paid a man physical education teacher on grounds that the only difference in their work was that the woman taught girls while the man taught boys. Another court might have said that the physical-education program for boys was more extensive than the program for girls, especially considering competitive sports such as football.

Cotter et al. v. City of Chelsea, 329 Mass. 314, 108 N. E. (2d) 47 (Massachusetts, 1952). [Controversy between city and school board as to validity of dependency allowances in salary plan.]

This is a petition by ten or more taxable inhabitants of the city under G.L.(Ter.Ed.) c. 71, § 34, as appearing in St.1939, c. 294, to require the city

to provide a sum of money (plus twenty-five per cent thereof) equal to an alleged "deficiency" resulting from the failure of the city to appropriate for public schools in 1950 the full amount estimated and requested by the school committee. . . .

On November 25, 1947, the school committee voted "that all married teachers who are the sole support of his own wife, her own husband or his or her own children under eighteen years of age be granted a dependency allowance of $300 per annum." The principal question presented is whether this vote was valid, so that the city was obliged to appropriate a sum sufficient to cover the so called allowances. . . .

The city has argued that this "dependency allowance" was a mere gift. We do not think so. It was not intended as a single payment for services previously rendered. It was evidently intended as a permanent future increase in the salaries of those entitled to it as a part of the compensation for their work. It was actually paid to them for more than two years before the city refused the necessary appropriation for the year 1950. It had fewer of the elements of a gift than did the so called "bonus" held valid in Attorney General v. Woburn, 317 Mass. 465, 58 N.E. 2d 746, or the pay for "sick leave" held valid in Averell v. City of Newburyport, 241 Mass. 333, 135 N.E. 463, and in Quinlan v. Cambridge, 320 Mass. 124, 68 N.E.2d 11, or the vacation pay held valid in Wood v. Haverhill, 174 Mass. 578, 55 N.E. 381. Compare Whittaker v. City of Salem, 216 Mass. 483, 104 N.E. 350.

It is also argued that the vote violates the equal pay law. We do not see that it does. . . . We do not think that the vote here in question does discriminate between the sexes. It does directly affect more men than women, but this must be because there are more married men teachers with dependents than there are married women teachers with dependents. Married women teachers with dependents, of whom there are a few, do share in the benefit on an exact level with the men.

We are now brought to the question whether the school committee had power to classify any teachers as to compensation with relation to their having or not having persons dependent upon them for support. School committees have "general charge" of public schools and undoubtedly have full power to make reasonable and proper contracts with teachers and to fix their pay. . . . But, as with other boards charged with the performance of public functions, all of their acts must be within the authority committed to them and must bear some rational relation to the furthering of the objects for which the board exists. . . . When a public board sets up standards of pay not directly related to the work performed but varying with the private personal status of the employee it is treading upon dangerous ground. . . . School committees are not charged with the task of ironing out the inequalities of life or setting up systems of social welfare. If the vote is to be held valid it must be because the committee could reasonably believe that it would be for the good of the school system to pay more for teachers having dependents. . . .

On the other hand, the court should be slow to decide that a public board has acted unreasonably or arbitrarily. The court should cast about to discover, if possible, some ground which reasonable men might deem proper on which the action can rest. And in the case before us there has been no

attempt wholly to exclude any class of persons from employment as teachers. It is simply a question whether making the amount of salary depend to some small extent upon the situation of the teacher with respect to dependents can be thought by a reasonable school committeeman to have some effect in producing more efficient schools. On the whole, we incline to the view that the vote can be sustained. It is not that married teachers with dependents are for that reason likely to be better teachers than other persons—a proposition which it might be difficult to maintain. Rather the reason is that in a time when many consider the teaching profession underpaid as compared to the rising cost of living, but when, nevertheless, there is great resistance to increased municipal tax rates, and when therefore the securing of the most competent teachers for the public schools has become a considerable problem, of the existence of which the court may take judicial notice, . . . it may be thought with some justification that the more mature, experienced, and competent teachers are those most likely to be married and to have dependents, and that some recognition of the additional burden which such teachers carry will have some effect in the long run in securing and in retaining for the public schools the services of teachers of that type. Whether in fairness unmarried teachers with dependents ought to have been included in the vote we think was a matter for the school committee to decide. We are not quite prepared to say that failure to include them renders the entire vote invalid. . . .

It is not to be assumed that in going as far as we have in supporting this slight incursion by the school committee, in conditions now known to exist, into the field of domestic economy we would support further or different incursions. . . .

The city concedes that, if the vote of the committee is valid, the amount of the deficiency is $32,816.50. A decree is to be entered in favor of the petitioners requiring the city to provide that sum or such part thereof as shall not already have been provided, together with a sum equal to twenty-five per cent thereof, all in accordance with the provisions of G.L.(Ter.Ed.) c. 71, § 34, as appearing in St.1939, c. 294.

So ordered.

Case note. The dependency allowance did not violate the equal pay statute because married women with dependents were eligible as well as men, the only distinction being numerical since more married men have dependents than do married women. The court felt that the board could base salaries upon reasonable classifications without violating the equal pay law, so long as the classifications were not dependent upon sex. The court justified the dependency allowance on the ground that the board could believe that the more mature, experienced and competent teachers would most likely be married and have dependents and that in the long run the extra salary would have the effect of securing and retaining teachers of that type. The board did not grant dependency allowances to unmarried teachers

with dependents. This, said the court, was a matter for the board to decide.

Note reference in the first paragraph of this opinion to Massachusetts law imposing a penalty on towns for failure to appropriate the sum fixed by the school board. So far as is known, no other state has such a law.

Parrish et al. v. Moss et al., 200 Misc. 375, 106 N. Y. S. (2d) 577 (New York, 1951) *aff'd* (without opinion) 279 A.D. 608, 107 N. Y. S. (2d) 580 (1951). [Extra duties at no extra pay.]

Petitioners seek an order directing the Board of Education of the City of New York to annul the resolutions adopted by the said board at a special meeting on May 24, 1951, and for a further order directing the superintendent of schools to refrain from carrying out or enforcing such resolutions.

'Resolved, That the following regulations submitted by the Superintendent of Schools and governing service of teachers outside of regular classroom instruction are hereby approved; and Resolved, That any inconsistent provisions of the By-Laws be, and they are hereby, suspended: Regulations Submitted by the Superintendent of Schools: 1. Every teacher is required to give service outside of regular classroom instruction in the performance of functions which are the essential duties of every teacher. 2. There is an area of teacher service which is important to the well rounded educational program of the students, but in which teachers participate in varied ways according to their interests, capabilities and school programs. The principal has the responsibility and duty to see to it that these activities are carried on. The principal may assign a teacher to reasonable amounts of such service beyond the specified hours of classroom instruction, and the teacher is required to render such service. 3. In the assignment of teachers to these activities, principals are directed to see to it that in so far as is practicable, such assignments are equitably distributed. 4. Principals are directed to keep records of all assignments and service under Regulation 2, including the type of service, date or dates, and approximate time spent beyond the regular hours of classroom instruction. Such records should be reported at the end of each school year to the associate superintendent in charge of a division with a copy to the assistant superintendent. Each teacher is to be given a copy of the report with respect to her own services. Blanks will be provided for such school and individual reports. 5. Questions as to the interpretation of the above rules and regulations should be referred by principals and teachers to the assistant superintendent for consideration.' . . .

Petitioners' third contention that the responsibility for the operation of the school activities program in each particular school has been improperly delegated by these regulations to the principals, without adequate safeguards for the teachers, is also untenable. . . .

The hours established in any case must be reasonable. "The broad grant of authority to fix 'duties' of teachers is not restricted to classroom instruc-

tion. Any teaching duty within the scope of the license held by a teacher may properly be imposed. The day in which the concept was held that teaching duty was limited to classroom instruction has long since passed. Children are being trained for citizenship and the inspiration and leadership in such training is the teacher. Of course, it is recognized that any bylaw of a board outlining teachers' duties must stand the test of reasonableness. Any teacher may be expected to take over a study hall; a teacher engaged in instruction in a given area may be expected to devote part of his day to student meetings where supervision of such teacher is, in the opinion of the board, educationally desirable. Teachers in the fields of English and Social Studies and undoubtedly in other areas may be expected to coach plays; physical training teachers may be required to coach both intramural and inter-school athletic teams; teachers may be assigned to supervise educational trips which are properly part of the school curriculum. The band instructor may be required to accompany the band if it leaves the building. These are illustrations of some of the duties which boards of education have clear legal justification to require of their employees. A board is not required to pay additional compensation for such services. The duty assigned must be within the scope of teachers' duties. Teachers may not be required, for instance, to perform janitor service, police service (traffic duty), school bus driving service, etc. These are not 'teaching duties.' The board may not impose upon a teacher a duty foreign to the field of instruction for which he is licensed or employed. A board may not, for instance, require a *mathematics* teacher to coach intramural teams. Where the service is not part of the duties of the teacher, there is nothing to prevent the board from arranging for such extra service and paying for the same in its discretion. It is pointed out that section 1709, subdivision 16, of the Education Law specifically notes that the board may utilize teachers for playground activities and may pay them extra compensation in so doing. There are some activities that are part of instruction but, by their very nature, may be performed after the close of the regular school session. The athletic program, for instance, in many instances takes place under such circumstances. It has, nevertheless, over the years been always regarded as part of the school curriculum (see Commissioner's Regulations section 155). As has been heretofore stated in departmental publication, 'athletic activities are a definite and integral part of the instruction program in physical education.' Coaching in athletic sports is teaching. It, therefore, does not follow that because an activity is conducted after regular class hours, it is not part of the regular curriculum." . . .

"The general rule is that mandamus will not lie to review the determination of public boards or officers in matters involving the exercise of discretion or judgment, if they have proceeded within their jurisdiction, and in substantial compliance with the forms of law."

In the light of the foregoing, I see no reason why this court should disturb the resolutions readopted by the board of education at its meeting of May 31, 1951. Petitioners' application is denied and the petition dismissed.

Case note. California courts have also upheld the right of a board to require extra duties of teachers, and the California court made no

distinction between extra duties which are within or outside the scope of the teacher's regular duties as did the New York court. Nor did the California court base its opinion on factors considered by the New York court such as that only reasonable amounts of outside service be assigned, that the assignments be equitably distributed, and that teachers who are aggrieved by their assignment have the right of appeal to the assistant superintendent. The school board has discretionary power to fix teachers' hours of service, which need not coincide with their hours of classroom instruction.

Fowler et al. v. Town of Enfield, 138 Conn. 521, 86 A. (2d) 662 (Connecticut, 1952). [Controversy among teachers, board of education, and municipal finance officers as to salary increases.]

The decisive question is whether the action of the board of education in entering into the purported amendment of its contracts with the plaintiffs providing a $250 increase in salary for the school year 1946-47 was valid and effective to render the defendant town liable for the unpaid $150 balance of this increase. In reaching our decision, we restrict our discussion of the facts found, the court's conclusions and the principles of law to those material and controlling in the determination of this issue. In May, 1946, the board of education entered into a contract with each of the plaintiffs for the school year 1946-47 specifying the salary at which he was employed by the town. The salaries so provided for, and subsequently paid, were larger than those budgeted and paid for the school year 1945-46. The contract provided that the plaintiffs should be notified of any adjustment of salary by the first of June preceding the opening of the school year in which the change was to become effective and that the plaintiffs agreed to accept and the town to pay the specified salary, and it included this further specific undertaking by each plaintiff: "I will abide by the terms of the contract given me at the time of this appointment." It further stated that either party might terminate the contract upon thirty days' written notice. After the board of education had entered into these contracts with the plaintiffs, it submitted its budget to the board of finance as the statute requires. General Statutes, § 1480. Incorporated in the budget was an item to meet the amount of the salaries to which the plaintiffs were entitled during the school year by virtue of their executed contracts. The budget was approved by the board of finance without material change and thereafter the town meeting made an appropriation to provide for the expenses so shown. The funds sought by the board of education were thus made available to it to meet all expenses for the operation of the schools, including the payment of the salaries for which the plaintiffs had agreed they would render services for the entire school year. The plaintiffs worked and were paid as agreed under these contracts for the entire school year of 1946-47. In addition they received the $100 adjustment referred to below. During the school year they gave no notice of intention to terminate their contracts.

On December 10, 1946, the welfare committee of the Enfield Teachers' Association appeared before the board of education, petitioned for a

"minimum salary adjustment of $500.00 retroactive to September 4, 1946" and demanded that the chairman of the committee be notified by December 18, 1946, of the board's action upon the petition. The board learned by informal inquiry of the board of finance that that body was not disposed to approve the increase demanded. On January 19, 1947, the board of education by formal vote requested approval from the board of finance of a salary increase of $250 for each full-time employee. In response to this vote, the latter board on February 5, 1947, advised the former that it had considered the demand for the salary increase and that it was denied. Meantime the teachers' welfare committee was also negotiating with the board of education for a requested salary increase of $500 for the year 1947-48. On February 11, 1947, after a full discussion in a joint meeting with representatives of the board of education, the acting superintendent of schools and the teachers' association, the board of finance declined to approve the increase for 1946-47. On February 24, 1947, the board of finance met again and considered not only the teachers' demand for an increase for the current year but also requests for increases by employees in other departments of the town. At this meeting the board voted to deny all requests for 1946-47 salary increases. Although on March 11, 1947, the board of education, notwithstanding the disapproval of the board of finance, "went on record" as favoring the $250 increase and requested a written decision on it from the board of finance, the latter did not alter its prior decision disapproving the demanded increases.

On March 16, 1947, the board of education met jointly with the teachers' welfare committee and the Connecticut State Teachers' Association, which had openly entered the controversy. The welfare committee and the state association were exerting the greatest possible pressure upon the board, insisting that definite action be taken upon the plaintiffs' demands and stating that otherwise "it was very probable an emergency would result." A representative of the state association who attended the meeting urged that the teachers' demands be complied with, stating that "otherwise the situation would become uncontrollable." For several days subsequent to March 16, 1947, the welfare committee and the state association continued to apply heavy pressure on the board of education to grant their demand for the salary increase, and it appeared to the board that "the teachers were prepared to take drastic steps." The board voted on March 21, 1947, to grant the demand for an increase of $250 for the current school year over and above the amounts for which the plaintiffs had respectively agreed to render services to the town. When this action was reported to a meeting of the board of finance on March 26, 1947, the latter adhered to its previous action disapproving the increase.

At the time of its meeting on April 8, 1947, the board of education recognized that if the salary increase was granted its appropriation would be exceeded and a deficit would result. Accordingly, it voted to defer further action until assured by counsel that its action would be legal. On April 15, 1947, however, the teachers' welfare committee gave the board of education the ultimatum that the committee had been authorized to "call a work stoppage at their discretion if the Board voted not to grant the increase" and that upon the denial of their demand "a work stoppage would un-

doubtedly follow very soon." These declarations constituted a clear threat to the board as the culmination of the long campaign of pressure to which it had been subjected. The statements neither referred to nor contemplated action pursuant to the contract provision regarding thirty days' notice of termination. Immediately upon receipt of this ultimatum the board of education voted to grant the plaintiffs' demand for an increase of $250 for the current school year and to amend the existing contracts accordingly, notwithstanding its knowledge that this would necessitate expenditures in excess of the appropriation for school purposes and result in a deficit. After the selectmen had advised the board of finance of this action by the board of education and of its request that the necessary measures be taken to obtain an additional appropriation of $23,250 to provide for it, the board of finance met on April 21, 1947, considered various departmental requests for the next fiscal year and conducted a detailed discussion of the board of education's budget, but it did not recede from its prior decision disapproving the demanded increase for the year 1946-47.

On May 9, 1947, each of the plaintiffs received, in addition to his regular pay for that pay-roll period under his original contract, the sum of $100, which purported to be on account of the $250 increase specified in a written "amendment" of his contract executed as of April 16, 1947, pursuant to the action by the board of education. The payment of these additional amounts resulted in an eventual deficit of $8311.16 in the board's total appropriation. Counsel for the Connecticut State Teachers' Association attended a meeting of the board of education on May 20, 1947. Pursuant to his advice, it was voted to notify the plaintiffs that the board could not make the payment of the $150 balance which had been voted May 13, 1947, because of lack of funds. The plaintiffs were so notified on May 20, 1947, and brought this action two days later. Payment of the $150 has never been made.

The question is whether the contract was rendered unenforceable by the refusal of the board of finance to recommend the requisite additional appropriation. A town board of education is an agency of the state in charge of education in the town, and broad powers are granted it by the legislature to that end. In the exercise of those powers or in the incurring of expense necessitated thereby to be paid by the town, the board of education is beyond control by the town or any of its officers except as limitations are found in the statutory provisions.

The controlling rule of law is thus stated in the Stamford case, supra, 127 Conn. 350, 16 A. 2d 601, 604: "[1] Where a town board of education includes in the estimates it submits to a board of finance expenditures for a purpose which is not within statutory provisions imposing a duty upon it nor within one which vests it with a discretion to be independently exercised, the board of finance may, if in its judgment, considering not only the educational purpose to be served but also the financial condition of the town, it finds that the expenditure is not justified, decline to recommend an appropriation for it; [2] where, however, the estimate is for an expenditure for a purpose which the statutes make it the duty of the board of education to effectuate or they vest in the board of education a discretion to be independently exercised as to the carrying out of some purpose, the town board

of finance has not the power to refuse to include any appropriation for it in the budget it submits and can reduce the estimate submitted by the board of education only when that estimate exceeds the amount reasonably necessary for the accomplishment of the purpose, taking into consideration along with the educational needs of the town, its financial condition and the other expenditures it must make. The board of finance in such a case must exercise its sound judgment in determining whether or to what extent the estimates of the board of education are larger than the sums reasonably necessary and if it properly exercises its discretion and the budget is approved by the town the board of education has no power to exceed the appropriations made." In applying the rule to the present case, the words "the estimates of the board of education" must be held to refer to the combined total of the original estimate upon which the appropriation was made and that for the salary increase which the board of finance refused to recommend.

Since there is no doubt that the providing of teachers is a duty imposed upon the board of education by the statutes, the validity of its action in granting the increase must be tested by (2) of the above rule. This resolves the question to whether or not the board of finance in refusing to recommend an appropriation for the salary increase exercised its sound judgment as required and properly exercised its discretion. In other words, was it warranted in deciding that the salary increase was beyond the amount reasonably necessary for the staffing of the schools for 1946-47, taking into consideration the educational needs of the town in connection with its financial condition and the other expenditures it must make? The vital fact involved was that the appropriation originally made was adequate to pay in full for this staffing under valid contracts executed by the plaintiffs before the school year began. When this fact exists, it is difficult to imagine a situation in which the refusal of the board of finance to make a recommendation for an additional appropriation would constitute an abuse of discretion as a matter of law. Certainly, no such conclusion is required in the case at bar. These contracts, in the absence of a breach thereof, or the giving of the thirty days' notice of termination provided for therein, guaranteed that the teaching staff would be available and would function for at least substantially the balance of the school year. The board of finance might reasonably have concluded that the plaintiffs would neither collectively commit the illegal act of striking nor individually be willing by giving thirty days' notice, to relinquish the positions which were then under the law assured to them for the remainder of the current school year. In other words, it might well have appeared to the board that the schools would continue to be operated by the same personnel without any increase in salaries. The court was fully warranted in its decisive conclusion that in reaching this decision the board of finance exercised its sound judgment and properly exercised its discretion. While this is decisive of the present appeal, the factual situation presented by the plaintiffs' conduct necessitates some further comment lest a mistaken implication be attributed to our decision.

Upon the facts which the court has found, the position of the plaintiffs implicit in their demands is one which neither legally nor morally commends itself. To accomplish their purpose, to coerce the board of education,

the plaintiffs threatened to cease work in disregard of the express provisions of their contracts. This was illegal. So too was their further threat to resort to a strike to enforce their demands. Norwalk Teachers' Ass'n v. Board of Education, 138 Conn. 269, 276, 83 A.2d 482. Neither by committing nor threatening to commit an illegal act or acts can one enhance his legal rights. The pleadings in the case at bar did not, however, present the issue whether illegal conduct of the plaintiffs caused the board of education to enter into the contracts with them for the $250 increase. We pointed out in the preceding paragraph that the board of finance might well have concluded that notwithstanding the threats of the plaintiffs they would not in fact have breached their contracts. It is not to be inferred from this statement that, had the board reached the opposite conclusion, disapproval by it of the increase would have constituted an abuse of its discretion. On the contrary, in a case like the present, if the court upon issue duly joined found that illegal conduct of the plaintiffs was the proximate cause of an increase granted to them by the board of education, in no event could a recommendation by the board of finance of an appropriation by the town to pay such an increase either render the plaintiffs' contracts therefor binding upon the town or warrant making an appropriation by it to provide for payment thereunder.

Case note. Here is another instance of collective bargaining by teachers in Connecticut. However, they brought such heavy pressure upon the board, even threatening to strike if their salary demands were not met, that the court condemned them on legal and moral grounds. Although the schools are under control of the boards of education, the town board of finance may refuse to recommend appropriations for expenditures it considers not justified. The board of finance in this case was influenced not only by lack of funds available to give the promised increases but also by the fact that the teachers had contracts for the year and were unlikely to breach them, even though they did threaten to do so.

The situation differs from state to state and, indeed, in some states among various classes of districts. Sometimes the financial officers of the municipality have right of review of the school district budget but have no right to decrease the total or any item in the budget—a hollow right—and sometimes the financial officers of the municipality have not even right of review. Fiscal independence of school districts is a goal not always achieved, however.

Johnston et al. v. Rapp, 103 Cal. App. (2d) 202, 229 P. (2d) 414 (California, 1951). [Salary increase during term of contract.]

Petitioner, Eugene M. Johnston, district superintendent of schools and principal of the Taft Union High School District, and the board of trustees of said district, by these proceedings, seek a writ mandate to

compel the auditor of Kern county to approve salary warrants issued to petitioner Johnston pursuant to an increase in his salary voted by the trustees.

The facts stipulated to by counsel for the respective parties are, in part, as follows: That at a regular meeting of the board of trustees of the Taft Union High School District, held on May 6, 1948, it was regularly moved, seconded and unanimously carried that the board give Mr. Eugene M. Johnston a four year written contract as district superintendent in accordance with the terms and provisions of the resolution incorporated in the minutes of said meeting; that thereafter a contract of employment was executed employing Johnston as district superintendent and principal of the Taft Union High School District for the period beginning July 1, 1948 and ending June 30, 1952; that the contract provided for an annual salary of $8,250, payable monthly, and contained the following provisions: "The board reserves the right to increase the salary during the four year period;" that at a regular meeting of said board held on May 5, 1949, the trustees unanimously voted to increase the salary of Johnston as district superintendent from $8,250 to $10,000 for the school year commencing July 1, 1949, and ending June 30, 1950; that thereafter warrants were drawn for Johnston's increased salary, which warrants were presented to the Kern county auditor, who refused to approve and return them; that because of the refusal of the auditor to approve and return the warrants, Johnston has not received his salary for his services as superintendent for the periods covered by the warrants.

It was alleged in an amendment to the petition, in paragraph four thereof, in addition to the foregoing stipulated facts, that the said increase in salary was made to compensate Johnston for various increases in his duties and responsibilities. . . .

The respondent auditor filed an answer in which he admitted the execution of the contract and alleged that the board of trustees had no legal power or authority to increase the said salary. He alleged that there were no changes or increases of any kind or character in the duties of petitioner Eugene M. Johnston for the school year commencing July 1, 1949 and ending June 30, 1950. . . .

However, he contends that once the salary has been fixed by contract for a prescribed period of time, it may not be increased during said period because of the provisions of sections 31 and 32 of article IV of the California Constitution, the pertinent parts of which are as follows:

Section 31. "The Legislature shall have no power . . . to make any gift or authorize the making of any gift, of any public money or thing of value to any individual, municipal or other corporation whatever. . . ."

Section 32. "The Legislature shall have no power to grant, or authorize any county or municipality authority to grant, any extra compensation or allowance to any public officer, agent, servant, or contractor, after service has been rendered, or a contract has been entered into and performed, in whole or in part, . . . and all such unauthorized agreements or contracts shall be null and void."

The constitutional provision in the above mentioned section is against "extra compensation or allowance." In the instant case the contract con-

tains the following provision: that the board "reserves the right to increase the salary during the four year period." Such a reservation clearly indicates that the named salary was subject to increase within the discretion of the board and was not, therefore, for a fixed amount for the entire four year period.

The effect of the increase voted by the board at the end of the first year of the contract was to fix the salary for the ensuing year. It did not constitute extra compensation for the services performed and was not prohibited by section 32 of article IV of the Constitution. The result obtained was the same as if a new contract had been executed for the school year commencing July 1, 1949 and ending June 30, 1950. . . .

It is apparent that the board in the instant case could have executed a new contract with petitioner at a salary of $10,000 per year, unless such action was arbitrary, discriminatory or unreasonable. Rible v. Hughes, supra, 24 Cal.2d at page 444, 150 P.2d at page 455, 154 A.L.R. 137. The record before us is devoid of any allegation of facts showing an abuse of such discretion. . . .

The increased salary voted to petitioner was for services to be rendered for a public purpose and in no sense a "gift" within the meaning of Section 31, article IV of the Constitution. The petitioner is not being paid more than provided in the contract for past or future services.

Appellant argues that since the answer denied that there were additional duties to be performed by plaintiff as alleged in the petition as reasons for the increased salary, that an issue of fact was presented which should have been determined at a trial of the action. However, it was stipulated that on May 5, 1949, the trustees at a regular meeting of the board voted to increase the salary of petitioner Johnston from $8,250 to $10,000 for the school year commencing July 1, 1949, and it appears from the pleadings that at the board meeting on May 6, 1948, the trustees reserved the right to increase the annual salary rate after the first year of service under the agreement for the subsequent years or any of them for any and all additional duties assumed by the said superintendent not otherwise imposed by law or by the rules and regulations of the said district at the time of the execution of the contract and for any and all substantial increases in the duties and responsibilities otherwise assumed by said superintendent at the time of the execution of the contract, such as increase in duties and responsibilities brought about by the increase in enrollment, addition in personnel, addition of schools, augmentation of the building program or *any other cause*, whether similar or otherwise to those enumerated. This specification of reasons for reserving the right is very broad and comprehensive in its scope. . . . It thus appears that there may have been sufficient reasons for said increase discussed and acted upon in addition to those alleged in the amendment to the petition. Under such circumstances it must be presumed that the board regularly performed its official duty.

Under the circumstances here shown and in view of what we have here said, we see no error in the granting of the motion for judgment on the pleadings.

The judgment is affirmed.

Case note. Technically, a cost-of-living increase or a bonus is illegal, being considered a gift or payment for past service, prohibited by the constitutions of more than half the states. Nevertheless, many such increases have been given, without judicial challenge.

Here, the contract of employment contained a right to increase the salary. Therefore, the contract was for a salary of $8,250 *or more* in each year of the four-year period the contract was to run. There have been other instances where courts have allowed increases during a term contract, when the contract did not include such a reservation, on the theory used in this case: that it was as if the board and superintendent had agreed to rescind the original contract and enter into a new one at the higher salary.

If it is legal for a board to reserve the right to increase a salary and do so, can it legally reserve the right to decrease a salary and do so? Some contracts contain a reservation allowing the board to decrease salaries, usually, however, only in the stipulated event of inadequate funds to pay the salary in full.

Thompson v. Board of Education of City of Syracuse, 11 Misc. (2d) 603, 107 N.Y.S. (2d) 80 (New York, 1950) *aff'd* (memorandum opinion) 279 A. D. 621, 107 N.Y.S. (2d) 584 (1950). [Computation of increased salary due.]

This case was tried December 7, 1949, and was held open at request of counsel for briefs and argument until October 23, 1950. The plaintiff, a teacher in the Syracuse public schools, has brought this action against the Board of Education, a corporate body, to recover an alleged unpaid balance of her salary. While the amount claimed is only $30, this is a test case to determine the rights of many other teachers similarly situated.

Briefly, this is the plaintiff's claim: She was entitled to a salary increase, from and after January 1, 1947, at the rate of $300 per year in addition to her salary as of June 30, 1945, and in addition to salary increments then or thereafter accruing. Education Law, § 3105, Subd. 2. The defendant, regarding the salary year from January 1 to December 31 as a period of ten months, excluding July and August, paid the plaintiff's annual salary in ten equal payments, one for each of the ten months, with no payment for July or August. Consequently, for the period of six months from January 1 to June 30 in each year the plaintiff received six of these checks, or six tenths of her annual salary. She therefore should have received, for the six months from January 1 to June 30, 1947, six tenths of the $300 increase, or $180. But the increase was paid to the plaintiff in such manner that she received only $150 thereof during said period of six months, leaving an alleged unpaid balance of $30 due on July 1, 1947.

The defendant does not admit all of these facts, and denies that there was any unpaid balance of the $300 increase due or owing to the plaintiff on July 1, 1947, or at any time thereafter. Without setting forth the

complicated facts claimed by the defendant, and assuming without deciding that the facts are as claimed by the plaintiff, the first question to be decided is the date on which the plaintiff's claim accrued.

Before deciding that this was the obvious date of July 1, 1947, due consideration has been given to the long period of negotiations for settlement between the parties and their legal representatives, and the question as to whether such negotiations operated to defer the accrual date of plaintiff's alleged claim until the defendant's final refusal to pay it, which refusal was less than three months before the plaintiff's verified claim was filed. I am obliged to hold as a matter of law that this accrual date was July 1, 1947, the date on which the alleged claim became due; and that said date was not deferred nor otherwise affected by said negotiations.

Since the plaintiff's claim accrued on July 1, 1947, and her written verified claim was not filed within three months thereafter, the defendant insists that said claim was absolutely barred at the expiration of said period of three months, and bases this defense squarely on Section 3813 of the Education Law, and on the decision in Todd v. Board of Education of City of Syracuse, 272 App.Div. 618, 74 N.Y.S.2d 468, affirmed 297 N.Y. 873, 79 N.E.2d 274.

In our case, therefore, I am forced to the conclusion, by Section 3813 of the Education Law as interpreted and applied by the Appellate Division and the Court of Appeals in the Todd case, that the plaintiff's action is barred by the undisputed fact that her written verified claim was not filed within three months after the claim accrued.

Complaint dismissed.

Case note. This case is a warning that procedural requirements are not taken lightly by the courts. When there is a statute of limitation before the running of which claims must be filed, the fact that negotiations for settlement outside of court were continued beyond the statutory time limit is no excuse for failing to file the claim on time. This principle is applicable to all kinds of claims, not just those for unpaid salary.

Greenup County Board of Education v. Harper, __ Ky. __, 256 S. W. (2d) 37 (Kentucky, 1953). [Reduction of salaries by uniform plan.]

The question presented in this case is whether a board of education has the right to reduce the salaries of its school principals without a reduction in the salaries of its other teaching personnel. The question requires a construction of KRS 161.760, which reads as follows:

"Each board of education shall cause notice to be given annually not later than August 1 to each teacher who holds a contract valid for the succeeding school year stating the best estimate as to the salary to be paid such teacher during such year. Such salary shall not be lower than the salary paid during the preceding school year unless such reduction be a part of a uniform plan affecting the entire district. But nothing herein shall prevent increases of salary after the board's annual notice has been given."

Eunice Harper was one of the Greenup County Board of Education's two high school principals. The Board reduced her salary and that of its other high school principal, along with the salaries of its two graded school principals. It is the contention of the Board that its action was justified under the statute because there was a uniform reduction plan affecting the entire supervisory staff. On the other hand, Eunice Harper contends that the language of the statute is unambiguous and means that a salary reduction must be a uniform plan affecting the entire teaching staff of the district. The lower court took that view of the case, and we think he did so correctly.

Eunice Harper was teaching under a continuing service contract. In the case of Williamson v. Cassady, 311 Ky. 666, 224 S.W.2d 934, we said that a principal teaching under a contract such as the one in question could be transferred from one school to another, but that his pay could not be reduced. The same reasoning applies in the case before us.

Judgment affirmed.

[Three judges] dissent because they believe the reduction of the salaries of all principals constituted a uniform plan for the reduction of salaries of a class affecting the entire district.

Case note. Many tenure laws prohibit reduction of salaries of tenure teachers except under designated circumstances, such as by a uniform plan. Then, the question is what constitutes a uniform plan. It is believed that many courts would agree that a reduction applicable to all the supervisory staff but not to the classroom teachers, or *vice versa*, followed a uniform plan.

Sources of Further Information

47 Am. Jur. "Schools" secs. 120-124, 135.

78 C. J. S. "Schools and School Districts" secs. 218-229.

A. L. R. "Schools" Topic Nos. 38-39.

American Digest System "Schools and School Districts" Key Nos. 143-145.

Work Sheet

1. What is the minimum salary legally payable in your state to public-school teachers?

2. Does the state law prescribe any schedule of salaries based on grades of certificate, length of service, or amount of professional preparation?

3. Is a salary schedule in effect in your district? If so, is it a single salary schedule?

4. Are increments in salary granted automatically for each succeeding year of experience or conditionally?

5. Have there been any local salary controversies involving any of the principles discussed in this chapter?

Chapter 7.

LEAVES OF ABSENCE

Editorial Comment

State laws permitting or requiring local school boards to grant leaves of absence for sickness or professional study or for other reasons have been enacted in more than half the states. Many local rules and regulations promulgated by local school boards so provide for the teachers in the particular districts. Even when there is a state law on the subject, a great deal is left to local discretion as only general guides for granting leaves of absence are contained in most of the state laws.

The major legal issues involved in this topic are three: (1) May an eligible teacher demand a leave of absence or is granting the leave within the discretion of the local board? (2) At the end of a leave of absence, duly granted, may a teacher demand reinstatement without loss of any salary, tenure, or retirement rights? (3) May a board require a teacher to take a leave of absence which the teacher has not requested?

As to the first question, the answer depends upon the purpose of the leave and the language of the law under which it is granted. In general, sick leave may be demanded as a right while leave for professional study is usually a privilege which may not be demanded but is granted within the discretion of the board.

Reinstatement at the end of a leave depends upon the terms of the agreement at the time the leave is granted, or upon the language of the law under which the leave is granted. Most tenure laws provide that a leave of absence, duly granted, does not disturb tenure rights. Usually a teacher on leave returns at the same salary which had been paid in the school year immediately preceding the leave. Retirement laws sometimes provide that a teacher on leave may pay into the retirement fund the amount of his contributions which would have been deducted from his salary had he been in active service and thus have the year's leave of absence counted as a year of service toward his retirement. However, not all retirement laws are framed in such a

way as to make this credit possible. If the teacher is paid full salary while on leave, the contributions of the employing board (or state) and the deductions from the teacher's salary would continue the same as if the teacher were in the classroom. So far as retirement credit is concerned, the difficulties arise when the teacher is on leave without pay.

It is universally held that a board may compel a teacher to take a leave of absence if the cause is illness or any type of physical or mental disability. A board also has the power to grant an unrequested leave of absence for other reasons, if they are reasonable.

Statutory Material

Florida Statutes Annotated, secs. 231.39-231.44.

Sec. 231.39. Any member of the instructional staff may secure leave of absence during the year when it is necessary to be absent from duty as prescribed by law and, under certain conditions may receive compensation during such period of absence. Any such leave of absence shall be classified as sick leave, illness-in-the-line-of-duty leave, professional leave, or personal leave. Subject to the provisions in the sections which follow, county boards shall prescribe regulations governing the granting of leaves of absence during the year. County boards shall also have authority to prescribe regulations for the granting, and with the approval of the trustees of the district in which the person is serving, to grant more extended leaves of absence, as follows:

(1) Extended professional leave.—Extended leave for professional improvement may be granted for a period of not to exceed one year to any member of the instructional staff who has served satisfactorily and successfully in the schools of the county for a period of three or more years; provided, that partial compensation may be authorized only when the person has served in the county for seven or more years.

(2) Military leave.—Any person called into military, naval or other service in defense of his country or volunteering for military or naval service of the United States may be granted military leave without compensation for such period or periods as may be authorized by the county board.

Sec. 231.40. Any member of the instructional staff employed in the public schools of the state who is unable to perform his duty in the school because of illness, or because of illness or death of father, mother, brother, sister, husband, wife, child, other close relative or member of his own household, and consequently has to be absent from his work shall be granted leave of absence for sickness by the county superintendent, or by someone designated in writing by him to do so. The following provisions shall govern sick leave:

(1) Each member of the instructional staff shall be entitled to not more than six days of sick leave during any one school year; provided, that such leave shall be taken only when necessary because of sickness as herein

prescribed. Such sick leave shall be cumulative from year to year; provided, that not more than seventy-two school days' sick leave, including sick leave for the current year and accumulated sick leave for previous years may be claimed in any one year; and provided, that unused sick leave credit for any year may not be claimed later than the end of the twelfth year thereafter; and provided, further, that at least half of this cumulative leave must be established within the same county school system. County school boards of the several counties may establish policies which will allow a teacher two days in each year for religious holidays; provided, that the use by the teacher of such days for religious holidays shall be charged to the sick leave provided for herein; and provided, further, that leave for religious holidays shall be non-cumulative.

(2) Any individual so employed shall receive full compensation for the time justifiably absent on sick leave as prescribed in subsections (1) and (3) hereof.

(3) Any member of the instructional staff who finds it necessary to be absent from his position because of illness shall notify the principal of his school if possible before the opening of school on the day on which he must be absent, or during that day except for emergency reasons recognized by the county board as valid. Any member of the instructional staff shall, before claiming and receiving compensation for the time absent from his or her duties while absent because of sick leave as prescribed in this section, make and file by the end of the school month following his return from such absence with the county superintendent of the county in which he is so employed a written certificate which shall set forth the day or days absent, that such absence was necessary and that such person is entitled to receive pay for such absence in accordance with the provisions of Sections 231.39-231.49; provided, however, that the county board of any county may prescribe regulations under which the county superintendent may require a certificate from a licensed physician or from the county health officer.

Sec. 231.41. Any member of the instructional staff shall be entitled to illness-in-line-of-duty leave when he has to be absent from his duties because of a personal injury received in the discharge of duty or because of illness from any contagious or infectious disease contracted in school work. The following requirements shall be observed:

(1) Leave of any such member of the instructional staff shall be authorized for a total of not to exceed ten school days during any school year for illness contracted from such causes as prescribed above; provided that county boards shall be authorized, when in the opinion of the county board it is desirable to do so, to carry insurance to safeguard the county board against excessive payments during any year.

(2) Any member of the instructional staff who has any claim for compensation while absent because of illness contracted or injury incurred as prescribed herein shall file a claim in the manner prescribed in Section 231.40, subsection (3), by the end of each month during which such absence has occurred. The county board of the county in which such person is employed shall approve such claims and authorize the payment thereof; provided that the county board shall satisfy itself that the claim

correctly states the facts and that such claim is entitled to payment in accordance with the provisions of this section.

Sec. 231.42. Any member of the instructional staff who finds it necessary to be absent from his duties for professional reasons or is assigned by the county superintendent under regulations of the county board to be absent for professional reasons may apply for professional leave during such absence. Such leave may be granted under regulations of the county board. The county board shall also prescribe by regulations, subject to any regulations of the state board, conditions under which compensation is to be allowed and the extent of compensation for such leave; provided that any leave granted under this section must be approved by the county superintendent.

Sec. 231.43. The county board of each county shall adopt regulations prescribing conditions under which members of the instructional staff shall be granted leave of absence for personal reasons. Any such leave of absence shall be approved by the county superintendent, subject to regulations of the county board. Any member of the instructional staff who is absent for personal reasons shall not be entitled to pay while absent.

Sec. 231.44. Any member of the instructional staff of any county who is wilfully absent from duty without leave shall forfeit compensation for the time of such absence, and his contract shall be subject to cancellation by the county board.

Statutory note. In some respects the quoted Florida law is more detailed than the average leave-of-absence law, most of which merely empower local districts to grant leaves of absence for stated causes. Not all laws prescribe a maximum length of time for which a teacher may be paid while absent because of sickness, and only half of the existing laws have cumulative provisions. Many states, having leave-of-absence laws for sickness or professional study, do not expressly authorize leaves for other causes. Where there are statutory provisions for leaves of absence for reasons other than sickness, they are usually very generally stated. California, Louisiana, and Pennsylvania have professional leave laws which are much more detailed than the others.

Case Material

State ex rel. Scoggins v. Vernon Parish School Board, __ La. __, 44 So. (2d) 385 (Louisiana, 1950). [Teacher's right to sabbatical leave.]

This is a mandamus proceeding in which the relator, Henry Y. Scoggins, is seeking to compel the Vernon Parish School Board to grant him a Sabbatical leave for one semester for cultural improvement for the school term of 1949-1950, beginning September 12th, 1949 and ending January 28th, 1950. The petition contained all necessary allegations and particularly that the relator complied with all the necessary requisites provided for by Sections 2, 3 and 4 of Act No. 319 of 1940 and amendments thereto, Act

No. 235 of 1946, Act No. 341 of 1948, and relator also alleged that he had filed two applications with the defendant school board and had been refused both times; that he had delivered these applications to the superintendent of the schools of Vernon Parish, Louisiana.

The defendant school board filed no answer but did file an exception of no cause of action levelled at relator's failure to send either of the applications to the Superintendent of Schools by registered mail as required by the Sabbatical Leave Act. . . .

Defendant school board has raised but two questions on this appeal, viz:

(1) Is the requirement that applications for Sabbatical Leave be sent to the superintendent of schools by registered mail . . . to be construed stricti juris? and

(2) Where less than five per centum of the total number of teachers employed in a given parish are taking Sabbatical Leave . . . does a School Board have authority to reject applications for Sabbatical Leave for any reason?

As to the first question, the evidence shows both applications for Sabbatical Leave were in accordance with law in all respects, but that both were delivered to the superintendent of schools personally rather than by registered mail as provided by the Act. The facts further show that both applications were presented by the superintendent to the School Board and the School Board acted upon these applications by refusing them. . . .

The purpose of sending an application by registered mail was to insure its delivery and a record of its being sent and delivered. The record shows that same purposes were accomplished by manual delivery. . . .

Counsel for the defendant school board has so phrased what he contends is the second question in this suit to be answered by the Court that it covers much more territory; that is, is much broader in scope than the actual question to be decided. It is not necessary to decide whether or not a school board has authority to reject applications for sabbitical leave for any reason; only is it necessary to decide whether this defendant school board in the present case, under the present facts and the law, had the right to reject relator's application.

It is shown by the record in this case that not one teacher employed by Vernon Parish School Board was on sabbitical leave at the time relator made his application, and at the time it was rejected, and, therefore, under Section 5 of Act No. 319 of 1940 and amendments thereto relator was clearly entitled to the leave for which he applied. It is contended, however, that the board did not have and could not get any qualified substitute teachers, and that this court should take judicial notice of the acute shortage of teachers and should hold that "in the face of such acute shortage the rights of the school children of this State to competent instruction must take precedence and priority over the rights of individual teachers who seek to take their sabbatical leave and increase their earning power at a time like this." In the first place, there is no testimony in the record except that of the Superintendent of Education that they did not have and could not get any qualified substitute teachers and there is no showing that any effort was made to get a substitute teacher and we cannot take judicial cognizance of the shortage of school teachers. It would appear to us that

the board could have found one teacher to employ if it made an effort and it was their duty to do so.

It is through no fault of the relator that the length of time necessary in order to obtain a final judgment in the case overlapped the period of time for which he had applied for such leave, and in view of the fact that his application was filed in accordance with law and in time prescribed thereby, we believe that we should affirm the judgment and order the defendant school board to grant relator sabbatical leave as requested in brief filed in his behalf for the school term of 1950 to 1951, beginning September 1950 and ending January 1951. . . .

Case note. With regard to *any* requirement that delivery be made by registered mail, courts will not disallow personal delivery. In fact, it is generally held that delivery by regular mail is sufficient if delivery is proved or acknowledged and the communication is received within the time limit.

On the question of rejection of applications for sabbatical leave, the court followed the usual practice of refusing to answer broad academic questions, keeping its decision to the facts in the case before it.

The sabbatical leave law provided that no more than five per cent of the staff in a given parish [county] could be on leave at the same time. It was because of this restriction that the board asked if it had the power to reject applications when fewer than five per cent were on leave.

The court here refused to take judicial notice of the shortage of teachers. Other courts have taken judicial notice of this condition.

School City of East Chicago v. Sigler, 219 Ind. 9, 36 N.E. (2d) 760 (Indiana, 1941). [Teacher sued for salary for period of unrequested leave of absence.]

Appellee was a tenure teacher in the schools of appellant. His last contract was dated September 6, 1937, was on the official form prescribed by the State Superintendent of Public Instruction and covered the school year beginning in the fall of 1937. It contained a provision that the teacher should "observe all rules and regulations of the properly constituted school authorities." In the afternoon of March 9, 1938, appellee mailed to the Secretary of State a declaration of appellee's candidacy for the nomination for the office of state representative. In the evening of the same day the school board of appellant passed a resolution reading, in part, "that on and after this date it is herby declared to be a rule governing such school system that any school employe who becomes a candidate for any elective political office, will be required to take a leave of absence, without pay, such leave becoming effective upon filing declaration of intention of becoming any such candidate for office and continuing for the duration of such political

activity, and during the period of active service in such office, if elected thereto."

This resolution was brought to the attention of all the teachers, including appellee, about a week later. The school board by letter to appellee dated March 29, 1938, notified him that it would enforce the rule so adopted, not as of the date of filing of his declaration, but as of April 2, 1938, the last day when under the law he was permitted to withdraw his candidacy. He had a conference with the school board but there was no compliance with the statutory provisions for notice and hearing as in the case of cancellation of a teacher's contract. He continued to be a candidate until he was defeated in the primary election on the third day of May. He was not permitted to teach from April 4 to May 3 when he returned to the schools and was there employed until January 1, 1940, when he voluntarily took a leave of absence. He was not paid for the month preceding the primary and brought this action for his salary. . . .

Appellant relies upon the rule adopted by the resolution of March 9, 1938, as a complete defense to the action. Appellee insists that the school board was without power to make the rule, that it conflicts with his contract which may not be impaired by any action of appellant subsequent to its execution, and that, if it was a valid rule, it could not be enforced without compliance with the same procedure required for cancellation of a tenure teacher's contract. . . .

It will be conceded that he has the same privilege as any other citizen to become a candidate for public office. Such candidacy should not be and is not ground for cancellation of his contract as a permanent teacher. But anyone who has been a candidate recognizes that political activity is apt to interfere with one's usual vocation and this fact, independent of any possible involvement of the school system in political controversies, affords a sound reason for a temporary severance of the candidate's connection with the schools. This rule, general in terms and applying to all teachers, does not to us seem such an unreasonable exercise of the board's powers as to warrant judicial interference. The board not the courts is charged with the duty of managing the school system and so long as it acts with fairness its decisions on matters within its discretion are not subject to judicial review.

To bind the teacher it is not necessary that the rule be made prior to the execution of his contract. In express terms it contains his agreement to "observe all rules and regulations of the school authorities." Without such provision we think this agreement would be read into the contract. The tenure law does not purport to take from the school authorities the management of the schools. If only such rules could be enforced as were in existence when the contract was signed the school system might be static for at least one year. New situations could not be met promptly. New problems would have to await solution until the close of the school year. We cannot find any such intent in the contract nor in the purpose behind the tenure law. "*All* rules and regulations" must, we think, include those adopted after as well as before the execution of the teacher's contract. Any other interpretation would unduly hamper the administration of the public-school system by the authorities charged with its management.

The title of the tenure Act, Acts 1927, c. 97, reads: "An act defining teachers and permanent teachers, providing for their employment and release, and defining, and providing for the making and cancelling of, indefinite contracts." The act is silent on the subject of temporary release until the fifth section . . . which reads:

"Any such school corporation, upon written request, may grant leaves of absence, for periods not exceeding one (1) year, to any permanent teacher for study or professional improvement or because of physical disability or sickness, subject to such rules and regulations governing leaves of absence as may be adopted by such corporation; Provided, That without written request any such school corporation may place a permanent teacher on leave of absence for periods of not exceeding one (1) year because of physical or other disability or sickness; Provided, That such teacher shall have a right to a hearing on *such* unrequested leave of absence in accordance with the provisions for hearing contained in Section 2 (sec. 28–4308) of this act." . . . [Italics added by court] The first proviso, therefore, prevents the school board from enforcing for a longer time than one year an involuntary leave of absence where the cause relates to physical ability of the teacher. Upon other involuntary leaves of absence the statute is silent. If there should be any further curtailment of the school board's general authority in the management of the schools the remedy is with the legislature.

We are supported in this reasoning by the express language of the second proviso in which the word "such" . . . confines the "provision for hearings" to only those unrequested leaves of absence as are occasioned by "physical or other disability or sickness." This, too, we think is a clause of limitation and not, as appellee contends, a recognition of the teacher's right to notice and hearing in all cases where the employer-employe relation is to be disturbed. It is true that wherever the act refers to any involuntary release, temporary or permanent, it provides for notice and hearing. It may be that such provision is desirable in the case of every unrequested leave, whether it is for a cause referred to in the statute or for any other cause. But we have no more right to read into the act a prohibition against involuntary leave without notice and hearing than to read in a prohibition against rules and regulations for involuntary leaves on other grounds than those specifically mentioned. In each case the statute is silent. . . .

Case note. This case illustrates that a school board may compel a tenure teacher to take an unrequested leave of absence by rules and regulations of the board, and unless the rule is considered unreasonable by the court, it will not interfere with the board's authority. Furthermore, rules and regulations promulgated after employment are of as much force for a particular teacher as those existing at the time of employment.

The court might have ruled that, because the statute mentioned unrequested leaves for "physical or other disability or sickness," the board had no power to compel a teacher to take unrequested leave

for reasons other than those mentioned in the statute; that specific mention of one thing implies exclusion of another thing. However, the general powers of the school board in the management of the schools and the teachers are such that the court found no lack of authority for the rule in question.

Sources of Further Information

Many implications for leaves of absence are contained in other sections of the law books, but the topic is rarely treated separately. 47 Am. Jur. "Schools" discusses compensation of a teacher on leave of absence in section 123. In the American Digest System Key No. 133.14 has been assigned to leaves of absence.

Work Sheet

1. Are you working under a leave-of-absence law?
2. If so, does it apply to sick leave only?
3. If your leave-of-absence law provides for leaves on account of several reasons, make a comparison of the requirements for and the benefits of each type of leave.

Chapter 8.

DEFAMATION OF CHARACTER

Editorial Comment

Any words tending to harm a person's reputation so as to lower him in the estimation of the community or to deter people from associating with him are "defamatory words." Under certain circumstances such words form the basis for a suit in which the person so injured seeks damages and the clearing of his reputation. Defamation may be a statement of fact, as "Miss X did thus and so"; or it may be the expression of a derogatory opinion based upon facts known, assumed, or undisclosed, as "I think Miss X should be fired for the betterment of the school."

School boards are authorized to dismiss permanent tenure teachers by provisions in tenure laws many of which include dismissal for personal reasons, such as immorality. Probationary teachers in tenure districts may be dismissed if they do not achieve the standards set by school boards and administrators, standards of personal conduct as well as professional. So also, teachers under contract for a specified term may be dismissed before the termination of the contract without liability for breach of contract on the part of the school board if certain charges can be upheld by sufficient evidence. Teaching certificates can be revoked. Applications for teaching certificates can be denied. Applications for teaching positions may be refused.

By any of these methods, a teacher may be excluded from the profession for which he has trained, upon charges of immorality, conduct unbecoming a teacher, dishonesty, intemperance, mental derangement, inefficiency, incompetency, etc. False charges of this type tend to defame the teacher's character and make it more difficult to secure other employment. Therefore, the question arises as to when a teacher can obtain legal redress from the responsible persons in a suit for defamation of character. In general, it must be remembered that only under certain circumstances will the court redress such a wrong.

Communication, oral or written, is called publication. If the words are spoken, they are called slander; if written, libel. A court action will not lie unless the slanderous words are of a certain nature. Written defamation, libel, is more easily redressed in the law courts than spoken defamation. Libel is frequently actionable even though the same words if spoken would not be actionable without special damage; that is, when the words are written, no injury to reputation need be proved. The mere publication of libel may be sufficient to maintain the action.

The words which historically were considered slanderous were (1) those imputing the commission of certain crimes; (2) those imputing certain diseases and contagious disorders; (3) any imputation affecting a person's reputation for skill in his business, office, trade, profession, or occupation which tended to cause his position to be prejudicially affected. To these three classes of slander another class has been added in modern times—words imputing unchastity to a woman. In these classes of defamation, no special injury need be proved—the words are enough. If the defamation does not fall into one of these classes, special injury must be proved—the words are not enough.

An action for slander will lie if one is accused of committing a crime which is punishable by imprisonment. The words to be actionable in this class must charge that the person has committed the crime; that he is a potential criminal is not a slanderous charge unless special damage can be proved. If the school law provides for discipline of a teacher convicted of a crime, conviction is conclusive of guilt for this purpose, and the teacher, even though injured in reputation thereby, cannot sue on an accusation which is based upon a fact.

The class of defamation imputing a disease arose because certain diseases were considered contagious and, when one was known to have any such, he was isolated. Leprosy, syphilis, and the plague are the historic diseases for which action would lie when the person was unjustly accused of having them. In modern times accusation of having any disease other than the three named is not usually actionable unless it is some deadly, communicable, and loathsome disease. An accusation that a person *has had* a disease of this sort is not actionable per se; that is, the words are not defamatory unless the person is accused of having the disease at the time the statement is made, or unless special damage can be proved to have resulted from an accusation of having had the disease at some time past.

In order for a communication to injure one's business or professional reputation, the words must relate directly to the person's official or business character and impute misconduct to him in that capacity.

For example, insolvency imputed to a businessman is always actionable as a businessman's good credit is necessary to the conduct of his
business; but to say that a professional man does not pay his debts is
not actionable since his private credit is unrelated to his professional
ability. The words must be specific and relate directly to the person's
ability in his work.

Under early common law in England, an imputation of unchastity
to a woman was not actionable per se except in one or two cities
where special conditions prevailed. Many states in the United States
have made slanderous imputation of unchastity to a woman actionable
per se. The common-law rule still applies to men, and any defamatory
words imputing unchastity to a man are not actionable per se unless
his conduct constitutes a sexual crime, and then his right to action
falls into the first class of defamatory words: those imputing the commission of a crime.

If a man teacher unjustly accused of unchastity can show special
damage, or that the defamation injured his reputation as a teacher, or
that the conduct of which he is accused constitutes a statutory crime
of which he is innocent, he can sue for slander. A woman, however,
need not show special damage or any other evidence than the untruth
of the statements.

An imputation of unchastity may be inferred from any words
which would naturally be understood by the hearers even though
the charge is not made in explicit terms. However, imputations of
immodesty which do not imply unchastity are not actionable, and
innuendos cannot be interpreted beyond their reasonable meaning.

Outside of the four named types of slander which are actionable
per se, defamatory words are actionable only when special injury can
be shown. This damage must be of a pecuniary or material nature,
not merely emotionable disturbance. However, when the words are
actionable per se, that is, when they fall into one of the four classes
discussed above, the injured person may recover because of the injury
to reputation even though no pecuniary or material damage was
suffered.

Words spoken directly to the one accused without any third person
present to hear is not publication, but disclosure to any person not
the one spoken of, even to a single person, may be publication in the
eyes of the law.

Truth is a complete defense to any action, unless the publication
of the truth was purely malicious. Usually, if the "slanderer" can
prove that the words were true, he is not liable and his words are not,

legally speaking, slanderous. Therefore, it is only when a teacher is unjustly accused that action should be considered, since malice is difficult to prove.

The second main defense of the slanderer is that the communication was "privileged." There is, first of all, the absolute privilege of legislators and witnesses. These persons cannot be brought into court for anything they say no matter how defiling it is, so long as their utterances are made in connection with their official duties. They are given this absolute privilege so as to free them from restrictions and dangers of suit in the conduct of their official business. Absolute privilege is rarely applicable to defamation of teachers, but frequently a communication defaming a teacher is "qualifiedly" privileged.

Where a person is so situated that it becomes right, in the interest of society, that he should tell to a third person certain facts, then, if he bona fide and without malice does tell the facts to that person, it is a privileged communication. If a sufficiently important public interest is affected and such public interest requires disclosure to a public officer or private citizen who is authorized or privileged to act if the defamatory matter is true, the occasion is qualifiedly privileged and the person "telling" is not liable for slander. Owing to the great interest of parents and other members of the community in the maintenance of high standards of morality and efficiency in the public schools, it is generally recognized that communications to the proper authorities in reference to school teachers are qualifiedly privileged. The communication is not privileged if made to one who has no authority or duty to remove the teacher or otherwise to take care of the situation.

Proceedings before school boards are also within the class having qualified privilege and are protected by such privilege when it is properly used and not abused. Proceedings before a school board may be published in the newspapers without liability, provided they are published correctly. Reports of one school official to another are privileged. Therefore, it is useless for a teacher to attempt to sue for defamation in official records of any school official or school board unless malice can be proved.

If the teacher can prove that the privilege was abused, the privilege will not save the one who abused it. A qualifiedly privileged communication is abused when the "teller" has no reasonable grounds for believing the communication. However, even rumors and suspicions may be published without abuse of privilege if the relationship of the parties and the importance of the interests affected and the harm

likely to be done thereto make the publication of the rumors and suspicions reasonable. This is true even though the person so publishing them reasonably doubts their truth or even knows of their falsity.

If the occasion is privileged but malice can be proved as the motivation behind the communication, the privileged character of the occasion is nullified. Malice may be inferred from the language itself or may be proved by extrinsic circumstances, but it must be proved. The mere fact that the statements are untrue does not prove malice, but if there is no ground for believing the communication, this evidence helps to prove that the publication was motivated by malice.

Owing to the public nature of the teaching profession, a teacher is not exempt from criticism, but accusations imputing to a teacher want of professional capacity, immorality, or unprofessional conduct are clearly actionable per se unless privileged. These comments go beyond the classification of "fair criticism." The private conduct or character of a teacher or of any person engaged in activities of public concern may be criticized so far as his private conduct or character affects his public conduct. The criticism, although defamatory, is privileged if it is based upon a true or privileged statement of fact, or upon facts generally known by the public. However, such criticism to be privileged must represent the actual opinion of the critic and not be made solely for the purpose of causing harm to the other. In addition, it must be criticism which a person of reasonable intelligence and judgment might make. Defamation, in order to fall into this class of fair comment, must meet all these requirements.

The law of defamation touches the teacher's career also from another angle. Can a pupil sue his teacher for defamation of character? The answer may be found in the principles discussed above with regard to the teacher's right to sue for defamation of *his* character.

False words spoken by a teacher about one of his pupils would be actionable unless the slanderous words were communicated under privileged circumstances. A teacher's report to the principal or other school official would certainly be privileged, as would also a communication to the pupil's parents or guardian. There would be no privilege, however, if a teacher slandered a pupil in the presence of other pupils, before the general public, to parents not involved in the situation, or to other teachers not teaching the pupil. The same distinctions would prevail between words actionable per se and those on account of which special injury must be proved in order to obtain damages.

Teachers are frequently asked for letters of recommendation on former students. Such letters are considered confidential, and honest comments are sometimes encouraged by prospective employers that they may better judge the potential worth of an applicant for employment. Dare a teacher write a derogatory letter without subjecting himself to suit for slander? If the letter expresses the teacher's honest opinion, reasonably based upon evidence which convinced the teacher of the truth of his estimate of the pupil and is not written with malicious intent to injure him, the communication under these circumstances is privileged; provided, of course, that the teacher does not show the letter to any other person, mails it to the prospective employer, and has no reason to know that any but the prospective employer will read it upon receipt. Communication by the employer after receipt of the letter may constitute slander on his part, depending upon the circumstances, but does not reflect back to the teacher who wrote the letter, unless he could have anticipated such publication. The same principles apply to letters of recommendation written by principals and superintendents concerning teachers.

Statutory Material

West's Wisconsin Statutes Annotated, secs. 263.37, 263.38, 328.33, 331.05.

Sec. 263.37. In an action for libel or slander it shall not be necessary to state in the complaint any intrinsic facts for the purpose of showing the application to the plaintiff of the defamatory matters out of which the cause of action arose; but it shall be sufficient to state generally that the same was published or spoken concerning the plaintiff, and if such allegation be controverted the plaintiff shall be bound to establish on the trial that it was so published or spoken.

Sec. 263.38. In an action for libel or slander the defendant may in his answer allege both the truth of the matter charged as defamatory and any mitigating circumstances to reduce the amount of damages; and whether he prove the justification or not he may give in evidence the mitigating circumstances.

Sec. 328.33. If the defendant in any action for slander or libel shall set up in his answer that the words spoken or published were true, such answer shall not be proof of the malice alleged in the complaint.

Sec. 331.05. (1) The proprietor, publisher, editor, writer or reporter upon any newspaper published in this state shall not be liable in any civil action for libel for the publication in such newspaper of a true and fair report of any judicial, legislative or other public official proceeding authorized by law or of any public statement, speech, argument or debate in the course of such proceeding. This section shall not be construed to exempt any such proprietor, publisher, editor, writer or reporter from liability for

any libelous matter contained in any headline or headings to any such report, or to libelous remarks or comments added or interpolated in any such report or made and published concerning the same, which remarks or comments were not uttered by the person libeled or spoken concerning him in the course of such proceeding by some other person.

(2) Before any civil action shall be commenced on account of any libelous publication in any newspaper, magazine or periodical, the libeled person shall first give those alleged to be responsible or liable for the publication a reasonable opportunity to correct the libelous matter. Such opportunity shall be given by notice in writing specifying the article and the statements therein which are claimed to be false and defamatory and a statement of what are claimed to be the true facts. The notice may also state the sources, if any, from which the true facts may be ascertained with definiteness and certainty. The first issue published after the expiration of one week from the receipt of such notice shall be within a reasonable time for correction. To the extent that the true facts are, with reasonable diligence, ascertainable with definiteness and certainty, only a retraction shall constitute a correction; otherwise the publication of the libeled person's statement of the true facts, or so much thereof as shall not be libelous of another, scurrilous, or otherwise improper for publication, published as a statement, shall constitute a correction within the meaning of this section. A correction, timely published, without comment, in a position and type as prominent as the alleged libel, shall constitute a defense against the recovery of any damages except actual damages, as well as being competent and material in mitigation of actual damages to the extent the correction published does so mitigate them.

Statutory note. Other than judicial procedure rules and guides for newspapers, there is little by way of statutory material in this field. The principles discussed in the *Editorial Comment* have to do with common-law slander and libel. Some states have written the same or similar principles into the statutes, but most have not, at least with the detail which has been established by case law over the years. No such statutes apply particularly to teachers. Some laws have been enacted to limit criticism of public officials to fair comment, but since teachers are not officers, these laws do not apply, strictly speaking. There is some case law, however, in which the common-law principles of fair comment have been invoked with regard to teachers.

Case Material

Spears v. McCoy, 155 Ky. 1, 159 S.W. 610 (Kentucky, 1913). [Teacher sued for slander.]

Plaintiff, Rediford Spears, brought this action against Mont McCoy to recover damage for slander. A demurrer was sustained to the petition and the petition dismissed. Plaintiff appeals.

The petition is as follows: "The plaintiff, Rediford Spears, states that he is a teacher of common schools by profession in Pike county, Kentucky, which county is his home and in which county he now resides; that he holds a first-class certificate to teach in the common schools of said county and has been a teacher for the last 10 years. He states that the defendant, Mont McCoy, in Pike County, Ky., on the____day of July, 1912, and in the presence and hearing of different and divers persons, spoke of plaintiff falsely and maliciously, wrongfully and unlawfully, these words to wit: 'I do not want such a teacher as Rediford Spears because he is all the time courting the girls and did court them last year in the school; that he would dismiss the boys last year in school and keep the girls in and give them candy and court them'—meaning thereby that the plaintiff who taught in Subdistrict No. 124, Pike county, Ky., last year had kept the girls who were his students in after the boys had been dismissed and had had carnal sexual intercourse with them; that plaintiff is now employed to teach in said subdistrict for the coming school year; that he makes his living by teaching in the common schools of Pike county; that said language which is false and untrue has greatly injured his reputation as a teacher and has caused him to suffer great mental anguish and humiliation and has greatly injured his character to his great damage in the full and just sum of $10,000. Wherefore plaintiff prays judgment against the defendant for the sum of $10,000 for costs and all proper relief."

While there is an attempt on the part of plaintiff to give a very strained construction to the words which it is alleged that the defendant spoke of him, it is well settled that an innuendo cannot extend the meaning of words beyond their natural import. It is only explanatory of some matter already expressed. It may show the application but cannot add to or enlarge or change the sense of the words. . . .

The question, therefore, turns on whether or not the words are actionable *per se*. Words are slanderous or actionable *per se* only in cases where they are falsely spoken and (1) impute the commission of a crime involving moral turpitude for which the party might be indicted and punished; (2) impute an infectious disease likely to exclude him from society; or (3) impute unfitness to perform the duties of an office or employment; or (4) prejudice him in his profession or trade; or (5) tend to discredit him.

In all other cases spoken words are either (a) not actionable at all or are only actionable (b) on proof of special damage. . . .

While it is true that the words in question do not impute the commission of a crime involving moral turpitude, for which plaintiff might be indicted and punished, the question is: Do they fall under either the third or fourth class; that is, do they impute to plaintiff unfitness to perform his duties in his office as teacher, or do they prejudice him in his profession of teacher?

It is clear that the words were spoken of him not in his individual capacity but in his capacity as a teacher. The charge is that he dismissed the boys and kept the girls in, gave them candy and courted them. Naturally the patrons of a school would not want such a teacher. They send their young daughters there to be instructed, not to be courted. A teacher

who indulges in such a practice would not be acceptable to the patrons and could not long continue in office. The charge is not only sufficient to show unfitness but to discredit his standing in his profession. We therefore conclude that the words are actionable.

It is insisted, however, that not only were no special damages alleged, but that as the petition shows that the plaintiff has again been employed to teach the same school, the petition fails to show that he has been damaged at all.

In answer to the first contention it is sufficient to say that where the words spoken impute unfitness to perform the duties of an office or employment, or prejudice him in his profession or trade, they are actionable *per se* and it is not necessary to allege and prove special damages. . . .

Nor is the fact that he has been already employed for the coming year conclusive of the question of damages. Notwithstanding this employment, he may be discharged or be otherwise discredited in his profession. It follows that the trial court should have overruled the demurrer to the petition.

[Judgment reversed, and cause remanded for proceedings consistent with this opinion.]

Case note. The court did not permit the teacher to use an interpretation of the spoken words which extended their meaning beyond a reasonable inference, but said that a reasonable inference was sufficient to make the words actionable without special damages shown. The case, therefore, would go back to the trial court for hearing on the merits of the case. The defense might be either truth of the actions charged, or that the communication was privileged because McCoy spoke in an official capacity. We do not, therefore, know the final outcome of the case. The opinion here did not identify McCoy. If he were a school trustee and was speaking to another school trustee or to a county superintendent or some school official of that sort, his communication would probably be privileged. If he were a patron only and spoke the words to another patron, his communication would not have been privileged, unless it could be defended on grounds of being fair criticism.

Brown v. McCann, 36 Ga. App. 812, 138 S.E. 247 (Georgia, 1927). [Teacher sued patron for slander.]

Mrs. B. B. Brown brought an action for slander against X. Y. McCann in the city court of Jesup, alleging that the defendant, about March, 1925, injured her in her profession as a teacher in the public schools by making to members of the school board and other persons named a false report that she was afflicted with a contagious disease, commonly known as tuberculosis. She alleged that as a result of such report she was summarily dismissed from the faculty of the Jesup public school, and was further damaged in that she was thereafter unable to obtain any other position as

teacher. The defendant in his answer denied the making of any such statements, but set up no affirmative defense as of privileged communication.

A. E. Knight, a member of the board of education of the school in which the plaintiff was teaching and in which a son of the defendant was a pupil, testified that in April 1925, the defendant came into his store and said to him "Have you heard the report on Mrs. Brown?" stating that Dr. Colvin had told him that she had consumption and asking the witness what the trustees "were going to do about it." The witness replied that the matter would have to come before the board and suggested that the defendant "appear before the board," whereupon the defendant said:

"No. I have nothing to do with it. . . . If she has tuberculosis I will take my boy out of school, as I do not want him exposed to it."

On a different occasion, seemingly a little later, the defendant voluntarily made to Mr. and Mrs. Anderson, at their home in Adams Park, Georgia, the following statement:

"A very unfortunate thing happened recently. Mrs. Brown's doctor told me that she had tuberculosis and asked me what I was going to do about it. . . . I told the doctor I couldn't do anything but stop my child, which I was going to do." . . .

The plaintiff testified that she had had no coughs and had not "suffered with anything except severe colds," and that she was now in October 1926, in perfect health. The trial court granted a nonsuit, and the plaintiff excepted.

Under the testimony submitted, the jury would have been authorized in finding that the defendant did, in fact, make the statements as charged, and, further, that these statements were false. This would make a *prima facie* case for the plaintiff, since the statements tended to show that the plaintiff was afflicted with a contagious disease, and since also they related to the plaintiff's profession and were calculated to injure her therein. . . . A false report of either character is actionable *per se*, unless the defendant comes forward and shows that it was privileged under the circumstances, this being a matter for defense. . . .

The fact that the defendant merely repeated the report of the doctor is no defense, since it is the law that "talebearers are as bad as talemakers." . . . Every repetition of a slander originated by a third person is a new publication of it.

Whether or not the publication was a privileged communication would depend upon the circumstances, including the intention with which it was published. If in good faith, with the sole purpose of protecting the interest of the defendant, it would be. If maliciously, for the purpose of injuring the reputation of the plaintiff, it would not be.

In view of the allegations of the petition the question of privilege is one which must be raised by plea and submitted to a jury as an issue of fact. . . . In order to make the defense complete, the defendant must show good faith, an interest to be upheld, a statement properly limited in its scope, a proper occasion and publication to proper persons only. . . . Whether the communication is made at the proper time and proper place and to a proper person and in good faith is usually a question for the jury to determine under the facts of the particular case. . . .

Assuming, without deciding, that it could be held as a matter of law, that the defendant's conversation with Knight, of the school board, was privileged . . ., the same is not true of the statements made to Mr. and Mrs. Anderson. Although the defendant did not plead privilege, the nonsuit would have been right if the defense had affirmatively and conclusively appeared from the plaintiff's own evidence. But it did not. The trial court therefore erred in granting the nonsuit.

Judgment reversed.

Case note. The communication to Mr. and Mrs. Anderson was obviously not privileged. The communication to Knight might or might not have been, depending upon the intent and the circumstances as outlined by the court in the decision. The establishment of privilege is, therefore, more complicated than merely showing that there might have been some official connection between the parties involved.

Sources of Further Information

33 Am. Jur. "Libel and Slander" secs. 46, 131.
58 A.L.R. 1165.
American Digest System "Libel and Slander" Key No. 9(5).

Work Sheet

Review some "gossip" which you have heard about some school teacher and determine if that teacher had grounds for a slander suit against the person who made the communication, applying the common-law principles discussed in this chapter.

Chapter 9.

BENEFITS FOR INJURIES AND
OTHER DISABILITIES

In this chapter will be discussed and illustrated three different kinds of benefits that some teachers may receive under designated circumstances. The first kind is under workmen's compensation acts; the second, under state or local retirement laws; and the third, under the federal Old-Age and Survivors' Insurance program. It is possible that a teacher who is disabled becomes eligible for benefits under all three programs. It is possible that a disabled teacher is eligible for workmen's compensation and retirement benefits, but not to payments from the Old-Age and Survivors' Insurance program. It is also possible that a disabled teacher is eligible for retirement benefits and payments from the Old-Age and Survivors' Insurance program, but not to workmen's compensation. These distinctions rest partly on the coverage of the particular teacher and partly on the type of disability, although other factors are sometimes pertinent.

First, workmen's compensation benefits will be described with some preliminary discussion of the reasons why workmen's compensation laws were enacted.

A. WORKMEN'S COMPENSATION BENEFITS

Editorial Comment

When compared with industrial occupations, public-school employment would seem to be nonhazardous, especially for professional employees. However, equipment in shops, cafeterias, and laboratories is sometimes dangerous. Supervision of football, rifle practice, and other activities exposes instructors to injury, while even classroom teachers may be placed in danger if the school building is out of repair, or in cases of emergency. Workmen's compensation laws are in operation in every state, and in many states these laws cover school employees as well as workmen in private industry.

Historically, an injured workman's only opportunity to obtain damages for injuries sustained at work rested upon proof of the employer's negligence. Under the fellow-servant doctrine, the employer could defend himself in a suit for damages brought by an injured employee merely by proving that the accident occurred through the negligence of another employee, even if the fellow servant was a supervisor or an administrator whom the injured workman had never seen.

Employers had another defense in the plea of contributory negligence. Under this theory, any injury caused wholly or in part by the workman's own negligence was not the responsibility of the employer.

A third defense was available to employers under the doctrine of assumption of risk. It was said that, since the ordinary risks of accident were considered and assumed by the workman at the time he made the contract of employment, the employer was not financially responsible for accidents arising out of such employment.

In short, the employer's liability was a weak reed upon which an injured workman could place little faith. He hesitated to risk the hazards of legal action which was based upon theories not designed to protect his interests. In order to obtain damages, it was necessary to show conclusive evidence in court that the employer had been negligent in not establishing safe working rules, in not providing a safe place to work, in not furnishing safe appliances, or in employing incompetent workmen.

Modifications in common-law liability of employers were made by statutes, the first step being the employer liability acts. These laws continued to recognize the necessity of fault on the part of the employer, but they limited certain of the defenses previously available to him and they extended somewhat the rights of the employees. Not until the enactment of workmen's compensation laws did injured workmen have any real protection from injuries sustained on the job.

The philosophy underlying workmen's compensation legislation is that industrial accidents are inevitable and the burden of such accidents should be borne by industry rather than by the injured workmen individually. The financial loss, distributed by insurance, enters into the cost of production. Workmen's compensation laws provide benefits for workmen injured while engaged in services for the employer. Injuries arising out of and in the course of, or resulting

from, the workman's employment by his employer are compensated for through the employer's insurance.

Accidents sometimes occur through no fault of either the employer or the employee; carelessness of a workman may be a contributing factor or the sole cause of the accident. Workmen's compensation laws fix for the employee an expeditious remedy regardless of fault. They are advantageous to employers also since the benefits are specified in the law and the employer is not exposed to the possibility of high damages recoverable in a single successful law suit.

Public employees, including teachers, never had even the remote opportunity available to workmen in private industry under the common-law principles, for use of the courts to collect damages when injured in line of duty, because public employers could not be sued in tort. Hence, the desirability of covering public employees under workmen's compensation acts is obvious. Not all such laws include public employees; some include only those employers who choose to be covered, or those employers who have a given number of employees, or those employees who engage in hazardous work. Yet, among teachers, a considerable number have workmen's compensation benefits available to them.

State industrial commissions usually decide claims under workmen's compensation laws, but a great many cases come before the courts on appeal. These cases for the most part have to do with the amount of damages. Another type of case arises out of disagreement as to whether or not the accident occurred in the course of employment, or whether or not the injured workman was covered at the time of the injury.

Statutory Material

United States Code Annotated. Title 33, Chapter 18.

Sec. 901. Short title.
Sec. 902. Definitions.
Sec. 903. Coverage.
Sec. 904. Liability for compensation.
Sec. 905. Exclusiveness of liability. The liability of an employer prescribed in section 904 of this title shall be exclusive and in place of all other liability of such employer to the employee, his legal representative, husband or wife, parents, dependents, next of kin, and anyone otherwise entitled to recover damages from such employer at law or in admiralty on account of such injury or death, except that if an employer fails to secure payment of compensation as required by this chapter, an injured

employee, or his legal representative in case death results from the injury, may elect to claim compensation under this chapter, or to maintain an action at law or in admiralty for damages on account of such injury or death. In such action the defendant may not plead as a defense that the injury was caused by the negligence of a fellow servant, nor that the employee assumed the risk of his employment, nor that the injury was due to the contributory negligence of the employee.

Sec. 906. Time for commencement of compensation.

(a) No compensation shall be allowed for the first three days of the disability, except the benefits provided for in section 907 of this title: *Provided, however,* That in case the injury results in disability of more than twenty-eight days the compensation shall be allowed from the date of the disability.

(b) Compensation for disability shall not exceed $54 per week and compensation for total disability shall not be less than $18 per week: *Provided, however,* That if the employee's average weekly wages, as computed under section 910 of this title, are less than $18 per week he shall receive as compensation for total disability his average weekly wages.

Sec. 907. Medical services and supplies.

(a) The employer shall furnish such medical, surgical, and other attendance or treatment, nurse and hospital service, medicine, crutches, and apparatus for such period as the nature of the injury or the process of recovery may require. If the employer fails to provide the same, after request by the injured employee, such injured employee may do so at the expense of the employer. The employee shall not be entitled to recover any amount expended by him for such treatment or services unless he shall have requested the employer to furnish the same and the employer shall have refused or neglected to do so, or unless the nature of the injury required such treatment and services and the employer or his superintendent or foreman having knowledge of such injury shall have neglected to provide the same; nor shall any claim for medical or surgical treatment be valid and enforceable, as against such employer, unless within twenty days following the first treatment the physician giving such treatment furnish to the employer and the deputy commissioner a report of such injury and treatment, on a form prescribed by the Secretary. The deputy commissioner may, however, excuse the failure to furnish such report within twenty days when he finds it to be in the interest of justice to do so, and he may, upon application by a party in interest, make an award for the reasonable value of such medical or surgical treatment so obtained by the employee. If at any time during such period the employee unreasonably refuses to submit to medical or surgical treatment, the deputy commissioner may, by order, suspend the payment of further compensation during such time as such refusal continues, and no compensation shall be paid at any time during the period of such suspension, unless the circumstances justified the refusal.

(b) Whenever in the opinion of the deputy commissioner a physician has not impartially estimated the degree of permanent disability or the extent of temporary disability of any injured employee, the deputy commissioner shall have the power to cause such employee to be examined by

a physician selected by the deputy commissioner and to obtain from such physician a report containing his estimate of such disabilites. If the report of such physician shows that the estimate of the physician has not been impartial from the standpoint of such employee, the deputy commissioner shall have the power in his discretion to charge the cost of such examination to the employer, if he is a self-insurer, or to the insurance company which is carrying the risk.

(c) All fees and other charges for such treatment or service shall be limited to such charges as prevail in the same community for similar treatment of injured persons of like standard of living, and shall be subject to regulation by the deputy commissioner.

(d) The liability of an employer for medical treatment as provided in this section shall not be affected by the fact that his employee was injured through the fault or negligence of a third party, not in the same employ, unless and until notice of election to sue has been given as required by section 933 (a) of this title or suit has been brought against such third party without the giving of such notice. The employer shall, however, have a cause of action against such third party to recover any amounts paid by him for such medical treatment in like manner as provided in section 933 (b) of this title.

Sec. 908. Compensation for disability. Compensation for disability shall be paid to the employee as follows:

(a) Permanent total disability. . . .

(b) Temporary total disability. . . .

(c) Permanent partial disability. . . .

(d) Any compensation to which any claimant would be entitled under subdivision (c) of this section excepting subdivision (c-21) of this section shall, notwithstanding death arising from causes other than the injury, be payable to and for the benefit of the persons following. . . .

(e) Temporary partial disability. . . .

(f) Injury increasing disability. . . .

(g) . . . .

(h) . . . .

(i) . . . .

Sec. 909. Compensation for death.

Sec. 910. Determination of pay.

Sec. 911. Guardian for minor or incompetent.

Sec. 912. Notice of injury or death.

Sec. 913. Time for filing of claims.

Sec. 914. Payment of compensation.

Sec. 915. Invalid agreements.

(a) No agreement by an employee to pay any portion of premium paid by his employer to a carrier or to contribute to a benefit fund or department maintained by such employer for the purpose of providing compensation or medical services and supplies as required by this chapter shall be valid, and any employer who makes a deduction for such purpose from the pay of any employee entitled to the benefits of this chapter shall be guilty of a misdemeanor and upon conviction thereof shall be punished by a fine of not more than $1,000.

(b) No agreement by an employee to waive his right to compensation under this chapter shall be valid.

Sec. 916. Assignment and exemption from claims of creditors.

Sec. 917. Compensation a lien against assets.

Sec. 918. Collection of defaulted payments; special fund.

Sec. 919. Procedure in respect of claims.

Sec. 920. Presumptions.

Sec. 921. Review of compensation orders.

Sec. 921a. Appearance of United States Attorney for Secretary of Labor or deputy commissioner.

Sec. 922. Modification of awards.

Sec. 923. Procedure before the deputy commissioner.

Sec. 924. Witnesses.

Sec. 925. Witness fees.

Sec. 926. Costs in proceedings brought without reasonable grounds.

Sec. 927. Powers of deputy commissioners.

Sec. 928. Fees for services.

Sec. 929. Record of injury or death. Every employer shall keep a record in respect of any injury to an employee. Such record shall contain such information of disease, other disability, or death in respect of such injury as the Secretary may by regulation require, and shall be available to inspection by the Secretary or by any State authority at such times and under such conditions as the Secretary may by regulation prescribe.

Sec. 930. Reports.

(a) Within ten days from the date of any injury or death or from the date that the employer has knowledge of a disease or infection in respect of such injury, the employer shall send to the Secretary a report setting forth (1) the name, address, and business of the employer; (2) the name, address, and occupation of the employee; (3) the cause and nature of the injury or death; (4) the year, month, day, and hour when and the particular locality where the injury or death occurred; and (5) such other information as the Secretary may require. A copy of such report shall be sent at the same time to the deputy commissioner in the compensation district in which the injury occurred.

(b) Additional reports in respect of such injury and of the condition of such employee shall be sent by the employer to the Secretary and to such deputy commissioner at such times and in such manner as the Secretary may prescribe.

(c) Any report provided for in subdivision (a) or (b) of this section shall not be evidence of any fact stated in such report in any proceeding in respect of such injury or death on account of which the report is made.

(d) The mailing of any such report and copy in a stamped envelope, within the time prescribed in subdivisions (a) or (b) of this section, to the Secretary and deputy commissioner, respectively, shall be a compliance with this section.

(e) Any employer who fails or refuses to send any report required of him by this section shall be subject to a civil penalty not to exceed $500 for each such failure or refusal.

(f) Where the employer or the carrier has been given notice, or the employer (or his agent in charge of the business in the place where the injury occurred) or the carrier has knowledge, of any injury or death of an employee and fails, neglects, or refuses to file report thereof as required by the provisions of subdivision (a) of this section, the limitations in subdivision (a) of section 913 of this title shall not begin to run against the claim of the injured employee or his dependents entitled to compensation, or in favor of either the employer or the carrier, until such report shall have been furnished as required by the provisions of subdivision (a) of this section.

Sec. 931. Penalty for misrepresentation. Any person who willfully makes any false or misleading statement or representation for the purpose of obtaining any benefit or payment under this chapter shall be guilty of a misdemeanor and on conviction thereof shall be punished by a fine of not to exceed $1,000 or by imprisonment of not to exceed one year, or by both such fine and imprisonment.

Sec. 932. Security for compensation.

Sec. 933. Compensation for injuries where third persons are liable.

Sec. 934. Compensation notice.

Sec. 935. Substitution of carrier for employer.

Sec. 936. Insurance policies.

Sec. 937. Certificate of compliance with chapter.

Sec. 938. Penalty for failure to secure payment of compensation.

Sec. 939. Administration.

Sec. 940. Deputy commissioners.

Sec. 941. Safety rules and regulations—Safe place of employment; installation of safety devices and safeguards.

Sec. 942. Traveling expenses.

Sec. 943. Annual report.

Sec. 944. Special fund.

Sec. 945. Administration fund.

Sec. 946. Appropriation.

Sec. 947. Availability of appropriations.

Sec. 948. Laws inapplicable.

Sec. 949. Effect of unconstitutionality.

Sec. 950. Separability provision.

Statutory note. Title 36, section 501, of the District of Columbia Code makes the Longshoremen's and Harbor Workers' Compensation Act applicable to employees of the District of Columbia. This is the compensation law here outlined. It is fairly typical. The details of benefits and qualifications for different kinds of benefits in each law are manifold, though there are not great differences from state to state as to the type of benefits. Workmen's compensation benefits are financed by employers; employees do not contribute.

Case Material

Whitney v. Rural Independent School District, 232 Iowa 61, 4 N.W. (2d) 394 (Iowa, 1942). [School district sought review of award to injured teacher under workmen's compensation act.]

The facts in this case have been stipulated. Evelyn M. Whitney on or about the 14th day of November 1939 entered into a written contract with the Board of Directors of the Rural Independent School District No. 4 of Lafayette Township, Bremer County, Iowa, to teach . . . at an agreed price of $60 per month. That on the 3d day of April 1940 at about 10:30 A.M., the same being during the forenoon recess of said school, one of the pupils attending the Rural Independent School District of Lafayette Township carelessly threw a hard piece of rubber across the school room, the same being a part of the wheel of a toy tractor. That the wheel of the toy tractor which was thrown by the student struck the glasses worn by the said Evelyn M. Whitney and also her left eye, injuring same. That it was further agreed that the uncorrected vision (vision without glasses) of the left eye of Evelyn M. Whitney prior to the injury was 87 percent but that with the aid of glasses her vision in the left eye was increased to 97 percent of normal. That it was agreed between the parties that if Dr. F. H. Reuling of Waterloo, Iowa, were placed on the stand, he would testify that there was a linear horizontal scar five millimeters in length and one millimeter in width on the cornea extending across the lower one-quarter of the pupil area of the left eye and that it was his opinion it was a permanent injury with a 40 percent loss of vision in the left eye. That Dr. R. E. Robinson, if he were placed on the stand, would testify in regard to the scar and that she has a loss of vision amounting to 50 percent of a normal seeing eye. That the use of glasses will not improve her vision in the left eye. That there was no injury to the right and that she is entitled to no compensation for said right eye. That the Rural Independent School District No. 4 of Lafayette Township is a school corporation existing by virtue of the statutes of the State of Iowa and that John Remley, August Ruth and Louis Graeser are the duly elected, qualified and now acting members of the Board of Directors. . . .

That the Deputy Industrial Commissioner, sitting as a Board of Arbitration, held that the claimant was entitled to compensation in the sum of $486.25 and interest thereon as provided by Section 1391 of the 1939 Code of Iowa in the sum of $26.79, making a total claim of $513.04. . . . That claimant sustained a permanent partial disability equal to a 46.8 percent loss of vision in her left eye and was entitled to weekly compensation benefits for a period of 46.8 weeks.

The Industrial Commissioner on Review affirmed the award and decision of the deputy industrial commissioner sitting as a board of arbitration.

The case was then appealed to the District Court of the State of Iowa in and for Bremer County and that court affirmed the decision of the Industrial Commissioner. The Rural Independent School District No. 4 of Lafayette Township being dissatisfied, has appealed to this court.

In a very able and elaborate brief the school district urges that the lower court erred in finding that claimant was not acting in an official position

or standing in a representative capacity within the meaning of the law [which excludes such persons.] . . . We come to the conclusion that she is an employe within the meaning of the Workmen's Compensation Act and entitled to its benefits. . . .

It is next claimed that the Industrial Commissioner erred in the amount of compensation allowed. Appellants claim that under the undisputed record the claimant sustained only a 32 percent loss of vision in her left eye as a result of said injury. This seems to be based upon the fact that the record shows that prior to the injury Evelyn M. Whitney had only an 87 percent vision in the left eye and that after the injury the uncorrected vision (vision of the left eye without glasses) was 55 percent, making a loss of 32 percent of vision due to the injury. With this we cannot agree.

It is true the record shows that the uncorrected vision prior to the injury was 87 percent, but the record shows that by the use of glasses the vision was corrected to 97 percent, and that after the injury, glasses would not help or aid her left eye. Appellants contend that we have to do simply with a normal eye. This it seems to us would be very unfair to Evelyn M. Whitney for with the aid of glasses she could correct, prior to the injury, the vision in her left eye to 97 percent, while after the injury glasses would not aid her in any way. The injury which she suffered was the injury to her eye. It was the loss of vision from 97 percent. Her injury is permanent. It will neither be better nor worse the doctors testify. In addition to this, there is the evidence stipulated to of Dr. Robinson, showing a loss of 51.1 percent vision in her left eye. Certainly there was sufficient evidence to sustain the verdict of the Industrial Commissioner as to the injury that this girl suffered. The purpose of the Workmen's Compensation Act was to reimburse the employe for the injury that that employe suffered. . . .

Case note. Most of the court cases involving workmen's compensation claims are quite complicated either with medical testimony or the arithmetical computation of benefits. The object of these laws is to give money damages for physical injuries. Therefore, the amount of damages due and the extent of the physical injuries sustained become the important issues in settling the claims.

Bower v. Industrial Commission, 61 Ohio App. 469, 22 N.E. (2d) 840 (Ohio, 1939). [Industrial Commission sought reversal of award granted by lower court to injured teacher under workmen's compensation act.]

At the time of her injury and for some years prior thereto, appellee was an employe of the Board of Education of Fremont, Ohio, as a teacher in the public schools of that city and on the day of her injury she was attending a teachers' institute at Toledo, Ohio. Her attendance there, with other teachers of Fremont, was at the express request and direction of the superintendent of schools of Fremont, the schools of that city being closed on that day to enable the teachers to attend the institute held on Friday and Saturday, and the teachers who did attend received

their regular pay for the day, while those who did not attend would forfeit a day's pay. Appellee was required to make a report of the sessions of the institute to her superintendent upon her return to Fremont on a form furnished by the superintendent. It appears also that attendance or non-attendance at these institutes gave the teachers credits or discredits in their rating for re-employment for succeeding years.

Appellee testified that she considered it compulsory on her part to attend the institute referred to herein. No transportation was provided for appellee or other teachers to Toledo and return, or were any accommodations provided for them in that city. Appellee drove there from Fremont in her car on the morning of October 26th, and attended the forenoon and afternoon sessions of the institute with another teacher, a Miss Gibbs, a friend whom she met there, also a non-resident of Toledo. After the afternoon session appellee placed her baggage in Miss Gibbs' car at her invitation, and Miss Gibbs offered to take appellee to the May apartments in Toledo where another friend of appellee's lived and with whom she testified she intended to attend the evening session of the institute, and then remain with her at the May apartments all night and attend the final sessions of the institute the next morning. Appellee states she had made these arrangements with her friend at the May apartments by letter some days before. She further states she did not know where the May apartments were located and was unfamiliar with the streets of Toledo. On the way to the May apartments the car of Miss Gibbs in which appellee was riding as a guest was struck by another car, resulting in serious and permanent injuries to appellee which are the basis of the claim she made before the commission.

Appellee's claim was rejected by the commission on the ground that her injuries were not suffered in the course of her employment and this is the point contended for here. . . .

It is the view of this court that the circumstances of the instant case show that at the moment of injury the appellee was performing duties incidental to her employment and a necessary part of her entire trip to Toledo to attend the institute as she had been directed to do by her employer, and that she was doing at the time what her employer would reasonably expect her to do; that the "employment had some casual connection with the injury, either through its activities, its conditions, or its environments. . . ." Appellee had to eat somewhere and had to sleep somewhere during her stay in Toledo, no such accommodations being provided for her by the employer, and to say she might have had her dinner and have slept elsewhere would be no answer and no defense, for no one can say what might have befallen her in such event.

We are aware, of course, of the different situation that would have been presented had appellee been injured in her home city while going from her home to the school where she taught, a fixed place of abode and a fixed situs of employment. . . .

We conclude that appellee was injured while doing an act incident to and reasonably within the course of her employment and duties and we find support for this view in [cases cited.] . . .

Some contention is made that Miss Gibbs in taking appellee to the May apartments did not take the most direct route from where she started with appellee, *viz:* the art museum in Toledo where the institute was held, but, instead, was first going to stop and see a cousin of hers on the way, and that the accident happened before arriving at the cousin's home. We do not think this material, particularly when the record shows that neither appellee nor Miss Gibbs knew just where the May apartments were located and neither was a resident of Toledo or familiar with its streets, and appellee testified she did not know Miss Gibbs was going to stop anywhere and supposed they were on the direct route to the place Miss Gibbs said she would take her, *viz:* the May apartments.

Case note. The last paragraph of the decision points to the principle that, if an employee is injured while on a "detour" from his regular line of duty, he is not injured in the course of his employment and no claim may be paid. Possibly had Miss Gibbs told Miss Bower that she planned to stop en route and visit a cousin, and Miss Bower agreed, the court would have denied the claim on the basis that the teacher was on a "detour." Possibly, also, had the teachers known the streets in Toledo and so deliberately took an indirect route, the claim might have been denied.

The ruling of this case has importance for all teachers who travel to association conventions and institutes. It should be pointed out, however, that an injury on the way to school is not compensable in the ordinary course of events.

B. DISABILITY RETIREMENT BENEFITS

Editorial Comment

Workmen's compensation benefits are payable only when the disability arose out of the performance of duties. Next will be discussed disability retirement benefits; they are not dependent upon injury in line of duty. A few retirement laws make special provision for disability because of injury in line of duty, making qualifications for eligibility lighter and payments larger than when the disability is nonduty-connected. Such provisions are rare. Frequently, these disability benefits are to be offset by benefits paid under the workmen's compensation law.

Disability retirement allowances apply to permanent disability only, with the exception of a very few laws which provide other benefits for temporary disability. Usually, a medical board must certify that the member is no longer physically or mentally capable of continuing in public-school teaching, and after retirement on disability a physical

examination is usually required periodically. Frequently the law provides that a person retired on disability may not, in another employment, earn more than the difference between the retirement allowance and the salary earned prior to retirement. Disability retirement is available to members of retirement systems after they have been members for a specified period of time, usually five or ten years. All these requirements are written into the law to prevent abuse of the provisions for disability retirement.

Disability benefits paid under the typical teacher retirement law may be the money-purchase type as for superannuation or service retirement, or a fixed benefit. If it is a money-doubled benefit, the accumulated contributions at the time the member becomes disabled are doubled by the state or city and the allowance calculated on the total, to be equal to the actuarial equivalent of that amount, payable in equal payments for the life of the retiring member. In plans providing a fixed benefit for superannuation or service retirement, disability benefits are usually a per cent of the allowance which would have been payable had the member continued in service until he met the qualifications for superannuation or service retirement.

Statutory Material

Revised Code of Washington, secs. 41.32.360, 41.32.540, 41.32.550, 41.32.560.

Sec. 41.32.360. Throughout each year during which he is employed each member who is employed on a full time basis shall have transferred from his contributions such sum as will, with regular interest, create a fund sufficient according to the actuarial tables adopted by the board of trustees to provide disability benefits for the members whose claims will be approved by the board of trustees during that year. These transfers shall be placed in the disability reserve fund.

Sec. 41.32.540. Upon application of a member in service or of his employer any member may be granted a temporary disability allowance by the board of trustees if the medical director, after a medical examination of such member, shall certify that such member is mentally or physically incapacitated for the further performance of duty. The disability allowance will be in the amount of seventy-five dollars per month payable from the disability reserve fund for a period not to exceed two years, but no payment shall be made for a disability period of less than sixty days.

Sec. 41.32.550. Should the board determine from the report of the medical director at the end of a two year disability period that a member's disability will continue, a member who had fifteen years or more of service credit when first granted the temporary disability allowance shall have the option of then receiving all accumulated contributions in

a lump sum payment and canceling his membership, or of accepting a retirement allowance because of disability. If the member elects to receive a retirement allowance because of disability he shall be paid an annuity which shall be the actuarial equivalent of his accumulated contributions at his age of retirement and a pension which shall be the actuarial equivalent of the pension to which he would be entitled at age sixty according to his years of service credit, but in no event shall the total allowance for disability be less than seventy-five dollars per month.

Sec. 41.32.560. Any former member of the retirement system or a former fund receiving permanent disability allowances on July 1, 1955, shall in lieu of all allowances provided by any former law receive a disability allowance adjusted for cost of living to seventy-five dollars per month to be paid from the pension fund. Any member of the retirement system receiving a temporary disability allowance on July 1, 1955, shall in lieu of the disability allowance provided by the former law receive a disability allowance adjusted for cost of living to seventy-five dollars per month to be paid from the disability reserve fund. Such disability allowances may be continued only upon recommendation of the medical director and approval of the board of trustees.

Statutory note. Washington's retirement disability provisions differ from practically all others by the separation of members' contributions for annuity and for disability; also few, if any, other state teachers' retirement systems pay disability benefits for temporary disability and permit the disabled teacher to withdraw accumulated contributions in a lump sum when the disability is determined to be permanent at the end of the second year. Of course, in other systems, a disabled member could resign and withdraw accumulated contributions rather than apply for a disability allowance; this, however, is different.

Qualifications for disability benefits differ and the method of computing these benefits differ. Many laws pay in the form of a disability benefit a portion of the benefit which would be available were the member able to continue in service until normal retirement age. Others have placed a floor of minimum disability benefits under the formula, and in some cases this has resulted in the payment of larger disability benefits than the member could obtain were he to continue in service until normal retirement age.

Case Material

Martin et al. v. Teachers' Retirement Board of City of New York. 70 N.Y.S. (2d) 593 (N. Y. 1947). [Teacher alleged to have been mentally incompetent at time of retirement.]

This action is brought to set aside the service retirement of the plaintiff's intestate as a teacher in the public schools of this city. The theory

of the action is that by reason of the teacher's "mental incompetency" at the time of filing his application for retirement, the retirement was null and void and that there is due the estate of the deceased teacher a sum representing his death benefits payable on the basis of his having died in service.

The intestate on November 1, 1939, had applied for retirement effective on November 13, 1939, on a maximum retirement annuity with no payment to his estate or a designated beneficiary upon his death. He died on January 5, 1940.

The law of the case was established by the decision of the Appellate Division (269 App. Div. 115, 54 N. Y. S. 2d 245, by Cohn, J.) holding the complaint sufficient: if he was incompetent Mr. Martin's act of retirement was voidable and could be disaffirmed by his administrators. But on the trial, the plaintiffs have failed to sustain the burden incumbent upon them of proving the deceased's incompetency; indeed, it may be fairly said that the greater weight of the evidence is with the defendant.

Unsoundness of mind or insanity sufficient to rescind a contract must be of such character that the incompetent had no reasonable perception or understanding of the nature and terms of the contract. . . . It seems clear that Mr. Martin knew what he was doing when he retired on a maximum retirement allowance; it may be readily conceived as a sound choice to gather for himself the greatest income he could under the then circumstances of his life—hindsight perhaps, not foresight, could presume to condemn it.

Apparently, the deceased had given the question of his retirement considerable thought and understood the nature and quality of the transaction he was making and the relationship he was entering into. He knew that no one was financially dependent upon him; he had always disdained medical assistance and with his optimistic nature assumed that he would live for many more years; he enjoyed life and wanted to get from the Retirement System as a retirement allowance the most that he could while he lived. Who can say that his choice was unjustified or unreasonable?

Though the plaintiffs make much of the fact that in 1939 their father was irritable, opinionated and forgetful, his colleagues—some of whom knew the deceased for almost forty years—and others affirmed that that condition was not unusual. Paul Martin, they aver, was a musical genius and had always been impulsive, volatile, enthusiastic—a brilliant teacher of music; as such, they imply, his display of temperament is imputable to a gifted personality. Divers idiosyncrasies are attributable to many, if not most, of mankind—the other fellow's singularity seems so surpassingly strange probably because it does not mirror our own. To hold these to evidence incompetency would be to render of dubious validity innumerable contracts under which valuable rights have been secured or solemn obligations incurred.

Annuity contracts could not be written if the heirs of short-living annuitants were permitted to rescind the annuity contract, when at the same time the Retirement System or the insurance company would be

compelled to continue payments to annuitants who live far beyond their life expectancy. . . .

The defendant is entitled to judgment dismissing the complaint on the merits. . . .

Case note. Most cases on disability retirement revolve around the medical evidence to prove disability. Sometimes the member's own physician disagrees with the physicians or the medical board appointed by the retirement system to evaluate all applications for disability retirement.

Most retirement laws have what is called a "death-bed" provision so that if death occurs before the first payment of a benefit check the decedent will be considered to have died in service—in which event his survivors would be entitled to return of his accumulated contributions. Several cases in New York State have been concerned with the issue of this case: when death occurs soon after retirement, the survivors claim that application for retirement was void because the former member was not of sound mind at the time he applied. The teacher in this case applied for regular retirement and to that extent the case hardly belongs in this chapter on disability benefits. However, it was placed here to indicate that mental incompetency is a disability for which a disability benefit is payable but that mental incompetency must be proved by adequate evidence. Furthermore, allegations that a deceased former member had an unsound mind cannot rescind an application for regular retirement, even though it is a general principle of contract law that any contract entered into by a mentally incompetent person is void.

C. FEDERAL SOCIAL SECURITY DISABILITY BENEFITS

Editorial Comment

In 1954 Congress amended the Social Security Act to establish the so-called disability "freeze" which is analogous to the waiver-of-premium provision in many insurance policies. Under that provision, one who is considered disabled will have his wage credits frozen so that when he reaches retirement age his benefit will not be diminished by the period of disability. In 1956 Congress added a program of cash benefits for disabled workers age 50 or over and in 1960 the age requirement was eliminated. The same standards of disability apply to both programs, except that blindness may result in a freeze but not in the payment of cash benefits.

The language of the Social Security Act is that the claimant for disability benefits must be unable to "engage in any substantial

gainful activity by reason of any medically determinable physical or mental impairment which can be expected to result in death or to be of long-continued and indefinite duration." Under regulations promulgated by the Department of Health, Education and Welfare (which has supervision of the social security program) the inability to engage in gainful employment must be because of a medically determinable physical or mental impairment and unemployment for any other reason does not qualify a claimant. The impairment need not be everlasting but must be of long-continued and indefinite duration or one expected to result in death. A condition which is remediable is a bar to benefits. The education and occupational experience of claimants is considered, together with their physical and mental condition. The claimant's education is a factor in the determination of whether or not he could be rehabilitated for work other than the kind he was accustomed to doing before becoming disabled.

All determinations are reviewed by the Bureau of Old-Age and Survivors' Insurance. Certain administrative remedies are available for appeal, and, finally, a dissatisfied claimant may go to the United States district courts. However, chances of getting a reversal of a denial of a claim do not seem very high, although there appears a slight tendency in the latest cases for the courts to be less strict than the Bureau referees. [No case material is included on this subject since no case has been found in which a school employee sought OASDI disability benefits and decisions in other applications would not likely be helpful. However, excerpts from the Social Security Act having to do with disability benefits are shown below.]

Statutory Material

United States Code Annotated. Title 42, secs. 421-423, as amended by P. L. 86-778 (1960).

Sec. 421. (a) In the case of any individual, the determination of whether or not he is under a disablity (as defined in section 416 (i) or 423 (c) of this title) and of the day such disability began, and the determination of the day on which such disability ceases, shall, except as provided in subsection (g) of this section, be made by a State agency pursuant to an agreement entered into under subsection (b) of this section. Except as provided in subsections (c) and (d) of this section, any such determination shall be the determination of the Secretary for purposes of this subchapter.

(b) The Secretary shall enter into an agreement with each State which is willing to make such an agreement under which the State agency or agencies administering the State plan approved under the Vocational Re-

habilitation Act, or any other appropriate State agency or agencies, or both, will make the determinations referred to in subsection (a) of this section with respect to all individuals in such State, or with respect to such class or classes of individuals in the State as may be designated in the agreement at the State's request.

(c) The Secretary may on his own motion review a determination, made by a State agency pursuant to an agreement under this section, that an individual is under a disability (as defined in section 416 (i) or 423 (c) of this title) and, as a result of such review, may determine that such individual is not under a disability (as so defined) or that such disability began on a day later than that determined by such agency, or that such disability ceased on a day earlier than that determined by such agency.

(d) Any individual dissatisfied with any determination under subsection (a), (c), or (g) of this section shall be entitled to a hearing thereon by the Secretary to the same extent as is provided in section 405 (b) of this title with respect to decisions of the Secretary, and to judicial review of the Secretary's final decision after such hearing as is provided in section 405 (g) of this title. . . .

(g) In the case of individuals in a State which has no agreement under subsection (b) of this section, in the case of individuals outside the United States, and in the case of any class or classes of individuals not included in an agreement under subsection (b) of this section, the determinations referred to in subsection (a) of this section shall be made by the Secretary in accordance with regulations prescribed by him.

Sec. 422. (a) It is declared to be the policy of the Congress that disabled individuals applying for a determination of disability, and disabled individuals who are entitled to child's insurance benefits, shall be promptly referred to the State agency or agencies administering or supervising the administration of the State plan approved under the Vocational Rehabilitation Act for necessary vocational rehabilitation services, to the end that the maximum number of such individuals may be rehabilitated into productive activity.

(b) [Deductions on account of refusal to accept rehabilitation services.] . . .

Sec. 423 (a) (1) Every individual who—

(A) is insured for disability insurance benefits (as determined under subsection (c) (1) of this section),

(B) has not attained the age of sixty-five,

(C) has filed application for disability insurance benefits, and

(D) is under a disability (as defined in subsection (c) (2) of this section) at the time such application is filed,

shall be entitled to a disability insurance benefit (i) for each month beginning with the first month after his waiting period (as defined in subsection (c) (3)) in which he becomes so entitled to such insurance benefits, or (ii) for each month beginning with the first month during all of which he is under a disability and in which he becomes so entitled to such insurance benefits, but only if he was entitled to disability insurance benefits which terminated, or had a period of disability (as de-

fined in section 416 (i) which ceased, within the 60-month period preceding the first month in which he is under such disability and ending with whichever of the following months is the earliest: the month in which he dies, the month in which he attains the age of sixty-five, or the third month following the month in which his disability ceases.

(2) Such individual's disability insurance benefit for any month shall be equal to his primary insurance amount for such month determined under section 415 of this title as though he had attained retirement age in—

(A) the first month of his waiting period, or

(B) in any case in which clause (ii) of paragraph (1) of this sub-section is applicable, the first month for which he becomes so entitled to such disability insurance benefits.

(b) No application for disability insurance benefits shall be accepted as a valid application for purposes of this section (1) if it is filed more than nine months before the first month for which the applicant becomes entitled to such benefits, or (2) in any case in which clause (ii) of paragraph (1) of subsection (a) is applicable, if it is filed more than six months before the first month for which the applicant becomes entitled to such benefits; and any application filed within such nine months' period or six months', as the case may be, shall be deemed to have been filed in such first month. An individual who would have been entitled to a disability insurance benefit for any month after June 1957 had he filed application therefor prior to the end of such month shall be entitled to such benefit for such month if he is continuously under a disability after such month and until he files application therefor, and he files such application.

(c) For purposes of this section—

(1) An individual shall be insured for disability insurance benefits in any month if he would have been a fully insured indivdual (as defined in section 414 of this title) had he attained retirement age and filed ap-plication for benefits under section 402 (a) of this title on the first day of such month.

(2) The term "disability" means inability to engage in any substantial gainful activity by reason of any medically determinable physical or mental impairment which can be expected to result in death or to be of long-continued and indefinite duration. An individual shall not be considered to be under a disability unless he furnishes such proof of the existence thereof as may be required.

(3) The term "waiting period" means, in the case of any application for disability insurance benefits, the earliest period of six consecutive calendar months—

(A) throughout which the individual who files such application has been under a disability which continues until such application is filed, and

(B) (i) which begins not earlier than with the first day of the eight-eenth month before the month in which such application is filed if such individual is insured for disability insurance benefits in such eighteenth month, or (ii) if he is not so insured in such month. which

begins not earlier than with the first day of the first month after such eighteenth month in which he is so insured.
Notwithstanding the preceding provisions of this paragraph, no waiting period may begin for any individual before January 1, 1957.

Statutory note. Acts of Congress are especially difficult to understand because of the congressional practice of amending by reference. The 1960 amendments to the disability provisions of the Social Security Act deleted the age requirement and liberalized the qualifications needed for eligibility for these benefits. Because the amendments referred to sections of the Social Security Act rather than to the United States Code Annotated, some editorial work needed to be done to weave the new material into the codified statute. For a simpler explanation of the OASDI disability benefits, a pamphlet may be obtained from the Bureau of Old-Age and Survivors' Insurance.[1]

Sources of Further Information

48 Am. Jur. "Social Security, Unemployment Insurance, and Retirement Funds" secs. 9 and 31.
99 C.J.S. "Workmen's Compensation" secs. 115-119.
A.L.R. "Social Security" Topic Nos. 1-16.
American Digest System "Social Security" secs. 241-242; "Workmen's Compensation" Key Nos. 225, 382.

Work Sheet

1. Are public-school teachers included in the workmen's compensation law of your state? Are there any limitations as to their coverage?
2. Outline the benefits of the workmen's compensation act.
3. Regardless of whether you are covered or not, review the contingencies in which such coverage would be beneficial to you in your particular type of school work.
4. If you know of someone who has been awarded benefits under a workmen's compensation act, ascertain from him the procedure followed in filing his claim and appeal, if made, for the benefits awarded.
5. What are the requirements for eligibility to disability retirement under the retirement system to which you belong?

---

[1] Address Bureau of Old-Age and Survivors' Insurance, Department of Health, Education, and Welfare, Washington 25, D. C.

6. How are disability benefits computed in your system?

7. Are you permitted to engage in other gainful employment after having been retired for disability? If so, is there a limitation on the amount earned?

8. Think of a disability which would make a teacher eligible for disability benefits under the Old-Age and Survivors' Insurance program. Is it possible that because teachers are highly educated in comparison with the population in general that the likelihood of their rehabilitation for other work might mean that teachers, generally, cannot benefit from the disability provisions of the federal program except during the period of rehabilitation?

Chapter 10.

RETIREMENT AND SOCIAL
SECURITY BENEFITS

Editorial Comment

By 1950 every regular full-time teacher in the public schools of the United States was covered by a state or local retirement or pension system. Until 1950 they were not eligible for coverage by the federal Social Security Act.

In 1960 about two-thirds of the teachers in the United States had both retirement-system membership and social security coverage. In some states social security coverage was adopted "on top" of the existing retirement plan—this is called "full supplementation." In other states the existing retirement plan was amended at the time social security coverage was adopted, although they are operated separately —this is called "coordination." In a few states the legislature determined by formula the amount of retirement income it wanted its teachers to have and provided that the retirement system would pay the difference between social security benefits and that amount—this is called the "offset method." Though social security coverage has spread widely throughout the 1950-60 decade, teachers in many states prefer not to be covered by the federal program lest it weaken the provisions of their retirement systems which, often but not always, pay benefits more generous than other retirement systems plus social security.

There are many variations in coordination and in offset formulas; undoubtedly, new ones will be developed. It is not the purpose of this brief discussion to examine any of these formulas; it should be pointed out, however, that complicated as they are, it behooves teachers to study their own formulas so that they will understand what they can expect upon reaching retirement age.

The remainder of this chapter is devoted to retirement laws. To describe the Social Security Act would be of no avail since that Act

is amended almost every year. Instead, the reader is advised to obtain from the Bureau of Old-Age and Survivors' Insurance[1] pamphlets which will explain the highlights and which will be currently up to date.

We shall now describe the typical teachers' retirement law which will be followed by *Statutory Material* and *Case Material* in this area.

Public-school teachers are provided with a plan for pension or retirement allowances in all states. There are also about 50 plans in operation on a city or county basis, and usually the teachers belonging to a city or county retirement system do not belong to the state plan in their state.

Practically all are joint-contributory, both members and employers contributing to the funds from which benefits are paid. Joint-contributory retirement plans are usually written on insurance principles, although there are several state and more city systems which have no such sound basis.

Insurance or actuarial types of retirement systems are not all alike, however. So far as public financing is concerned, there are three general types: (1) pay-as-you-go or cash disbursement plans, (2) partially reserve plans, and (3) fully funded plans.

In a pay-as-you-go system, the state or city appropriates the money for payment of its share of the benefits each year as it is needed for those who are on retirement, or, if more than enough for the current payments is appropriated, at least there is no relation between the amount of appropriations and future needs.

In a partially reserve system, the state or city appropriates, at the time a member goes on retirement, sufficient funds to carry the benefits due that member in the future so long as he lives.

In a fully funded or reserve system, the appropriation from public funds each year is an amount calculated to be sufficient, when added to past and future appropriations with interest, to accumulate before the member retires an amount which will be then available to pay the benefits due the member thereafter, so long as he lives.

Note that these distinctions refer only to the state or city appropriations. The terms do not refer to that part of the plan having to do with the members' contributions. Other distinctions apply to members' contributions.

Some retirement laws provide that the member shall contribute a fixed per cent of salary, *e.g.*, 4 per cent, or 4 per cent of salary

---

[1] Address Bureau of Old-Age and Survivors' Insurance, Department of Health, Education, and Welfare, Washington 25, D. C.

up to a designated ceiling. Other laws provide that the member's contribution shall be fixed by the actuary, to be such rate of contribution as will provide, with interest, at the time the member retires an accumulation sufficient to pay his share of the benefits thereafter.

Benefits in retirement plans are of three kinds: (1) superannuation or service retirement allowance, (2) disability retirement allowance, and (3) death benefits.

Superannuation or service retirement allowance provisions provide that when a member has reached a specified age, e.g., sixty, or has served a specified number of years, e.g., 30, or has met whatever qualifications for retirement are set down in the law, he shall be eligible to receive an allowance based in part on his own accumulated contributions and in part on the appropriations from the state or city. If it is a fully funded system, the appropriations are in the retirement fund waiting for him when he meets qualifications for retirement.

The allowance payable may be of the money-purchase type, or the fixed-benefit type. A money-purchase benefit in retirement systems means that the benefit payable is calculated by the actuary to be the allowance which is equal to the actuarial equivalent of accumulated contributions of the member and the appropriations on his behalf from state or city funds. When the accumulated contributions of the member are matched by an equal amount from public funds, it is called a money-doubled plan.

The fixed-benefit type of retirement system, as its name implies, states that the allowance shall be either an amount of money, e.g., $1,200 (this is rare), or an allowance calculated by some formula involving a percent of the final average salary multiplied by the number of years of service. Final average salary is usually the average salary paid in the last five or ten years, or sometimes during the best five years while the teacher was a member of the system.

Most retirement laws also provide that when a member retires he may choose one of several options for the payment of his retirement allowance, so that under some of these options he may provide survivors' benefits for his dependents.

If a member withdraws from the teaching profession, or from the jurisdiction covered by a particular retirement law, he may withdraw his accumulated contributions. If he dies before meeting the qualifications for retirement, his accumulated contributions are paid to his estate or to a named beneficiary. In neither case is any

part of the state or city appropriation on his behalf paid to the withdrawing member or to his estate. However, many laws now provide fixed amounts as death benefits either in addition to or in lieu of refund of the member's own contributions with interest. Some of these death benefits are lump sum payments; others are in the form of monthly payments to named beneficiaries or to unnamed dependent children and widows.

Administering a retirement system is "big business" involving the investment of large amounts of money, actuarial calculations of the most detailed sort, and record keeping which must be meticulous. Retirement boards are usually established for this purpose. The law prescribes the types of investments in which the reserves must be invested and the frequency with which actuarial surveys must be conducted to determine if the funds will be available when needed to pay the promised benefits. Administrative expenses run into large figures in some systems where the membership and the type of law require considerable personnel to manage the records.

Because modern courts have held that the payment of a joint-contributory retirement allowance constitutes a contract which the state may not impair by lowering it after retirement, the question has arisen as to the legislature's power to increase these benefits after retirement. A contract is binding on both parties. Most state constitutions contain a provision prohibiting the payment of anything of value for past services. This provision has prevented increasing allowances of those already retired, even though higher cost of living has dwindled the living that can be purchased with retirement income fixed when cost of living was much lower. On the other hand, a number of states have increased allowances payable to retired teachers without having had their action challenged in the courts. When there has been a judicial challenge several courts based their decisions on the moral obligation of the state to help retired teachers meet high costs of living. Occasionally a court holds that such an increase is valid for those who joined the retirement system voluntarily. After adverse opinions, several states have effectuated increases by creating a new contract with retired teachers—their allowances for past services were not increased, theoretically, but they received additional payments for additional contributions to the system or for the promise to give additional services.

Statutory Material

New York Education Law, Article 11. State Teachers' Retirement System for Public School Teachers.

Sec. 501 Definitions
Sec. 502 Retirement system
Sec. 503 Membership of system
Sec. 504 Retirement board; members; terms of office; vacancies
Sec. 505 Election of elected members of board
Sec. 506 Board meetings; oath of office; quorum; expenses
Sec. 507 Officers of board; custody of funds
Sec. 508 Investment of funds; interest; accounts; reports
Sec. 509 Statements of teachers' service; determination of service creditable; service certificates
Sec. 510 Superannuation retirement

1. Retirement upon a superannuation allowance shall be made under the following conditions:

a. A member who is a present teacher and who has completed twenty-five years of total service and who has attained the age of sixty years or over while in service, or a member who is a new entrant who has completed twenty-five years of total state service and who has attained the age of sixty years or over while in service, or any member who has completed thirty-five years of total service shall be retired, if he files with the retirement board a statement duly attested setting forth at what time not less than thirty days nor more than sixty days subsequent to the execution and filing thereof he desires such retirement.

b. Any member who has attained age seventy may be retired at his own request or at the request of his employer if he or his employer files with the retirement board a statement duly attested setting forth at what time subsequent to the execution and filing thereof retirement is desired, and if throughout the year immediately preceding the filing of such statement he shall have been in service as a teacher in this state. The retirement board shall retire said member as of the date so specified or as of such other time within thirty days thereafter as the retirement board may find advisable.

2. Upon superannuation retirement a member shall receive a super-annuation retirement allowance which shall consist of:

a. An annuity which shall be the actuarial equivalent of his accumulated contributions at the time of his retirement, and

b. A pension of one quarter (1/4) of his final average salary or if his total service is less than twenty-five years, a pension of one one-hundredth (1/100) of his final average salary multiplied by the number of years of total service, and

c. If the member has attained age sixty at the time of retirement, a further pension of one one-hundred fortieth (1/140) of his final average salary multiplied by the number of years of total state service in excess of thirty-five years, and

d. If the member be a present teacher, a further pension of one one-hundred fortieth (1/140) of his final average salary multiplied by the

number of years of total service certified on his prior service certificate, and

e. If the member has contributed pursuant to paragraph c of subdivision three of section five hundred sixteen, a further pension of one one-hundred twentieth (1/120) of his final average salary for each year of total service in excess of twenty-five years but not in excess of thirty-five years, nor in excess of the number of years for which credit is allowed under paragraph d of subdivision three of section five hundred sixteen, and

f. A further pension, of such amount as shall be required to bring the total retirement allowance of members with twenty-five or more years of state service up to four hundred dollars per annum, and

g. The provision of paragraph (c) of subdivision two of this section shall apply only to members retiring on and after the date on which paragraph (c) of subdivision two of this section becomes operative and prior to July first, nineteen hundred sixty-five.

Sec. 511 Disability retirement

1. Retirement on account of disability shall be made under the following conditions: A member who has completed at least fifteen years of total state service or a member who is a present teacher and who has completed twenty years of service, the last ten of which were state service, may be retired on account of disability either upon the application of his employer or upon his own application or that of a person acting in his behalf, if the retirement board, after a medical examination of said member, made at the place of his residence within the state or other place mutually agreed upon, by a physician or physicians designated by said board shall determine upon the basis of a report submitted by said physician or physicians that the said member is physically or mentally incapacitated for the performance of duty, that he was incapacitated at the time he ceased teaching and that said member ought to be retired. . . .

3. Once each year during the first five years following the retirement of the teacher on a disability allowance the retirement board may, and upon his application shall, require any disability beneficiary to undergo medical examination by a physician or physcians designated by the retirement board, said examination to be made at the place of residence of said beneficiary or other place mutually agreed upon. Should any disability beneficiary refuse to submit to a medical examination, his retirement allowance shall be discontinued until his withdrawal of such refusal, and should such refusal continue for one year, all his rights in and to his pension shall be forfeited.

4. Should the physician or physicians designated by the retirement board report and certify to the retirement board that such disability beneficiary is engaged in or is able to engage in a gainful occupation paying more than the difference between his retirement allowance and his final average salary, and should the retirement board concur in such report, then the amount of his pension shall be reduced to an amount which, when added to the amount earnable by him, together with his annuity shall equal the amount of his final average salary. Should his earning capacity be later changed, then the amount of his pension may be further altered; provided, that the new pension shall not exceed the

amount of the pension originally granted nor an amount which when added to the amount earned by the beneficiary, together with his annuity equals the amount of his final average salary. A beneficiary restored to active service at a salary less than the final average salary or upon the basis of which he was retired shall not become a member of the retirement system while receiving a reduced pension. Notwithstanding any other provision of this article until July first, nineteen hundred sixty-one, the term "final average salary" as used in this subdivision four, shall mean either "final average salary" as defined by subdivision eleven of section five hundred one, or the maximum salary or compensation which the retired member currently would be receiving in the position from which he was last retired for disability, if he had not been so retired, whichever is greater, provided, however, that if the position from which he was so retired has been abolished, the retirement board, upon the basis of salary or compensation currently paid by the retired member's last employer to persons in similiar or comparable position, shall determine, for the purposes of this subdivision four, the maximum amount of salary or compensation which such retired member currently would be receiving in such position.

Sec. 511-a Special service retirement

Sec. 511-b Privilege of certain retired members to undertake public employment

Sec. 512 Withdrawal and death benefits

a. A member who withdraws from service or ceases to be a teacher for any cause other than death or retirement shall be paid on demand the accumulated contributions standing to the credit of his individual account in the annuity savings fund.

b. 1. Should a contributor die before retirement, his accumulated contributions shall be paid to his estate or to such person as he shall have nominated to receive such benefit. In the event such designated beneficiary does not survive him, or if he shall not have so designated a beneficiary, such benefit shall be payable to the deceased member's estate or as provided in section one hundred three-a of the decedent estate law. Such nomination must be by written designation duly executed and filed with the retirement board. 2. In addition to the return of accumulated contributions, a death benefit also shall be payable upon the death of a member who died before the effective date of his retirement, and was in service upon which his membership was based when he died or was on the payroll in such service and paid within a period of twelve months prior to his death and had not been otherwise gainfully employed since he ceased to be on such payroll; provided, he had credit for one or more years of service while actually a member. The amount of the death benefit shall be computed by multiplying one-twelfth of the compensation earnable by such member during his last twelve months of service while a member by the number of years, not to exceed twelve, of his total credit for service as a teacher in this state. The death benefit shall be paid to such person as he shall have nominated to receive such benefit. In the event such designated beneficiary does not survive him, or if he shall not have so designated a beneficiary, such benefit shall be payable to the deceased

member's estate or as provided in section one hundred three-a of the decedent estate law. Such nomination must be by written designation duly executed and filed with the retirement board. The provisions of this paragraph two of subdivision b of this section shall apply only to deaths occurring on and after July first, nineteen hundred fifty-nine and prior to July first, nineteen hundred sixty-four.

c. The member or, within ninety days after his death, the person nominated by him to receive any benefit payable on his account, may file with the retirement board a written designation, duly executed, providing that such benefit shall be paid in the form of an annuity to the person so nominated. Such annuity shall be determined as the actuarial equivalent of the benefit otherwise payable, on the basis of the interest rate and the mortality tables adopted by the retirement board for use in the calculations of such annuities. Such annuity shall be payable throughout the life of the person so nominated, with no payments at his death unless the member or, within ninety days after his death, the person nominated by him to receive his benefit, shall elect to have the actuarial equivalent of such annuity paid in the form of a reduced annuity payable for life with the provision that if the person so nominated should die before the annuity payments received by him are equal to such actuarial equivalent, the balance thereof shall be paid in a lump sum to such beneficiary's estate or to such person as such member or his nominee shall have designated. Such designation of a beneficiary to receive such benefit may be made or changed at any time by the person who made it. Such election or change shall be made by written designation duly executed and filed with the retirement board. Notwithstanding the foregoing provisions, the retirement board reserves the right to pay any benefit in the form of a lump sum payment if the annuity determined as the actuarial equivalent of the benefit otherwise payable is less than twenty-five dollars per month.

Sec. 513 Optional allowances

1. With the exception that no election of an optional benefit shall become effective in case a member dies within thirty days after the filing of an application for a retirement allowance, until the first payment on account of any benefit becomes normally due, any member, at the time of his retirement, may elect to receive his benefits in a retirement allowance payable throughout life or he may on retirement elect to receive the actuarial equivalent at that time of his retirement allowance in a lesser retirement allowance, payable throughout life with the provision that:

Option 1. If he die before he has received in payments the present value of his retirement allowance as it was at the time of his retirement, the balance shall be paid to his legal representatives or to such person as he shall nominate by written designation duly acknowledged and filed with the retirement board.

Option 2. Upon his death, his retirement allowance shall be continued through the life of and paid to such person as he shall nominate by written designation duly acknowledged and filed with the retirement board at the time of his retirement.

Option 3. Upon his death, one-half of his retirement allowance shall be continued throughout the life of and paid to such person as he shall nominate by written designation duly acknowledged and filed with the retirement board at the time of his retirement.

Option 4. Some other benefit or benefits shall be paid either to the member or to such person or persons as he shall nominate, provided such other benefit or benefits, together with the lesser retirement allowance, shall be certified by the actuary to be of equivalent actuarial value to his retirement allowance and shall be approved by the retirement board.

2. If any retired member who has not elected an optional benefit, or who has elected a benefit under Option 4 providing for the payment at death of the amount, if any, by which his accumulated contributions at the time of his retirement exceed the aggregate amount of his annuity payments, dies within thirty days after the date his retirement becomes effective, notwithstanding any other provisions of this law to the contrary, benefits shall be paid in accordance with subdivision (b) or (c) of section five hundred twelve, except that the amount of his accumulated contributions payable under paragraph (1) of said subdivision (b) shall be reduced by any annuity payments received by him prior to his death and the benefit payable under paragraph (2) of said subdivision (b) shall be reduced by any pension payments received by him prior to his death. The amounts payable shall be paid to the beneficiary or beneficiaries entitled thereto as provided under section five hundred twelve, except that if the member has elected Option 4, as provided above, the beneficiary nominated under such Option 4 shall be substituted for any beneficiary previously nominated and all amounts payable shall be paid to the beneficiary nominated under such Option 4.

3. The provisions of subdivision two of this section shall apply only to deaths occurring after the date on which said subdivision two becomes operative and prior to July first, nineteen sixty-five.

Sec. 514 Benefits to participants in old retirement fund
Sec. 515 Funds enumerated
Sec. 516 Annuity savings fund; contributions and payments
Sec. 517 Annuity reserve fund; pension accumulation fund
Sec. 518 Pension reserve fund
Sec. 519 Expense fund
Sec. 520 Duties of employer
Sec. 521 Collection of contributions
Sec. 522 Transfer of contributions between retirement systems
Sec. 523 State supervision
Sec. 524 Exemption from taxation and execution
Sec. 525 Protection against fraud
Sec. 526 Merger of local teachers' retirement and pension systems with the state system
Sec. 527 Determination of annuities of teachers retired prior to August 28, 1958
Sec. 528 Pensions-providing-for-increased-take-home-pay

1. Notwithstanding any other provision of law to the contrary, beginning with the payroll period the first day of which is nearest to April first,

nineteen hundred sixty, and ending with the payroll period immediately prior to that the first day of which is nearest to April first, nineteen hundred sixty-one, the contribution of each member of the retirement system who is a teacher within the provisions of subdivision four of section five hundred one of this article in the employ of the state of New York shall be reduced by five per centum of the compensation paid such member, provided, however, where a member's rate of contribution is less than five per centum his contribution shall be discontinued. A member whose rate of contribution shall be reduced pursuant to the provisions of this subdivision shall be deemed to have elected to have his rate so reduced unless he files an election pursuant to the provisions of subdivision two of this section.

2. Any member whose rate of contribution is reduced pursuant to the provisions of subdivision one of this section may by a written notice, duly acknowledged and filed with the retirement board within one year after such reduction or within one year after he last became a member, whichever is later, elect to make an additional contribution in addition to other contributions otherwise allowed in this article equal to the amount of such reduction. One year or more after the filing of such notice a member may withdraw such election by filing a written notice duly acknowledged and filed with the retirement board.

3. For a period of time as the provisions of this section shall be in effect, contributions for each member of the system whose rate of contribution is reduced by virtue of the provisions of subdivision one of this section shall be made to the pension accumulation fund by the state of New York in the same manner and at the same time as other contributions made by the state as employer of members of the retirement system at a rate fixed by the actuary which shall be computed to be sufficient to provide pensions-providing-for-increased-take-home-pay and other benefits which become payable on account of members in the employ of the state. The actuary engaged by the retirement board shall compute an additional contribution to be known as the "special deficiency contribution to provide a reserve-for-increased-take-home-pay." The amount of the reserve-for-increased-take-home-pay shall be the present value of five per centum of the member's compensation paid to him during the period for which his rate of contribution was reduced as provided in subdivision one, plus regular interest thereon to the date that pension and other benefits become payable.

4. Upon retirement a member whose rate of contribution shall be reduced pursuant to the provisions of subdivision one of this section will receive, in addition to the annuity and other pension benefits provided by this article, a pension which is the actuarial equivalent of the reserve-for-increased-take-home-pay to which he may be entitled, if any.

5. In addition to the return of accumulated contributions and the death benefit provided by the provisions of section five hundred twelve of this article, upon the death of a member who died before the effective date of his retirement and was in service upon which his membership was based when he died or was on the payroll in such service and paid within a period of twelve months prior to his death and had not been other-

wise gainfully employed since he ceased to be on such payroll, and provided further, he had credit for one or more years of service while actually a member, then the reserve-for-increased-take-home-pay attributable to such member shall be paid in the same manner and at the same time as the death benefit is paid by reason of such member's membership in the retirement system.

6. The reserve-for-increased-take-home-pay shall be a portion of the pension accumulation fund and upon the retirement of a new entrant an amount equal to the reserve-for-increased-take-home-pay for such member shall be transferred from the pension accumulation fund to the pension reserve fund.

7. If a person has been a member of the retirement system and contributions have been made by the state as his employer to provide a reserve-for-increased-take-home-pay and such person has ceased to be a member of the system and upon rejoining the retirement system claims credit for such period, the member shall not be required to pay for such years of service as a contribution shall have been made by the state for pensions-providing-for-increased-take-home-pay pursuant to the provisions of this section.

Statutory note. It can hardly be said that any retirement law is typical although certain features are common; *e.g.*, options for the payment of benefits, refund of contributions to withdrawing members, inclusion of disability provisions, administration by a board of trustees. Formulas for contributions and for benefits, however, differ greatly—except that practically all fall into the categories mentioned in the *Editorial Comment*. Because retirement laws are so difficult for laymen to understand, most retirement systems issue a "primer" or some sort of pamphlet, often in question and answer style, so that members can study their retirement plan in simplified language. It is suggested that each teacher obtain such a pamphlet from the retirement office of the system to which he belongs.

Case Material

Dodge v. Board of Education of Chicago, 302 U. S. 74 (1937). [Teachers challenged constitutionality of amendment reducing their pensions.]

The appellants challenge an act of Illinois which they assert impairs the obligation of contracts in contravention of Article 1, section 10, of the Constitution of the United States and deprives them of a vested right without due process contrary to the Fourteenth Amendment. The statute decreased the amount of annuity payments to retired teachers in the public schools of Chicago.

Since 1895 the State has had legislation creating a teachers' pension and retirement fund originally the fruit of teachers' contributions and gifts of legacies but later augmented by allotments from interest received

and from taxes. With this fund and the benefit payments thereunder we are not concerned. . . .

In 1926 an Act, known as the "Miller Law," became effective. This provided for compulsory retirement and for the payment of annuities to retired teachers. By Section 1 the Board of Education was directed to retire teachers from active service. . . . Section 2 provided:

"Each person so retired from active service who served in the public schools of such city for twenty or more years prior to such retirement shall be paid the sum of Fifteen hundred dollars ($1,500) annually and for life from the date of such retirement from the money derived from the general tax levy for educational purposes. . . ."

In 1927, a third section was added permitting teachers who had served for twenty-five years or more, and were sixty-five years of age or over, who had not reached the age of compulsory retirement to be retired upon request and to be paid from One thousand dollars to Fifteen hundred dollars per annum, depending upon the age at retirement. . . .

July 12, 1935, a further amendment of the Miller Law was adopted requiring the Board presently to retire teachers then in service who were sixty-five years of age or over, and in the future to retire teachers as they attained that age. Each person so retired was to be paid Five hundred dollars annually for life from date of retirement . . . . Section 3 of the Miller Law, permitting voluntary retirement between the ages of sixty-five and seventy, was repealed. As construed by the State Supreme Court, the new law reduced to $500 the annuities of teachers theretofore retired, or eligible for retirement under the Miller Law, as well as those to be retired subsequent to its enactment.

Some of the appellants filed a class bill, in which the others intervened as co-plaintiffs, alleging that their rights to annuities were vested rights of which they could not be deprived; that the Miller Law constituted an offer which each of them had accepted by remaining in service until compulsory retirement or by retiring; that the obligation of the contract had thus been perfected and its attempted impairment by the later enactment was ineffective; and praying that the Board be commanded to rescind action taken pursuant to the Act of 1935, and enjoined from complying with its provisions. The appellee Board of Education filed an answer in which it denied the existence of a contract and asserted that the payments to be made to appellants were pensions, subject to revocation or alteration at the will of the legislature. The appellee City of Chicago filed a motion to dismiss for want of equity. After a hearing at which testimony was taken on behalf of the appellants, the trial court dismissed the bill.

The Supreme Court of the State affirmed, holding that, notwithstanding the payments under the Miller Law are denominated annuities, they cannot be differentiated from similar payments directed by law to be made to other retired civil servants of the State and her municipalities, and are in fact pensions or gratuities involving no agreement of the parties and subject to modification or abolition at the pleasure of the legislature.

The parties agree that a State may enter into contracts with citizens, the obligations of which the legislature cannot impair by subsequent enactment. They agree that legislation which merely declares a state

policy, and directs a subordinate body to carry it into effect, is subject to revision or repeal in the discretion of the legislature. The point of controversy is as to the category into which the Miller Law falls. . . .

[The court quoted the language of the Miller Law, and then continued as follows:] . . . Appellants admit that this is not the normal language of a contract but rely on the circumstances that they, as teachers, especially those who voluntarily retired when otherwise they would not have been required to do so, rightly understood the State was pledging its faith that it would not recede from the offer held out to them by the statue as an inducement to become teachers and to retire, and that the use of the term "annuities" rather than "pensions" was intended as a further assurance of a vested contractual right.

The Supreme Court [of the state] answered this contention by referring to the fact that for years prior to the adoption of the Miller Law, and by a uniform course of decision, it had held that acts indistinguishable from the Miller Law, establishing similar benefit systems, did not create contracts or vested rights and that the State was free to alter, amend, and repeal such laws, even though the effect of its action was to deprive the pensioner or annuitant for the future, of benefits then enjoyed. The cases to which the court refers so decide.

The court further held that the legislature presumably had the doctrine of these cases in mind when it adopted the act now under review and that the appellants should have known that no distinction was intended between the rights conferred on them and those adjudicated under like laws with respect to other retired civil servants. We cannot say that this was error.

The appellants urge that the Miller Law, contrary to most of the acts that preceded it, omitted to use the word "pension" and instead used the word "annuity," a choice of terminology based on contract rather than on gift, and implying a consideration received as well as offered. The State Supreme Court (364 Ill. 547, 5 N.E. (2d) 84, 88) answered the contention by saying: "We are unable to see the distinction. The plan of payment is the same, the purposes are evidently the same, and the use of the term 'annuity' instead of 'pension'—which is but an annuity—does not seem to us to result in the distinction for which counsel for appellants contend."

We are of the same opinion particularly as an examination of the Illinois statutes indicates that in acts dealing with the subject, the legislature has apparently used the terms "pensions," "benefits," and "annuities" interchangeably as having the same connotation.

Case note. This case caused considerable disturbance when it was decided by the United States Supreme Court, but the decision merely pointed out the distinction between a pension, noncontributory type of plan, and a joint-contributory retirement system. The confusion arose because of misuse of terms in the Miller Law, and the fact that there was another law creating a joint-contributory retirement system for the teachers in Chicago.

That pensions are gratuities which may be reduced or abolished is an accepted principle. It does not follow that all annuities based upon joint contributions of employee and employer are contracts which the state may not modify. On this score there is difference of opinion among the courts, especially in the older cases. The modern view is that a joint-contributory retirement system creates for its members a vested right which cannot be impaired by the legislature or by the retirement board in its by-laws, at least after a member has retired.

The New York State Constitution was amended in 1938 to provide that all retirement benefits provided in part by public funds create a contractual relation between the members and the state and cannot be impaired by the legislature. This constitutional provision was interpreted to mean that the retirement board could not adopt new actuarial tables necessitated by increased longevity, as authorized in the retirement law, because the new tables would have resulted in lower benefits (to spread the reserve over a longer life) and thus impaired the contractual obligation.

State ex rel. Thomson, Attorney General v. Giessel, 265 Wis. 558, 61 N. W. (2d) 903 (Wisconsin, 1953) [Increase of benefits for those already retired.]

As a reading of the act will disclose, after reciting in its preamble the reasons for its enactment and providing a number of directions for its administration it authorizes the engagement of retired teachers of a class therein described for stand-by service as substitute teachers or for other educational services.

Respondent's principal contention is that the law by its own terms discloses a purpose on the part of the legislature to grant to certain retired teachers extra compensation for services already performed, in violation of Section 26, art. IV, Wisconsin Constitution, and that what we said and held in State ex rel. Thomson v. Giessel, 262 Wis. 51, 53 N. W. (2d) 726 is applicable and requires that we declare that Chapter 434 is invalid. We had for consideration in that case Chapter 551, Laws of 1951, by the enactment of which and in unambiguous terms the legislature sought to grant to retired teachers added benefits under the Teachers' Retirement Law without any requirement that they render or hold themselves available for additional future service. His attack must be construed as a suggestion that the 1953 legislature was motivated by a purpose to avoid by subterfuge the effect of the decision in the case to which reference has been made. It is elementary that if the statute appears on its face to be constitutional and valid, we may not inquire into the motives of the legislature, and that all doubts as to its constitutionality must be resolved in favor of its validity. . . .

That we might suspect that the real purpose of the legislature in enacting chapter 434 was to accomplish what it failed to accomplish by its enactment of Chapter 551, Laws of 1951 and which in the former case we declared to be invalid is immaterial. . . .

Our search must be for a means of sustaining the act, not for reasons which might require its condemnation.

The act must be construed as authorizing a contract by which the state rehires retired teachers. That the state may bind itself by contract for the performance of one of its functions cannot be questioned. One of its major functions is to provide and promote an efficient educational system. It appears from the provisions of the body of the act that the legislature in enacting the law in question considered that it would promote the efficiency of the schools of the state. That appears also from its own expression contained in the preamble of the act which, while it is not conclusive on the court, is persuasive. . . . It appears just as clearly that the legislature considered that, because of a shortage of active and prospective teachers, an emergency exists; that to engage and compensate retired teachers for "stand-by" service would in some degree promote the efficiency of the school system and make it possible to equip the schools with teachers now concededly unavailable. It should be noted that at least some of the teachers who have retired have done so under statutory compulsion and that absent the provisions of Chapter 434 the state is without authority to reengage them—their services are not available except as they may be reobtained by virtue of the provisions of the chapter.

The payments provided by the act are not intended to be compensation for past services. Its terms disclose an intent and purpose to make is possible to reengage teachers who have left the service and to induce them to hold themselves available for reemployment, thereby giving to the public the benefit of their experience and supplying a source to draw upon in this period when there exists an alarming shortage of qualified persons. We say that the act was intended as an inducement to the persons of the class designated therein to make themselves available for reemployment; that appears from the fact that not all the persons of the class described are entitled by mere enactment of the act to the payments therein provided—the compensation is to be paid only to those of the group who apply to the state superintendent for registration upon the roster of substitute teachers or to those who offer themselves for other educational services. . . .

We conclude that Chapter 434, Laws of 1953, is a valid enactment.

Case note. Wisconsin tried to increase allowances of retired teachers in 1951. The attorney general was sympathetic with the plight of retired teachers whose allowances were meager, but it was his responsibility to test the law as to its constitutionality because, if unconstitutional, payments of public funds for these increases would have been malfeasance on the part of the state officials authorizing the payments. The court held that it was illegal to give additional

compensation for services rendered in the past. In 1953 the legislature achieved the same end by constitutional means—it created a new contract with retired teachers. For every contract there must be "consideration." The consideration on the part of the teachers already retired was making themselves available as substitutes or for other service *in the future;* in exchange, the consideration on the part of the state was the payment of money, resulting in increased allowances for those retired teachers who placed their names on the roster as available.

Several other teachers' retirement laws have created new contracts for retired teachers so as to increase their allowances by providing that those who made a new contribution of several hundred dollars with or without interest would be entitled to the payment of an annuity in a stated amount.

As was said in the *Editorial Comment* many states have increased allowances of retired teachers without having their actions challenged in the courts. However, no matter how low a retirement benefit, it was fixed by the law at the time of retirement; at that time a contract is created. The state may not decrease—or increase—the amount. Since retirement formulas are set up to pay a specific sum of money it, legally, matters not how many loaves of bread that amount can buy. The *legal* way to increase benefits after retirement is to create a new contract between retirants and the state; any other way is open to challenge.

Sources of Further Information

48 Am. Jur. "Social Security, Unemployment Insurance, and Retirement Funds" secs. 9-38.

78 C.J.S. "Schools and School Districts" secs. 231-236.

A.L.R. "Schools" Topic No. 48; "Social Security" Topic Nos. 1-16.

American Digest System "Schools and School Districts" Key No. 148; "Social Security" Key Nos. 121-151.

Work sheet

Study the retirement system for the district in which you are employed before answering the following questions:

1. Is the system joint-contributory?

2. Does the state or city contribute sufficient funds to accumulate reserves adequate to match the annuities granted to the survivors of each year's contributors who qualify for retirement?

3. Does the law require that a reserve be built up to meet future costs?

4. Is the plan a money-purchase or fixed-benefit plan? If a money-purchase plan, is it a money-doubled formula?

5. Are actuarial valuations of the system required periodically?

6. Is the contribution from public funds fixed by the actuary?

7. Is the retirement allowance based upon mortality tables? If not, is the contribution fixed by the actuary?

8. Were teachers in service at the time the system was established given due credit for service rendered prior to the establishment of the system?

9. When a teacher withdraws from the profession or dies in service, are all his own contributions returned, and with interest?

10. Does the system give a teacher about to retire a choice of several ways of receiving his allowance?

11. Is retirement possible for a teacher who is disabled prior to meeting the requirements (age and/or years of service) for super-annuation or service retirement?

12. Do the members have a vested interest in the retirement system?

Obtain a pamphlet on social security benefits and attempt to compute the benefit to which you may be entitled at retirement age, on the assumption that your current salary is continued until then. As of 1960, the OASDI benefits can be found from a table in the law; the computation, therefore, revolves around "average monthly wage" which is often a complicated computation.

Chapter 11.

MISCELLANEOUS RIGHTS OF AND RESTRICTIONS ON TEACHERS

In this chapter we shall discuss and illustrate health requirements, residence requirements, right to engage in political activities, and right to appeal from school-board decisions.

A. HEALTH REQUIREMENTS

Editorial Comment

Many states require a general health certificate for certification; some do not demand more than a chest X-ray. Aside from certification requirements, a number of states require either a general health certificate, a chest X-ray, or both, prerequisite to employment. The health certificate sometimes refers only to tuberculosis or other communicable diseases, but in other instances a complete physical and mental examination is required. These statutory provisions have been in force in some states for many years.

More recently, state legislatures and local school boards have required periodic examinations, sometimes annually and sometimes when deemed necessary by the local school board. Although chest X-ray is the most commonly used method for detection of tuberculosis and is the most common requirement, intradermal tuberculosis tests may be substituted in several states.

It should be pointed out that even when the state law is silent the general powers of local school boards are sufficiently broad to enforce regulations regarding the health of its employees or prospective employees, especially with regard to communicable diseases.

Statutory Material

General Statutes of North Carolina, sec. 115-143.

Any person serving as county superintendent, city superintendent, supervisor, district principal, building principal, teacher, or any other

179

employee in the public schools of the State, shall file in the office of the county or city superintendent each year, before assuming his or her duties, a certificate from the county physician, local health director, or other reputable physician, certifying that the said person does not have tuberculosis in the communicable form, or other communicable disease, or any disease, physical or mental, which would impair the ability of the said person to perform effectively his or her duties.

The examining physician shall make the aforesaid certificate on an examination form supplied by the State Superintendent of Public Instruction. The certificate shall be issued only after a physical examination has been made at the time of the certification, and such examination shall be in accordance with rules and regulations adopted by the State Superintendent of Public Instruction, with approval of the State Health Director, and such rules and regulations may include the requirement of an X-ray chest examination.

It shall be the duty of the county or city superintendent of the school in which the person is employed to enforce the provisions of this section.

Any person violating any of the provisions of this section shall be guilty of a misdemeanor and subject to a fine or imprisonment in the discretion of the court.

Statutory note. It cannot be said that this type of law is common among the states, although there are a number of similar enactments. There is no question as to its validity; a health requirement is within the police power of the state.

Case Material

Groad v. Jansen et al., 13 Misc. (2d) 741, 173 N. Y. S. (2d) 946 (New York, 1958). [Principal's request that teacher be given health examination insufficient without particulars.]

The letter dated December 17, 1957, addressed to the Superintendent of Schools, requesting that petitioner "be examined in accordance with the By-Laws of the Board of Education" is not a report within the meaning of section 2568 of the Education Law which provides as follows:

"The superintendent of schools of a city having a population of one million or more shall be empowered to require any person employed by the board of education of such city to submit to a medical examination by a physician or school medical inspector of the board, in order to determine the mental or physical capacity of such person to perform his duties, whenever it has been recommended in a report in writing that such examination should be made. Such report to the superintendent may be made only by a person under whose supervision or direction the person recommended for such medical examination is employed. The person required to submit to such medical examination shall be entitled to be accompanied by a physician or other person of his own choice. . . ." A "report" envisages more than a mere request and should contain some facts and circumstances upon which the recommendation for the medical

examination is predicated. The legislative intent to protect employees of the Board of Education from needless harassment, while overcoming the effect of the holding in Board of Education of City of New York v. Graves, 175 Misc. 205, 24 N.Y.S.2d 644, affirmed 261 App. Div. 1115, 27 N.Y.S.2d 404, clearly indicates that more than a request is required. If it were intended that a simple request were to suffice, the statute could have readily so provided. Under the circumstances, therefore, petitioner was not guilty of insubordination and the action of the Superintendent and the Associate Superintendent of Schools in suspending her, was arbitrary.

Case note. Should a teacher refuse to submit to a physical examination required by the state or the school board, his refusal would be governed by the same principles as laid down in cases dealing with refusal of parents to have their children vaccinated [see *Anderson et al. v. State,* page 271.] In addition, there is the principle that an employer has the right to make reasonable demands of its employees, especially when those demands are intended for the general welfare of other employees and the pupils in the school. In such cases the police power overrides even religious objections.

Frequently, school principals hear rumors of or have evidence of ill health of a teacher under their supervision. It is then the principal's responsibility to notify the proper authorities. In this case the court points out that in making such a report the principal should include substantiating evidence and not merely register a request that the teacher in question be given a physical examination. Because the teacher in this case refused to submit to an examination on the basis of the principal's inadequate "report," she was suspended for insubordination. The court set aside the suspension because it held that there was no insubordination in refusing to comply with a mere request. The case is included to show principals that notices of ill health of their teachers should be more specific than the notice this principal sent. However, it is not certain that courts of other states would agree. It is possible that failure to comply with even a request might be considered insubordination.

B. RESIDENCE REQUIREMENTS

Editorial Comment

A few years ago it was common for local school boards to require its teachers to live within the boundaries of the district. The theory was that money earned from the taxpayers in a locality should be spent in that locality. Probably the growth of suburbia has ameliorated

this requirement. Few school boards now have residence requirements. However, it has been upheld as reasonable in several recent cases; but, on a different theory—that the teachers should be living close enough to be readily available out of school hours.

So far as is known, no state law requires teachers to live in the districts where they are employed; in fact, several states provide that no discrimination can be made on the basis of race, religion, national background, or *residence*.

Statutory Material

Burns Indiana Statutes Annotated, sec. 28-4337.

It shall be unlawful for the governing agencies of school corporations of this state to adopt requirements for the residence of teachers or other school employees in the employment, assignment, and/or reassignment for duties within any prescribed area.

Failure to observe the provisions of this act [sec. 28-4337] shall cause the said school corporation to become ineligible for state funds under all acts relating to that subject. . . .

Statutory note. The chief state school officer is charged with responsibility of withholding state-aid funds otherwise due a district which imposes residence requirements on teachers. How could the punitive procedure be instituted? What proof would substantiate violation of the law?

Case Material

Appeal of Sinton, 154 Pa. Super. 233, 35 A. (2d) 542 (Pennsylvania, 1944). [Teachers required to live in district where employed.]

. . . After a brief discussion of those facts the court concluded that appellant's "negligence in failing to comply with the board's regulation was persistent and wilful, and in violation of the school laws of the Commonwealth."

The order is amply sustained by the evidence. The resolution of the board, especially after the amendment which afforded the teacher time until June 1, 1941, to establish a residence within the township, was a reasonable regulation. Jones v. Kulpmont Borough School District, 333 Pa. 581, 3 A.2d 914. Nothing on its face indicates arbitrary or capricious action. If it is unreasonable, extraneous circumstances make it so, and the burden of proving such factors rests upon the party who asserts their existence. That is, appellant carried the burden of proof; she was obliged to show that the resolution was unreasonable or that the manner of its enforcement was unreasonable and arbitrary. She might have discharged that obligation by showing that suitable housing accommodations were not

available in the township. Instead, she testified that she had inquired of several fellow teachers about vacant houses. . . .

After these feeble attempts to find a house, she addressed a letter to the board, dated May 23, 1941, expressing her willingness to comply with the resolution, that she had not been able to find an available house and requested permission to remain at her home in Llewellyn "until such accommodations can be furnished me." The day following the close of the school term of 1941, she joined her husband at Langley Field, Virginia, and after that date she exerted no effort to find a home in Cass Township. It was her duty to comply with the resolution; the duty of finding a home was upon her; the board was not required to find a house for her. Nevertheless, the supervising principal, on behalf of the board, wrote to her on July 7, 1941, that a house was available at Pine Knot, "consisting of eight rooms and bath, with ideal surroundings" and adding that the owner "will take our recommendation for a tenant for this home." He requested her to inspect the home and to "answer as to your intentions of moving into this home on or before Saturday, July 12, 1941." On July 10, 1941, writing from Langley Field, she said, in part, "I wish to state that it would be a hardship for me to return to Pennsylvania at this time to inspect a house. If this house, or any other suitable house, is vacant when I return to Pennsylvania the day preceding the opening of school I shall be glad to look it over and make my decision regarding it at that time." A fair construction of the letter is that, although she was in default since June 1, 1941, in failing to establish residence in the township, she intended to do nothing about the house which was open to her inspection, and would make no effort to find a house until she returned to her school work on the first day of the new school term. With no expression of thanks for the board's voluntary effort to assist her in finding a home, she cooly informed it that she would give the matter attention when she returned to Pennsylvania. Thus, to her default which began on June 1, 1941, when she failed to establish a residence in conformity to the resolution, she added an expression which at the least indicated complete indifference to her duty of complying with the resolution. . . .

At the hearing before the school board upon the charges it had preferred against her, she testified that she was unwell when the letter of the school board was received and that, because of that condition and because she and her husband were contemplating moving to other quarters, it would have been a hardship to travel to Pennsylvania. Possibly, a frank statement of these conditions to the board in her reply of July 10th might have produced a further extension of time. Be that as it may, the fact is that, as pointed out by the court below, by her letter she expressely reserved to herself the right to make her decision on the day preceding the opening of the next school term. In effect, she was telling the board that she would not inspect the house; would not attempt to comply with its resolution until she returned to Pennsylvania; and was herself choosing the time when she would comply with the board's resolution. This is the very core of the case. There was not only one act of negligence, as her counsel argues; she was negligent on every day after June 1, 1941; it was continuing and, therefore, persistent negligence; and it became wilful when

she announced that she would make a decision at her own pleasure, and not before she returned to Pennsylvania.

Case note. The court was influenced to hold the board's residence requirement reasonable by the fact that the board gave each teacher five months in which to comply. Though the teacher in this case contended that no suitable house was available, her contention was overridden by her neglect to look at the one the board found for her.

C. RIGHT TO ENGAGE IN POLITICAL ACTIVITIES

Editorial Comment

Restrictions on teachers' membership in and activities with subversive groups and the Communist Party have been discussed in Chapter 3 on Loyalty. The following discussion concerns the other side of the coin—the right of teachers whose loyalty is unquestioned to engage in normal political activities.

In 1939 Congress enacted the Hatch Act which applied to federal employees; in 1940 it was extended to state and local employees who are employed "in connection with any activity which is financed in whole or in part by loans or grants made by the United States or by any such department, independent agency, or other agency of the United States." Thus, vocational education teachers and certain others were covered. However, in 1942 the Hatch Act was amended to delete its application, generally, to teachers. Today, the Hatch Act applies to teachers only with regard to several specified acts with which few teachers, if any, are likely to be concerned.

Shortly after the original enactment of the federal Hatch Act, many state legislatures passed what were called "Little Hatch Acts" applicable to some or all of their state and local employees. Few of these state laws restrict teachers from normal political activity. In fact, where such laws do apply to teachers, the restriction may be considered more protective than objectionable. For example, several states have prohibited teachers from soliciting funds or services for political purposes and prohibit others from soliciting teachers on school premises or during school hours. On the other hand, several states have specifically denied the right of employers to restrict normal political activities of teachers so long as these activities are carried on outside of school premises and outside of school hours.

Undoubtedly, unwritten laws (mores and social pressures) sometimes restrict teachers in this area. These restrictions are not based on law, and a teacher who has the courage to disregard them might well obtain

their judicial disapproval. Perhaps there are a few restrictive local school board regulations; if brought before a court such regulations would need to meet the measure of reasonableness.

Statutory Material

Massachusetts General Laws Annotated. Chapter 71, sec. 44.

No committee [school board] shall by rule, regulation, or otherwise, restrict any teacher in, or dismiss him for, exercising his right of suffrage, signing nomination papers, petitioning the general court [state legislature] or appearing before its committees, to the extent that such rights, except voting, are not exercised on the school premises during school hours, or when their exercise would actually interfere with the performance of school duties.

Statutory note. Although there are few such laws, it is expected that a court would hold that a teacher has similar rights merely because he is a citizen, and that the right to engage in activities which the Massachusetts legislature spelled out is a constitutional guarantee of all citizens. Possibly, the purpose of this enactment was to prohibit the exercise of these activities, except voting, on school premises during school hours or when they would interfere with the performance of school duties. However, even in the absence of such legislation, it would seem that a board could dismiss a teacher for neglect of duty in the event that he used school time or school property for political activities.

Case Material

Adams v. State ex rel. Sutton, 69 So. (2d) 309 (Florida, 1954). [Political activity of teachers.]

This appeal was taken from a final judgment and peremptory writ of mandamus commanding the appellants to nominate the relator for the position of principal of one of the Duval County schools.

A superintendent who had recently been defeated in a spirited, if not acrimonious campaign, recommended the relator for the principalship and was asked by the appellants to recommend someone else. The superintendent failed or refused to comply with the request and at a subsequent meeting the appellants rejected the recommendation on the grounds that the relator was not qualified and had too violently opposed the candidate who was successful in unseating the superintendent who selected her for the place. It is significant that the request for a new recommendation was made three months before the trustees actually rejected the recommendation of the relator. As we shall now see there was no authority for the request until the superintendent's original recommendation had been formally disapproved. . . .

We will dispose of the first objection by simply stating that the record abundantly supports the view of the circuit judge that lack of qualification of the relator was not substantiated, therefore no "good cause" had been shown for rejection of the recommendation on that ground.

The second ground, that is the political activity of the relator, seems to be the one more deserving of consideration and discussion by this court.

According to the return to the alternative writ the relator was, during the election of a superintendent in 1952, active in the dissemination of literature which reflected on the character of the victorious candidate who is now serving as Superintendent of Public Instruction. The appellants took the position that the attacks sponsored by a committee of which relator was a member were so intemperate that in appellants' opinion, the functioning of the schools would be impaired by placing her in the position of principal in the system supervised by the present superintendent and that in this situation they were justified in disapproving the recommendation.

The problem is a delicate one because the equilibrium of the school system should not be disturbed by an inordinate participation in political campaigns, particularly those for the election of school officials, and, on the other hand, the members of the profession should not be throttled in voicing their preference in such contests. We are also concerned with the precedent that might be set were it to appear, even, that teachers on the losing side were penalized for their efforts while those on the winning side were rewarded. Surely there could be no blending of the school and spoils systems.

There is no hint in this record that the appellants were actuated by any motive but to protect and improve the functioning of the school in their district but the danger of a ruling too strenuously curtailing the participation of teachers in school elections is lurking in this controversy, nonetheless.

The only law cited to us carrying a restriction of teachers' participation in politics is the Teachers Tenure Act, Chapter 21197, Laws of Florida, Special Acts of 1941, which provides in Section 11: "Teachers are expressly prohibited from engaging in any political activity *during the regular school hours of any school day*" (Italics supplied.) The circuit judge recited that there was conflicting evidence about the relator's taking part in the distribution of "violent and scurrilous literature" in the campaign but he declared "There was no evidence by either side that the political activities of [relator] occurred during school hours."

We agree with the circuit judge in his disposition of this controversy. Inasmuch as none of relator's energies in behalf of her candidate were expended during school hours, there was no violation by her of any provision of law peculiar to the political activities of school teachers. So it is clear to us as it was to the circuit judge that school teachers may engage in political campaigns precisely as other persons may so long as they confine their activities to periods that do not fall in "school hours of any school day"; that there is no ground for disciplining them as school teachers so long as they observe the inhibition of the act we have quoted. For transgressions of election laws generally they would, of course, fall in the same category as persons not members of their profession.

We subscribe to what the circut judge held with reference to the charge that the position of the newly elected superintendent would be "undermined, weakened and made less effective if [relator] should be appointed as principal of a district school." This apprehension is necessarily speculative as it is based on the premise that the ill feeling generated in the campaign might result in the relator's being disloyal to the person whom she sought to defeat. If the relator proves insubordinate, inefficient or incompetent she may be dismissed regardless of the reason for her misdeeds or her unfitness, but there is no logical reason now to determine that because of animosity growing out of the election the relator will inevitably be so recalcitrant that she should be excluded from a position of authority.

As we have already written, we fear an endorsement of such a principle would set a precedent that would itself be dangerous to the efficiency of the school system. We must conclude that the circuit judge was correct when he held that the relator was not "rejected for good cause."

Affirmed.

Case note. Although this case illustrates the point that the school trustees had no power to request a new recommendation before the county superintendent's original recommendation had been formally disapproved, it is included at this point to illustrate teachers' (and principals') rights to engage in political activity even in an election for a school officer. The court said that a school system should not be disturbed by "inordinate" participation of school employees in political campaigns of school officials (and what that means is anybody's guess) but held that school employees should not be "throttled" in voicing preferences in school elections. When there was no violation of law, either the restriction of teachers' political activities to periods outside the school hours or the general election laws, teachers were said to have the same rights as other members of society to participate in political campaigns.

D. RIGHT TO APPEAL FROM SCHOOL BOARD DECISIONS

Editorial Comment

In the study of tenure laws, mention was made of the teacher's right to appeal from dismissal decisions of the school board. In most states, teachers have the right to appeal from other decisions made by their employers, although in some states this right operates in designated circumstances only. For example, in Oklahoma a teacher may appeal when a certificate has been revoked on charges of inculcating disloyalty to the flag and to the United States Government.

Appeal is usually to a higher school authority: the county superintendent, the county board of education, the state superintendent, or

the state board of education. In some states, all these may be called upon for review of decisions of those lower in authority. Then, in some states the school law provides for original appeal to the local courts. In a few states, there is no statutory provision for appeal, and only the common-law remedies would be available.

Some laws providing for appeal procedure to higher school authorities also provide for judicial review of the appeal. Even when there is no such provision, resort may usually be had to the courts. A general rule might be stated that courts will not review discretionary decisions of school authorities; but when the controversy raises questions of the constitutionality of a statute or of a school board decision, or when the jurisdiction or right of the school officer or school board to make the decision or to give an order is involved, the courts usually will pass upon the question. The courts recognize the desirability of placing the responsibility for decisions in professional controversies in the hands of educationally trained rather than legally trained persons. Furthermore, appeal to school authorities is a much less expensive matter than a court proceeding.

Statutory Material

Code of Georgia Annotated, secs. 32-414 and 32-910.

Sec. 414. The state board of education shall have appellate jurisdiction in all school matters which may be appealed from any county or city board of education, and its decisions in all such matters shall be final and conclusive. Appeals to the Board must be made in writing through the county superintendent of schools, or the secretary of the Official Board of Independent Systems, and must distinctly set forth the question of law, as well as the facts in the case. The Board shall provide by regulation for notice to the opposite party and for hearing on the appeal.

Sec. 910. The county board of education shall constitute a tribunal for hearing and determining any matter of local controversy in reference to the construction or administration of the school law, with power to summon witnesses and take testimony if necessary; and when they have made a decision, said decision shall be binding upon the parties. Either of the parties shall have the right of appeal to the State Board of Education, and said appeal shall be made through the county superintendent of schools in writing and shall distinctly set forth the question in dispute, the decision of the county board and testimony as agreed upon by the parties to the controversy, or if they fail to agree, upon the testimony as reported by the county superintendent of schools. . . .

New York Education Law, secs. 310-312.

Sec. 310. Any person conceiving himself aggrieved may appeal or petition to the commissioner of education who is hereby authorized and

required to examine and decide the same; and the commissioner of education may also institute such proceedings as are authorized under this article and his decision in such appeals, petitions or proceedings shall be final and conclusive, and not subject to question or review in any place or court whatever. Such appeal or petition may be made in consequence of any action: . . . 7. By any other official act or decision of any officer, school authorities, or meetings concerning any other matter under this chapter, or any other act pertaining to common schools.

Sec. 311. The commissioner, in reference to such appeals, petitions or proceedings, shall have power: 1. To regulate the practice therein. 2. To determine whether an appeal shall stay proceedings, and prescribe conditions upon which it shall or shall not so operate. 3. To decline to entertain or to dismiss an appeal, when it shall appear that the appellant has no interest in the matter appealed from, and that the matter is not a matter of public concern, and that the person injuriously affected by the act or decision appealed from is incompetent to appeal. 4. To make all orders, by directing the levying of taxes or otherwise, which may, in his judgment, be proper or necessary to give effect to his decision.

Sec. 312. The commissioner shall file, arrange in the order of time, and keep in his office, so that they may be at all times accessible, all the proceedings on every appeal or petition to him under this article, including his decision and orders founded thereon; and copies of all such papers and proceedings, authenticated by him under his seal of office, shall be evidence equally with the originals.

Statutory note. Very frequently included in the statutory sections dealing with the powers and duties of the state board of education, the state superintendent, the county board of education, and the county superintendent, are brief provisions of a few words only, stating that appeals may be made to these school officers. Rarely are the provisions for appeal detailed. The Georgia quotation is as extensive as almost any of these provisions.

New York State is the only one where aggrieved teachers must choose between appealing to the chief state school officer for review of a board's decision and going to court. If a teacher elects to use the state department of education as his forum, he is barred from further appeal to the courts unless it can be shown that the commissioner's decision was arbitrary and capricious. Such a showing is practically impossible, especially since courts give great weight to the presumption of reasonableness in administrative rulings. It has been held, even, that when a group of teachers are affected by a particular decision of their employing board, those who appeal to the commissioner of education preclude the others from going to the courts because the issue is then *res adjudicata. Gable et al. v. Raftery et al.*, 65 N. Y. S. (2d) 513 (New York, 1945).

Case Material

Baron v. O'Sullivan et al., 258 F. (2d) 336 (C.C.A., 3d, 1958). [Administrative remedies for aggrieved teachers.]

Appellant Rose Baron is a teacher holding a certificate of eligibility to teach in the elementary schools of the State of New Jersey. A further written examination and oral interview is required to teach in the schools of Jersey City. Appellant filed a complaint against the members of the Board of Examiners of Jersey City, alleging a conspiracy under color of state law to deprive her of the privilege of receiving a certificate as a permanent teacher in Jersey City. The action is based upon the Civil Rights Act, 42 U.S.C.A. sec. 1983, with jurisdiction conferred by Section 1343 of Title 28 of the United States Code. After answer was filed, the district court granted defendants' motion for judgment on the pleadings and dismissed the action on the ground that the complaint did not spell out a denial of "any right, privilege or immunity secured by the Constitution and laws of the United States, but of a right or privilege created by or under a law or laws of the State of New Jersey." This appeal followed.

The complaint alleges that plaintiff availed herself of two administrative reviews, both before the Board of Examiners of Jersey City. However, the fourth separate defense in the answer alleges that plaintiff has not exhausted the state administrative remedies available to her.

Chapter 3 of Title 18 of the Revised Statutes of New Jersey, Section 14, N. J. S.A. 18:3-14, grants to the Commissioner of Education the power to decide controversies arising under school laws. Specifically it reads:

"The commissioner shall decide without cost to the parties all controversies and disputes arising under the school laws, or under the rules and regulations of the state board or of the commissioner. . . .

"The decision shall be binding until a decision thereon is given by the state board on appeal."

Section 15 of the same chapter provides for review of the commissioner's decision by the state board. These two steps in the statutory scheme of administrative review were not taken by appellant here, although clearly they were open to her. In re Masiello, 1958, 25 N.J. 590, 138 A.2d 393.

May a litigant properly seek the remedy of a federal court under the Civil Rights Act before exhausting the available administrative remedies of the state? We think not.

There is no longer any doubt that where a person's federally-protected civil or constitutional rights are abridged, "resort to a federal court may be had without first exhausting the *judicial* remedies of state courts." . . . If, however, the state court in fact is applying an administrative rather than a judicial remedy, resort must first be had to the state court before suit can be brought in the federal court. Prentis v. Atlantic Coast Line Co., 1908, 211 U.S. 210, 29 S.Ct. 67, 53 L.Ed. 150.

Certainly in the grant or denial of a teaching certificate by a state board, no judicial process is involved. Such boards, created to review subordinate decisions in their own ranks, are exercising a strictly legislative function with which this court cannot interfere.

Although the usual reason given for the requirement of the exhaustion of administrative remedies is the hesitation of the courts to interfere with state legislative processes, there is a more compelling one, as is apparent here. Appellant alleges a denial of a federally-protected privilege. The decision of the Board of Examiners of Jersey City, reviewable as it is both by the commissioner and the state board, is in a true sense interlocutory. It is merely a tentative determination subject to revision at the discretion of other agencies which are an integral part of the same legislative scheme. We cannot know, therefore, whether the privilege asserted has been denied until the state board has finally made its decision. The present action was premature.

The judgment of the district court will be affirmed.

Case note. This case is complicated by the fact that the teacher brought it in a federal court alleging denial of a right under the federal Civil Rights Act. That point may be disregarded in studying the case. The holding is that *all* administrative remedies must be exhausted before a court will hear the grievance of a teacher. This is typical in all states except New York. Most state boards of education or the chief state school officer have appellate jurisidiction to decide controversies between teachers and their employers. This court held that the decision of the local board was merely interlocutory until reviewed by the state school officers.

Sources of Further Information

These miscellaneous rights and duties of teachers are not usually separately identified in the law books. Some information will be found "buried" in the following citations:

47 Am. Jur. "Schools" sec. 109 (health); sec. 139 (political activities); sec. 141 (right of appeal).

78 C.J.S. "Schools and School Districts" secs. 208-217 (right of appeal).

A.L.R. "Schools" Topic No. 43 (political activities).

American Digest System "Schools and School Districts" Key No. 59 (health); Key Nos. 47, 48(7), 61 (right of appeal).

Work Sheet

1. Were you required to pass a physical examination before certification? Before employment?

2. Are periodic physical examinations required of teachers in your district? If so, is this examination complete or merely a chest X-ray?

3. Does your school board require its employees to live within the district?

4. Have you or your acquaintances in the school system felt any restrictions on the exercise of normal political activities?

5. Does the school law of your state provide for appeal through the county and state school officers?

6. If so, is there any limitation on the type of issue which these school officers may review?

7. If these administrative remedies are exhausted first, may an aggrieved teacher appeal to the courts?

8. If you have a choice, by law, would you prefer to appeal to the court directly from the school board's decision rather than to go through administrative channels? Why?

Part II

PROBLEMS OF PUPIL PERSONNEL

Chapter 12.

ADMISSION AND ATTENDANCE

Editorial Comment

Constitutional mandates requiring state legislatures to establish and maintain free public schools do not mean necessarily that all persons who wish may attend free of charge. The legislature may set standards to be met as a qualification for free attendance. Some constitutions themselves contain these standards, and of course, statutory qualifications can add to but not contradict constitutional provisions. However, the constitution in most states sets only general requirements, and the specific qualifications for admission to the public schools are matters of state or local legislation.

By constitution or state law, free attendance at the public schools is restricted to children of certain ages. Most commonly, children above age six and below age twenty-one are entitled to free school attendance under these provisions; and as a general principle, tuition may be charged or pupils be excluded outside these age limits.

In recent years, many states have authorized early childhood education as part of the public-school system, and first kindergarten, then nursery schools, have become integrated into the typical public-school system, especially in the larger districts. At the other end of the usual age limit, exceptions were made by legislation providing for veterans' education. Even states which have constitutional free-school age limits may by legislation provide for free attendance outside the constitutional free-school age limits, since the constitutional provisions do not imply a legislative prohibition to extending those limits.

Residence is another legal requirement for free public-school attendance. Residence for school purposes is broader than domicile required for other purposes, such as voting. Any more or less permanent dwelling establishes the right to attend the public schools of the district. Even temporary residence suffices if the reason for the temporary

residence is not primarily so that the children may attend a particular school.

Since constitutional and statutory provisions require that the schools shall be free, for those children qualified for admission, a school district cannot charge a matriculation fee of residents, but incidental fees, such as for laboratory or athletic equipment, may be charged without violating the requirement of free schooling.

Attendance is not free to nonresidents; generally speaking, tuition is paid in order that children may attend a school outside their resident district. When the school district arranges for its children to attend a school across a district line, tuition is paid for them out of the public funds of the resident district. When a parent arranges for his own children to attend a school outside his district instead of the school which by law is available to them free, the parent pays the tuition.

Even with the payment of tuition, however, there may not be admission to a particular school. The receiving school has the power to refuse admission; frequently legislation prescribes also some other authority whose approval must be obtained, e.g., the county superintendent.

Another frequent requirement for admission to the public schools is vaccination or other health certificate. If a parent refuses to permit his child to be vaccinated, the school board may exclude the child. He must then attend a private school, if he can be admitted to a private school without the certificate.

Parents have the legal right to send their children to a nonpublic school if they prefer. The state cannot compel all children of school age to attend the public schools, but it can compel all children of school age to attend some school, or be educated by private tutors. Compulsory school attendance has been held to be within the police power of the state. More than half the states require children between ages seven and sixteen to attend school; in the other states, other age limits apply, but all states have had a compulsory attendance law of some sort. The existence of compulsory attendance legislation today is somewhat uncertain in one or two states which have taken steps to avoid desegregation.

Penalties for violation of the compulsory attendance law are imposed upon the parents of children who do not attend as required. When attendance officers seek the aid of a court in the enforcement of a compulsory attendance law, they may seek a judgment which takes the form of a fine or imprisonment of the parents, or they may at-

tempt to have the child committed to a children's home on the theory that he is "neglected."

Many exceptions are allowed by law in a few states, and in a few other states there seem to be no statutory exceptions to compulsory attendance during the ages specified in the law. In the majority of states, children who attain a specified level of instruction are usually permitted to leave school regardless of age. In some states those who live a great distance from school are excused from attendance unless transportation facilities are provided. Special attendance provisions have usually been enacted for the physically and mentally handicapped. Child labor laws affect but do not always coincide with compulsory school attendance laws.

Formerly there were 17 states where constitutional or statutory provisions prohibited the public-school mingling of white and Negro pupils. Separate schools were maintained in the District of Columbia also, by act of Congress. Racial segregation of pupils in public schools had been upheld against the contention that it violates the Fourteenth Amendment to the Federal Constitution, but the United States Supreme Court also said that the education offered in schools for Negroes must be equivalent to that offered in schools for white pupils.

In 1954 the Supreme Court decided the "Segregation Cases" which were consolidated from four states. Since the educational opportunity for Negro pupils was equal or nearly equal to those afforded white pupils, the Court was faced squarely with the question of whether separate but equal educational opportunity violates the Fourteenth Amendment. It held that it did. Because of the necessity for administrative change to desegregate the schools, the Court asked the attorneys in these cases and attorneys general from other states which had operated segregated schools and the attorney general of the United States to submit briefs on the best way to implement the 1954 decision. These briefs resulted in the second segregation decision, in 1955. It held, in effect, that schools should be desegrated with "deliberate speed"—that is, as soon as practically possible.

Since then, there have been many cases in the lower federal courts, some of which were appealed, where state legislation attempting to circumvent the Court's decision in pupil placement laws, by tuition grants, and by similar methods, were challenged as being in defiance of the Court's direction for desegregation with "deliberate speed." Most of these subterfuges were struck down by the courts. Such cases have been too numerous to mention and do not lend themselves to illustration because each is based upon a particular set of facts.

Statutory Material

Oklahoma Statutes Annotated, Title 70, secs. 10-10 and 10-11.

Sec. 10. It shall be unlawful for a parent, guardian, custodian or other person having control of a child who is over the age of seven (7) years and under the age of eighteen (18) years, and who has not finished four (4) years of high school work, to neglect or refuse to cause or compel such child to attend and comply with the rules of some public, private or other school, unless other means of education are provided for the full term the schools of the district are in session; and it shall be unlawful for any child who is over the age of sixteen (16) years and under the age of eighteen (18) years, and who has not finished four (4) years of high school work, to neglect or refuse to attend and comply with the rules of some public, private or other school or receive an education by other means for the full term the schools of the district are in session. Provided, that this Section shall not apply (1) if any such child is prevented from attending school by reason of mental or physical disability, to be determined by the board of education of the district upon a certificate of the school physician or public health physician, or if no such physician is available, a duly licensed and practicing physician, or (2) if any such child is excused from attendance at school, due to an emergency, by the principal teacher of the school in which such child is enrolled, at the request of the parent, guardian, custodian or other person having control of such child. It shall be the duty of the supervisor of school census and attendance to enforce the provisions of this Section. Any parent, guardian, custodian, child or other person violating any of the provisions of this Section shall be guilty of a misdemeanor, and upon conviction thereof shall be punished by a fine of not more than Fifty Dollars ($50.00), or by imprisonment in the county jail for not more than ten (10) days, or by both such fine and imprisonment.

Sec. 11. It shall be the duty of the principal or head teacher of each public, private or other school in the State of Oklahoma to keep a full and complete record of the attendance of all children at such school and to notify the supervisor of school census and attendance of the district in which such school is located of the absence of such children from the school together with the causes thereof, if known; and it shall be the duty of any parent, guardian or other person having charge of any child of compulsory attendance age to notify the child's teacher concerning the cause of any absences of such child. Such supervisor of school census and attendance and teacher shall be required to report to the school health officer all absences on account of illness with such information respecting the same as may be available by report or investigation; and after investigation of all facts relating to the absence of any child or children from such school, the supervisor of school census and attendance shall, if justified by the circumstances, promptly give written notice to the parent, guardian or custodian of any child who has not complied with the provisions of this article, that the attendance of such child is required at some public, private or other school as herein provided. If within five days thereafter such parent, guardian or custodian of such child does not comply with

the provisions of this article, then such supervisor shall make complaint against the parent, guardian or custodian of such child in a court of competent jurisdiction for such violation, which violation shall be a misdemeanor.

Statutory note. There is nothing unusual about the Oklahoma law; it is fairly typical of compulsory attendance laws. Some others have more exceptions and some have no exceptions.

Case Material

Pierce v. Society of Sisters; Pierce v. Hill Academy, 268 U. S. 510 (1925). [Sisters operating parochial schools and owners of a military school sought to restrain enforcement of Oregon compulsory school law, which required all children to attend public schools.]

. . . there are no controverted questions of fact. Rights said to be guaranteed by the federal Constitution were specially set up, and appropriate prayers asked for their protection.

The challenged Act, effective September 1, 1926, requires every parent, guardian, or other person having control or charge or custody of a child between eight and sixteen years to send him "to a public school for the period of time a public school shall be held during the current year" in the district where the child resides; and failure so to do is declared a misdemeanor. . . . The manifest purpose is to compel general attendance at public schools by normal children, between eight and sixteen, who have not completed the eighth grade. And without doubt enforcement of the statute would seriously impair, perhaps destroy, the profitable features of appellees' business and greatly diminish the value of their property.

Appellee, the Society of Sisters, is an Oregon corporation, organized in 1880 with power to care for orphans, educate and instruct the youth, establish and maintain academies or schools, and acquire necessary real and personal property. It has long devoted its property and effort to the secular and religious education and care of children, and has acquired the valuable good will of many parents and guardians. It conducts inter-dependent primary and high schools and junior colleges, and maintains orphanages for the custody and control of children between eight and sixteen.

In its primary schools many children between those ages are taught the subjects usually pursued in Oregon public schools during the first eight years. Systematic religious instruction and moral training according to the tenets of the Roman Catholic Church are also regularly provided. All courses of study, both temporal and religious, contemplate continuity of training under appellee's charge; the primary schools are essential to the system and the most profitable. It owns valuable buildings, especially constructed and equipped for school purposes. The business is remunerative—the annual income from primary schools exceeds $30,000—and the successful conduct of this required long-time contracts with teachers and

parents. The Compulsory Education Act of 1922 has already caused the withdrawal from its schools of children who would otherwise continue, and their income has steadily declined. The appellants, public officers, have proclaimed their purpose strictly to enforce the statute.

After setting out the above facts the Society's bill alleges that the enactment conflicts with the right of parents to choose schools where their children will receive appropriate mental and religious training, the right of the child to influence the parents' choice of a school, the right of schools and teachers therein to engage in a useful business or profession, and is accordingly repugnant to the Constitution and void. And, further, that unless enforcement of the measure is enjoined the corporation's business and property will suffer irreparable injury.

Appellee, Hill Military Academy, is a private corporation organized in 1908 under the laws of Oregon, engaged in owning, operating and conducting for profit an elementary, college preparatory and military training school for boys between the ages of five and twenty-one years. The average attendance is one hundred, and the annual fees received for each student amount to some eight hundred dollars. The elementary department is divided into eight grades, as in the public schools; the college preparatory department has four grades, similar to those of the public high schools; the courses of study conform to the requirements of the State Board of Education. Military instruction and training are also given, under the supervision of an Army officer. It owns considerable real and personal property, some useful only for school purposes. The business and incident good will are very valuable. In order to conduct its affairs long time contracts must be made for supplies, equipment, teachers and pupils. Appellants, law officers of the State and County, have publicly announced that the Act of November 7, 1922, is valid and have declared their intention to enforce it. By reason of the statute and threat of enforcement appellee's business is being destroyed and its property depreciated; parents and guardians are refusing to make contracts for the future instruction of their sons, and some are being withdrawn.

The Academy's bill states the foregoing facts and then alleges that the challenged Act contravenes the corporation's right guaranteed by the Fourteenth Amendment and that unless appellants are restrained from proclaiming its validity and threatening to enforce it irreparable injury will result. The prayer is for an appropriate injunction.

The [state] court ruled that the Fourteenth Amendment guaranteed appellees against the deprivation of their property without due process of law consequent upon the unlawful interference by appellants with the free choice of patrons, present and prospective. It declared the right to conduct schools was property and that parents and guardians, as a part of their liberty, might direct the education of children by selecting reputable teachers and places. Also, that these schools were not unfit or harmful to the public, and that enforcement of the challenged statute would unlawfully deprive them of patronage and thereby destroy their owners' business and property. Finally, that the threats to enforce the Act would continue to cause irreparable injury; and the suits were not premature.

No question is raised concerning the power of the State reasonably to regulate all schools, to inspect, supervise and examine them, their teachers and pupils; to require that all children of proper age attend some school, that teachers shall be of good moral character and patriotic disposition, that certain studies plainly essential to good citzenship must be taught, and that nothing be taught which is manifestly inimical to the public welfare.

The inevitable practical result of enforcing the Act under consideration would be destruction of appellees' primary schools, and perhaps all other private primary schools for normal children within the State of Oregon. These parties are engaged in a kind of undertaking not inherently harmful, but long regarded as useful and meritorious. Certainly there is nothing in the present records to indicate that they have failed to discharge their obligations to patrons, students or the State. And there are no peculiar circumstances or present emergencies which demand extraordinary measures relative to primary education.

Under the doctrine of *Meyer v. Nebraska*, 262 U.S. 390, we think it entirely plain that the Act of 1922 unreasonably interferes with the liberty of parents and guardians to direct the upbringing and education of children under their control. As often heretofore pointed out, rights guaranteed by the Constitution may not be abridged by legislation which has no reasonable relation to some purpose within the competency of the State. The fundamental theory of liberty upon which all governments in this Union repose excludes any general power of the State to standardize its children by forcing them to accept instruction from public teachers only. The child is not the mere creature of the State; those who nurture him and direct his destiny have the right, coupled with the high duty, to recognize and prepare him for additional obligation. . . .

Generally it is entirely true, as urged by counsel, that no person in any business has such an interest in possible customers as to enable him to restrain the exercise of proper power of the State upon the ground that he will be deprived of patronage. But the injunctions here sought are not against the exercise of any *proper* power. Plaintiffs asked protection against arbitrary, unreasonable and unlawful interference with their patrons and the consequent destruction of their business and property. Their interest is clear and immediate. . . .

Case note. This case is frequently quoted as an example of religious liberty and the right of parents to send their children to a school in which sectarianism is taught as well as the regular secular school curriculum. The case does so hold; but it is usually forgotten that a private military school joined with the Society of Sisters in their complaint and that the case really upholds the existence of private schools, secular as well as sectarian. The decision was based upon the due-process clause of the Constitution, not, except indirectly, upon the First Amendment and its guarantee of religious liberty.

People v. Turner et al., 121 Cal. App. (2d) 861, 263 P. (2d) 685 (California, 1953). [Home instruction as a substitute for school attendance.]

Defendants were convicted of violating section 16601 of the Education Code in that they neglected and refused to send their three children to a public school, and each was sentenced to pay a fine of $10 on each of three counts. The section in question reads as follows: "Each parent, guardian, or other person having control or charge of any child between the ages of eight and 16 years, not exempted under the provisions of this chapter, shall send the child to the public full-time day school for the full time for which the public schools of the city, city and county, or school district in which the child resides are in session."

"16625. Children not attending a private full-time day school, and who are being instructed in study and recitation for at least three hours a day for 170 days each calendar year by a private tutor or other person, in the several branches of study required to be taught in the public schools of this State and in the English language shall be exempted. The tutor or other person shall hold a valid State credential for the grade taught. The instruction shall be offered between the hours of 8 o'clock a.m. and 4 o'clock p.m."

Defendants' main contention, however, is that the statute in question is unconstitutional in that it deprives parents of the right to determine how and where their children may be educated. There can be no doubt that if the statute, without qualification or exception required parents to place their children in public schools, it would be unconstitutional. Pierce v. Society of Sisters, 1925, 268 U.S. 510, 45 S.Ct. 571, 69 L.Ed. 1070, 39 A.L.R. 468. The statute here, however, unlike that involved in the case cited, does not so provide. It recognizes the right of parents not to place their children in public schools if they elect to have them educated in a private school or through the medium of a private tutor or other person possessing certain specified qualifications. We see no basis therefore upon which to predicate a holding of unconstitutionality unless such a holding is compelled because the statute denies the right of parents to educate their children unless such parents possess the qualifications prescribed therein.

The question here, therefore, may be narrowed down as to whether or not it is within the competency of the State to require parents to place their children in public schools or, in the alternative, a private school meeting certain prescribed conditions, or that the children be instructed by a private tutor or other person possessing qualifications and in the manner prescribed by section 16625. We believe that the answer must be in the affirmative.

It is not without significance that, although it has been said that "only eleven of the forty-eight states permit by statute that instruction may be given at home by their parent or tutor," and "such home instruction moreover is specifically conditioned except in two states" (Parental Right in Educational Law, Loughery, Catholic University of America Press, 1952), we have been unable to find a single case in which it has been held that so-called compulsory attendance statutes are rendered unconstitutional

and void merely by reason of a failure to recognize home instruction as an alternative to attendance in the public schools.

Nor do we see any merit in the claim of defendants that the statute under consideration is unreasonable or arbitrary in that, while exempting private schools, it does not require teachers therein to "hold a valid state credential for the grade taught," but a private tutor or other person in order to be exempted under section 16625 must possess such a certificate. If, as we have seen, the state might have refused to grant an exemption in the case of children being instructed at home by their parents or a private tutor without rendering the statute vulnerable to the charge of unconstitutionality, we see no reason why objection can be raised to a statute which, while granting an exemption in such cases, conditions the same by requiring such parents or tutors to possess certain qualifications even if these be stricter than those required of teachers in private schools. In the light of this, defendants may not be heard to assert that they have been discriminated against because the legislature conditioned the exemption granted to private instruction outside of a public or private school by requiring persons so undertaking to teach outside of such schools to possess qualifications different from those prescribed for teachers in private schools. Were it otherwise, however, it may not be said that there is not a reasonable basis for the distinction in question. The most obvious reason for such difference in treatment is that pointed out in Hoyt v. State, supra, namely, the difficulty in supervising without unreasonable expense a host of individuals, widely scattered, who might undertake to instruct individual children in their homes as compared with the less difficult and expensive supervision of teachers in organized private schools. Also the legislature might reasonably have concluded that teachers in private schools would be under direct supervision of their school authorities at all times, and that the interests of the persons conducting the same would compel the maintenance of the required standard of instruction by competent instructors for otherwise the school would fail to qualify for the exemption granted thereby, and without pupils it could not continue to exist.

Case note. The court here upheld the California statute requiring that instruction by a private tutor, as a substitute for school attendance, be by one who is qualified as a teacher. Many courts would agree even if the statute were less specific, because most such laws require education outside of the public schools to be equivalent to public-school education. The New Jersey courts, however, have held that home instruction can never be equivalent since the children are denied association with others of their age and interests, thus losing valuable intangibles of school attendance.

Sulzen v. School District No. 36 of City of Lecompton, 144 Kans. 648, 62 P. (2d) 880 (Kansas, 1936). [Requirement of residence for free attendance.]

This was an action to restrain and enjoin the officers and directors of School District No. 36 in Douglas county, Kan., and the principal of said school from interfering with plaintiff's children attending said school, which is located within the city of Lecompton.

The petition alleged that plaintiff was an actual bona fide resident of the city of Lecompton, that he and his wife were the owners of a home in said city, that he and his family have occupied said home and his children have been attending said school for more than 2 years last past, and that the defendants have discharged and dismissed his children from said school because he and his family were not residents of the city and school district No. 36. The answer of the defendants denied specifically the allegations as to the residence of plaintiff and family.

The first finding concerns the existence of School District No. 36 and its being within the corporate limits of the city of Lecompton. The remaining findings are as follows:

"2. The plaintiff, T. J. Sulzen, is the head of a family consisting of himself, wife and five minor children. He owns 160 acres of land in Lecompton Township, Douglas County, Kansas, and in School District No. 19 of said county. There is situated on the 160 acres a house suitable for domicile. The plaintiff's wife owns two lots in the city of Lecompton on which there is a house suitable for domicile.

"3. Mrs. Sulzen spent the summer of 1935 on the farm with her husband and family in Lecompton Township. She came to the city of Lecompton just before the beginning of the school year in District No. 36, in September of 1935 and set up a menage with three of her minor children on the property owned by her in said city. Mrs. Sulzen stays in the city of Lecompton and resides and lives there with her three children a major portion of the time. Ordinarily on week ends she goes out to the farm where her husband lives. Occasionally Mr. Sulzen during the week and sometimes at week ends stays in the house in the city of Lecompton. The three minor children have been going to school in School District No. 36.

"4. The plaintiff, T. J. Sulzen, is a resident of Lecompton Township in the technical sense of the term and he also resides in School District No. 19 in Lecompton Township a major portion of the time. Mrs. Sulzen is a resident of the city of Lecompton, Kansas, and School District No. 36.

"5. At the time of the school census in 1935 the plaintiff listed his five children in School District No. 19. Both the plaintiff and his wife voted in the city election in the city of Lecompton in the spring of 1935."

The conclusions of law are as follows:

"1 The three minor children of the plaintiff mentioned in the conclusions of fact reside in School District No. 36 of the city of Lecompton, Douglas county, Kansas, under such circumstances that they are entitled to attend school in the said district and might be compelled to do so, under the provisions of the statutes of Kansas relative to schools.

"2. The injunction prayed for should be allowed."

It was distinctly understood that the question of whether or not the plaintiff may be compelled to pay for the tuition of his minor children

while attending School District No. 36 was not at issue and no ruling was made thereon.

The finding that plaintiff was a resident of Lecompton township and school district No. 19 in Douglas county is contrary to the allegations of the petition, and, aside from the question of paying tuition under some of our statutes, would make his right to maintain such an action rather questionable, but one that need not here be decided. However, the pleadings and findings recognize residence as being the determinative issue in the case. R.S. 72–1107 makes the district schools of the state at all times equally free and accessible to all children resident therein over 6 and under the age of 21 years. The conclusion that the three minor children of the plaintiff were residents of district No. 36 could not rest upon the residence of the father who was found to have been a resident of another district.

The finding that the wife of the plaintiff was a resident of the city of Lecompton and School District No. 36 is inconsistent with the finding of the residence of the plaintiff elsewhere and that he was the head of a family consisting of himself, his wife, and children. A wife's residence or domicile follows that of her husband. . . .

There are certain circumstances which permit husband and wife to have separate legal residences or domiciles, but no such facts were pleaded in this case and no finding shows such a situation, but they are all to the contrary, so that, without the existence of such special circumstances having been found, the residence or domicile of the wife was necessarily at the same place as that of her husband, and the fact that she owned property or even voted elsewhere would not change her place of residence.

The first conclusion of law as to the residence of the three minor children being in the city of Lecompton and school district No. 36 is not supported by the findings of fact, because the minor children have no right to select or make a different residence for themselves than that of their parents. Their residence is necessarily the same as that of their father, unless they come within one of the few exceptions which permit of a change, none of which are mentioned in the pleadings or findings.

We cannot avoid concluding that these minor children were not residents of School District No. 36 and holding there was inconsistency in the findings, and that they would not support the conclusion as to the residence of the minor children.

The claim that the defendants are estopped from questioning the right of these minor children to attend school in district No. 36, because of having permitted them to do so for 2 years before discharging them is not well founded nor supported by any cited authorities.

Case note. The residence of a minor whose father is living is at the father's residence (with few exceptions, such as when the parents are divorced and the mother has custody of the children). This is a case where the mother took the children to a different school district ostensibly for the purpose of establishing her residence there so that

the children could attend that school. A mother who is not divorced from her husband cannot establish a separate residence for herself or for her children. Nor can a child establish a separate residence for himself until he reaches majority or is emancipated. Nonresidents may be required to pay tuition. It is true that some school boards are lax on this point and permit nonresident children to attend school if they are living away from home with a relative or friend of the family. However, the board usually requires tuition unless the relative, or friend of the family, legally adopts the child.

Brown et al. v. Board of Education, 347 U. S. 483 (1954). [The segregation cases.]

These cases come to us from the States of Kansas, South Carolina, Virginia, and Delaware. They are premised on different facts and different local conditions, but a common legal question justifies their consideration together in this consolidated opinion.

In each of the cases, minors of the Negro race, through their legal representatives, seek the aid of the courts in obtaining admission to the public schools of their community on a nonsegregated basis. In each instance, they had been denied admission to schools attended by white children under laws requiring or permitting segregation according to race. This segregation was alleged to deprive the plaintiffs of the equal protection of the laws under the Fourteenth Amendment. In each of the cases other than the Delaware case, a three-judge federal district court denied relief to the plaintiffs on the so-called "separate but equal" doctrine announced by this Court in *Plessy* v. *Ferguson,* 163 U.S. 537. Under that doctrine, equality of treatment is accorded when the races are provided substantially equal facilities, even though these facilities be separate. In the Delaware case, the Supreme Court of Delaware adhered to that doctrine, but ordered that the plaintiffs be admitted to the white schools because of their superiority to the Negro schools.

The plaintiffs contend that segregrated public schools are not "equal" and cannot be made "equal," and that hence they are deprived of the equal protection of the laws. Because of the obvious importance of the question presented, the Court took jurisdiction. Argument was heard in the 1952 Term, and reargument was heard this Term on certain questions propounded by the Court.

Reargument was largely devoted to the circumstances surrounding the adoption of the Fourteenth Amendment in 1868. . . . This discussion and our own investigation convince us that, although these sources cast some light, it is not enough to resolve the problem with which we are faced. At best, they are inconclusive.

In the instant cases, that question is directly presented. Here, . . . there are findings below that the Negro and white schools involved have been equalized, or are being equalized, with respect to buildings, curricula, qualifications and salaries of teachers, and other "tangible" factors. Our

decision, therefore, cannot turn on merely a comparison of these tangible factors in the Negro and white schools involved in each of the cases. We must look instead to the effect of segregation itself on public education.

In approaching this problem, we cannot turn the clock back to 1868 when the Amendment was adopted, or even to 1896 when *Plessy* v. *Ferguson* was written. We must consider public education in the light of its full development and its present place in American life throughout the Nation. Only in this way can it be determined if segregation in public schools deprives these plaintiffs of the equal protection of the laws.

Today, education is perhaps the most important function of state and local governments. Compulsory school attendance laws and the great expenditures for education both demonstrate our recognition of the importance of education to our democratic society. It is required in the performance of our most basic public responsibilities, even service in the armed forces. It is the very foundation of good citizenship. Today it is a principal instrument in awakening the child to cultural values, in preparing him for later professional training, and in helping him to adjust normally to his environment. In these days, it is doubtful that any child may reasonably be expected to succeed in life if he is denied the opportunity of an education. Such an opportunity, where the state has undertaken to provide it, is a right which must be made available to all on equal terms.

We come then to the question presented: Does segregation of children in public schools solely on the basis of race, even though the physical facilities and other "tangible" factors may be equal, deprive the children of the minority group of equal educational opportunities? We believe that it does. . . .

Such considerations apply with added force to children in grade and high schools. To separate them from others of similar age and qualifications solely because of their race generates a feeling of inferiority as to their status in the community that may affect their hearts and minds in a way unlikely ever to be undone. The effect of this separation on their educational opportunities was well stated by a finding in the Kansas case by a court which nevertheless felt compelled to rule against the Negro plaintiffs:

> "Segregation of white and colored children in public schools has a detrimental effect upon the colored children. The impact is greater when it has the sanction of the law; for the policy of separating the races is usually interpreted as denoting the inferiority of the negro group. A sense of inferiority affects the motivation of a child to learn. Segregation with the sanction of law, therefore, has a tendency to [retard] the educational and mental development of negro children and to deprive them of some of the benefits they would receive in a racial[ly] integrated school system."

Whatever may have been the extent of psychological knowledge at the time of *Plessy* v. *Ferguson*, this finding is amply supported by modern authority. Any language in *Plessy* v. *Ferguson* contrary to this finding is rejected.

We conclude that in the field of public education the doctrine of "separate but equal" has no place. Separate educational facilities are inherently unequal. Therefore, we hold that the plaintiffs and others similarly situated for whom the actions have been brought are, by reason of the segregation complained of, deprived of the equal protection of the laws guaranteed by the Fourteenth Amendment. This disposition makes unnecessary any discussion whether such segregation also violates the Due Process Clause of the Fourteenth Amendment.

Because these are class actions, because of the wide applicability of this decision, and because of the great variety of local conditions, the formulation of decrees in these cases presents problems of considerable complexity. On reargument, the consideration of appropriate relief was necessarily subordinated to the primary question—the constitutionality of segregation in public education. We have now announced that such segregation is a denial of the equal protection of the laws. . . .

Case note. The cases from Kansas, South Carolina, and Virginia arose because Negro children were denied admission to schools for white children; the Delaware case arose because the State Board of Education had ruled that educational opportunities for Negroes were unequal to those for white children and therefore that the Negroes should be admitted to the white schools. While these cases were pending, another case concerning segregated schools in the District of Columbia was initiated and was taken over by the Supreme Court without its going through the normal judicial procedure.

The segregation cases decided that equality in educational opportunity is broader than equality in facilities, qualification of teachers, and the like—that mere separation constitutes a psychological barrier which results in inequality. Though it may be said, loosely, that this decision overruled *Plessy v. Ferguson,* that is not strictly true because *Plessy v. Ferguson* dealt with segregation in transportation. However, in the Plessy decision the Court referred to the unlikelihood that segregated schools would be considered unconstitutional. This was dictum in the Plessy case but it formed the foundation for arguments that led the Supreme Court to uphold segregated schools previous to this decision.

Brown et al. v. Board of Education, 349 U. S. 294 (1955). [Implementation of 1954 segregation cases.]

These cases were decided on May 17, 1954. The opinions of that date declaring the fundamental principle that radical discrimination in public education is unconstitutional, are incorporated herein by reference. All provisions of federal, state, or local law requiring or permitting such discrimination must yield to this principle. There remains for consideration the manner in which relief is to be accorded. . . .

Full implementation of these constitutional principles may require solution of varied local school problems. School authorities have the primary responsibility for elucidating, assessing, and solving these problems; courts will have to consider whether the action of school authorities constitutes good faith implementation of the governing constitutional principles. Because of their proximity to local conditions and the possible need for further hearings, the courts which originally heard these cases can best perform this judicial appraisal. Accordingly, we believe it appropriate to remand the cases to those courts.

In fashioning and effectuating the decrees, the courts will be guided by equitable principles. Traditionally, equity has been characterized by a practical flexibility in shaping its remedies and by a facility for adjusting and reconciling public and private needs. These cases call for the exercise of these traditional attributes of equity power. At stake is the personal interest of the plaintiffs in admission to public schools as soon as practicable on a nondiscriminatory basis. To effectuate this interest may call for elimination of a variety of obstacles in making the transition to school systems operated in accordance with the constitutional principles set forth in our May 17, 1954, decision. Courts of equity may properly take into account the public interest in the elimination of such obstacles in a systematic and effective manner. But it should go without saying that the vitality of these constitutional principles cannot be allowed to yield simply because of disagreement with them.

While giving weight to these public and private considerations, the courts will require that the defendants make a prompt and reasonable start toward full compliance with our May 17, 1954, ruling. Once such a start has been made, the courts may find that additional time is necessary to carry out the ruling in an effective manner. The burden rests upon the defendants to establish that such time is necessary in the public interest and is consistent with good faith compliance at the earliest practicable date. To that end, the courts may consider problems related to administration, arising from the physical condition of the school plant, the school transportation system, personnel, revision of school districts and attendance areas into compact units to achieve a system of determining admission to the public schools on a nonracial basis, and revision of local laws and regulations which may be necessary in solving the foregoing problems. They will also consider the adequacy of any plans the defendants may propose to meet these problems and to effectuate a transition to a racially nondiscriminatory school system. During this period of transition, the courts will retain jurisdiction of these cases. . . .

It is so ordered.

Case note. Lower federal courts would have been saved much time and consternation had the Supreme Court in its 1955 decision held that all schools must be desegregated immediately, at the beginning of the next school year, within a designated period of time, or given some other specific instruction. However, the Court could not see its way to upset the educational systems of many states by such

an upheaval; also, the Court recognized that some schools could be desegregated more quickly than others. It was for these reasons rather than because of the social opposition of majorities in some states that led the Court to its 1955 decision granting time for schools to be desegregated in an orderly manner. It seems certain that the Court anticipated some of the troubles which followed its decision. Even had it anticipated riots, closing of the schools, and federal troops to enforce its decision, it is likely that the 1954 decision would have been made since the United States has held itself out as a stronghold of democracy in favor of the rights of minority groups. Just as the world situation probably influenced the Court in its flag-salute case in 1943 [see *West Virginia State Board of Education v. Barnette,* p. 217], it was probably influenced by the world situation in its segregation decisions.

Cooper v. Aaron, 358 U.S. 1 (1958). [The Little Rock Story.]

As this case reaches us it raises questions of the highest importance to the maintenance of the Federal system of Government. It necessarily involves a claim by the Governor and Legislature of a State that there is no duty on state officials to obey Federal court orders resting on this Court's considered interpretation of the United States Constitution.

Specifically it involves actions by the Governor and Legislature of Arkansas upon the premise that they are not bound by our holding in *Brown v. Board of Education,* 347 U.S. 483. . . .

We are urged to uphold a suspension of the Little Rock School Board's plan to do away with segregated public schools in Little Rock until state laws in effect upset and nullify our holding in *Brown v. Board of Education* have been further challenged and tested in the court. We reject these contentions. . . .

The following are the facts and circumstances so far as necessary to show how the legal questions are presented.

On May 17, 1954, this Court decided that enforced racial segregation in the public schools of a State is a denial of the equal protection of the laws enjoined by the Fourteenth Amendment. . . . The Court postponed, pending further argument, formulation of a decree to effectuate this decision. That decree was rendered May 31, 1955. . . . In the [1955 opinion] "Courts of equity may properly take into account the public interest in the elimination of such obstacles in a systematic and effective manner. But it should go without saying that the vitality of these constitutional principles cannot be allowed to yield simply because of disagreement with them. . . ."

Under such circumstances, the District Courts were directed to require "a prompt and reasonable start toward full compliance," and to take such action as was necessary to bring about the end of racial segregation in the public schools "with all deliberate speed." . . . Of course, in many locations, obedience to the duty of desegregation would require the immediate

general admission of Negro children, otherwise qualified as students for their appropriate classes, at particular schools. On the other hand, a District Court, after analysis of the relevant factors (which, of course, excludes hostility to racial desegregation), might conclude that justification existed for not requiring the present nonsegregated admission of all qualified Negro children. In such circumstances, however, the court should scrutinize the program of the school authorities to make sure that they had developed arrangements pointed toward the earliest practicable completion of desegregation, and had taken appropriate steps to put their program into effective operation. . . .

On May 20, 1954, three days after the first *Brown* opinion, the Little Rock District School Board adopted, and on May 23, 1954, made public, a statement of policy entitled "Supreme Court Decision—Segregation in Public Schools." In this statement the board recognized that

"It is our responsibility to comply with Federal constitutional requirements and we intend to do so when the Supreme Court of the United States outlines the method to be followed."

Thereafter the Board undertook studies of the administrative problems confronting the transition to a desegregated public school system at Little Rock. It instructed the superintendent of schools to prepare a plan for desegregation, and approved such a plan on May 24, 1955, seven days before the second *Brown* opinion. . . .

Following the adoption of this plan, the Superintendent of Schools discussed it with a large number of citizen groups in the city. As a result of these discussions, the Board reached the conclusion that "a large majority of the residents" of Little Rock were of "the belief that the plan, although objectionable in principle," from the point of view of those supporting segregated schools, "was still the best for the interests of all pupils in the district."

Upon challenge by a group of Negro plaintiff's desiring more rapid completion of the desegregation process, the District Court upheld the School Board's plan. . . .

While the school Board was thus going forward with its preparation for desegregating the Little Rock school system, other state authorities, in constrast, were actively pursuing a program designed to perpetuate in Arkansas the system of racial segregation which this court had held violated the Fourteenth Amendment. First came, in November, 1956, an amendment to the State Constitution flatly commanding the Arkansas General Assembly to oppose "in every constitutional manner the un-constitutional desegregation decisions of May 17, 1954 and May 31, 1955 of the United States Supreme Court," Ark. Const., Amend. 44, and, through the initiative, a Pupil Assignment Law, Ark. Stat. 80-1519 to 80-1524. This state Constitutional command, relieving school children from compulsory attendance at racially mixed schools, Ark. Stat. 80-1525, and a law establishing a State Sovereignty Commission, Ark. Stat. 6-801 to 6-824, was enacted by the General Assembly in February 1957.

The School Board and the Superintendent of Schools nevertheless continued with preparations to carry out the first stage of the desegregation program. Nine Negro children were scheduled for admission in September

1957 to Central High School, which has more than 2,000 students. Various administrative measures, designed to assure the smooth transition of this first stage of desegregation were undertaken.

On Sept. 2, 1957, the day before these Negro students were to enter Central High, the school authorities were met with drastic opposing action on the part of the Governor of Arkansas who dispatched units of the Arkansas National Guard to the Central High School grounds and placed the school "off limits" to colored students. As found by the District Court in subsequent proceedings, the Governor's action had not been requested by the school authorities and was entirely unheralded. . . .

The Board's petition for postponement in this proceeding states: "The effect of that action [of the Governor] was to harden the core of opposition to the Plan and cause many persons who theretofore had reluctantly accepted the Plan to believe that there was some power in the State of Arkansas which, when exerted, could nullify the Federal law and permit disobedience of the decree of this [District] Court, and from that date hostility to the Plan was increased and criticism of the officials of the [School] District has become more bitter and unrestrained." The Governor's action caused the School Board to request the Negro students on Sept. 2 not to attend the high school until the legal dilemma was solved." The next day, Sept. 3, 1957, the Board petitioned the District Court for instructions, and the court, after a hearing, found that the Board's request of the Negro students to stay away from the high school had been made because of the stationing of the military guards by the state authorities. The court determined that this was not a reason for departing from the approved plan, and ordered the School Board and Superintendent to proceed with it.

On the morning of the next day, Sept. 4, 1957, the Negro children attempted to enter the high school but, as the District Court later found, units of Arkansas National Guard "acting pursuant to the Governor's order, stood shoulder to shoulder at the school grounds and thereby forcibly prevented the nine Negro students . . . from entering," as they continued to do every school day during the following three weeks. . . .

That same day, Sept. 4, 1957, the United States Attorney for the Eastern District of Arkansas was requested by the District Court to begin an immediate investigation in order to fix responsibility for the interference with the orderly implementation of the District Court's direction to carry out the desegregation program. Three days later, Sept. 7, 1957, the District Court denied a petition of the School Board and the Superintendent of Schools for an order temporarily suspending continuance of the program.

Upon completion of the United States Attorney's investigation, he and the Attorney General of the United States, at the District Court's request, entered the proceedings and filed a petition on behalf of the United States, as *amicus curiae*, to enjoin the Governor of Arkansas and officers of the Arkansas National Guard from further attempts to prevent obedience to the court's order. After hearings on the petition, the District Court found that the School Board's plan had been obstructed by the Governor through the use of National Guard troops, and granted a preliminary injunction on Sept. 20, enjoining the Governor and the officers of the Guard from

preventing the attendance of Negro children at Central High School, and from otherwise obstructing or interfering with the orders of the court in connection with the plan. . . . The National Guard was then withdrawn from the school.

The next school day was Monday, Sept. 23, 1957. The Negro children entered the high school that morning under the protection of the Little Rock Police Department and members of the Arkansas State Police. But the officers caused the children to be removed from the school during the morning because they had difficulty controlling a large and demonstrating crowd which had gathered at the high school. . . . On September 25, however, the President of the United States dispatched Federal troops to Central High School and admission of the Negro students to the school was thereby effected. Regular Army troops continued at the high school until Nov. 27, 1957. They were then replaced by Federalized National Guardsmen who remained throughout the balance of the school year. Eight of the Negro students remained in attendance at the school through-out the school year.

We come now to the aspect of the proceeding presently before us. On Feb. 20, 1958, the School Board and the Superintendent of Schools filed a petition in the District Court seeking a postponement of their program for desegregation. Their position in essence was that because of extreme public hostility, which they stated had been engendered largely by the official attitudes and actions of the Governor and the Legislature, the maintenance of a sound educational program at Central High School, with the Negro students in attendance, would be impossible.

The Board therefore proposed that the Negro students already admitted to the school be withdrawn and sent to segregated schools, and that all further steps to carry out the Board's desegregation program be postponed for a period later suggested by the Board to be two and one-half years.

After a hearing the District Court granted the relief requested by the Board. . . . The Negro respondents appealed to the Court of Appeals for the Eighth Circuit. . . . The Court of Appeals . . . reversed the District Court. . . . On Aug. 21, 1958, the Court of Appeals stayed its mandate to permit the School Board to petition this Court for certiorari. Pending the filing of the School Board's petition for certiorari, the Negro respond-ents on Aug. 23, 1958, applied to Mr. Justice Whittaker, as Circuit Justice for the Eighth Circuit, to stay the order of the Court of Appeals with-holding its own mandate and also to stay the District Court's judgment. In view of the nature of the motions, he referred them to the entire Court. Recognizing the vital importance of a decision of the issues in time to permit arrangements to be made for the 1958-59 school year . . . we con-vened in special term on Aug. 28, 1958, and heard oral argument on the respondents' motions, and also argument of the Solicitor General who, by invitation, appeared for the United States as *amicus curiae*, and asserted that the Court of Appeals' judgment was clearly correct on the merits, and urged that we vacate its stay forthwith. . . . On Sept. 12, 1958, as already mentioned, we unanimously affirmed the judgment of the Court of Appeals. . . .

In affirming the judgment of the Court of Appeals, which reversed the

District Court, we have accepted without reservation the position of the School Board, the Superintendent of Schools, and their counsel that they displayed entire good faith in the conduct of these proceedings and in dealing with the unfortunate and distressing sequence of events which has been outlined.

We likewise have accepted the findings of the District Court as to the conditions at Central High School during the 1957-58 school year, and also the findings that the educational progress of all the students, white and colored, of that school has suffered and will continue to suffer if the conditions which prevailed last year are permitted to continue.

The significance of these findings, however, is to be considered in the light of the fact, indisputably revealed by the record before us, that the conditions they depict are directly traceable to the actions of legislators and executive officials of the State of Arkansas, taken in their official capacities, which reflect their own determination to resist this Court's decision in the *Brown* case and which have brought about violent resistance to that decision in Arkansas. . . .

The constitutional rights of respondents are not to be sacrificed or yielded to the violence and disorder which have followed upon the actions of the Governor and Legislature. . . . Thus law and order are not here to be preserved by depriving the Negro children of their constitutional rights. . . .

The controlling legal principles are plain. The command of the Fourteenth Amendment is that no "State" shall deny any person within its jurisdiction the equal protection of the laws. "A State acts by its legislative, its executive, or its judicial authorities. It can act in no other way. The Constitutional provision, therefore, must mean that no agency of the State, or of the officers or agents by whom its powers are exerted, shall deny to any person within its jurisdiction the equal protection of the law. . . ." Thus the prohibitions of the Fourteenth Amendment extend to all action of the State denying equal protection of the laws; whatever the agency of the state taking the action. . . . In short, the Constitutional rights of children not to be discriminated against in school admission on grounds of race or color declared by this Court in the *Brown* case can neither be nullified openly and directly by state legislators or state executive or judicial officers, nor nullified indirectly by them through evasive scheme for segregation whether attempted "ingeniously or ingenuously. . . ."

What has been said, in the light of the facts developed is enough to dispose of the case. However, we should answer the premise of the actions of the Governor and Legislature that they are not bound by our holding in the *Brown* case. It is necessary only to recall some basic Constitutional propositions which are settled doctrine.

Article VI of the Constitution makes the Constitution the "supreme Law of the Land." In 1803, Chief Justice Marshall, speaking for a unanimous Court, referring to the Constitution as "the fundamental and paramount law of the nation," declared in the notable case of *Marbury v. Madison*, 1 Cranch 137, 177, that "it is emphatically the province and duty of the judicial department to say what the law is." This decision declared the basic principle that the Federal judiciary is supreme in the exposition of the

law of the Constitution, and that principle has ever since been respected by this Court and the Country as a permanent and indispensable feature of our Constitutional system.

It follows that the interpretation of the Fourteenth Amendment enunciated by this Court in the *Brown* case is the supreme law of the land, and Art. VI of the Constitution makes it binding on the states "any Thing in the Constitution or Laws of any State to the Contrary notwithstanding."

Every state legislator and executive and judicial officer is solemnly committed by oath taken pursuant to Art. VI, Cl. 3, "to support this Constitution. . . ." No state legislator or executive or judicial officer can war against the Constitution without violating his undertaking to support it. Chief Justice Marshall spoke for a unanimous Court in saying that: "If the legislatures of the several states may, at will, annul the judgment of the courts of the United States, and destroy the rights acquired under those judgments, the Constitution itself becomes a solemn mockery. . . ."

A Governor who asserts a power to nullify a Federal Court order is similarly restrained. If he has such power, said Chief Justice Hughes, in 1932, also for a unanimous Court, "it is manifest that the fiat of a State Governor, and not the Constitution of the United States, would be the supreme law of the land; that the restrictions of the Federal Constitution upon the exercise of state power would be but impotent phrases. . . ."

It is, of course, quite true that the responsibility for public education is primarily the concern of the States, but it is equally true that such responsibilities, like all other state activity, must be exercised consistently with Federal Constitutional requirements as they apply to state action. The Constitution created a Government dedicated to equal justice under law. The Fourteenth Amendment embodied and emphasized that ideal.

State support of segregated schools through any arrangement, management, funds, or property cannot be squared with the Amendment's command that no State shall deny any person within its jurisdiction the equal protection of the laws. The right of a student not to be segregated on racial grounds in schools so maintained is indeed so fundamental and pervasive that it is embraced in the concept of due process of law. . . . The principles announced in that [Brown] decision and the obedience of the states to them, according to the command of the Constitution, are indispensable for the protection of the freedoms guaranteed by our fundamental charter for all of us. Our Constitutional ideal, of equal justice under law, is thus made a living truth.

Case note. There is not much to be said about this case; the facts are given in full for the world to read. It is unbelievable that such a thing could happen in the United States. However, that comment and all other comments the author feels like writing, are sociological and political rather than legal. The legal point of the case is that the Constitution of the United States and its interpretations by the Supreme Court of the United States are the supreme law of the land which no state can disregard. Immediately after the segregation decisions, there

was much talk in some states about interposition. There can be no such thing, as this case shows.

Commonwealth v. Smoker, 77 Pa. Super. 435, 110 A. (2d) 740 (Pennsylvania, 1955). [Compulsory education laws and religious liberty.]

Samuel L. Smoker, defendant, was convicted for violating the provisions of the Public School Code of March 10, 1949, P.L. 30, 24 P.S. sec. 1-101 et seq. He is the father of Mervin Smoker who was assigned to the elementary school in Leacock Township, Lancaster County, Pennsylvania. The testimony disclosed that defendant refused his son attendance to school because of religious belief which prevents parents of the Amish faith from sending their children to school after they attain the age of fourteen and have completed the eighth grade of public school. Mervin finished eighth grade and was over fourteen years of age.

On or about December 29, 1953, defendant filed with the Secretary of the School District of the above township an application for a farm work permit for Mervin on the ground that it was necessary for him to be at home to help with the work, and to assist in taking care of defendant's sick father. The permit, with the Secretary's approval, was sent to the Superintendent of Public Instruction of the Commonwealth of Pennsylvania. On January 6, 1954, permit was refused on the ground that there was an older son available for the purposes requested in the application.

It is contended that compulsory school attendance as applied here is contrary to the First and Fourteenth Amendments of the United States Constitution and Article I, Section 3, Constitution of Pennsylvania, P.S., in respect to the guarantees of religious freedom. This question has already been decided by this Court in Commonwealth v. Beiler, 168 Pa. Super. 462, 79 A. 2d 134. The Beiler case likewise involved Amish defendants with children who had completed the eighth grade and attained the age of fourteen. We held that the Public School Code was not violative of our Constitution and that decisions of the United States Supreme Court were clear on the issue and determined the matter. We adhere to our decision and to the reasoning so lucidly set forth by Judge Reno in the Beiler case.

Defendant also contends that he is not guilty because his son should have been granted a work permit. Section 1330 of the Public School Code, 24 P.S. sec. 13-1330, provides for exemption from compulsory school attendance if a child is fourteen years old, has completed the eighth grade, and has received a work permit. Pursuant to the Code, the Superintendent of Public Instruction issued Rules and Regulations pertaining to work permits. These Regulations provide that a permit be issued only where the child's family is "in dire financial circumstances." The Superintendent refused a permit to defendant's son because of an absence of a showing of dire financial circumstances. There is no merit to defendant's contention that these Regulations are unreasonable and arbitrary and an attempt by the Superintendent to legislate. The Superintendent of Public Instruction as an administrative officer, may properly be invested with a reasonable amount of discretion in determining individual fact situations and in issu-

ing rules to govern his administration. Weaverland Independent School District Case, 378 Pa. 449, 106 A. 2d 812. The Public School Code is obviously intended to require school attendance up to a certain age. However, the legislature recognized that strict compliance with such requirement could work hardship in certain cases. Hence, Section 1330 provides for some exemptions based on age and engagement in farm or domestic work on permits issued "in accordance with regulations which the Superintendent of Public Instruction is hereby authorized to prescribe." The Regulations promulgated pursuant to the Code, in requiring "dire financial circumstances" before a work permit shall issue, are reasonable in that they recognize and uphold the basic purpose of the Code in requiring school attendance. Undue hardship to a given family is an eminently reasonable restriction to the approval of an exemption. To issue permits merely on the convenience of a family or because of a different religious belief would result in subversion of the intent of the legislature in requiring school attendance. It follows that the permit was properly refused in this case, pursuant to Regulations promulgated in accordance with the law.

Case note. When a family's religion disapproves of education beyond a particular limit, the family's religious liberty is not violated by a compulsory attendance law which requires a child to attend beyond that limit. The state regulation permitted work permits to be issued to children under the compulsory attendance age only when the child's family is in such financial circumstances as to need the child out of school to help with the family's support. This distinction was held to be reasonable and not arbitrary.

West Virginia State Board of Education v. Barnette, 319 U. S. 624 (1943). [Compulsory flag salute and religious freedom.]

Following the decision by this Court on June 3, 1940, in *Minersville School District v. Gobitis,* 310 U. S. 586, the West Virginia legislature amended its statutes to require all schools therein to conduct courses of instruction in history, civics, and in the Constitution of the United States and of the State "for the purpose of teaching, fostering and perpetuating the ideals, principles and spirit of Americanism, and increasing the knowledge of the organization and machinery of the government." Appellant Board of Education was directed, with advice of the State Superintendent of Schools, to "prescribe the courses of study covering these subjects" for public schools. The Act made it the duty of private, parochial and denominational schools to prescribe courses of study "similar to those required for the public schools."

The Board of Education on January 9, 1942, adopted a resolution containing recitals taken largely from the Court's *Gobitis* opinion and ordering that the salute to the flag become "a regular part of the program of activities in the public schools," that all teachers and pupils "shall be required to participate in the salute honoring the Nation represented by

the Flag; provided, however, that refusal to salute the Flag be regarded as an act of insubordination, and shall be dealt with accordingly." . . .

Failure to conform is "insubordination" dealt with by expulsion. Readmission is denied by statute until compliance. Meanwhile the expelled child is "unlawfully absent" and may be proceeded against as a delinquent. His parents or guardians are liable to prosecution, and if convicted are subject to fine not exceeding $50 and jail term not exceeding thirty days.

Appellees, citizens of the United States and of West Virginia, brought suit in the United States District Court for themselves and others similarly situated asking its injunction to restrain enforcement of these laws and regulations against Jehovah's Witnesses. The Witnesses are an unincorporated body teaching that the obligation imposed by law of God is superior to that of laws enacted by temporal government. Their religious beliefs include a literal version of Exodus, Chapter 20, verses 4 and 5, which says: "Thou shalt not make unto thee any graven image, or any likeness of anything that is in heaven above, or that is in the earth beneath, or that is in the water under the earth; thou shalt not bow down thyself to them nor serve them." They consider that the flag is an "image" within this command. For this reason they refuse to salute it.

. . . The question which underlies the flag salute controversy is whether such a ceremony so touching matters of opinion and political attitude may be imposed upon the individual by official authority under powers committed to any political organization under our Constitution. We examine rather than assume existence of this power and, against this broader definition of issues in this case, reexamine specific grounds assigned for the *Gobitis* decision.

1. It was said that the flag-salute controversy confronted the Court with "the problem which Lincoln cast in memorable dilemma: 'Must a government of necessity be too *strong* for the liberties of its people, or too *weak* to maintain its own existence?'" and that the answer must be in favor of strength. *Minersville School District v. Gobitis*, supra, at 596.

We think these issues may be examined free of pressure or restraint growing out of such considerations.

It may be doubted whether Mr. Lincoln would have thought that the strength of government to maintain itself would be impressively vindicated by our confirming power of the State to expel a handful of children from school. Such oversimplification, so handy in political debate, often lacks the precision necessary to postulates of judicial reasoning. If validly applied to this problem, the utterance cited would resolve every issue of power in favor of those in authority and would require us to override every liberty thought to weaken or delay execution of their policies.

Government of limited power need not be anemic government. Assurance that rights are secure tends to diminish fear and jealousy of strong government, and by making us feel safe to live under it makes for its better support. Without promise of a limiting Bill of Rights it is doubtful if our Constitution could have mustered enough strength to enable its ratification. To enforce those rights today is not to choose weak government over strong government. It is only to adhere as a means of strength

to individual freedom of mind in preference to officially disciplined uniformity for which history indicates a disappointing and disastrous end.

The subject now before us exemplifies this principle. Free public education, if faithful to the ideal of secular instruction and political neutrality, will not be partisan or enemy of any class, creed, party, or faction. If it is to impose any ideological discipline, however, each party or denomination must seek to control, or failing that, to weaken the influence of the educational system. Observance of the limitations of the Constitution will not weaken government in the field appropriate for its exercise.

2. It was also considered in the *Gobitis* case that functions of educational officers in States, counties and school districts were such that to interfere with their authority "would in effect make us the school board for the country." *Id.* at 598.

The Fourteenth Amendment, as now applied to the States, protects the citizen against the State itself, and all of its creatures—Boards of Education not excepted. These have, of course, important, delicate, and highly discretionary functions, but none that they may not perform within the limits of the Bill of Rights. That they are educating the young for citizenship is reason for scrupulous protection of Constitutional freedom of the individual, if we are not to strangle the free mind at its source and teach youth to discount important principles of our government as mere platitudes.

Such Boards are numerous and their territorial jurisdiction often small. But small and local authority may feel less sense of responsibility to the Constitution, and agencies of publicity may be less vigilant in calling it to account. The action of Congress in making flag observance voluntary and respecting the conscience of the objector in a matter so vital as raising the Army contrasts sharply with these local regulations in matters relatively trivial to the welfare of the nation. There are village tyrants as well as village Hampdens, but none who acts under color of law is beyond reach of the Constitution.

3. The *Gobitis* opinion reasoned that this is a field "where courts possess no marked and certainly no controlling competence," that it is committed to the legislatures as well as the courts to guard cherished liberties and that it is constitutionally appropriate to "fight out the wise use of legislative authority in the forum of public opinion and before legislative assemblies rather than to transfer such a contest to the judicial arena," since all the "effective means of inducing political changes are left free." *Id.* at 597-598, 600.

The very purpose of a Bill of Rights was to withdraw certain subjects from the vicissitudes of political controversy, to place them beyond the reach of majorities and officials and to establish them as legal principles to be applied by the courts. One's right to life, liberty, and property, to free speech, a free press, freedom of worship and assembly, and other fundamental rights may not be submitted to vote; they depend on the outcome of no elections.

Children of this faith have been expelled from school and are threatened with exclusion for no other cause. Officials threaten to send them to reformatories maintained for criminally inclined juveniles. Parents of such

children have been prosecuted and are threatened with prosecutions for causing delinquency.

The Board of Education moved to dismiss the complaint setting forth these facts and alleging that the law and regulations are an unconstitutional denial of religious freedom, and of freedom of speech, and are invalid under the "due process" and "equal protection" clauses of the Fourteenth Amendment to the Federal Constitution. The cause was submitted on the pleadings to a District Court of three judges. It restrained enforcement as to the plaintiffs and those of that class. The Board of Education brought the case here by direct appeal.

This case calls upon us to reconsider a precedent decision, as the Court throughout its history often has been required to do.

Whether the First Amendment to the Constitution will permit officials to order observance of ritual of this nature does not depend upon whether as a voluntary exercise we would think it to be good, bad or merely innocuous. Any credo of nationalism is likely to include what some disapprove or to omit what others think essential, and to give off different overtones as it takes on different accents or interpretations. If official power exists to coerce acceptance of any patriotic creed, what it shall contain cannot be decided by courts, but must be largely discretionary with the ordaining authority, whose power to prescribe would no doubt include power to amend. Hence validity of the asserted power to force an American citizen publicly to profess any statement of belief or to engage in any ceremony of assent to one, presents questions of power that must be considered independently of any idea we may have as to the utility of the ceremony in question.

In weighing arguments of the parties it is important to distinguish between the due process clause of the Fourteenth Amendment as an instrument for transmitting the principles of the First Amendment and those cases in which it is applied for its own sake. The test of legislation which collides with the Fourteenth Amendment, because it also collides with the principles of the First, is much more definite than the test when only the Fourteenth is involved. Much of the vagueness of the due process clause disappears when the specific prohibitions of the First become its standard. The right of a State to regulate, for example, a public utility may well include, so far as the due process test is concerned, power to impose all of the restrictions which a legislature may have a "rational basis" for adopting. But freedoms of speech and of press, of assembly, and of worship may not be infringed on such slender grounds. They are susceptible of restriction only to prevent grave and immediate danger to interests which the State may lawfully protect. It is important to note that while it is the Fourteenth Amendment which bears directly upon the State it is the more specific limiting principles of the First Amendment that finally govern this case.

Nor does our duty to apply the Bill of Rights to assertions of official authority depend upon our possession of marked competence in the field where the invasion of rights occurs. True, the task of transisting the majestic generalities of the Bill of Rights, conceived as part of the pattern of liberal government in the eighteenth century, into concrete restraints

on officials dealing with the problems of the twentieth century, is one to disturb self-confidence. These principles grew in soil which also produced a philosophy that the individual was the center of society, that his liberty was attainable through mere absence of governmental restraints, and the government should be entrusted with few controls and only the mildest supervision over men's affairs. We must transplant these rights to a soil in which the *laissez-faire* concept or principle of non-interference has withered at least as to economic affairs, and social advancements are increasingly sought through closer integration of society and through expanded and strengthened governmental controls. These changed conditions often deprive precedents of reliability and cast us more than we would choose upon our own judgment. But we act in these matters not by authority of our competence but by force of our commissions. We cannot, because of modest estimates of our competence in such specialties as public education, withhold the judgment that history authenticates as the function of this Court when liberty is infringed.

4. Lastly, and this is the very heart of the *Gobitis* opinion, it reasons that "National unity is the basis of national security," that the authorities have "the right to select appropriate means for its attainment," and hence reaches the conclusion that such compulsory measures toward "national unity" are constitutional. *Id.* at 595. Upon the verity of this assumption depends our answer in this case.

National unity as an end which officials may foster by persuasion and example is not in question. The problem is whether under our Constitution compulsion as here employed is a permissible means for its achievement.

Struggles to coerce uniformity of sentiment in support of some end thought essential to their time and country have been waged by many good as well as by evil men. Nationalism is a relatively recent phenomenon but at other times and places the ends have been racial or territorial security, support of a dynasty or regime, and particular plans for saving souls. As first and moderate methods to attain unity have failed, those bent on its accomplishment must resort to an ever-increasing severity. As governmental pressure toward unity becomes greater, so strife becomes more bitter as to whose unity it shall be. Probably no deeper division of our people could proceed from any provocation than from finding it necessary to choose what doctrine and whose program public educational officials shall compel youth to unite in embracing. Ultimate futility of such attempts to compel coherence is the lesson of every such effort from the Roman drive to stamp out Christianity as a disturber of its pagan unity, the Inquisition, as a means to religious and dynastic unity, the Siberian exiles as a means to Russian unity, down to the fast failing efforts of our present totalitarian enemies. Those who begin coercive elimination of dissent soon find themselves exterminating dissenters. Compulsory unification of opinion achieves only the unanimity of the graveyard.

It seems trite but necessary to say that the First Amendment to our Constitution was designed to avoid these ends by avoiding these beginnings. There is no mysticism in the American concept of the State or of the

nature or origin of its authority. We set up government by consent of the governed, and the Bill of Rights denies those in power any legal opportunity to coerce that consent. Authority here is to be controlled by public opinion, not public opinion by authority.

The case is made difficult not because the principles of its decision are obscure but because the flag involved is our own. Nevertheless, we apply the limitations of the Constitution with no fear that freedom to be intellectually and spiritually diverse or even contrary will disintegrate the social organization. To believe that patriotism will not flourish if patriotic ceremonies are voluntary and spontaneous instead of a compulsory routine is to make an unflattering estimate of the appeal of our institutions to free minds. We can have intellectual individualism and the rich cultural diversities that we owe to exceptional minds only at the price of occasional eccentricity and abnormal attitudes. When they are so harmless to others or to the State as those we deal with here, the price is not too great. But freedom to differ is not limited to things that do not matter much. That would be a mere shadow of freedom. The test of its substance is the right to differ as to things that touch the heart of the existing order.

If there is any fixed star in our constitutional constellation, it is that no official, high or petty, can prescribe what shall be orthodox in politics, nationalism, religion, or other matters of opinion or force citizens to confess by word or act their faith therein. If there are any circumstances which permit an exception, they do not now occur to us.

We think the action of the local authorities in compelling the flag salute and pledge transcends constitutional limitations on their power and invades the sphere of intellect and spirit which it is the purpose of the First Amendment to our Constitution to reserve from all official control.

The decision of this Court in *Minersville School District* v. *Gobitis* and the holdings of those few *per curiam* decisions which preceded and foreshadowed it are overruled, and the judgment enjoining enforcement of the West Virginia Regulation is

Affirmed

Concurring opinions: (1) Words uttered under coercion are proof of loyalty to nothing but self-interest. Love of country must spring from willing hearts and free minds, inspired by a fair administration of wise laws enacted by the people's elected representatives within the bounds of express constitutional prohibitions. These laws must, to be consistent with the First Amendment, permit the widest toleration of conflicting viewpoints consistent with a society of free men.

Neither our domestic tranquillity in peace nor our martial effort in war depend on compelling little children to participate in a ceremony which ends in nothing for them but a fear of spiritual condemnation. If, as we think, their fears are groundless, time and reason are the proper antidotes for their errors. The ceremonial, when enforced against conscientious objectors, more likely to defeat than to serve its high purpose, is a handy implement for disguised religious persecution. As such, it is inconsistent with our Constitution's plan and purpose.

(2) I am unable to agree that the benefits that may accrue to society from the compulsory flag salute are sufficiently definite and tangible to justify the invasion of freedom and privacy that is entailed or to compensate for a restraint on the freedom of the individual to be vocal or silent according to his conscience or personal inclination. The trenchant words in the preamble to the Virginia Statute for Religious Freedom remain unanswerable: ". . . all attempts to influence [the mind] by temporal punishments, or burdens, or by civil incapacitations, tend only to beget habits of hypocrisy and meanness, . . ." Any spark of love for country which may be generated in a child or his associates by forcing him to make what is to him an empty gesture and recite words wrung from him contrary to his religious beliefs is overshadowed by the desirability of preserving freedom of conscience to the full. It is in that freedom and the example of persuasion, not in force and compulsion, that the real unity of America lies.

Dissenting opinion: Under our constitutional system the legislature is charged solely with civil concerns of society. If the avowed or intrinsic legislative purpose is either to promote or to discourage some religious community or creed, it is clearly within the constitutional restrictions imposed on legislatures and cannot stand. But it by no means follows that legislative power is wanting whenever a general non-discriminatory civil regulation in fact touches conscientious scruples or religious beliefs of an individual or a group. Regard for such scruples or beliefs undoubtedly presents one of the most reasonable claims for the exertion of legislative accommodation. It is, of course, beyond our power to rewrite the State's requirement, by providing exemptions for those who do not wish to participate in the flag salute or by making some other accommodations to meet their scruples. That wisdom might suggest the making of such accommodations and that school administration would not find it too difficult to make them and yet maintain the ceremony for those not refusing to conform, is outside our province to suggest. Tact, respect, and generosity toward variant views will always commend themselves to those charged with the duties of legislation so as to achieve a maximum of good will and to require a minimum of unwilling submission to a general law. But the real question is, who is to make such accommodations, the courts or the legislature? . . . Judges should be very diffident in setting their judgment against that of a state in determining what is and what is not a major concern, what means are appropriate to proper ends, and what is the total social cost in striking the balance of imponderables. . . .

An act compelling profession of allegiance to a religion, no matter how subtly or tenuously promoted, is bad. But an act promoting good citizenship and national allegiance is within the domain of governmental authority and is therefore to be judged by the same considerations of power and of constitutionality as those involved in the many claims of immunity from civil obedience because of religious scruples. . . .

The subjection of dissidents to the general requirement of saluting the flag, as a measure conducive to the training of children in good citizenship, is very far from being the first instance of exacting obedience to general

laws that have offended deep religious scruples. Compulsory vaccination, see *Jacobson* v. *Massachusetts*, 197 U.S. 11, food inspection regulations, see *Shapiro* v. *Lyle*, 30 F. 2d 971, the obligation to bear arms, see *Hamilton* v. *Regents*, 293 U.S. 245, 267, testimonial duties, see *Stansbury* v. *Marks*, 2 Dall. 213, compulsory medical treatment, see *People* v. *Vogelgesang*, 221 N. Y. 290, 116 N.E. 977—these are but illustrations of conduct that has often been compelled in the enforcement of legislation of general applicability even though the religious consciences of particular individuals rebelled at the exaction. . . . One may have the right to practice one's religion and at the same time owe the duty of formal obedience to laws that run counter to one's beliefs. Compelling belief implies denial of opportunity to combat it and to assert dissident views. Such compulsion is one thing. Quite another matter is submission to conformity of action while denying its wisdom or virtue and with ample opportunity for seeking its change or abrogation.

In *Hamilton* v. *Regents*, 293 U. S. 245, this Court unanimously held that one attending a state-maintained university cannot refuse attendance on courses that offend his religious scruples. That decision is not overruled today, but is distinguished on the ground that attendance at the institution for higher education was voluntary and therefore a student could not refuse compliance with its conditions and yet take advantage of its opportunities. But West Virginia does not compel the attendance at its public schools of the children here concerned. West Virginia does not so compel, for it cannot. This Court denied the right of a state to require its children to attend public schools. *Pierce* v. *Society of Sisters*, 268 U. S. 510. As to its public schools, West Virginia imposes conditions which it deems necessary in the development of future citizens percisely as California deemed necessary the requirements that offended the student's conscience in the *Hamilton* case.

. . . And for me it still remains to be explained why the grounds of Mr. Justice Cardozo's opinion in *Hamilton* v. *Regents, supra,* are not sufficient to sustain the flag salute requirement. Such a requirement, like the requirement in the *Hamilton* case, "is not an interference by the state with the free exercise of religion when the liberties of the constitution are read in the light of a century and a half of history during days of peace and war." 293 U. S. 245, 266. The religious worshiper, "if his liberties were to be thus extended, might refuse to contribute taxes . . . in furtherance of any other end condemned by his conscience as irreligious or immoral. The right of private judgment has never yet been so exalted above the powers and the compulsion of the agencies of government." *Id.*, at 268. . . .

We are told that a flag salute is a doubtful substitute for adequate understanding of our institutions. The states that require such a school exercise do not have to justify it as the only means for promoting good citizenship in children, but merely as one of diverse means for accomplishing a worthy end. We may deem it a foolish measure, but the point is that this Court is not the organ of government to resolve doubts as to whether it will fulfill its purpose. Only if there be no doubt that any reasonable mind could entertain can we deny to the states the right to resolve doubts their way and not ours.

That which to the majority may seem essential for the welfare of the state may offend the consciences of a minority. But, so long as no inroads are made upon the actual exercise of religion by the minority, to deny the political power of the majority to enact laws concerned with civil matters, simply because they may offend the consciences of a minority, really means that the consciences of a minority are more sacred and more enshrined in the Constitution than the consciences of a majority.

Case note. The flag-salute requirement swept the country during World War I by state laws, state department of education regulations, and local school board rules. The original voluntary character of the salute and pledge was soon lost, and participation in the ceremony became compulsory. Its constitutionality was never questioned until 1937 but had been litigated since then in at least 13 states. Members of Jehovah's Witnesses contended that the flag salute was unconstitutional as applied to them because their religious belief prohibited them from bowing down before any graven image.

State courts were moved by sociological issues as much as by the threat of infringement of religious freedom. Actions brought against parents to punish them for their children's refusal to salute the flag, under statutes imposing a penalty for contributing to the delinquency of minors, or under the compulsory school attendance laws, resulted in the setting aside of convictions in the lower courts in four out of five cases. Likewise, five cases brought against pupils on grounds of their being delinquent or "habitual school offenders" set aside the convictions of the lower courts which, if affirmed, would have resulted in the commitment of the children to state institutions. Even though nine of these ten courts refused to enforce the punishment imposed by statute, six of the cases upheld the flag-salute requirement as valid and not unconstitutional.

State courts also refused in five other cases to compel the school boards concerned to reinstate pupils who had been expelled for refusal to salute the flag. Although the power of the school board in discretionary matters was discussed in these cases, the primary consideration was given to the question of whether the flag salute was patriotic or religious in nature. In all five cases, it was held that the flag salute was in no sense religious.

The question went to the United States Supreme Court in 1940 in the case of *Minersville v. Gobitis*, 310 U.S. 586, referred to in the West Virginia decision quoted above. In the Gobitis case the Court seemed to be concerned principally with the propriety of passing upon an educational policy. It did not state in that case whether or not the salute should be considered a religious rite, nor whether

the compulsory nature of the regulation violated the religious freedom guaranteed by the Constitution. The decision was based rather on the theory that national unity demanded certain sacrifices of individual freedoms, including possibly religious freedom.

In the West Virginia decision the Supreme Court overruled the Gobitis case, with three dissenting justices. The Court held in substance that a school board in compelling pupils to salute and pledge allegiance to the American flag transcends constitutional limitations on its power and "invades the sphere of intellect and spirit which it is the purpose of the First Amendment to our Constitution to reserve from all official control."

Sources of Further Information

47 Am. Jur. "Schools" secs. 147, 151-159, 191-199, 216-219.
79 C.J.S. "Schools and School Districts" secs. 445-482.
A.L.R. "Schools" Topic Nos. 50-57, 59.
American Digest System "Schools and School Districts" Key Nos. 148-162.

Work Sheet

1. Between what ages are children in your state *permitted* to attend public schools free of charge?
2. Between what ages are they *required* to attend school?
3. What, if any, are the qualifications for admission to the public schools in your district in addition to age and residence?
4. What are the legal exceptions to compulsory school attendance?
5. In what occupations may children of compulsory school age be employed? During what hours and how many hours a week? Do these provisions conflict with school attendance?

Chapter 13.

TRANSPORTATION AT PUBLIC EXPENSE

Editorial Comment

Since some children live a distance from school, the availability of transportation facilities is an important part of the whole question of school attendance.

Some courts held that without express statutory power a school district cannot legally provide transportation at public expense; however, a more modern view is that general powers to do all things necessary for the government of the schools includes the power to pay for transportation. Since every state now provides statutory authority for pupil transportation, the power of a school district to do so without statutory authority is practically an academic question.

Of more importance, nowadays, is the issue of whether or not a school board is compelled to provide transportation in particular instances. Many states by statute require that local school boards furnish transportation at public expense for children who live as much as a certain distance from school. Most commonly the distance is two miles. However, some statutes do not prescribe any specified distance for pupil transportation and, instead, require that transportation be furnished if the pupil lives an unreasonable distance from school, or if his home is remote. Under such laws it is sometimes necessary for the court to interpret what is "unreasonable" or "remote." Courts have frequently supported school boards which require pupils to walk some distance to meet the bus on its route.

In connection with pupil transportation laws, or in separate enactments dealing with motor-vehicle regulations, standards of safety for school-bus equipment and the safe operation of school buses have been established in many states. Qualifications for school-bus drivers are frequently fixed by law or by state board of education regulation. In the absence of such standards set by legal authorities, parents of pupils

227

who must ride in school buses have no way to complain at law if
the school board uses unsafe equipment or careless drivers. All such
matters must be regulated by legislation, directly or indirectly. In
the absence of statutory standards, as for example in states where at
most the legislative requirement is merely that transportation be
comfortable and safe, only gross abuse of discretion in the eyes of
the law would give judicial relief to the parents who seek to obtain
safer equipment or more careful drivers.

Statutory Material

Kentucky Revised Statutes, sec. 158.110.

Boards of education shall furnish transportation from their general
funds or otherwise for pupils of elementary grade who do not reside
within reasonable walking distance of the school provided for them, and
any board of education may provide transportation from its general
funds or otherwise for any pupil of any grade who does not live within
a reasonable walking distance from the school provided for him. The
boards of education shall adopt such rules and regulations as will insure
the comfort, health and safety of the children who are transported,
consistent with the rules and regulations of the State Board of Education dealing with the transportation of pupils.

Statutory note. Kentucky is one of very few states which does not
provide for transportation, at least of elementary-school pupils, for
a specifically designated distance, such as two miles. Here, local
school boards are given discretionary power to determine when transportation is to be furnished and questions arise as to what the legislature meant by "a reasonable walking distance." The *Case Material*
points out the problem.

Notice in the first sentence that the board *shall* furnish transportation for elementary-school pupils and *may* furnish transportation for
others; but, in each case the crux of the mandate and the authority
rests on what the board considers to be a reasonable walking distance.

Many pupil transportation laws spell out details of how the comfort, health and safety of the children who are transported are to
be achieved. Kentucky leaves these questions to the state and local
boards of education.

Code of Virginia, secs. 22-284 through 22-294.

Sec. 22-284. No county, city or other public school unit (sometimes
herein referred to as "locality" or "localities"), in which any school pupils
or personnel are transported at public expense to or from any public
school supported in whole or in part by State funds, in any vehicle

owned or operated by, or owned or operated by any person under contract with, the locality or its school board, shall receive any State school funds, unless it complies with all applicable requirements of this article and full compliance therewith and satisfactory evidence to the Superintendent of Public Instruction of the effectuation of all requisite insurance are expressly made conditions precedent to the distribution of State school funds to localities.

Sec. 22-285. (1) Every vehicle so used shall be covered in a policy of public liability and property damage insurance, issued by an insurance carrier authorized to transact business in this State in the amounts of at least fifteen thousand dollars for injury, including death, to one person, one hundred thousand dollars for injury, including death, to all persons injured in any one accident, and five thousand dollars for damage, including destruction, to the property of any person, other than the insured.

(2) The insurance so effected is to be subject to all laws of this State regulating insurance.

(3) This insurance is not required in cases when pupils are transported on a common carrier if it be covered by a policy of insurance affording substantially the protection required by this article.

Sec. 22-286. In any case in which a vehicle used for transportation of school pupils and personnel regularly transports less than ten pupils the policy of insurance may be in amounts of (1) fifteen thousand dollars for injury, including death, to one person, (2) fifty thousand dollars for injury, including death, to all persons in any one accident, (3) one thousand dollars for damages, including destruction, to property of any person except that of the insured, and shall be subject to other provisions of this article.

Sec. 22-287. In every case in which a locality or its school board fails to obtain, or to require vehicles operated under contract with it to be covered by, the requisite insurance, by the first of August of any year, or fails to notify the Superintendent of Public Instruction of the effectuation of requisite insurance on or before the tenth of August, it shall be the duty of the Superintendent of Public Instruction, on or before the tenth of September, to obtain insurance complying with the requirements of this article on all vehicles to be used, as far as known to or reasonably ascertainable by him, for school pupil and personnel transportation in the ensuing session, and to expend for this purpose the requisite amount out of any State school funds otherwise distributable, or becoming distributable, to the particular locality so in default.

Sec. 22-288. Every policy of insurance issued in pursuance of the provisions of this article, in addition to compliance with other requirements of this article and with the requirements of other applicable laws, shall cover:

(1) Injury, including death, to school pupils and personnel, except the driver when not a pupil, riding as passengers on any of the vehicles so insured when used to transport such persons to or from any school at which they are required to be by State law or school regulations;

(2) Injury, including death, to any persons not passengers on any such vehicle;

(3) Damage, including destruction, to property of any person, other than the insured.

Sec. 22-289. In case any school pupil or personnel, except the driver when not a pupil, whether riding in the vehicle or not, or any other person suffers injury, including death, or property damage, including destruction, through the ownership, maintenance, use or operation of the vehicle it shall be sufficient, in any action for recovery upon the policy, to prove such facts and circumstances as are required to be shown in order to recover damages for death or injury to person or property, caused by the negligent operation of privately owned motor vehicles, in Virginia; provided that such pupils and personnel shall not be considered as guests, and section 8-646.1 shall not apply to them.

Sec. 22-290. In case the locality or the school board is the owner, or operator through medium of a driver, of, or otherwise is the insured under the policy upon, the vehicle involved in an accident the locality or school board shall be subject to action up to, but not beyond, the limits of valid and collectable insurance in force to cover the injury complained of and the defense of governmental immunity shall not be a bar to action or recovery, and in case of several claims for damages arising out of a single accident involving the vehicle, the claims of pupils and school personnel, excluding driver when not a pupil, shall be first satisfied, but in no event shall school funds be used to pay any claim or judgment or any person for any injury arising out of the operation of any such vehicle. The locality or school board so responsible may be sued alone, or jointly with the driver, provided that in no case shall any member of a school board be liable personally in the capacity of school trustee solely.

Sec. 22-291. In case the vehicle involved is not owned by the locality or school board but is operated under contract with the locality or school board and is involved in an accident, recovery may be had as provided for in section 22-289.

Sec. 22-292. If insurance be obtained but lapses while the vehicle is still being used or is proposed to be used to transport school pupils or personnel no school funds remaining to be distributed to the locality so in default shall be distributed to it until the terms of this article in this regard have been fully complied with.

Sec. 22-293. When the Superintendent of Public Instruction effects insurance as required by this article, he shall nevertheless not make any distribution of State school aid funds to the locality or school board so in default until he has been furnished with satisfactory assurances that all vehicles required by this article to be covered by insurance have been duly insured.

Sec. 22-294. The provisions of this article apply to all vehicles used in transporting school pupils and personnel at public expense to any public free school whether or not the requirements of the State Department of Education for its approval of vehicles for this use have been complied with, and irrespective of whether or not any State aid for transporting school pupils and personnel in the particular vehicle has been, is, or will be allocable.

Statutory note. Many, but not all, pupil transportation laws provide that school buses shall be insured. The Virginia law is one of the more specific; it includes a provision that if the local school board does not obtain insurance the state superintendent shall do so and withhold state-aid funds due the district so long as it is in default. The Virginia law is unusual also in that it permits suit to be brought to the extent of the insurance, though the defense of governmental immunity is denied.

At one time it was thought that denying the defense of governmental immunity solved the problem and Minnesota was one of the first states to require such an endorsement on all school-bus insurance policies; yet, the court said that governmental immunity could not be so waived.

General Statutes of North Carolina, secs. 115-193 through 115-197.

Sec. 115-193. The State Board of Education is hereby authorized and directed to set up in its budget for the operation of the public schools of the State a sum of money which it deems sufficient to pay the claims hereinafter authorized and provided for. The Board is hereby authorized and directed to pay out of said sum provided for this purpose to the parent, guardian, executor or administrator of any pupil who may be injured or whose death results from injuries received while such pupil is boarding, riding on, or alighting from a school bus owned and operated by any county or city administrative unit, and transporting pupils to or from the public schools of the State, or sustained as a result of the operation of a school bus on the grounds of the school in which such pupil is enrolled, medical, hospital, surgical, and funeral expenses incurred on account of such injuries or death of such pupil in an amount not to exceed six hundred dollars ($600.00). This section shall not apply to injuries sustained as a result of the operation of any activity bus as distinguished from a regular school bus.

Sec. 115-194. The State Board of Education is hereby authorized and empowered, under such rules and regulations as it may promulgate, to approve any claim authorized herein, and when such claim is so approved, such action shall be final: Provided, that the total benefits for hospitalization, medical treatment, and funeral expenses shall in no case exceed six hundred dollars ($600.00) for any pupil so injured.

Sec. 115-195. The claims authorized herein shall be paid by the said State Board of Education, regardless of whether the injury received by said pupil shall have been due to the negligence of the driver of the said school bus: Provided, that whenever there is recovery on account of said accident by the father, mother, guardian, or administrator of such pupil against any person, firm or corporation, the amount expended by the State Board of Education hereunder shall constitute a paramount lien on any judgment recovered by said parent, guardian, or administrator,

and shall be discharged before any money is paid to said parent, guardian, or administrator, on account of said judgment.

Sec. 115-196. Nothing in this article shall be construed to mean that the State shall be liable for sickness, or disease, or for personal injuries sustained otherwise than by reason of the operation of such bus.

Sec. 115-197. The right to compensation as authorized herein shall be forever barred unless a claim be filed with the State Board of Education within one year after the accident, and if death results from the accident, unless a claim be filed with the said Board within one year thereafter.

Statutory note. North Carolina and Alabama have set up in the state government claims offices for the payment of damages to injured pupils, thus avoiding the problem of governmental immunity. These statutes have been on the books of these states for many years, but the idea did not spread to other states even though many of them have had great difficulty in compensating injured pupils. The chief objection to the North Carolina statute is the meager amount payable; also, payments are limited to injuries sustained in transportation accidents. [The Alabama law applies to injuries regardless of where or how sustained.]

Case Material

Schmidt et al. v. Payne et al., 304 Ky. 58, 199 S.W. (2d) 990 (Kentucky, 1947). [Parents sought mandamus to compel school board to furnish transportation.]

Louis Payne and others, appellees, who are parents of 10 elementary school children of the independent school district of Shelbyville, sought a writ of mandamus to require Paul Schmidt and others, appellants, who are members of the board of education of the same district, to furnish school transportation for appellees' children. The chancellor having granted the writ, the board members are now appealing.

The chief contention of this appeal is that the trial court's judgment should be reversed because there exists no statutory authority requiring boards of *independent* school districts to furnish school transportation for any pupils of such districts. . . .

The evidence for appellees shows that their children, all of immature age, live on a hard surfaced but rather hazardous road, at distances varying from about 2 to 3 miles, leading southward from Shelbyville and from this school; that these parents have heretofore transported their children in their own conveyances to school rather than have them risk the hazards of sharp curves, motor traffic, a railroad crossing and bad weather. . . .

Appellees contend that KRS 158.110 requires *all* boards of education in this state to furnish school transportation to all elementary pupils who do not live within a reasonable walking distance of their respective schools.

Appellant board members contend that this statutory provision, which uses the words "boards of education," without further particularity, should

be interpreted to mean only *county* boards of education, not to mean *independent* school district boards, such as this one at Shelbyville. . . .

[After reviewing the history of school law in Kentucky, the court held that KRS 158.110 "wraps its mandatory force around these appellants as members of this independent school district at Shelbyville."]

But even though KRS 158.110 applies to independent schools, yet these schools, along with all other public schools facing the same problem, have, appellants further contend, a broad discretion in deciding whether or not appellees' children actually live within a reasonable walking distance of their school. . . .

So, now looking at the conditions of this specific case, we find that these young children were walking distances of 2 to 3 miles to their school at Shelbyville. We find that there was and is a tortuous road presenting a possible peril upon its pedestrians, particularly little children, in almost every furlong of its length. This road has neither sidewalks nor graveled berm. This route is one of heavy travel, both by trucks and other vehicles. This route crosses a narrow bridge, a railroad, a federal highway where fast-moving traffic continually chants a funeral dirge for the unwary. Now it does seem entirely possible to consider that one school route of 2 miles might constitute a reasonable walking distance while another and different school route of only 1 mile might constitute an unreasonable walking distance. The hazards and highway conditions of any particular route should certainly enter into a proper determination of what constitutes a reasonable walking distance. These hazards and highway conditions may be more decisive as determining factors in a question of this kind than the mere distance involved. Because of both the hazards and the distances proven in this specific case and as to appellees' particular route, we believe that appellants abused their discretion in deciding that appellees' chldren are within a reasonable walking distance of their school. . . .

Case note. The reasoning of this opinion suggests the idea that transportation laws providing for transportation of pupils who live a designated distance from school might be improved by deleting the specific distance or adding to it the provision that transportation shall be furnished when the pupil lives an unreasonable distance from school. However, sound as this court's reasoning seems to be, there would be no assurance that another court would look at the word "reasonable" in the same way. Probably the best safeguard would be to include in the transportation statute a definition of reasonable and unreasonable so as to require transportation over short but dangerous distances as well as long but safe distances. No transportation law is as specific as that, however.

Gandt v. Joint School District No. 3, 4 Wis. (2d) 419, 90 N. W. (2d) 549 (Wisconsin, 1958). [Measurement of distance for pupil transportation purposes.]

Sec. 40.53, Stats. provides that school boards of all school districts operating public elementary schools shall provide transportation to and from school for all pupils residing in the district two miles or more from the nearest public school they may attend. In Pagel v. School Dist., 1924, 184 Wis. 251, 199 N.W. 67, it was held that travel on a private road is included in ascertaining the distance between home and school.

The question involved is whether or not the distance between the home of the plaintiff and the school attended by his children entitles him to compensation for the cost of transporting his children.

Plaintiff's farm home is located south of a public road running east and west. The school house is to the east thereof. During the school years commencing in 1953 and 1954 plaintiff had a driveway located east of his house which the children used in going to and from school. On February 20, 1954 plaintiff and two members of the school board measured the distance between the house and the school as eleven feet short of two miles. Plaintiff claimed that the measurement deviated from the usually traveled route by cutting across his lawn. Before the commencement of the 1955 school year plaintiff established a driveway west of his house.

On June 13, 1957 the distance between house and school was remeasured. Several measurements were made and the route via the east driveway, as well as that via the west driveway, was found to be in excess of two miles. . . .

It is defendant's position that the 1954 measurement prevails. That was a question of fact for the trial court. It found that during each of the three school years involved the distance between home and school, measured along the "closest usually traveled route," was in excess of two miles. The 1954 measurement admittedly did not follow the east driveway but cut across the lawn to the back door of plaintiff's home. The children's mother testified that at that time the usually traveled route of the children was the east driveway and that there was no path across the lawn where the measurement was made. From the trial court's finding it is apparent that it rejected the 1954 measurement as not being the usually traveled route. The evidence supports the finding.

Defendant points out that there is no explanation in the record why plaintiff rerouted his driveway, and cites 22 Op. Attys. Gen. 783 to the effect that a private road lengthening the distance from home to school should not be used in measuring that distance if the lengthening of the private road was "palpably fraudulent and taken solely for the purpose of coming within the purview [sic] of the school transportation law. If the trial court had concluded that the 1954 measurement was to be accepted, it might have drawn the inference that the west driveway was established by the plaintiff for the purpose of coming within the statute, but it did not do so. The trial court having found, however, that the distance of the "closest usually traveled route" was more than two miles even before the west driveway was put in, there was no room for the inference that the driveway was changed to come within the statute. . . .

Case note. In contrast with the Kentucky statute and court decision thereunder, this case shows what can result when the statute names a specific distance beyond which pupils are not entitled to transportation. It is easy to imagine the local controversy that ended in the Gandt case; there were probably hard feelings on both sides. Even though the court found that the driveway was not changed so that the Gandt children would come within the two-mile limit, the facts indicate that two people measuring the shortest distance between two points can get different results.

Everson v. Board of Education of Ewing Township et al., 330 U.S. 1 (1947). [Transportation of parochial-school pupils at public expense.]

A New Jersey statute authorizes its local school districts to make rules and contracts for the transportaton of children to and from schools. The appellee, a township board of education, acting pursuant to this statute, authorized reimbursement to parents of money expended by them for the bus transportation of their children on regular busses operated by the public transportation system. Part of this money was for the payment of transportation of some children in the community to Catholic parochial schools. These church schools gave their students, in addition to secular education, regular religious instruction conforming to the religious tenets and modes of worship of the Catholic Faith. The superintendent of these schools is a Catholic priest.

The appellant, in his capacity as a district taxpayer, filed suit in a state court challenging the right of the Board to reimburse parents of parochial school students. He contended that the statute and the resolution passed pursuant to it violated both the State and the Federal Constitutions. That court held that the legislature was without power to authorize such payment under the state constitution. . . . The New Jersey Court of Errors and Appeals reversed, holding that neither the statute nor the resolution passed pursuant to it was in conflict with the State constitution or the provisions of the Federal Constitution in issue. . . .

The only contention here is that the state statute and the resolution, in so far as they authorized reimbursement to parents of children attending parochial schools, violate the Federal Constitution in these two respects, which to some extent overlap. *First.* They authorize the State to take by taxation the private property of some and bestow it upon others, to be used for their own private purposes. This, it is alleged, violates the due process clause of the Fourteenth Amendment. *Second.* The statute and the resolution forced inhabitants to pay taxes to help support and maintain schools which are dedicated to, and which regularly teach, the Catholic Faith. This is alleged to be a use of state power to support church schools contrary to the prohibition of the First Amendment which the Fourteenth Amendment made applicable to the states.

First. The due process argument that the state law taxes some people to help others carry out their private purposes is framed in two phases.

The first phase is that a state cannot tax A and reimburse B for the cost of transporting his children to church schools. This is said to violate the due process clause because the children are sent to these church schools to satisfy the personal desires of their parents, rather than the public's interest in the general education of all children. This argument, if valid, would apply equally to prohibit state payment for the transportation of children to any non-public school, whether operated by a church, or any other non-government individual or group. But, the New Jersey legislature has decided that a public purpose will be served by using tax-raised funds to pay the bus fares of all school children, including those who attend parochial schools. The New Jersey Court of Errors and Appeals has reached the same conclusion. The fact that a state law, passed to satisfy a public need, coincides with the personal desires of the individual most directly affected is certainly an inadequate reason for us to say that a legislature has erroneously appraised the public need.

It is true that this Court has, in rare instances, struck down state statutes on the ground that the purpose for which tax-raised funds were to be expended was not a public one. . . . But the Court has also pointed out that this far reaching authority must be exercised with the most extreme caution. . . . Otherwise, a state's power to legislate for the public welfare might be seriously curtailed, a power which is a primary reason for the existence of states. Changing local conditions create new local problems which may lead a state's people and its local authorities to believe that laws authorizing new types of public services are necessary to promote the general well-being of the people. The Fourteenth Amendment did not strip the states of their power to meet problems previously left for individual solution. . . .

It is much too late to argue that legislation intended to facilitate the opportunity of children to get a secular education serves no public purpose. The same thing is no less true of legislation to reimburse needy parents, or all parents, for payment of the fares of their children so that they can ride in public busses to and from schools rather than run the risk of traffic and other hazards incident to walking or "hitchhiking." . . . Nor does it follow that a law has a private rather than a public purpose because it provides that tax-raised funds will be paid to reimburse individuals on account of money spent by them in a way which furthers a public program. . . . Subsidies and loans to individuals such as farmers and home-owners, and to privately owned transportation systems, as well as many other kinds of businesses, have been commonplace practices in our state and national history.

Insofar as the second phase of the due process argument may differ from the first, it is by suggesting that taxation for transportation of children to church schools constitutes support of a religion by the State. But if the law is invalid for this reason, it is because it violates the First Amendment's prohibition against the establishment of religion by law. This is the exact question raised by appellant's second contention, to consideration of which we now turn.

Second. The New Jersey statute is challenged as a "law respecting an establishment of religion." The First Amendment, as made applicable to

the states by the Fourteenth, *Murdock v. Pennsylvania*, 319 U. S. 105, commands that a state "shall make no law respecting an establishment of religion, or prohibiting the free exercise thereof. . . ." These words of the First Amendment reflected in the minds of early Americans a vivid mental picture of conditions and practices which they fervently wished to stamp out in order to preserve liberty for themselves and for their posterity. Doubtless their goal has not been entirely reached; but so far has the Nation moved toward it that the expression "law respecting an establishment of religion," probably does not so vividly remind present-day Americans of the evils, fears, and political problems that caused that expression to be written into our Bill of Rights. Whether this New Jersey law is one respecting the "establishment of religion" requires an understanding of the meaning of that language, particularly with respect to the imposition of taxes. Once again, therefore, it is not inappropriate briefly to review the background and environment of the period in which that constitutional language was fashioned and adopted.

A large proportion of the early settlers of this country came here from Europe to escape the bondage of laws which compelled them to support and attend government-favored churches. The centuries immediately before and contemporaneous with the colonization of America had been filled with turmoil, civil strife, and persecutions, generated in large part by established sects determined to maintain their absolute political and religious supremacy. With the power of government supporting them, at various times and places, Catholics had persecuted Protestants, Protestants had persecuted Catholics, Protestant sects had persecuted other Protestant sects, Catholics of one shade of belief had persecuted Catholics of another shade of belief, and all of these had from time to time persecuted Jews. In efforts to force loyalty to whatever religious group happened to be on top and in league with the government of a particular time and place, men and women had been fined, cast in jail, cruelly tortured, and killed. Among the offenses for which these punishments had been inflicted were such things as speaking disrespectfully of the views of ministers of government-established churches, non-attendance at those churches, expressions of non-belief in their doctrines, and failure to pay taxes and tithes to support them.

These practices of the old world were transplanted to and began to thrive in the soil of the new America. The very charters granted by the English Crown to the individuals and companies designated to make the laws which would control the destinies of the colonials authorized these individuals and companies to erect religious establishments which all, whether believers or non-believers, would be required to support and attend. An exercise of this authority was accompanied by a repetition of many of the old-world practices and persecutions. Catholics found themselves hounded and proscribed because of their faith; Quakers who followed their conscience went to jail; Baptists were peculiarly obnoxious to certain dominant Protestant sects; men and women of varied faiths who happened to be in a minority in a particular locality were persecuted because they stead-fastly persisted in worshipping God only as their own conscience dictated. And all of these dissenters were compelled to pay

tithes and taxes to support government-sponsored churches whose ministers preached inflammatory sermons designed to strengthen and consolidate the established faith by generating a burning hatred against dissenters.

These practices became so commonplace as to shock the freedom-loving colonials into a feeling of abhorrence. The imposition of taxes to pay ministers' salaries and to build and maintain churches and church property aroused their indignation. It was these feelings which found expression in the First Amendment. No one locality and no one group throughout the Colonies can rightly be given entire credit for having aroused the sentiment that culminated in adoption of the Bill of Rights' provisions embracing religious liberty. But Virginia, where the established church had achieved a dominant influence in political affairs and where many excesses attracted wide public attention, provided a great stimulus and able leadership for the movement. The people there, as elsewhere, reached the conviction that individual religious liberty could be achieved best under a government which was stripped of all power to tax, to support, or otherwise to assist any or all religions, or to interfere with the beliefs of any religious individual or group.

The movement toward this end reached its dramatic climax in Virginia in 1785-86 when the Virginia legislative body was about to renew Virginia's tax levy for the support of the established church. Thomas Jefferson and James Madison led the fight against this tax. Madison wrote his great Memorial and Remonstrance against the law. In it, he eloquently argued that a true religion did not need the support of law; that no person, either believer or non-believer, should be taxed to support a religious institution of any kind; that the best interest of a society required that the minds of men always be wholly free; and that cruel persecutions were the inevitable result of government-established religions. Madison's Remonstrance received strong support throughout Virginia, and the Assembly postponed consideration of the proposed tax measure until its next session. When the proposal came up for consideration at that session, it not only died in committee, but the Assembly enacted the famous "Virginia Bill for Religious Liberty" originally written by Thomas Jefferson. The preamble to that Bill stated among other things that

> "Almighty God hath created the mind free; that all attempts to influence it by temporal punishments, or burthens, or civil incapacitations, tend only to beget habits of hypocrisy and meanness, and are a departure from the plan of the Holy author of our religion, who being Lord both of body and mind, yet chose not to propagate it by coercions on either . . .; that to compel a man to furnish contributions of money for the propagation of opinions which he disbelieves, is sinful and tyrannical; that even the forcing him to support this or that teacher of his own religious persuasion, is depriving him of the comfortable liberty of giving his contributions to the particular pastor, whose morals he would make his pattern. . . ."

And the statute itself enacted

"That no man shall be compelled to frequent or support any religious worship, place, or ministry whatsover, nor shall be enforced, restrained, molested, or burthened, in his body or goods, nor shall otherwise suffer on account of his religious opinions or belief. . . ."

This Court has previously recognized that the provisions of the First Amendment, in the drafting and adoption of which Madison and Jefferson played such leading roles, had the same objective and were intended to provide the same protection against governmental intrusion on religious liberty as the Virginia statute. . . . Prior to the adoption of the Fourteenth Amendment, the First Amendment did not apply as a restraint against the states. Most of them did soon provide similar constitutional protections for religious liberty. But some states persisted for about half a century in imposing restraints upon the free exercise of religion and in discriminating against particular religious groups. In recent years, so far as the provision against the establishment of a religion is concerned, the question has most frequently arisen in connection with proposed state aid to church schools and efforts to carry on religious teachings in the public schools in accordance with the tenets of a particular sect. Some churches have either sought or accepted state financial support for their schools. Here again the efforts to obtain aid or acceptance of it have not been limited to any one particular faith. The state courts, in the main, have remained faithful to the language of their own constitutional provisions designed to protect religious freedom and to separate religions and governments. Their decisions, however, show the difficulty in drawing the line between tax legislation which provides funds for the welfare of the general public and that which is designed to support institutions which teach religion.

The meaning and scope of the First Amendment, preventing establishment of religion or prohibiting the free exercise thereof, in the light of its history and the evils it was designed forever to suppress, have been several times elaborated by the decisions of this Court prior to the application of the First Amendment to the states by the Fourteenth. The broad meaning given the Amendment by these earlier cases has been accepted by this Court in its decisions concerning an individual's religious freedom rendered since the Fourteenth Amendment was interpreted to make the prohibitions of the First applicable to state action abridging religious freedom. There is every reason to give the same application and broad interpretation to the "establishment of religion" clause. The interrelation of these complementary clauses was well summarized in a statement of the Court of Appeals of South Carolina, quoted with approval by this Court, in *Watson v. Jones*, 13 Wall. 679, 730: "The structure of our government has, for the preservation of civil liberty, rescued the temporal institutions from religious interference. On the other hand, it has secured religious liberty from the invasions of the civil authority."

The "establishment of religion" clause of the First Amendment means at least this: Neither a state nor the Federal Government can set up a church. Neither can pass laws which aid one religion, aid all religions,

or prefer one religion over another. Neither can force nor influence a person to go to or to remain away from church against his will or force him to profess a belief or disbelief in any religion. No person can be punished for entertaining or professing religious beliefs or disbeliefs, for church attendance or non-attendance. No tax in any amount, large or small, can be levied to support any religious activities or institutions, whatever they may be called, or whatever form they may adopt to teach or practice religion. Neither a state nor the Federal Government can, openly or secretly, participate in the affairs of any religious organizations or groups and *vice versa*. In the words of Jefferson, the clause against establishment of religion by law was intended to erect "a wall of separation between Church and State." . . .

We must consider the New Jersey statute in accordance with the foregoing limitations imposed by the First Amendment. But we must not strike that state statute down if it is within the State's constitutional power even though it approaches the verge of that power. New Jersey cannot consistently with the "establishment of religion" clause of the First Amendment contribute tax-raised funds to the support of an institution which teaches the tenets and faith of any church. On the other hand, other language of the amendment commands that New Jersey cannot hamper its citizens in the free exercise of their own religion. Consequently, it cannot exclude individual Catholics, Lutherans, Mohammedans, Baptists, Jews, Methodists, Non-believers, Presbyterians, or the members of any other faith, *because of their faith, or lack of it,* from receiving the benefits of public welfare legislation. While we do not mean to intimate that a state could not provide transportation only to children attending public schools, we must be careful, in protecting the citizens of New Jersey against state-established churches, to be sure that we do not inadvertently prohibit New Jersey from extending its general State law benefits to all its citizens without regard to their religious belief.

Measured by these standards, we cannot say that the First Amendment prohibits New Jersey from spending tax-raised funds to pay the bus fares of parochial school pupils as a part of a general program under which it pays the fares of pupils attending public and other schools. It is undoubtedly true that children are helped to get to church schools. There is even a possibility that some of the children might not be sent to the church schools if the parents were compelled to pay their children's bus fares out of their own pockets when transportation to a public school would have been paid for by the State. The same possibility exists where the state requires a local transit company to provide reduced fares to school children including those attending parochial schools, or where a municipally owned transportation system undertakes to carry all school children free of charge. Moreover, state-paid policemen, detailed to protect children going to and from church schools from the very real hazards of traffic, would serve much the same purpose and accomplish much the same result as state provisions intended to guarantee free transportation of a kind which the state deems to be best for the school children's welfare. And parents might refuse to risk their children to the serious danger of traffic accidents going to and from parochial schools, the approaches

to which were not protected by policemen. Similarly, parents might be reluctant to permit their children to attend schools which the state had cut off from such general government services as ordinary police and fire protection, connections for sewage disposal, public highways and sidewalks. Of course, cutting off church schools from these services, so separate and so indisputably marked off from the religious function, would make it far more difficult for the schools to operate. But such is obviously not the purpose of the First Amendment. That Amendment requires the state to be a neutral in its relations with groups of religious believers and non-believers; it does not require the state to be their adversary. State power is no more to be used so as to handicap religions, than it is to favor them.

This Court has said that parents may, in the discharge of their duty under state compulsory education laws, send their children to a religious rather than a public school if the school meets the secular educational requirements which the state has power to impose. See *Pierce v. Society of Sisters*, 268 U. S. 510. It appears that these parochial schools meet New Jersey's requirements. The State contributes no money to the schools. It does not support them. Its legislation, as applied, does no more than provide a general program to help parents get their children, regardless of their religion, safely and expeditiously to and from accredited schools.

The First Amendment has erected a wall between church and state. That wall must be kept high and impregnable. We could not approve the slightest breach. New Jersey has not breached it here.

Affirmed.

Dissenting opinions: (1) . . . In fact, the undertones of the opinion, advocating complete and uncompromising separation of Church from State, seem utterly discordant with its conclusion yielding support to their commingling in educational matters. The case which irresistibly comes to mind as the most fitting precedent is that of Julia who, according to Byron's reports, "whispering 'I will ne'er consent,'—consented." . . . The state cannot maintain a Church and it can no more tax its citizens to furnish free carriage to those who attend a Church. The prohibition against establishment of religion cannot be circumvented by a subsidy, bonus or reimbursement of expense to individuals for receiving religious instruction and indoctrination. . . . Of course, the state may pay out tax-raised funds to relieve pauperism, but it may not under our Constitution do so to induce or reward piety. It may spend funds to secure old age against want, but it may not spend funds to secure religion against skepticism. It may compensate individuals for loss of employment, but it cannot compensate them for adherence to a creed. . . . A policeman protects a Catholic, of course—but not because he is a Catholic; it is because he is a man and a member of our society. The fireman protects the Church school—but not because it is a Church school; it is because it is property. . . . That there is no parallel between police and fire protection and this plan of reimbursement is apparent from the incongruity of the limitation of this Act if applied to police and fire service. Could we sustain an act that said the police shall protect pupils on the

way to or from public schools and Catholic schools but not while going
to and coming from other schools. . . .?

(2) . . . Legislatures are free to make, and courts to sustain, appropriations only when it can be found that in fact they do not aid, promote,
encourage or sustain religious teaching or observances, be the amount
large or small. No such finding has been or could be made in this case.
The Amendment has removed this form of promoting the public welfare
from legislative and judicial competence to make a public function. It is
exclusively a private affair. . . . It was to create a complete and permanent
separation of the spheres of religious activity and civil authority by com-
prehensively forbidding every form of public aid or support for religion.
. . . In view of this history no further proof is needed that the Amendment forbids any appropriation, large or small, from public funds to
aid or support any and all religious exercises.

Case note. The last dissenting opinion included an extensive history
of the separation of church and state, including Madison's "Remonstrance against Religious Assessments" and other historic papers. Both
dissenting opinions expressed the view that the Court in its majority
opinion had laid down certain principles and then decided the case
contrary to its principles.

The majority seem to have decided this case on the same theory of
child benefit as was used by the Court in the Cochran textbook case
(see p. 251). The New Jersey transportation law authorized the
payment of transportation costs of all children attending public or
private schools, except private schools operated for profit. Thus the
language of the New Jersey statute is different from that of the
Louisiana textbook law—yet sufficiently like it to have justified the
majority decision were it not for the fact that the township school
board resolution, implementing the statute, definitely and explicitly
provided for the payment of fares of children attending the Catholic
schools only. When the resolution and the statute are considered together, the majority opinion does not seem to be good reasoning.

Sources of Further Information

47 Am. Jur. "Schools" secs. 160-166.
79 C.J.S. "Schools and School Districts" secs. 475-482.
A.L.R. "Schools" Topic No. 58.
American Digest System "Schools and School Districts" Key No.
159½.

Work Sheet

Find the transportation law of your state before answering the
following questions:

1. Under what circumstances may the school board in your district furnish free transportation for pupils?

2. Is the furnishing of free pupil transportation under these circumstances mandatory, or is it within the discretion of the local district?

3. Are standards of bus equipment set forth in the law? If not, has the state board of education or the motor-vehicle department of the state issued any such standards?

4. Is school-bus insurance permitted or required?

5. Have specific rules of the road been promulgated for safety of pupils in transportation?

6. What are the qualifications for school-bus drivers?

7. Does the pupil transportation service, and its equipment, in your district satisfy all requirements for the safety of pupils served?

Chapter 14.

TEXTBOOKS AND CURRICULUM

Editorial Comment

Historically, the courts at first conceded the power of school boards to furnish such materials as dictionaries, where one copy would do for many pupils, under general powers to furnish "educational appliances," but refused the boards' contention that they had a right under such general statutes to purchase books for individual pupils. In the absence of a permissive statute, the courts have denied that school boards have implied power even to furnish textbooks at reduced rates, since school boards have only the powers granted by express or implied language of the statutes. Hence statutory authorization for free textbooks has been enacted in most states.

Free textbooks are supplied to public-school pupils in most states, although frequently the initial step was required to be taken by the electorate. In at least three states, the state board of education has discretionary power, by statute, to furnish free textbooks. In some states only elementary-school books are furnished free.

Providing free textbooks does not prevent a school board from requiring a deposit from financially able pupils to cover textbooks used, when the deposit is refunded if the books are returned in a reasonable condition, due allowance made for ordinary wear and tear but deductions made for unreasonable usage. Legal justification for such a deposit charge lies in the express or implied responsibility of the board for the proper care and preservation of the books.

The textbooks which are furnished public-school pupils are sometimes state-adopted or county-adopted; that is, all the texts for a particular level and subject are the same throughout the state, or the county, and the law prohibits the use of any other textbooks. More often, each local school board may select the books it wishes to use from a list prepared by the state or county board of education; it can use any book on the list but no other. These prohibitions do not

extend to books for supplementary reading, although occasionally a particular book is banned as objectionable.

Some states print their own textbooks for the public schools; others provide by law for contracts with publishers. It is usually provided that school officers and employees cannot have any financial interest in these contracts, this in order to prevent the adoption of books regardless of quality which would benefit any of the persons authorized to approve adoption. When a textbook has been adopted, it may not be changed sooner than the law permits, this to conserve the finances of the textbook fund. Other provisions regarding the adoption and use of textbooks may be found in the textbook law quoted in the *Statutory Material* in this chapter.

Some states have state-adopted courses of study prescribed by law or by state board of education regulation; in other states there is meager prescription at the state level as to the content of courses. However, practically every state has some statutory requirements as to subjects to be taught in the public schools. When the curriculum is fixed by state law or state board of education regulation, parents cannot compel the local school board to modify the state standards for their own children; nor can local school boards avoid the minimum standards fixed by state law or regulation. A prescribed course cannot be discontinued.

By way of illustration of the types of curriculum prescriptions sometimes found in state laws, the following may be mentioned: physiology and hygiene, the nature and effects of alcoholic drinks and narcotics, the United States Constitution, American history, civics, citizenship, state history, patriotism, forestry and allied agricultural subjects, and humane treatment of animals. A few state laws also enumerate the subjects to be taught in elementary grades, but in most states this matter is left to state board regulation.

Although a legislature can prohibit the teaching of a subject in the public schools, it cannot prohibit children from learning a subject outside the public schools. In the absence of a state prescription, local school boards have discretion as to whether or not a course is to be offered. In the absence of a state-adopted or locally prescribed course of study or syllabus, teachers have some discretionary authority in the outline of their courses.

One of the most controversial curriculum questions has to do with sectarian education in the public schools. Twelve state constitutions prohibit sectarian instruction or influence in the public school. A num-

ber of states, including some of these twelve with constitutional provisions, have enacted legislation to the same effect.

These constitutional provisions have been invoked in controversies over sectarian instruction in a number of quite different circumstances. Most states by law either require or permit the reading of the Bible in the schools, and the majority of the courts have held that Bible reading is not sectarian education. Bible reading, within the meaning of these statutes and as interpreted by these courts, refers only to the reading of a passage as a part of the opening exercises. Study of the Bible as a textbook with an examination following was held to be invalid and contrary to the Washington State Constitution.

Since the use of public-school funds for sectarian education is expressly unconstitutional in many states, and impliedly unconstitutional in most other states, a plan which has come to be known as "released time" was devised some 45 years ago. Under such a plan, pupils are usually released from the regular school curriculum for an hour or so a week to attend whichever church their parents choose for religious education under the auspices of the church. The Supreme Court of the United States and several state supreme courts have upheld this type of released-time plan.

The Supreme Court, however, invalidated a different type of released-time plan which, although less common, has been used in a number of districts, exemplified by Champaign, Ill. In the Champaign program, which the Court declared to be unconstitutional, the church-sponsored teachers of religion were brought into the school buildings where they conducted classes in religion with the cooperation of the school board and its staff. This type of religious education, the Court held to violate the First Amendment to the Federal Constitution (see p. 260).

Statutory Material

Baldwin's Ohio Revised Code, secs. 3329.01, 3329.05 through 3329.11.

Sec. 3329.01. Any publisher of schoolbooks in the United States desiring to offer schoolbooks for use by pupils in the public schools of Ohio, before such books may be adopted and purchased by any school board, must file in the office of the superintendent of public instruction, a copy of each book proposed to be so offered, together with the published list wholesale price thereof. No revised edition of any such book shall be used in public schools until a copy of such edition has been filed in the office of the superintendent together with the published list wholesale price thereof. The superintendent must carefully preserve in his office all such copies of books and the price thereof.

Sec. 3329.05. Sections 3329.01 to 3329.04, inclusive, and section 3329.08 of the Revised Code do not apply to the purchase of supplementary reading books, library books, reference books, or any other books except textbooks, required by the board of education. All of such books except textbooks required by the board, shall be ordered, received, examined, and paid for in the same manner and by the same persons as other supplies and equipment.

Sec. 3329.06. The board of education of each city, exempted village, and local school district shall furnish, free of charge, the necessary textbooks to the pupils attending the public schools. Pupils wholly or in part supplied with necessary textbooks shall be supplied only as other or new books are needed. A board may limit its purchase and ownership of books needed for its schools to six subjects per year, the cost of which shall not exceed twenty-five per cent of the entire cost of adoption. All textbooks furnished as provided in this section shall be the property of the district, and loaned to the pupils on such terms as each such board prescribes. . . .

Sec. 3329.07. The board of education of each city, exempted village, and local school district shall cause it to be ascertained and at a regular meeting determine which, and the number of each of the textbooks the schools under its charge require. The clerk at once shall order the books agreed upon from the publisher, who on the receipt of such order must ship them to the clerk without delay. He forthwith shall examine the books, and, if found right and in accordance with the order, remit the amount to the publisher. The board must pay for the books so purchased and in addition all charges for the transportation of the books out of the general fund of said district or out of such other funds as it may have available for such purchase of textbooks. If such board at any time can secure from the publishers books at less than such maximum price, they shall do so, and without unnecessary delay may make effort to secure such lower price before adopting any particular textbooks.

Sec. 3329.08. At a regular meeting, held between the first Monday in February and the first Monday in August, the board of education of each local school district, from lists adopted by the county board of education and the board of education of city and exempted village school districts shall determine by a majority vote of all members elected which of such textbooks so filed shall be used in the schools under its control. No textbooks shall be changed, nor any part thereof altered or revised, nor any other textbook substituted therefor, within four years after the date of selection and adoption thereof, as shown by the official records of such boards, except by the consent, at a regular meeting, of four-fifths of all members elected thereto. Books so substituted shall be adopted for the full term of four years.

Sec. 3329.09. Each city, exempted village, and local board of education shall make all necessary provisions and arrangements to place the books purchased within easy reach of and accessible to all the pupils in their district. In city and exempted village school districts the superintendent of schools and in local school districts the clerk of the board of education shall be the custodian of all schoolbooks purchased for the use of and

furnished free to all the pupils attending public schools of such district. They shall distribute such books, keep such records, maintain such accounts, and make such reports as the board requires. The board may employ such additional help as is necessary to properly administer this section.

This section does not prohibit any pupil, or the parent of any pupil, from purchasing textbooks for their own use, or the use of their children or wards in the schools of the district in which such purchaser resides. The board in each school district upon the request of a pupil, or the parent of any pupil, shall sell to such individual making the request textbooks of the kind requested at a price not to exceed the cost paid therefor plus ten per cent. The proceeds of such sales shall be credited to the fund from which payments are made by the board for the purchase of textbooks.

Sec. 3329.10. A superintendent, supervisor, principal, or teacher employed by any board of education shall not act as sales agent, either directly or indirectly, for any person, firm, or corporation whose school textbooks are filed with the superintendent of public instruction, or for school apparatus or equipment of any kind for use in the public schools. A violation of this section shall work a forfeiture of their certificates to teach in the public schools.

Sec. 3329.11. No person shall offer or give a reward or consideration, or make a present or reduction in price to a person employed in a public school, or to an officer having authority or control over it, for favoring, recommending, or advocating the introduction, adoption, or use in such school, of a textbook, map, chart, globe, or other school supply, or shall induce him to do so, or, no employee or officer of such school shall accept, offer, or agree to receive or accept a reward, consideration, present, gift, or reduction in price for so doing.

Statutory note. The Ohio law is fairly typical. Most states have enacted procedures for the adoption of textbooks; they provide that these procedures do not apply to supplementary and library books; they prohibit school employees from having an interest in the books proposed for adoption or acting as salesmen for the publisher. The limitation on frequency of changing adopted textbooks is necessary for financial reasons.

New Jersey Statutes Annotated, secs. 18:14-83.1, 18:14-85.1 through 18:14-85.3, 18:19-3, 18:19-8, 18:19-9.

18:14-83.1 Courses in civics, geography, history and responsibilities of citizenship. Each board of education shall adopt a course of study in community civics, the geography, history and civics of New Jersey, and the privileges and responsibilities of citizenship as they relate to community and national welfare, which course shall be taken by all pupils in the public elementary schools in the grade or grades in which it is given, with the object of producing the highest type of patriotic citizenship. 18:14-85.1 History of United States in high school. The superintendent of schools in each school district shall prepare and recommend to the

board of education of the district, and the board of education shall adopt, when approved by the State Board of Education on the recommendation of the Commissioner of Education, a suitable two-year course of study in the history of the United States to be given to each student during the last four years of high school.

18:14-85.2 Nature and purpose of history course. Such course of study shall include instruction in the priniciples and ideals of the American form of representative government as expressed by the framers of the Declaration of Independence and of the Constitution of the United States, in said documents and particularly in the Bill of Rights, and in the history of the origin and growth of the social, economic and cultural development of the United States, of American family life, and of the high standard of living and other privileges enjoyed by the citizens of the United States, and in such other events in the history of the United States as will tend to instill, into every girl and boy, a determination to preserve these principles and ideals as the principles and ideals of citizens of the United States, and an appreciation of their solemn duty and obligation to exercise the privilege of the ballot, upon their reaching voting age, to the end that such principles and ideals may be so preserved.

18:14-85.3 Instruction in humanity. Each board of education may teach, by special courses or by emphasis in appropriate places of the curriculum in a manner adapted to the ages and capabilities of the pupils in the several grades and departments, the principles of humanity as the same apply to kindness, and avoidance of cruelty, to animals and birds, both wild and domesticated.

18:19-3 Instruction in prevention. All boards of education and boards or persons having control of other schools in this State shall provide for instruction in accident prevention adapted to the understanding of the pupils of the various grades and classes in such schools.

18:19-8 Regular courses in all schools. Regular courses of instruction in the constitution of the United States shall be given in all public and private schools.

18:19-9 Grades and courses wherein instruction required. Instruction shall begin not later than the opening of the seventh grade, or in private schools a grade equivalent thereto, and shall continue in the high school course and in courses in state colleges, universities, and the educational departments of state and municipal institutions, to an extent to be determined by the state commissioner of education.

Statutory note. Even these many quotations from New Jersey law are not exhaustive of the curriculum prescriptions of that state and some other states have a greater number of prescriptions.

It should be noted that private as well as public schools must teach certain subjects, such as the Constitution of the United States. It is within the constitutional power of a legislature to prescribe courses in private schools, although it cannot proscribe any subject which is not harmful to the pupils. The police power enables a legislature to

require that all children be prepared for good citizenship, regardless of the school they attend.

Purdon's Pennsylvania Statutes Annotated. Title 24, sec. 15-1516, as amended in 1959.

At least ten verses from the Holy Bible shall be read, without comment, at the opening of each public school on each school day. Any child shall be excused from such Bible reading, or attending such Bible reading, upon the written request of his parent or guardian.

Statutory note. The Pennsylvania law was amended to permit objecting pupils to be excused from Bible reading after a federal lower court held that the Pennsylvania law was an unconstitutional denial of religious liberty. Many Bible-reading statutes do not contain this specific point; some of them operate illegally by requiring all pupils to participate; others tacitly excuse pupils who object.

Case Material

Cochran v. Louisiana State Board of Education, 281 U.S. 370 (1930). [Taxpayers sought to restrain state board of education from supplying free textbooks to children attending nonpublic schools.]

The appellants, as citizens and taxpayers of the State of Louisiana, brought this suit to restrain the State Board of Education and other state officials from expending any part of the severance tax fund in purchasing school books and in supplying them free of cost to the school children of the State, under Acts No. 100 and No. 143 of 1928, upon the ground that the legislation violated specific provisions of the constitution of the State and also Section 4 of Article IV and the Fourteenth Amendment of the Federal Constitution. The Supreme Court of the State affirmed the judgment of the trial court, which refused to issue an injunction. 168 La. 1030.

Act No. 100 of 1928 provided that the severance tax fund of the State, after allowing funds and appropriations as required by the state constitution, should be devoted "first, to supplying school books to the school children of the state." The Board of Education was directed to provide "school books for school children free of cost to such children." Act. No. 143 of 1928 made appropriations in accordance with the above provisions.

The Supreme Court of the State, following its decision in *Borden v. Louisiana State Board of Education,* 168 La. 1005, held that these acts were not repugnant to either the state or the Federal Constitution. . . .

The contention of the appellant under the Fourteenth Amendment is that taxation for the purchase of school books constituted a taking of private property for a private purpose. . . . The purpose is said to be to aid private, religious, sectarian, and other schools not embraced in the public educational system of the State by furnishing text-books free to the children attending such private schools. The operation and effect of

the legislation in question were described by the Supreme Court of the State as follows (168 La., p. 1020):

"One may scan the acts in vain to ascertain where any money is appropriated for the purchase of school books for the use of any church, private, sectarian or even public school. The appropriations were made for the specific purpose of purchasing school books for the use of the school children of the state, free of cost to them. It was for their benefit and the resulting benefit to the state that the appropriations were made. True, these children attend some school, public or private, the latter, sectarian or non-sectarian, and that the books are to be furnished them for their use, free of cost, whichever they attend. The schools, however, are not the beneficiaries of these appropriations. They obtain nothing from them, nor are they relieved of a single obligation, because of them. The school children and the state alone are the beneficiaries. It is also true that the sectarian schools, which some of the children attend, instruct their pupils in religion, and books are used for that purpose, but one may search diligently the acts, though without result, in an effort to find anything to the effect that it is the purpose of the state to furnish religious books for the use of such children. . . . What the statutes contemplate is that the same books that are furnished children attending public schools shall be furnished children attending private schools. This is the only practical way of interpreting and executing the statutes, and this is what the state board of education is doing. Among these books, naturally, none is to be expected, adapted to religious instruction."

The Court also stated, although the point is not of importance in relation to the Federal question, that it was "only the use of the books that is granted to the children or, in other words, the books are lent to them."

Viewing the statute as having the effect thus attributed to it, we cannot doubt that the taxing power of the State is exerted for a public purpose. The legislation does not segregate private schools, or their pupils, as its beneficiaries or attempt to interfere with any matters of exclusively private concern. Its interest is education, broadly; its method, comprehensive. Individual interests are aided only as the common interest is safeguarded.

Affirmed.

Case note. As usual, much depends upon the language of a statute. Here the legislative intent might have been to provide free textbooks to children attending parochial as well as public schools, so that the parochial-school pupils would not be "discriminated against" by a benefit which would otherwise be available to children attending public schools only. At any rate, the statute was so stated that, on the ground of the child-benefit theory, the courts found nothing unconstitutional in it.

Since this decision, the Louisiana law was amended to provide other school supplies such as paper and pencils to the children of the state

free of charge, and these supplies are furnished to the children attending the parochial schools also.

It is quite possible that the Court would rule otherwise if the language of a statute provided free textbooks and supplies to be furnished to sectarian schools for their pupils, although even that may be doubtful in view of the Everson decision (see p. 235).

Meyer v. State of Nebraska, 262 U.S. 390 (1923). [Private-school teacher was arrested for teaching in German, contrary to state law.]

Plaintiff in error was tried and convicted in the District Court for Hamilton County, Nebraska, under an information which charged that on May 25, 1920, while an instructor in Zion Parochial School, he unlawfully taught the subject of reading in the German language to Raymond Parpart, a child of ten years, who had not attained and successfully passed the eighth grade. The information is based upon "An act relating to the teaching of foreign languages in the State of Nebraska," approved April 9, 1919, . . .

The Supreme Court of the State affirmed the judgment of conviction. 107 Neb. 657. It declared the offense charged and established was "the direct and intentional teaching of the German language as a distinct subject to a child who had not passed the eighth grade." . . . And it held that the statute forbidding this did not conflict with the Fourteenth Amendment, but was a valid exercise of the police power. . . .

The challenged statute forbids the teaching in school of any subject except in English; also the teaching of any other language until the pupil has attained and successfully passed the eighth grade, which is not usually accomplished before the age of twelve. The Supreme Court of the State has held that "the so-called ancient or dead languages" are not "within the spirit or the purpose of the act." . . . Latin, Greek, Hebrew are not proscribed; but German, French, Spanish, Italian and every other alien speech are within the ban. Evidently the legislature has attempted materially to interfere with the calling of modern language teachers, with the opportunities of pupils to acquire knowledge, and with the power of parents to control the education of their own.

It is said the purpose of the legislation was to promote civic development by inhibiting training and education of the immature in foreign tongues and ideals before they could learn English and acquire American ideals; and "that the English language should be and become the mother tongue of all children reared in this state." It is also affirmed that the foreign born population is very large, that certain communities commonly use foreign words, follow foreign leaders, move in a foreign atmosphere, and that the children are thereby hindered from becoming citizens of the most useful type and the public safety is imperiled.

That the State may do much, go very far indeed, in order to improve the quality of its citizens, physically, mentally, and morally, is clear; but the individual has certain fundamental rights which must be respected. The protection of the Constitution extends to all, to those who speak

other languages as well as to those born with English on the tongue. Perhaps it would be highly advantageous if all had ready understanding of our ordinary speech, but this cannot be coerced by methods which conflict with the Constitution—a desirable end cannot be promoted by prohibited means.

For the welfare of his Ideal Common-Wealth, Plato suggested a law which should provide: ". . . That the proper officers will take the off-spring of the good parents to the pen or fold, and there they will deposit them with certain nurses who dwell in a separate quarter; but the off-spring of the inferior, or the better when they chance to be deformed, will be put away in some mysterious, unknown place, as they should be." In order to submerge the individual and develop ideal citizens, Sparta assembled the males at seven into barracks and intrusted their subsequent education and training to official guardians. Although such measures have been deliberately approved by men of great genius, their ideas touching the relation between individual and State were wholly different from those upon which our institutions rest; and it hardly will be affirmed that any legislature could impose such restrictions upon the people of a State without doing violence to both letter and spirit of the Constitution. The desire of the legislature to foster a homogeneous people with American ideals prepared readily to understand current discussions of civic matters is easy to appreciate. Unfortunate experiences during the late war and aversion toward every characteristic of truculent adversaries were certainly enough to quicken that aspiration.

But the means adopted, we think, exceed the limitations upon the power of the State and conflict with rights assured to plaintiff in error. The interference is plain enough and no adequate reason therefor in time of peace and domestic tranquility has been shown.

The power of the State to compel attendance at some school and to make reasonable regulations for all schools, including a requirement that they shall give instructions in English is not questioned. Nor has challenge been made of the State's power to prescribe a curriculum for institutions which it supports. Those matters are not within the present controversy. Our concern is with the prohibition approved by the Supreme Court. . . . No emergency has arisen which renders knowledge by a child of some language other than English so clearly harmful as to justify its inhibition with the consequent infringement of rights long freely enjoyed. We are constrained to conclude that the statute as applied is arbitrary and without reasonable relation to any end within the competency of the State.

As the statute undertakes to interfere only with teaching which involves a modern language, leaving complete freedom as to other matters, there seems no adequate foundation for the suggestion that the purpose was to protect the child's health by limiting his mental activities. It is well known that proficiency in a foreign language seldom comes to one not instructed at an early age, and experience shows that this is not injurious to the health, morals or understanding of the ordinary child.

The judgment of the court below must be reversed and the cause remanded for further proceedings not inconsistent with this opinion.

Case note. Many states have statutes prohibiting the teaching of any subject except in English, but such a provision was not before the Court in this case. In fact, there was dictum of approval of this kind of regulation. It might even be enforced in private schools.

Several states also have restrictions on teaching foreign languages to young children, but under the ruling of this case these laws must be applied only in the public schools, even if not explicitly so stating. A legislature may not prevent a child from learning anything not harmful to the state, so long as the teaching is outside of the public schools. However, the state may restrict the subjects taught in the public schools, as evidenced by the following case.

Scopes v. State, 154 Tenn. 105, 289 S.W. 363 (Tennessee, 1927). [Teacher convicted of teaching the theory of evolution in the public schools, contrary to law, appealed from the conviction.]

Scopes was convicted of a violation of Chapter 27 of the Acts of 1925, for that he did teach in the public schools of Rhea County a certain theory that denied the story of the divine creation of man, as taught in the Bible, and did teach instead thereof that man has descended from a lower order of animals. After a verdict of guilty by the jury, the trial judge imposed a fine of $100, and Scopes brought the case to this court by an appeal in the nature of a writ of error. . . .

While the act was not drafted with as much care as could have been desired, nevertheless there seems to be no great difficulty in determining its meaning. . . . Evolution, like prohibition, is a broad term. In recent bickering, however, evolution has been understood to mean the theory which holds that man has developed from some preexisting lower type. This is the popular significance of evolution, just as the popular significance of prohibition is prohibition of the traffic in intoxicating liquors. It was in that sense that evolution was used in this act. . . .

So interpreted, the statute does not seem to be uncertain in its meaning nor incapable of enforcement for such a reason, notwithstanding the argument to the contrary. The indictment herein follows the language of the statute. The statute being sufficiently definite in its terms, such an indictment is good. . . .

It is contended that the statute violates Section 8 of Article 1 of the Tennessee Constitution, and Section 1 of the Fourteenth Amendment of the Constitution of the United States—the law of the land clause of the state constitution, and the due process of law clause of the Federal Constitution, which are practically equivalent in meaning.

We think there is little merit in this contention. The plaintiff in error was a teacher in the public schools of Rhea County. He was an employe of the State of Tennessee or of a municipal agency of the state. He was under contract with the state to work in an institution of the state. He had no right or privilege to serve the state except upon such terms as the state prescribed. His liberty, his privilege, his immunity to teach and pro-

claim the theory of evolution elsewhere than in the service of the state was in no way touched by this law.

The statute before us is not an exercise of the police power of the state undertaking to regulate the conduct and contracts of individuals in their dealings with each other. On the other hand, it is an act of the state as a corporation, a proprietor, an employer. It is a declaration of a master as to the character of work the master's servant shall, or rather shall not, perform. In dealing with its own employes engaged upon its own work, the state is not hampered by the limitations of Section 8 of Article 1 of the Tennessee Constitution nor of the Fourteenth Amendment to the Constitution of the United States. . . .

But it is urged that Chapter 27 of the Acts of 1925 conflicts with Section 12 of Article 11, the educational clause, and Section 3 of Article 1, the religious clause, of the Tennessee Constitution. . . .

The relevant portion of Section 12 of Article 11 of the constitution is in these words: ". . . It shall be the duty of the General Assembly in all future periods of this government, to cherish literature and science." The argument is that the theory of the descent of man from a lower order of animals is now established by the preponderance of scientific thought and that the prohibition of the teaching of such theory is a violation of the legislative duty to cherish science. . . .

In no case can the court directly compel the legislature to perform its duty. . . . If the legislature thinks that, by reason of popular prejudice, the cause of education and the study of science generally will be promoted by forbidding the teaching of evolution in the schools of the state, we can conceive of no ground to justify the court's interference. The courts cannot sit in judgment on such acts of the Legislature or its agents and determine whether or not the omission or addition of a particular course of study tends "to cherish science."

The last serious criticism made of the act is that it contravenes the provision of Section 3 of Article 1 of the constitution, "That no preference shall ever be given by law, to any religious establishment or mode of worship." . . .

We are not able to see how the prohibition of teaching the theory that man has descended from a lower order of animals gives preference to any religious establishment or mode of worship. So far as we know, there is no religious establishment or organized body that has in its creed or confession of faith any article denying or affirming such a theory. . . . Belief or unbelief in the theory of evolution is no more a characteristic of any religious establishment or mode of worship than is belief or unbelief in the wisdom of the prohibition laws. It should appear that members of the same churches quite generally disagree as to these things. . . .

Dissenting opinion: . . . I am of the opinion that it [the statute forbidding the teaching of evolution in the public schools] is invalid for uncertainty of meaning. I therefore respectfully dissent from the contrary holding of my associates.

[Although the court approved the grounds for the conviction, the case was reversed because Tennessee law requires the jury to assess any

fine over $50. Here the judge had fined Scopes $100. In reversing on this technicality, the court suggested that the attorney general drop the case which had interfered with the "peace and dignity of the state."]

Case note. At the time of this decision it received headline publicity over the entire country. The emphasis was on the teaching of the theory of evolution rather than upon the powers of the state to prescribe public-school curriculum and proscribe the teaching of a subject in the public schools. Undoubtedly it was for this reason that the court suggested that the attorney general drop the case.

There is no question but that the state has full power in regulating the public-school curriculum, although it was shown in the Nebraska case that the state cannot prevent a child from learning a subject not harmful to the state if it is learned outside the public schools.

Kaplan v. Independent School District of Virginia, 171, Minn. 142, 214 N. W. 18 (Minnesota, 1927). [Parent challenged the constitutionality of Bible reading in the public schools.]

The school board of the independent school district of Virginia, Minn., was requested by the Ministerial Association of that city to place a copy of the Bible in every schoolroom and to direct the superintendent to make suitable selections to be read daily, without note or comment, by the teacher in each room at the opening of school. In the request it was asserted that our nation was founded upon Christian principles; that the association had a firm conviction that this nation can prosper only when its citizenship is guided by the teachings of the Bible; and that the youth of the community will receive moral and spiritual help therefrom. By resolution the school board concurred in the resolution or request presented by the association, provided each schoolroom with a copy of what is known as King James' version of the Bible, the superintendent made suitable selections from the Old Testament only, and of those selections a portion is read by the teacher in the lower grades at the opening of school each morning, and in the upper grades at some time during the day. Where a parent of any pupil or the pupil objects to listening to such reading, he may retire from the room. The parents of the children attending the school include Protestants, Roman Catholics, Christian Scientists, and Jews. This action was brought to enjoin the reading of these selections in the schools. The court after finding the above-stated facts, in substance, found:

"That the purpose of the defendant school board in having the Bible read in the public schools was to implant in the minds of the pupil higher moral and ethical standards and a knowledge of the Bible and was not for the purpose of teaching the doctrines of any religious sect."

And as conclusions of law:

"That the reading of the Bible in the public schools does not constitute any infringement of the plaintiff's constitutional rights and is lawful,"— and denied the injunction with costs . . . and plaintiff appeals.

This state has from the beginning fostered public schools, deeming the education of its citizens essential to their own happiness and welfare, to the peace and prosperity of the nation, and to an intelligent participation in the government of a republic and a proper exercise of the right of suffrage. . . . What is to be taught and the method of conducting the schools and institutions of learning have, in the main, been left to the judgment of the local school boards, supervised by the county and state superintendents, and by constituted boards and faculties. The Legislature has, however, seen the need of moral training and of instruction in the care of body and mind. Section 2906, G.S. 1923, reads:

"The teachers in all public schools shall give instruction in morals, in physiology and hygiene, and in the effects of narcotics and stimulants."

What more natural than turning to that Book for moral precepts which for ages has been regarded by the majority of the peoples of the most civilized nations as the fountain of moral teachings? . . .

. . . The only thing with which this court is concerned is whether the practice adopted by authorities of this school, as above stated, infringes any constitutional rights of appellant. . . .

It is claimed that reading extracts from the Bible, as here done, is worship and converts the schoolhouse into a place of worship contrary to the constitutional provision:

"nor shall any man be compelled to attend, erect or support any place of worship."

We submit it to be a strained construction to hold that because the teacher reads a short extract from the Bible each day the schoolroom is converted into a place of worship. . . . Nor, except by a strained and narrow construction, can it be claimed that because the few minutes the teacher reads the extracts mentioned there is an expenditure of public funds forbidden [by the constitution] . . . from being appropriated for denominational schools and . . . the teaching of the distinctive doctrines of any sect or creed in the public schools maintained by the state. . . .

. . . So long as no pupil is compelled to worship according to the tenets of any creed, or at all, and no sectarian belief is taught, courts should not hold that there is any violation of the constitutional guarantee of religious liberty. . . .

Dissenting opinion: I agree that the reading of the Bible in the schools does not require a taxpayer to "support a place of worship." The [state] Constitution not only says that every man may "worship God according to the dictates of his own conscience," but it says:

"Nor shall any control of or interference with the rights of conscience be permitted."

"Rights of conscience" means what? By conscience we mean that internal conviction or self-knowledge that tells us that a thing is right or wrong. It is that faculty or power within us which decides on the right or wrong of an act and approves or condemns. . . . Each person is governed by his own views. The "rights of conscience," in religious matters, means the privilege of resting in peace or contentment according to one's own judgment. . . .

Of course, the thing of which complaint is here made will not directly prevent him from worshipping God according to the dictates of his own conscience when he is in his own sanctuary or home, but how soon will it pervert the child from the parental belief? No one knows. . . . He, at least, sincerely believes that there is danger of this result and he worries. He is dissatisfied and discontented. Why? Because something is being done which to him is a real "interference with the rights of conscience," which the Constitution expressly says shall not be permitted. If this constitutional barrier to unfortunate controversies must be broken down, it should be by a constitutional amendment, rather than have the evil, at which the Constitution was aimed, break out, with its ancient vigor, through judicial construction. . . .

Case note. The majority opinion represents the majority rule among state courts which generally hold that Bible reading in the public schools, without comment, is not religious teaching contrary to the constitutional provisions guaranteeing religious liberty or proscribing sectarian education in the public schools.

Note that in the Minnesota case, the superintendent chose the selections from the Bible for the teachers to read, and his selections were made from the Old Testament only. It may be that such a procedure makes Bible reading even more nonsectarian than it would possibly be if the selections were chosen by individual teachers who might be influenced by their own beliefs in selecting the passages to be read. Also, reading from the New Testament has been held occasionally to violate the religious liberty of Jews. Thus both these contingencies were avoided in the Minnesota situation.

Theoretically, it would seem that Bible reading has possibilities for sectarianism in the public schools and that the constitutional question must be answered according to the circumstances in each case. If the Bible is treated as a historical book or a treatise on ethics and morals, there should be no objection to its use. If it is used to indoctrinate pupils, even in the general precepts of Christianity, there may be a question of the legality of its use in this way.

In 1963, the Supreme Court of the United States declared Bible-reading in the public schools to be unconstitutional. (*School District of Abington Township, Pennsylvania v. Schempp; Murray v. Curlett,* 83 S. Ct. 1560.) The *Murray* case came from Maryland. The Court said that although religion has been identified with our history and government, religious freedom is likewise deeply imbedded in our public and private life. This decision is contrary to the majority rule in state courts. Distribution of Gideon Bibles in the public schools has been held invalid.

Tudor v. Board of Education and Gideons International, 14 N.J. 31, 100 A. (2d) 857 (New Jersey, 1953).

A lower court in New York held in 1959 that a nondenominational prayer was not illegal. *Engel v. Vitala,* New York Superior Court, Nassau County.

Illinois ex rel. McCollum v. Board of Education of School District No. 71, Champaign County, Illinois, 333 U. S. 203 (1948). [Validity of released-time plan.]

The appellant, Vashti McCollum, began this action for mandamus against the Champaign Board of Education in the Circuit Court of Champaign County, Illinois. Her asserted interest was that of a resident and taxpayer of Champaign and of a parent whose child was then enrolled in the Champaign public schools. Illinois has a compulsory education law which, with exceptions, requires parents to send their children, aged seven to sixteen, to its tax-supported public schools where the children are to remain in attendance during the hours when the schools are regularly in session. Parents who violate this law commit a misdemeanor punishable by fine unless the children attend private or parochial schools which meet educational standards fixed by the State. District boards of education are given general supervisory powers over the use of the public school buildings within the school districts. Ill. Rev. Stat. ch. 122, §§ 123, 301 (1943).

Appellant's petition for mandamus alleged that religious teachers, employed by private religious groups, were permitted to come weekly into the school buildings during the regular hours set apart for secular teaching, and then and there for a period of thirty minutes substitute their religious teaching for the secular education provided under the compulsory education law. The petitioner charged that this joint public-school religious-group program violated the First and Fourteenth Amendments to the United States Constitution. The prayer of her petition was that the Board of Education be ordered to "adopt and enforce rules and regulations prohibiting all instruction in and teaching of religious education in all public schools in Champaign School District Number 71, . . . and in all public school houses and buildings in said district when occupied by public schools."

Although there are disputes between the parties as to various inferences that may or may not properly be drawn from the evidence concerning the religious program, the following facts are shown by the record without dispute. In 1940 interested members of the Jewish, Roman Catholic, and a few of the Protestant faiths formed a voluntary association called the Champaign Council on Religious Education. They obtained permission from the Board of Education to offer classes in religious instruction to public school pupils in grades four to nine inclusive. Classes were made up of pupils whose parents signed printed cards requesting that their children be permitted to attend; they were held weekly; thirty minutes for the lower grades, forty-five minutes for the higher. The council employed the religious teachers at no expense to the school

authorities, but the instructors were subject to the approval and supervision of the superintendent of schools. The classes were taught in three
separate religious groups by Protestant teachers, Catholic priests, and a
Jewish rabbi, although for the past several years there have apparently
been no classes instructed in the Jewish religion. Classes were conducted
in the regular classrooms of the school building. Students who did not
choose to take the religious instruction were not released from public
school duties; they were required to leave their classrooms and go to
some other place in the school building for pursuit of their secular studies.
On the other hand, students who were released from secular study for
the religious instructions were required to be present at the religious
classes. Reports of their presence or absence were to be made to their
secular teachers.

The foregoing facts, without reference to others that appear in the
record, show the use of tax-supported property for religious instruction
and the close cooperation between the school authorities and the religious
council in promoting religious education. The operation of the State's
compulsory education system thus assists and is integrated with the program of religious instruction carried on by separate religious sects. Pupils
compelled by law to go to school for secular education are released in
part from their legal duty upon the condition that they attend the religious classes. This is beyond all question a utilization of the tax-established
and tax-supported public school system to aid religious groups to spread
their faith. And it falls squarely under the ban of the First Amendment. . . .
For the First Amendment rests upon the premise that both religion and
government can best work to achieve their lofty aims if each is left free
from the other within its respective sphere. Or, as we said in the *Everson*
case, the First Amendment has erected a wall between Church and State
which must be kept high and impregnable.

Here not only are the State's tax-supported public school buildings used
for the dissemination of religious doctrines. The state also affords sectarian groups an invaluable aid in that it helps to provide pupils for their
religious classes through use of the State's compulsory public school
machinery. This is not separation of Church and State.

The cause is reversed and remanded to the State Supreme Court for
proceedings not inconsistent with this opinion.

Case note. There was considerable discussion of this case following
its decision. Differing opinions were held among educators, lawyers,
and church officers, as groups and as individuals. One point of
view was, and still is, that the illegality of the Champaign program
lay in the fact that the classes were held in the school buildings.
Champaign continued its released-time plan without change except
that the classes were taken out of public-school buildings after this
decision. Other released-time programs have continued in some places,
even in school buildings, on the ground that some difference between
the Champaign plan and their own makes the decision inapplicable to

them. Districts where classes have always been held outside school buildings have for the most part continued after the decision was rendered.

A few local districts and one or two states, by state board of education regulation, have ceased conducting released-time programs even when held off school property, on the ground that the decision was broader than a restriction to the use of school property.

Some fear has been expressed that the McCollum decision required the abandonment of Bible reading in the public schools also. The fact of the matter is that the majority opinion was clothed in such general terms that no one was certain of the extent to which the decision was to be applied.

The McCollum decision caused a reexamination of the relationship between the schools and religious groups in other respects also. New Mexico and North Dakota have taken steps to prohibit public-school teachers from wearing the garb of religious orders; the Catholic Church has responded by permitting nuns to discard their religious garb while teaching in the public schools.

Educators and religious leaders sought curriculum materials and methods of presenting them which would likely be constitutional under the McCollum decision, and undoubtedly the case developed a new emphasis upon character education in the public schools and upon sectarian education through church facilities outside of school time.

Although some educators are concerned with the uncertainty of the legality of their programs, and probably some existing programs are unconstitutional, the McCollum decision does not seem to preclude any religious education which is nonsectarian. The teaching of spiritual values and ethics apart from religion was not disturbed by the Court in this opinion. Nor was Bible-reading, though later outlawed. Character education which the public schools have carried on over the years without segregation of pupils into sectarian groups for instruction in the particular beliefs of certain groups was not affected. There is no need to change this sort of "religious" education in the public schools.

Zorach et al. v. Clauson et al., 343 U. S. 306 (1952). [Validity of released-time plan.]

New York City has a program which permits its public schools to release students during the school day so that they may leave the school buildings and school grounds and go to religious centers for religious

instruction or devotional exercises. A student is released on written request of his parents. Those not released stay in the classrooms. The churches make weekly reports to the schools, sending a list of children who have been released from public school but who have not reported for religious instruction.

This "released time" program involves neither religious instruction in public school classrooms nor the expenditure of public funds. All costs, including the application blanks, are paid by the religious organizations. The case is therefore unlike *McCollum v. Board of Education,* 333 U. S. 203, which involved a "released time" program from Illinois. In that case the classrooms were turned over to religious instructors. We accordingly held that the program violated the First Amendment which (by reason of the Fourteenth Amendment) prohibits the states from establishing religion or prohibiting its free exercise.

Appellants, who are taxpayers and residents of New York City and whose children attend its public schools, challenge the present law, contending it is in essence not different from the one involved in the *McCollum* case. Their argument, stated elaborately in various ways, reduces itself to this: the weight and influence of the school is put behind a program for religious instruction; public school teachers police it, keeping tab on students who are released; the classroom activities come to a halt while the students who are released for religious instruction are on leave; the school is a crutch on which the churches are leaning for support in their religious training; without the cooperation of the schools this "released time" program, like the one in the *McCollum* case, would be futile and ineffective. The New York Court of Appeals sustained the law against this claim of unconstitutionality. 303 N. Y. 161, 100 N. E. 2d 463. The case is here on appeal. 28 U. S. C. § 1257 (2).

It takes obtuse reasoning to inject any issue of the "free exercise" of religion into the present case. No one is forced to go to the religious classroom and no religious exercise or instruction is brought to the classrooms of the public schools. A student need not take religious instruction. He is left to his own desires as to the manner or time of his religious devotions, if any.

There is a suggestion that the system involves the use of coercion to get public school students into religious classrooms. There is no evidence in the record before us that supports that conclusion. The present record indeed tells us that the school authorities are neutral in this regard and do no more than release students whose parents so request. If in fact coercion were used, if it were established that any one or more teachers were using their office to persuade or force students to take the religious instruction, a wholly different case would be presented. Hence we put aside that claim of coercion both as respects the "free exercise" of religion and "an establishment of religion" within the meaning of the First Amendment.

Moreover, apart from that claim of coercion, we do not see how New York by this type of "released time" program has made a law respecting an establishment of religion within the meaning of the First Amendment. There is much talk of the separation of Church and State in the history

of the Bill of Rights and in the decisions clustering around the First Amendment. See *Eversion v. Board of Education,* 330 U. S. 1; *McCollum v. Board of Education, supra.* There cannot be the slightest doubt that the First Amendment reflects the philosophy that Church and State should be separated. And so far as interference with the "free exercise" of religion and an "establishment" of religion are concerned, the separation must be complete and unequivocal. The First Amendment within the scope of its coverage permits no exception; the prohibition is absolute. The First Amendment, however, does not say that in every and all respects there shall be a separation of Church and State. Rather, it studiously defines the manner, the specific ways, in which there shall be no concert or union or dependency one on the other. That is the common sense of the matter. Otherwise the state and religion would be aliens to each other—hostile, suspicious, and even unfriendly. Churches could not be required to pay even property taxes. Municipalities would not be permitted to render police or fire protection to religious groups. Policemen who helped parishioners into their places of worship would violate the Constitution. Prayers in our legislative halls; the appeals to the Almighty in the messages of the Chief Executive; the proclamations making Thanksgiving Day a holiday; "so help me God" in our courtroom oaths—these and all other references to the Almighty that run through our laws, our public rituals, our ceremonies would be flouting the First Amendment. A fastidious atheist or agnostic could even object to the supplication with which the Court opens each session: "God save the United States and this Honorable Court."

We would have to press the concept of separation of Church and State to these extremes to condemn the present law on constitutional grounds. The nullification of this law would have wide and profound effects. A Catholic student applies to his teacher for permission to leave the school during hours on a Holy Day of Obligation to attend a mass. A Jewish student asks his teacher for permission to be excused for Yom Kippur. A Protestant wants the afternoon off for a family baptismal ceremony. In each case the teacher requires parental consent in writing. In each case the teacher, in order to make sure the student is not a truant, goes further and requires a report from the priest, the rabbi, or the minister. The teacher in other words cooperates in a religious program to the extent of making it possible for her students to participate in it. Whether she does it occasionally for a few students, regularly for one, or pursuant to a systematized program designed to further the religious needs of all the students does not alter the character of the act.

We are a religious people whose institutions presuppose a Supreme Being. We guarantee the freedom to worship as one chooses. We make room for as wide a variety of beliefs and creeds as the spiritual needs of man deem necessary. We sponsor an attitude on the part of government that shows no partiality to any one group and that lets each flourish according to the zeal of its adherents and the appeal of its dogma. When the state encourages religious instruction or cooperates with religious authorities by adjusting the schedule of public events to sectarian needs, it follows the best of our traditions. For it then respects the religious nature

of our people and accommodates the public service to their spirtual needs. To hold that it may not would be to find in the Constitution a requirement that the government show a callous indifference to religious groups. That would be preferring those who believe in no religion over those who do believe. Government may not finance religious groups nor undertake religious instruction nor blend secular and sectarian education nor use secular institutions to force one or some religion on any person. But we find no constitutional requirement which makes it necessary for government to be hostile to religion and to throw its weight against efforts to widen the effective scope of religious influence. The government must be neutral when it comes to competition between sects. It may not thrust any sect on any person. It may not make a religious observance compulsory. It may not coerce anyone to attend church, to observe a religious holiday, or to take religious instruction. But it can close its doors or suspend its operations as to those who want to repair to their religious sanctuary for worship or instruction. No more than that is undertaken here. . . .

In the *McCollum* case the classrooms were used for religious instruction and the force of the public school was used to promote that instruction. Here, as we have said, the public schools do no more than accommodate their schedules to a program of outside religious instruction. We follow the *McCollum* case. But we cannot expand it to cover the present released time program unless separation of Church and State means that public institutions can make no adjustments of their schedules to accommodate the religious needs of the people. We cannot read into the Bill of Rights such a philosophy of hostility to religion.

Affirmed.

Case note. This decision seemed to confirm the opinion of those who had believed the McCollum case outlawed only those classes in religion which were held on school property. The language of the New York statute, however, made it possible for the Court to hold that if a single pupil can be excused from school for a religious rite, a group can be excused for religious instruction—a distinction without a difference in the eyes of the Court.

Sources of Further Information

47 Am. Jur. "Schools" secs. 200-215.

78 C.J.S. "Schools and School Districts" sec. 90; 79 C.J.S. "Schools and School Districts" secs. 487-492.

A.L.R. "Schools" Topic Nos. 64 and 67.

American Digest System "Schools and School Districts" Key Nos. 86(1), 163-168.

Work Sheet

1. Are textbooks furnished free to all public-school pupils in all grades of your district?

2. Is a refundable deposit fee charged for the use of the books?

3. How are textbooks selected in your state?

4. How often *may* uniformly adopted textbooks be changed? How often *are* they usually changed?

5. Has there been any complaint from patrons as to the contents of any books? If so, what action has been taken by the board, if any?

6. Examine the state laws in your state to ascertain what subjects are prescribed for your school level.

7. Is the state board of education or the state superintendent required by law to prepare a syllabus for teachers to follow? Are teachers required to follow such a syllabus? Does the syllabus you are following, if any, coincide with the state law prescriptions?

8. Is the Bible read in your school? If so, who selects the passages? Are the passages you read of a nonsectarian nature?

9. Does your school operate a "released-time" plan? If so, are the classes held on school property? Have any pupils or parents objected to the released-time program in your district?

10. Compare your released-time plan, if any, with the program operated in Champaign and judge the validity of your own plan according to the elements found unconstitutional by the Court in the Champaign program.

Chapter 15.

CONTROL OF PUPILS' CONDUCT

Editorial Comment

Pupils have the responsibility of obeying the school laws and the rules and regulations of the state and local governing officials; they have the duty of submitting to the orders of their teachers and other school authorities. Failure to do so may result in corporal punishment, suspension, or expulsion. Corporal punishment usually falls within the scope of the teacher's authority; suspension and expulsion are usually within the discretionary powers of the school board. In the power to regulate pupils' conduct, the teacher stands *in loco parentis*; that is, the teacher is conditionally privileged to take disciplinary steps under certain circumstances and for certain purposes.

Corpus Juris Secundum (79 C. J. S. 493) gives the following explanation of the position of the teacher with regard to disciplinary control of pupils:

> As a general rule a school teacher, to a limited extent at least, stands *in loco parentis* to pupils under his charge, and may exercise such powers of control, restraint, and correction over them as may be reasonably necessary to enable him properly to perform his duties as teacher and accomplish the purposes of education, and is subject to such limitations and prohibitions as may be defined by legislative enactment. . . .

State statutes which deal with the corporal punishment of pupils are of several definite types. In the District of Columbia and New Jersey, corporal punishment is prohibited by law. Many local school districts have so ruled also, by school board regulation. In the absence of prohibitory legislation, state or local, a teacher may administer corporal punishment because he stands *in loco parentis*. There are certain common-law principles in this regard; *e.g.*, that the punishment be not unreasonable, nor excessive in view of the age and sex of the pupil, nor excessive in view of the gravity of the offense, nor

administered maliciously. These common-law principles are either written into statutes or implied in more general statutory language.

Almost all states have laws forbidding cruelty to children, and if corporal punishment administered by a school teacher be excessive or administered with a dangerous instrument or in an improper manner, the teacher is liable to apprehension under such laws which usually provide a penalty of a fine or imprisonment.

A third type of law bearing on the teacher's authority consists of sanctions for moderate and reasonable punishment through the definition of assault and battery or homicide in the penal codes of a number of states. These laws define assault and battery as the use of force or violence upon or toward another person, with the proviso that force or violence shall not be considered assault and battery when committed in certain instances, including the lawful exercise of authority to restrain a pupil. Even death of a pupil resulting from corporal punishment may be excused in law if the teacher's conduct was within limits set forth in certain statutes defining homicide.

Thus a teacher who chastises a pupil may be subject to dismissal for violation of a school law or school board regulation in some districts; is subject to fine or imprisonment and to a civil action by the parent of the pupil, if the punishment is unreasonable, malicious, or otherwise unlawful.

Another disciplinary measure is suspension or expulsion. Pupils may be expelled from school for violation of reasonable rules and regulations of the school board. Usually a teacher, principal, or superintendent may suspend a pupil temporarily only—action of the school board being necessary to expel a pupil. Parents rarely challenge the right of a school board to suspend a pupil temporarily for violation of a school board rule, but when a pupil is expelled the parents must send the child to a private school because of the compulsory attendance law. Therefore, parents frequently challenge the right of the school board to expel children for violation of rules which the pupils or their parents consider unreasonable. Until the United States Supreme Court spoke in 1943, pupils could be expelled for refusal to salute the American flag. School board rules and state laws forbidding membership in high-school fraternities have also been before the courts many times.

Statutory Material

New Jersey Statutes Annotated, sec. 18:19-1.

No person employed or engaged in a school or educational institution, whether public or private, shall inflict or cause to be inflicted corporal

punishment upon a pupil attending such school or institution. Every resolution, by-law, rule, ordinance, or other act or authority permitting or authorizing corporal punishment to be inflicted upon a pupil attending a school or educational institution shall be void.

Burns Indiana Statutes Annotated, sec. 10-807.

Any person who shall cruelly ill-treat, abuse, overwork or inflict unnecessary cruel punishment upon any infant or minor child, and any person having the care, custody or control of any minor child who shall wilfully abandon or neglect the same, shall be guilty of a misdemeanor, and upon conviction thereof by any justice of the peace . . . shall be fined not less than five dollars [$5] nor more than fifty dollars [$50] for each offense to which may be added imprisonment not exceeding thirty [30] days.

Colorado Revised Statutes, sec. 40-2-18.

Excusable homicide by misadventure is when a person is doing a lawful act without any intention of killing, yet unfortunately kills another; as . . . where a parent is moderately correcting a child, or a master his servant or scholar, . . . and happens to occasion death, it is only a misadventure, for the act of correction was lawful; but if a parent or master exceeds the bounds of reason or moderation, . . . either in the manner, the instrument or quantity of punishment, and death ensue, it will be manslaughter or murder, according to the circumstances of the case.

Virginia State Board of Education Regulations, No. 17.

Teachers shall require of pupils cleanliness of person, punctuality, diligence and good behavior during their attendance at school and on their way thither and back to their homes. In the enforcement of discipline teachers have authority, subject to such regulations as the school boards may prescribe, to inflict reasonable penalties, and for a sufficient cause they may suspend pupils from school until the case is decided by the board; provided, that in all such cases of suspension the teacher shall promptly report the facts in writing to the school board and to the parent or guardian of the pupil suspended.

Maryland State Department of Education Bylaws, No. 73.

No pupil enrolled in a public school in any county of Maryland shall be a member of a fraternity or sorority or any other secret, exclusive, self-perpetuating social organization composed in whole or part of public-school pupils, which seeks to organize and perpetuate itself by taking in members from among the pupils enrolled in such school in which they are pupils, upon the basis of decision of the membership of such organization, rather than from the free choice of any pupils in such school who are otherwise qualified to fill the special aims of such an organization.

The county board of education is hereby authorized, upon finding that any pupil is a member of a high-school fraternity, sorority, or social

organization as above defined, to exclude such pupil from representing the school in any public activity, contest, or exhibition, such as athletic, literary, or dramatic, and from participating in any school activity other than class attendance, and from holding a position of authority in any school or class organization.

Nothing in this regulation shall be deemed as prohibiting the county board of education from excluding any pupil from class in those instances where the behavior of such pupil is detrimental to school discipline.

Statutory note. These four illustrations of statutes and regulations having the force of law, run the gamut from one extreme to another with respect to corporal punishment. In New Jersey, a teacher may not lay a hand on a pupil as a disciplinary measure; in Colorado, death resulting from corporal punishment may be excused under some circumstances. Most statutes permitting corporal punishment are couched in language which would require the punishment to be reasonable, even as in Colorado, and the common-law principles of what is reasonable punishment are used by the courts in evaluating the pupil's and the teacher's behavior when the latter is challenged.

The antifraternity rule from Maryland is less severe than many others.

Case Material

Suits v. Glover, 260 Ala. 449, 71 So. (2d) 49 (Alabama, 1954). [Assault and battery charged on ground of corporal punishment.]

Tort action by appellant, a schoolboy suing by his father as next friend, against appellee, a former schoolteacher, claiming damages in three counts of the complaint for assault and battery. A jury trial was had resulting in a verdict in favor of appellee. . . .

There was no conflict but that certain punishment was administered to the appellant, a school pupil, by the appellee, a schoolmaster. The evidence was, however, conflicting as to the type of instrument used to administer the punishment; the appellant's evidence tending to show that he was whipped with a slat from an apple crate and the appellee's evidence tending to show that the instrument used was a ping-pong paddle, commonly used by the school for administering such punishment. There was evidence that the appellee was responsible for maintaining order and discipline and to administer corporal punishment as was deemed necessary as punishment for infractions of the school rules. Further, there was evidence of an infraction of the school rules by the appellant, the nature of which was insubordination and scuffling in the school hall. The appellant's medical expert testified that in his opinion there was no permanent injury and the evidence showed that the appellant remained in school the remainder of the school day the incident occurred (February 22nd) and did not miss any time from school, at least until March 9th, except the day following the incident (February 23rd). The evidence further showed that the appellant

was eight and a half years old, well developed, fat and in good health; and there was evidence warranting the inference that the appellee was in no wise angry or aggravated with the appellant when he administered the spanking. The evidence was also conflicting on the issue of the severity of the punishment, the appellee's evidence tending to show that the appellant was paddled on his buttocks only, the skin was not broken, and approximately only five licks were administered.

A schoolmaster is regarded as standing in *loco parentis* and has the authority to administer moderate correction to pupils under his care. To be guilty of an assault and battery, the teacher must not only inflict on the child immoderate chastisement, but he must do so with legal malice or wicked motives or he must inflict some permanent injury. In determining the reasonableness of the punishment or the extent of malice, proper matters for consideration are the instrument used and the nature of the offense committed by the child, the age and physical condition of the child, and the other attendant circumstances. . . .

It appears from the foregoing there was evidence which, if believed by the jury, justified the verdict and we conclude that the trial court committed no error.

Case note. Exasperated as a teacher might be by the inattention and vagrancies of a class, he must remember that the court will think of the individual pupil only and not recognize that the annoyance the teacher feels in a particular instance is multiplied many times in a school day. A teacher does not have the moral right to become angry with a child; he does not have the legal right to express that anger, at least by physical blows. Punishment should never be motivated by anger or malice. If anger or malice can be proved, the other principles of common law with regard to reasonable punishment of pupils are of no avail as defense.

In this case there was no evidence of exasperation or malice on the part of the teacher. Therefore, the court could decide the issue on the common-law standards of reasonable punishment that may be inflicted by a teacher on a pupil. The instrument used and the severity of the punishment were the deciding factors. Although the evidence was conflicting, there was sufficient evidence, said the appellate court, for the jury to decide in favor of the teacher.

Anderson et al. v. State, 84 Ga. App. 259, 65 S. E. (2d) 848 (Georgia, 1951). [Expulsion for refusal to be vaccinated.]

The undisputed evidence on the trial of the case was that the defendants' children were by them enrolled in Collins High School in Tattnall County at the beginning of the school term and remained for about seven days; that at that time the county nurse under the direction of the County Board of Education attempted to vaccinate the children against certain

contagious diseases, to which the defendants objected on the ground that it was against their religious beliefs; that they do not believe in taking vaccine or immunization against disease but do believe in divine healing through faith; that the matter was taken up at a meeting of the County Board of Education, which indicated its willingness to dispense temporarily with the vaccination requirement if the parents and pastor of their church signed a certificate stating that their religious sect was opposed to the use of medicine in the treatment of disease; that the pastor refused to sign this certificate on the ground that the opposition to the use of medicine and immunization were not a part of the church creed, but a belief embraced by certain of its members individually, including these defendants; that the parents were notified to put their children in school; that the children came back to school but were not allowed to be vaccinated, whereupon the teachers were ordered not to accept them until they were vaccinated; that they returned home and have not attended school since. The defendant made a statement in which he contended that he was being tried on a religious issue; that it was his individual belief that healing is through faith and not by medicine, and that it was not his intention to violate the law.

. . . Code, sec. 32-911, as amended by the Act of 1946, Ga. L. 1946, pp. 206, 207, provides as follows: "The boards of education of each county and independent school system may make such regulations as in their judgment shall seem requisite to insure the vaccination of the pupils in their respective schools and may require all scholars or pupils to be vaccinated as a prerequisite to admission to their respective schools." Similar statutes have been widely held to be valid delegations of legislative power to the designated county or municipal authorities for the purpose of requiring vaccination as a prerequisite to school attendance, or as a health measure. . . . Here, the following excerpt from the minutes of the Tattnall County Board of Education was admitted in evidence without objection: "The superintendent reported that the County Board of Health has requested the County Board of Education to require children entering school to take the immunizations for smallpox, diphtheria and typhoid at least. Mr. Rabun moved that as a requisite to the further attending of any pupil in school [he] be required to take the immunization of all infectious diseases required by the County Board of Health. This . . . was carried." The objection appears to be, not to the sufficiency of evidence of the resolution of the county board of education, but because of a failure to show any immunization requirements of the county board of health. Since Code Ann. Supp. sec. 32-911, supra, empowers the board of education without regard to any rules or regulations promulgated by the board of health to require as prerequisite to admission in the public schools over which it has jurisdiction the vaccination of children, the fact that its action was taken here pursuant to a request by the county board of health is immaterial. The board of education could have taken the same.

The defendant further contends that the court, even without request, should have charged Art. I, Sec. I, Par. XII of the Constitution of Georgia, Code § 2-112, as follows: "All men have the natural and inalienable right to worship God, each according to the dictates of his own conscience,

and no human authority should, in any case, control or interfere with such right of conscience." The defendants contend that they are members of a religious sect which permits them to choose for themselves the application of the tenets of their sect; that they interpret their religious instruction to mean that they should not use medicinal aids; that this is a part of their religion and to deprive them of it is to deprive them of their freedom of worship; that they do not wish to deprive their children of an education but when forced to make a choice between depriving them of an education and allowing them to receive medical treatment they must choose the former. The ill effects of contagious disease, and its power to wipe out entire populations, is a matter of history. Many of these scourges of the past have been completely dissipated by the preventive methods of medical science. The purpose of the legislature in passing the statute embodied in Code Supp. § 32-911 was to prevent the spread of these diseases, not only for the protection of those actually immunized but for the protection of others with whom they might come in contact. The refusal of the defendants here to have their children vaccinated amounted to a transgression of the rights of others.

Liberty of conscience is one thing. License to endanger the lives of others by practices contrary to statutes passed for the public safety and in reliance upon modern medical knowledge is another. The validity of the statute is not questioned, and the wisdom of the legislative enactment is not a matter for the decision either of this court or of any individual citizen. The opinion of the defendants that they should practice healing without the aid of medicine is not a legal justification for refusal to abide by the statutes of this state and regulations passed pursuant thereto, and for this reason freedom of worship was not an issue in the case. The failure of the court to charge on this subject was not error.

Code Supp. § 32-2104 imposes upon parents of children between the ages of seven and sixteen years the duty of enrolling and sending such children to a public or private school. Code Supplement § 32-9914 fixes the penalty for noncompliance with this duty. As hereinbefore pointed out, Code and Supplement § 32-911 empowers the county boards of education to fix rules and regulations insuring the vaccination of such school children as a prerequisite to admission. These provisions of our statute law therefore impose upon the parents the duty of sending the children to school and upon the school authorities the duty of fixing the rules and regulations under which they shall attend. The defendants in this case sought to comply with their duty to send their children to school but at the same time usurp the prerogative of the school authorities, and also undertook to fix the rules under which they should attend. Their contention therefore that they did actually enroll the children unvaccinated constitutes no valid defense. It is the same contention urged in State v. Drew, supra, where the offer to send the children unvaccinated to the school was sought to be treated as a "legal tender" and the rejection as sought to be treated as an estoppel of the school board. Such a contention is unsound for the reason that an offer to do a thing only upon waiver of the conditions precedent thereto amounts to no offer at all. Further, our statute specifically provides, not only that the child shall be enrolled, but kept in

school for a minimum of 175 days or the full session thereof, subject to certain exceptions. Under these circumstances, the action of the parents in refusing to meet the prerequisites of attendance in public school constituted a violation of the statute and the court did not err in so charging.

The judgment of the trial court overruling the motion for new trial as amended is without error.

Judgment affirmed.

Case note. Vaccination certificates and health reports of more extensive detail are required nowadays in many school districts, by local regulation. A few states prescribe the vaccination as a prerequisite for admission to the public schools. The requirements have been challenged in courts, not frequently, but sufficiently often to have laid down a generally accepted principle that such regulations are within the police power of the state. The local school board is an agent of the state. The state has police power and may delegate some of its police power to its agents and agencies.

Hughes et al. v. Caddo Parish School Board et al., 57 F. Supp. 508 (D. C. La. 1944) *aff'd* (per curiam) 323 U.S. 685 (1945). [Antifraternity law.]

The complaint is by the four parents of children attending the Byrd High School of Shreveport, Louisiana, who are members of national Greek-letter fraternities, chapters of which have been in public existence at this school for a number of years. Act No. 342 of the Legislature of Louisiana for 1944, granting to the various parish school boards the power and authority to abolish high school fraternities and sororities, is attacked as being unconstitutional, null and void for the following reasons:

"(1) Said Statute is violative of the 14th Amendment to the Constitution of the United States in that it deprives plaintiffs and their children of vested rights without due process of law, abridges their privileges and immunities, deprives them of the equal protection of the laws, and attempts to grant special privileges to a class, limiting the privilege of free education to students who are not members of Greek-letter fraternities and sororities."

There are five other reasons of unconstitutionality alleged under the constitution of the state of Louisiana; and, finally, a seventh reason, wherein both constitutions federal and state, are involved:

"(7) Said Statute, as originally introduced in the House of Representatives, expressly declared that high school fraternities were inimical to the public good and to the welfare of the public high schools of Louisiana, but this language was stricken from said Act by the House of Representatives: that the Legislature, having failed to find said organizations detrimental to the general welfare, and on the contrary, having in effect found otherwise, said Statute has no legal basis on which to rest, and constitutes a violation of the inherent personal rights guaranteed to every citizen by the state and Federal Constitutions." The complaint alleges that:

Under date of September 6, 1944, at its regular session, the Caddo Parish School Board, proceeding under said Act No. 342 for 1944 of the Legislature, adopted a resolution abolishing high school fraternities and sororities, and making it the duty of the principals of the various high schools in the Parish of Caddo to suspend or expel from said schools any pupil who might be or remain a member of any high school fraternity of [sic] sorority.

So, it is our opinion that the state court of final arbitrament having ruled that the Act and the two local school board resolutions were not in violation of the state constitution, the whole attack based on state grounds of want of constitutionality is settled for us. . . .

The items of the complaint left for us to consider, therefore, are those where there are alleged violations of the fourteenth amendment to the Constitution of the United States. . . .

Thus, the instant situation is exactly the same in principle as with the student Waugh in Mississippi when the state required him, already a member of a Greek-letter fraternity, though at another college, to renounce his allegiance to and affiliation with such fraternity. The United States Supreme Court held that Waugh could be so obliged without denying him due process of law or his privileges or immunities as a citizen of the United States under the fourteenth amendment.

Because of the strikingly similar facts in the two cases, we adopt the following principles of the Waugh case from the Supreme Court of the United States:

"It is said that the fraternity to which complainant belongs is a moral and of itself a disciplinary force. This need not be denied. But whether such membership makes against discipline was for the state of Mississippi to determine. It is to be remembered that the University was established by the state, and is under the control of the state, and the enactment of the statute may have been induced by the opinion that membership in the prohibited societies divided the attention of the students, and distracted from that singleness of purpose which the state desired to exist in its public educational institutions. It is not up to us to entertain conjectures in opposition to the views of the state, and annul its regulations upon disputable considerations of their wisdom or necessity. Nor can we accommodate the regulations to the assertion of a special purpose by the applying student, varying, perhaps, with each one, and dependent alone upon his promise.

"This being our view of the power of the legislature, we do not enter upon a consideration of the elements of complainant's contention. It is very trite to say that the right to pursue happiness and exercise life and liberty are subject in some degree to the limitations of the law, and the condition upon which the state of Mississippi offers the complainant free instruction at its University, that while a student is there he renounce affiliation with a society which the state considers inimical to discipline, finds no prohibition in the 14th amendment." . . .

Case note. The Supreme Court of the United States upheld an antifraternity law enacted in Mississippi as it applied to the state

university. The essential point in all these cases is that freedoms guaranteed by the Constitution may be limited if the limitation is reasonable and in the interest of public welfare. Occasionally, a court will intimate that the wisdom of an antifraternity rule may be in question, but it is not within the province of a court to evaluate the wisdom of legislation. One court said that pupils have the option of withdrawing from their fraternity or submitting to the penalty. Penalties differ: from participation in extracurricular activities to suspension or even expulsion.

Only one state has held that antifraternity rules are unreasonable— Missouri in 1922—where the court said that the detrimental effects of membership in fraternities and sororities had not been sufficiently proved. *Wright v. Board of Education of St. Louis*, 295 Mo. 466, 246 S.W. 43 (Missouri, 1922). The Texas court followed the majority rule with regard to banning fraternities during the school term, but held that application of the rule to summer vacations was unreasonable because during that period the pupils were under control of their parents, not the school authorities, and, furthermore, it would be impracticable for the school board to attempt to enforce the rule during summer vacations when the students are dispersed. *Wilson et al. v. Abilene Independent School District*, ——Tex. Civ. App.——, 190 S. W. (2d) 406 (Texas, 1945).

Sources of Further Information

47 Am. Jur. "Schools" secs. 167-188.

79 C.J.S. "Schools and School Districts" secs. 493-505.

A.L.R. "Schools" Topic Nos. 60-62.

American Digest System "Schools and School Districts" Key Nos. 169-177.

Restatement of the Law of Torts, Vol. I, Chapter 6, Topic 2, secs. 147-155.

Work Sheet

1. May a teacher administer corporal punishment in your district?

2. If so, are there statutory limitations or procedures to be observed?

3. For what reasons does your state law permit the school board to suspend or expel pupils?

4. Is there an antifraternity rule?

5. Examine the rules and regulations in your school for the regulation of pupils' conduct to ascertain if any, in your judgement, infringe upon any constitutional rights of the pupils.

Chapter 16.

REDRESS FOR INJURY THROUGH NEGLIGENCE OF TEACHER OR SCHOOL BOARD

Editorial Comment

In this chapter we will first discuss the liability of a teacher whose negligence results in injury to a pupil and then take up the legal responsibility of the school board.

The extent to which a teacher is liable for injuries sustained by a pupil depends upon the common-law principles of negligence. Public-school teachers have no special immunity because they are public employees. In fact, they may be held even more accountable than the ordinary person because pupils are in their care and they have the duty to prevent pupil injuries so far as possible.

Some injuries are caused by what the law calls a "pure accident"; that is, it was unforeseeable, unavoidable, and no one was to blame. Other injuries are caused by another person's negligence in allowing or in not preventing the injury. If a teacher's negligence can be proved, he can be held for damages in a tort action brought by the pupil or his parents; if the teacher can prove that there was no negligence but the injury was caused by a pure accident, there is no recovery of damages. It is therefore necessary to examine what might be called negligence by the courts.

Negligence at law is any conduct which falls below standard for the protection of others against unreasonable risk of harm. Negligence may be acts of commission or of omission, and liability is conditioned upon both the character of the conduct and the nature of the results. The amount of caution required is proportionate to the amount of threatened or apparent danger.

The first test to determine if there has been negligence is the test of foreseeability. When a reasonably prudent person could have fore-

277

seen the harmful consequences of his act, the actor, in disregarding the foreseeable consequences, is liable for negligent conduct. This is the general rule. Applying it to the teacher-pupil relationship, we may say that if a reasonably prudent teacher could have foreseen that a pupil might be injured by some act of his own or another's, the teacher is liable if he disregards these foreseeable consequences.

There may be many antecedent events leading to an injury, each in its major or minor way contributing to the cause, but some of these antecedent events have no legal bearing on the cause of the injury. The one or more causes without which the injury would not have happened is or are the actual causes among all the antecedent events. Among these actual causes, the legal cause is that cause which in the natural and continuous sequence of events produced the result, provided there has been no interference of an independent superseding cause.

A negligent person is relieved of legal responsibility if some other event breaks the connection between his act and the harm done, in such a way as to be considered by the court as a superseding cause of the harm, but the determination that an act is a superseding cause involves complicated legal principles.[1]

When a teacher is sued for negligent conduct which has caused injury to a pupil, one defense may be contributory negligence. Contributory negligence is conduct on the part of the injured person which falls below the standard to which he should conform for his own protection, and which is a contributing factor bringing about the person's injury. Minors are not held to the same degree of care as is demanded of adults. The standard required of children is that degree of care which the great mass of children of like age, intelligence, and experience would ordinarily exercise under the same circumstances. A pupil's youth and inexperience increase the precaution necessary on the part of the teacher to avoid an unreasonable risk toward the child.

Although a teacher is not liable for pupil injuries unless it can be shown that the teacher was negligent, once negligence has been proved, there are far-reaching implications of liability. That is, for example, a person whose negligence has caused an injury to another may be held liable also for physical harm resulting from fright or shock or other similar and immediate emotional disturbances caused by the injury; or for additional bodily harm resulting from acts done by third persons in rendering aid irrespective of whether the subsequent acts are

---

[1] Principles of superseding cause are outside the scope of this textbook.

done in a proper or negligent manner; or for a disease contracted because of lowered vitality resulting from the injury; or for harm sustained in a subsequent accident which would not have happened had the injured's bodily efficiency not been impaired by the negligent person. Furthermore, a teacher may be liable for injuries resulting from his conduct where the prior physical condition of the pupil is unknown.

Because accidents do occur to public-school pupils and because teachers are sued because of these accidents, several states have attempted to relieve them of the burden of paying judgments in such suits; one state is New York whose law is quoted in the *Statutory Material* provided later in this chapter.

This chapter examines also the legal consequences of pupil injuries from the point of view of the school board on the theory that pupils are injured under circumstances in which no individual teacher could be held liable and suit would be brought against the school board—if suits against school boards were permitted at law.

The general rule is that a school district, or a school board, is not liable for injuries to pupils in the absence of a statute imposing liability. In *Chicago v. Chicago*, 243 Ill. App. 327 (1927) the court said: "There are two reasons for this rule: (1) that a school board acts *nolens volens* as an agent of the state, performing a purely public or governmental duty imposed upon it by law, for the benefit of the public and for the performance of which it receives no profit or advantage; (2) since the property which it possesses is held in trust, the payment of judgments in tort would amount to a diversion, or, in some cases, a destruction, of the trust." There is a third and older reason: the traditional immunity of government from tort actions.

Court decisions over the country by the hundreds have upheld the principle of governmental immunity when injured pupils and their parents have sued school districts. There is no redress at common law. No school district can accept liability voluntarily and waive its immunity. The state can do so, for itself or for its subdivisions, but a school district is a subordinate unit without power to make itself liable. This is the general rule.

Only Arizona, Illinois, and New York courts have departed from this common-law rule without legislative authorization to do so. Legislatures of Massachusetts, Oregon, and Wyoming have authorized school districts to assume liability imposed on a teacher because of negligence, but these statutes are permissive. The Minnesota legislature abrogated governmental immunity in 1963. New York courts applied *respondeat*

superior even before the legislation which required school districts to pay judgments against their employees.

In all other states, the courts have followed the common-law rule of governmental immunity in the absence of statutory abrogation of this principle.

Several states have modified the traditional common-law rule by statute. Some of these enactments have not been interpreted by the courts in such a way as to give judicial aid to injured pupils, because being in abrogation of the common law, they are strictly construed.

"Safe-place" statutes in a few states cover public buildings and grounds. Again the courts have been strict in applying these statutes to school districts, and there has been considerable inconsistency among them. In general, without a "safe-place" statute, and even under some such laws, improper construction of a school building does not make the school board liable for injuries to pupils resulting from the faulty construction. Nor is there liability for failure to repair, for defective appliances, or dangerous condition of grounds; nor for any injury occasioned by the negligence of the school board or its employees. There are hundreds of court cases which uphold this theory of immunity.

On the other hand, there does seem to be some theoretical trend toward the abolition or modification of the theory of nonliability. A number of court opinions and legal authorities in their treatises have admitted the injustice of the common-law immunity. Yet, as mentioned by the Illinois court above, there are practical reasons why the development of legislation imposing liability has been slow, and outside of several states, the lag of legal theory exemplified by judicial decisions has impeded the effectiveness of what little legislation has been attempted.

The implications of governmental immunity from tort action are manifold. Among the many problems is the question of whether or not a school board may carry insurance in order to have funds available for the payment of damages to injured pupils. Most courts have said that without legislation enabling the purchase of accident insurance, a school board has no such right under its general powers; that having no liability there is nothing to insure; that even with enabling legislation permitting the school board to buy insurance protection for its pupils, suit cannot be taken against the board to establish the amount of damages for the insurance company to pay; that a statute authorizing the purchase of insurance does not abrogate the common-law

governmental immunity of the school board. It has been only recently that injured pupils have been permitted in some jurisdictions to collect on insurance carried by their school boards, if it was necessary to go to the court to settle the claim. Probably nowhere in the entire body of school law is there more uncertainty, more realization of the gap between the moral and the legal duty of the school board—between the social and the legal rights of the public-school pupil.

Statutory Material

New York Education Law, sec. 3023.

Notwithstanding any inconsistent provision of law, general, special or local, or the limitation contained in the provisions of any city charter, it shall be the duty of each board of education, trustee or trustees, in any school district having a population of less than one million, and each board of cooperative educational services established pursuant to section nineteen hundred fifty-eight of this chapter, to save harmless and protect all teachers and members of supervisory and administrative staff or employees from financial loss arising out of any claim, demand, suit or judgment by reason of alleged negligence or other act resulting in accidental bodily injury to any person within or without the school building, provided such teacher or member of the supervisory or administrative staff or employee at the time of the accident or injury was acting in the discharge of his duties within the scope of his employment and/or under the direction of said board of education, trustee, trustees, or board of cooperative educational services; and said board of education, trustee, trustees, or board of cooperative educational services may arrange for and maintain appropriate insurance with any insurance company created by or under the laws of this state, or in any insurance company authorized by law to transact business in this state, or such board, trustee, trustees, or board of cooperative educational services may elect to act as self-insurers to maintain the aforesaid protection. A board of education, trustee, board of trustees, or board of cooperative educational services, however, shall not be subject to the duty imposed by this section, unless such teacher, or member of the supervisory and administrative staff or employee shall, within ten days of the time he is served with any summons, complaint, process, notice, demand or pleading, deliver the original or a copy of the same to such board of education, trustee, board of trustees, or board of cooperative educational services.

Statutory note. Somewhat similar laws have been enacted in New Jersey and Connecticut. Also, Wyoming has authorized local school districts to "save teachers harmless," within the discretionary power of each local district. In many other states, insurance protection is by individual or group action, unsupported by public funds. A few districts contribute from public funds to pay up to half the premium

costs, the teachers themselves paying the balance. And, many teachers still have no insurance protection covering this type of risk.

Principles of negligence outlined in general terms in the *Editorial Comment* of this chapter are not written into statutory law but are the rules which have evolved through legal tradition.

Deering's California Education Code, secs. 903, 904, 906, 1041-1044.

Sec. 903. The governing board of any school district is liable as such in the name of the district for any judgment against the district on account of injury to person or property arising because of the negligence of the district, or its officers or employes.

Sec. 904. The governing board of any school district shall pay any judgment for debts, liabilities, or damages out of the school funds to the credit of the district, subject to the limitation on the use of the funds provided in the Constitution. If any judgment is not paid during the tax year in which it was recovered:

(a) and if, in the opinion of the board, the amount is not too great to be paid out of taxes for the ensuing tax year, the board shall include in its budget for the ensuing tax year a provision to pay the judgment, and shall pay it immediately upon the obtaining of sufficient funds for that purpose.

(b) If, in the opinion of the board, the amount of the judgment is so great that undue hardship will arise if the entire amount is paid out of taxes for the next ensuing tax year, the board shall provide for the payment of the judgment in not exceeding three annual installments with interest thereon, at a rate not exceeding 4 percent per annum, up to the date of each payment, and shall include provision for the payment in each budget for not exceeding three consecutive tax years next ensuing. Each payment shall be of an equal portion of the principal of the judgment.

Sec. 906. The district attorney of the county in which a school district is located shall, without fee or other charge, defend the district in any suit brought for injury to any pupil for any cause.

Sec. 1041. No member of the governing board of any school district shall be held personally liable for accidents to children going to or returning from school, or on the playgrounds, or in connection with school work.

Sec. 1042. No member of the governing board of any school district shall be held personally liable for the death of, or injury to, any pupil enrolled in any school of the district, resulting from his participation in any classroom or other activity to which he has been lawfully assigned as a pupil in the school unless negligence on the part of the member of the governing board is the proximate cause of the injury or death.

Sec. 1043. If suit is brought against any member of the governing board of any school district as an individual, for any act, or omission, in the line of his official duty as a member of the board, or suit is brought against any employe of any school district for any act performed in the course of his employment, the district attorney of the county shall defend the

member of the board or the individual employe upon request of the governing board of the school district, without fee or other charge.

Sec. 1044. The governing board of any school district shall insure against the liability (other than a liability which may be insured against under the provisions of Divisions 4 and 5 of the Labor Code) of the district and against the personal liability of the members of the board and of the officers and employes of the district, for damages to property or damage by reason of the death of or injury to, any person or persons, as the result of any negligent act by the district, or by a member of the board, or any officer or employe when acting within the scope of his office or employment. The insurance may be written in any insurance company authorized to transact the business of insurance in the State or in a nonadmitted insurer to the extent and subject to the conditions prescribed by section 1763 of the Insurance Code.

Statutory note. California has gone farther than any other state in abrogating its governmental immunity for injured pupils. It allows direct suit against the school board and requires the board to pay damages out of school funds. On occasion, judgments in California cases have been high and to pay them out of the current budget would be impossible. The legislature has taken care of this problem also.

It is a general principle of law that members of an official board, like a school board, are not personally liable for damages on account of injuries resulting from negligence of the board; it has been less well publicized, however, that if the injury resulted from the *personal* negligence of a board member, he can be held liable. The California statute spells out these principles.

Oklahoma Statutes Annotated. Title 70, sec. 9-7.

The board of education of any school district authorized to furnish transportation may purchase insurance for the purpose of paying damages to persons sustaining injuries proximately caused by the operation of motor vehicles used in transporting school children. The operation of said vehicles by school districts, however, is hereby declared to be a public governmental function, and no action for damages shall be brought against a school district under the provisions of this Section but may be brought against the insurer, and the amount of the damages recoverable shall be limited in amount to that provided in the contract of insurance between the district and the insurer and shall be collectible from said insurer only. The provisions of this Section shall not be construed as creating any liability whatever against any school district which does not provide such insurance.

Statutory note. The Oklahoma statute creates a situation of doubtful acceptance in general insurance law. If the contract is between the insurer and the school district, the injured party cannot usually sue

the insurer, but must sue the insured, even if only as a preliminary step to ascertain the amount of the claim. However, any carrier wishing to do business with Oklahoma school districts must accept the possibility of direct suit by the injured, since this specific statutory provision would override any contrary provisions in the general insurance laws of the state and any provision in the policy contract.

Though Oklahoma authorizes school bus insurance, it does not abrogate its governmental immunity thereby. It is a common-law state in other areas as well.

Nevada Revised Statutes, sec. 392.440.

1. As used in this section, "injury" shall include injury resulting in death within 1 year.

2. The purpose of this section is to provide, if practicable, protection to student members of athletic teams of public schools from loss arising out of injuries received by them in the course of athletic competition or practice under the immediate charge of school coaches or authorities and injuries received by them in travel for such purposes.

3. Whenever any insurance company authorized to do business in this state submits a plan for group insurance of students in the public schools against loss in circumstances referred to in subsection 2, for a blanket annual premium charge not greater than one-half of any amount which may be appropriated for 2 years by the legislature for this purpose, the commissioner of insurance and the superintendent of public instruction shall study the plan and ask the opinion of the attorney general concerning the legality of the plan. If the commissioner of insurance and the superintendent of public instruction certify that the proposed rates and the policy of insurance as executed meet the requirements of this section, a claim for the annual premium shall be presented to the state board of examiners for audit and allowance as provided by law. If more than one qualified insurance company submit identical or substantially identical plans and rates, the insurance may be divided equitably among them.

4. The superintendent of public instruction and school authorities throughout the state shall cooperate in reporting the total number of students to be included in the group insured, and in certifying the membership of an individual student on athletic teams should he be injured.

5. Nothing in this section shall be deemed to admit any liability on the part of the state or the school districts therein for any injury.

Statutory note. It will have been noted that some insurance laws cover transportation injuries only and some cover all kinds of injuries. The Nevada law illustrates insurance coverage for school athletes. Like many other states, including Oklahoma as shown in the preceding quotation, Nevada clings to its governmental immunity.

Case Material

Guerrieri v. Tyson et al., 147 Pa. Super. 239, 24 A. (2d) 468 (Pennsylvania, 1942). [Parents sued for damages resulting from injury to son caused by teachers' medical treatment.]

On June 15, 1938 the minor plaintiff, then 10 years old, was a pupil in a public school in which the defendants were acting as teachers, in the employ of the school district. The little finger of the boy's right hand had been infected but this condition did not prevent him from playing baseball during the noon recess. During the afternoon session of that day, defendant Myrtle Tyson, noticing the inflamed condition of the finger, asked the boy to report at the school office after school. There, if we give the plaintiffs the benefit of the favorable inferences from the testimony, she heated a pan of water to the boiling point and with the assistance of defendant Elinor Rae immersed the boy's hand in the scalding water against his will and held it there for about ten minutes. The testimony is that Miss Rae held a paper towel over the boy's eyes while Miss Tyson kept the boy's hand in the water. When the hand was removed is was covered with blisters which Miss Tyson opened with a needle. The boy then was suffering intense pain. He was later taken home in Miss Rae's automobile. His parents immediately sent for a doctor and on his advice the boy was removed to a hospital where he remained for twenty-eight days. The scalding aggravated the infection, and the scar tissue resulting from the boiling water permanently disfigured the hand. There is medical testimony that these conditions were the direct result of the treatment which the boy received at the school from defendants Tyson and Rae.

Under the circumstances, we think it clear that these defendants are legally liable for the damages resulting from their tort. These teachers stood in loco parentis to the child, but there is nothing in that relationship which will justify defendants' acts. Under the delegated parental authority implied from the relationship of teacher and pupil, . . . there is no implied delegation of authority to exercise her lay judgment, as a parent may, in the matter of the treatment of injury or disease suffered by a pupil.

Treatment of the minor plaintiff's hand was not necessary in this case; defendants were not acting in an emergency. The defendants were not school nurses and neither of them had any medical training or experience. Whether treatment of the infected finger was necessary was a question for the boy's parents to decide. The status of a parent, with some of the parent's privileges, is given a school teacher by law in aid of the education and training of the child . . . and ordinarily does not extend beyond matters of conduct and discipline. There is nothing in the teacher-pupil relationship between the defendants in this case and the minor plaintiff which can relieve them from responsibility for their acts. The court properly refused to enter judgment in their favor.

Case note. When a pupil becomes ill, it is the teacher's duty to send him to the school nurse or to his parents for medical treatment by the

family physician. If the illness is sufficiently severe, the pupil might be removed to a hospital, after the parents are notified. Under no *such* circumstances should a teacher attempt medical treatment because he may be liable for damages if his treatment causes the pupil to be in a worse condition than he was before the teacher's voluntary treatment.

However, it is necessary to make the important distinction between illness as exemplified in the Guerrieri case to which the principles set down in the preceding paragraph apply, and an emergency in which first aid is needed without delay. In the latter circumstances, a teacher would be considered negligent if he did not attempt to act for the benefit of the pupil. Teachers owe their pupils the duty of first-aid care in cases of emergency, provided, of course, a nurse or physician is not immediately available. If a person with medical training is available, the teacher, untrained in more than the rudiments of first-aid treatment, should not attempt to act; but if no person with medical training is available and the pupil needs immediate attention which cannot wait for the arrival of a doctor or nurse, the teacher would be derelict in his duty if he did not render first aid. Yet, the treatment the teacher gives the pupil under these circumstances must be such as not to worsen his condition, or the teacher might be held liable for causing him greater injury than he originally sustained.

Livingston v. Regents of the New Mexico College of Agriculture and Mechanic Arts, 64 N. Mex. 306, 328 P. (2d) 78 (New Mexico, 1958). [Pupil injury in common-law state.]

The appellant, Sheila Livingston, who was the plaintiff below, was a student at the New Mexico College of Agriculture and Mechanic Arts. While in the college cafeteria on September 14, 1956, she was injured as a result of the alleged negligence of Carlos Gallegos, an employee of the defendant college.

The complaint set forth the injury and alleged damages suffered by the plaintiffs as a proximate result of defendants' negligence, and it then further alleged:

"The defendant, A & M Regents, at the time of said incident . . . carried liability insurance with the United States Fidelity and Guaranty Company, fully protecting said defendant and insuring it against liability to plaintiffs, arising out of the facts herein alleged, up to and including the limits of the policy issued by said company, which policy was and, at all times material hereto, has been in full force and effect.

To this complaint the defendant Board of Regents filed a motion to dismiss, contending that the defendant Board was immune from suit.

We have a well established rule in this state that a state institution, as is the defendant Board of Regents in this case, is not subject to an action in damages for the negligence of its employees.

The appellants recognize this rule but argue strenuously that a suit demanding judgment only to the extent that the state agency is protected by liability insurance does not violate the rule of immunity.

Appellants rely most heavily upon Thomas v. Broadlands Community Consol. School Dist., 348 Ill. App. 567, 109 N.E.2d 636; Tracy v. Davis, D.C.E.D. Ill., 123 F. Supp. 160; and Williams v. Town of Morristown, 32 Tenn. App. 274, 222 S.W.2d 607, modified, 189 Tenn. 124, 222 S.W.2d 615.

The Broadlands case held that an action in tort by a student injured on a playground would lie against the defendant school district inasmuch as the district carried liability insurance. While upholding the historical rule of sovereign immunity from suit, the Illinois court reasoned that liability insurance, to the extent that it protects public funds, removes the reason for such immunity.

As argued by appellees, however, the majority of the courts seem to hold contrary to the authorities relied upon by appellants.

It is to be noted that in 1941 the legislature provided for the recovery of damages for the negligence of employees of this state in specific instances, and we are impressed by the manner in which this was done:

"The state board of finance is authorized to require all officials or the administrative heads of all departments to purchase and secure public liability and property damage insurance in such sums as they may deem advisable, protecting the state against property loss and the public against injury to property or persons because of the negligent operation of automobiles, trucks, trailers, tractors, graders or other motor vehicles by employees, agents or officials of the state, or any of its institutions, agencies or political subdivisions." (§ 64-25-8, N.M.S.A. 1953.)

"No action shall be brought or entertained in any court of this state *against the state or any of its institutions, agencies, or political subdivisions* for injury or damage caused by the operation of such vehicles, but the action for any such injury or damage shall be brought against the person operating such vehicle at the time of the injury or damage. Every policy of insurance upon such vehicles shall contain a provision that the defense of immunity from tort liability because the insured as a governmental agency or an employee of a governmental agency, or because the accident arose out of the performance of a governmental function, shall not be raised against any claim covered by such policy, Provided the claimant, or plaintiff in the event suit is instituted, shall file with the insured and the company issuing such policy of insurance a release in writing of any amount of such claim in excess of the limit stated in the policy, and a further statement that any such release shall not be construed as an admission of liability, nor may it be offered in evidence for any purpose, and that no attempt may be made in the trial of any case to suggest the existence of any insurance which covers in whole or in part any judgment or award in favor of the claimant."

We admit that the logic of appellants' argument might very well justify a change in the public policy of this jurisdiction. We feel, however, that the appellants' argument should be addressed to the legislature and not to this court.

Are we to say that the legislature should have expanded the provisions of the 1941 Act so as to have permitted recovery in an action such as this; and that the legislature having failed to do so, we will declare such to be the policy of this state?

To do this, we think, would usurp the functions of the legislative branch of our government.

We hold that a suit based upon tort against a state agency such as the Regents, demanding judgment only to the extent that such agency is protected by liability insurance, violates the rule of governmental immunity from suit. The order of the lower court dismissing the action as to the defendant Board of Regents is affirmed.

Case note. This is the traditional judicial view. Even though insurance is carried, suit cannot be brought against a public agency, even to the extent of the insurance, unless the legislature has abrogated its immunity at least to that extent. An exception to application of this rule among common-law states is Illinois (see Molitor case, p. 296).

Notice that the 1941 statute quoted by the court in the New Mexico case (Livingston) requires waiver of the defense of governmental immunity, as in the Virginia law quoted on page 228. However, as was pointed out in the *Statutory note* following the Virginia quotation, such a waiver was held by the Minnesota court to be of no avail.

Sestero et al. v. Town of Glastonbury, 19 Conn. Sup. 156, 110 A. (2d) 629 (Connecticut, 1954). [Nuisance as an exception to governmental immunity in general.]

In this action the plaintiff seeks damages against the town of Glastonbury, the board of education of the town of Glastonbury, and a teacher employed in the Glastonbury schools. The plaintiff, a pupil in a Glastonbury elementary school, claims to have sustained injuries during a school recess as the result of a push by classmates which caused him to fall on the school playground. The defendants pleaded in abatement that in the maintenance and management of public schools the town board of education is the agent of the state and not of the town. The defendant board of education has demurred to the complaint because in the maintenance and management of the public schools, it is a quasi corporation acting in the course of governmental or public duty and therefore immune or relieved thereby from liability for the harm alleged in the complaint.

The authorities cited by the defendant town of Glastonbury regarding the respective legal positions of towns and boards of education and the status of boards of education as agencies of the state and not of the towns in the maintenance and management of public schools would appear to support the legal position taken by the defendant town of Glastonbury. . . .

The demurrer of the defendant board of education is based upon the defense of governmental immunity which attaches to the performance by a municipality or public body of a public duty for the public benefit and not for its own corporate profit. . . .

The defense of governmental immunity, however, does not avail against a cause of action founded on a nuisance created by a governmental body by positive act. . . .

The complaint to which the demurrer has been filed is in one count which sets out numerous ways in which it is alleged that the defendant was negligent. "A nuisance may have its origin in negligence. . . . It is not always easy to determine when the nuisance as distinguished from the negligence arises. . . ." While the pleader has avoided the use of the word "nuisance" in the complaint, it does appear that the allegations of the complaint are sufficiently broad to set forth, in addition to an allegation of ordinary negligence, the essentials of a claim of nuisance. . . . In addition to the allegations of failure to act, it is alleged that the condition or situation complained of was created by the positive act of the defendant and increased greatly the probability of injury or harm "creating a hazardous and dangerous condition." While it is true that most of the allegations of the complaint alleges a failure on the part of the defendant to take some action, positive acts of negligence on the part of the defendant creating and maintaining the alleged hazardous and dangerous conditions are alleged and since the defense of governmental immunity does not avail as against a cause of action founded on a nuisance created by positive act, the demurrer is overruled.

Case note. In the last decade a few cases have allowed suit against school boards in common-law states when the injury was caused by a "nuisance"; other states have held that governmental immunity prevails even when the injury is caused by a nuisance. An unguarded bayou was held not to have created a nuisance by the Louisiana court which implied that even if the unguarded bayou could be called a nuisance the school board would not have been liable for damages when a little child fell in and was drowned, because the board was immune from suit in general. *Whitfield v. East Baton Rouge Parish School Board*, ____La. App.____, 23 So. (2d) 708 (Louisiana, 1945). In that case the board was charged with maintaining an attractive nuisance. An attractive nuisance is one which attracts children's curiosity and invites them to play on, in, over, or with it. The theory began with railroad turntables. The one responsible for leaving an attractive nuisance may be held liable for damages if children are injured; he owes children a duty to have such a danger guarded in some way to prevent injuries to children who are attracted to it by their natural curiosity.

The playground of a school should be kept in safe condition. Maintenance of a dangerous condition on the playground may be called a

nuisance, as in this Connecticut case, where the court said that if the jury found the playground in a dangerous condition and that that condition caused the pupil's injury, the board could be held liable for damages for maintaining a nuisance even though Connecticut has not abrogated its governmental immunity.

Dutcher v. City of Santa Rosa High School District, Rehe v. City of Santa Rosa High School District, 156 Cal. App. (2d) 256, 319 P. (2d) 14 (California, 1957). [Pupil injury in state which has abrogated common-law immunity.]

Vinton H. Dutcher and his wife, parents of Paul Dutcher, deceased, commenced an action against the city of Santa Rosa High School District and Rollo Norris, an instructor employed by the school to recover damages for the death of their son. In another action, Dennis Rehe, a minor, by his guardian ad litem, brought an action against the school district and Norris for damages for personal injuries suffered by him in the same accident. His father sued for expenses incurred. Both boys were members of a class in auto mechanics which the respondent Norris was teaching. Each complaint charges negligence on the part of Norris. The answers of respondents in each case denied any negligence on their part and also pleaded the defenses of contributory negligence and unavoidable accident. The two cases were consolidated for trial. . . .

On December 11, 1952, Paul Dutcher and Dennis Rehe, as students at Santa Rosa High School, were attending their regular fifth period auto shop class which was held between 12:40 and 1:40 p.m. During the first part of the period the class was being instructed by respondent Rollo Norris, the class instructor for approximately 8 years, on the method of removing the valves from an automobile motor which was on a work bench. This motor was some 30 feet from an automobile owned by Donald Saunders to which Norris had his back, and his vision of Saunders' car was partially obstructed by another car. Following the completion of the instructions Norris was picking up the valve springs and equipment and putting them in a box while the students walked away toward other parts of the shop. Rehe and Dutcher stopped at Saunders' car. They saw Saunders inside the car doing some cutting with a torch and they stood and watched him. While they were standing alongside the car, the gas line tank of the Saunders car exploded and a fire resulted, causing the severe injuries to the boys from which Dutcher ultimately died.

Just prior to the explosion Norris had left the work bench and had gone to the car owned by a student, parked some 6 or 7 feet to the rear of and at right angle to Saunders' car. He got under this car on the side nearest the rear of Saunders' car by the use of a "creeper," upon which the person lies down and pulls himself head first under the car. On getting out from under the car by use of the "creeper" Norris pulled himself feet first in the direction of the Saunders' car and when arising from the "creeper" would necessarily face toward that car where Dutcher and Rehe were grouped around it watching Saunders work. He arose from

the "creeper," turned to go back to the bench and had taken a few steps when the explosion occurred.

Donald Saunders was a regular member of the second period class in the auto shop and a regular member of the fifth period gymnasium class, and after answering roll call in his fifth period gymnasium class he left the class without permission or knowledge of his teacher and went to the auto shop at about 1:00 p.m. He had done this on other occasions during the semester. On two previous occasions Saunders had come to the shop during the fifth period when he did not have any conflicting class and Norris had given him permission to return. Respondents contend that Norris did not actually know that Saunders was in the shop during this particular fifth period. However, appellants point to the evidence, that when Saunders entered the shop he stopped and talked to several of the students and then went to the bench where Norris was instructing. Saunders stood there for a while and then went to the tool room and obtained a cutting torch from one of the student monitors. He passed by the work bench again and went to the oxygen and acetylene tanks which were about midway between the work bench where Norris was instructing the group and the left rear of Saunders' parked car. Saunders attached the cutting torch and lit it. After adjusting the flame, he walked to his car with a lighted torch and began burning a hole in its floor.

Norris had given general safety instructions to all of his students about removing the gas tank before welding or cutting on a car. Saunders had removed the gas tank from his car about two weeks before the accident, placing the tank against the wall of the building. During the second period on December 11, 1952, Norris advised Saunders to take his gasoline tank and replace it up on the frame so the janitor could sweep around the area. Saunders did not comply with this request. Saunders did not know where the gas tank was located when the explosion occurred.

Appellants contend that respondent Norris, the instructor in charge, failed to live up to his duty. They state that he failed to observe that Saunders was in the class although Saunders was within a few feet of him on several occasions and at one point stood with a lighted torch; and that he failed to observe the group around Saunders' car and the noise and light from the torch which should have caused him to investigate because the boys were supposed to be working on other projects. Appellants argue that a serious laxity existed in the instructor's supervision by permitting so dangerous an instrument as a cutting torch to be handed out to anyone who came to the tool room, even a non-member of the class. Even more serious, they state, is the instructor's indifference to the danger presented by the gas tank being in such proximity to the car. . . .

We believe that the question of whether or not respondent Norris, the class instructor, was guilty of negligence which proximately caused the injuries to appellants was a question of fact to be submitted to the jury under proper instructions.

The next and most serious contention of appellants is that the court erred in giving the following instructions on assumption of risk:

"We have a legal principle commonly referred to by the term 'assumption of risk.' It will now be explained to you:

"A person is said to assume a risk when he freely, voluntarily and knowingly manifests his assent to dangerous conduct or to the creation or maintenance of a dangerous condition, and voluntarily exposes himself to that danger, or when he knows that a danger exists in either the conduct or condition of another, or in the condition, use or operation of property, and voluntarily places himself, or remains, within the area of danger.

"A person who thus assumed a risk is not entitled to recover for damages caused without intention and which resulted from the dangerous condition or conduct to which he thus exposed himself.

"In determining whether or not a person had knowledge of a dangerous situation and whether, with such knowldege, he assented to or assumed a risk so as to bar recovery by him of damages for injury, you may consider his age, experience and capacity along with all the other surrounding circumstances as shown by the evidence. . . ."

Appellants do not question the correctness of the principles stated in the said instructions but they contend that the court should not have given any instructions on assumption of risk. . . .

Respondents seek to justify the giving of the challenged instructions upon the theory that the boys knew that there were hazards attached to the burning of a torch as they had received safety instructions and they were mature students mechanically. Respondents rely upon testimony of Saunders to the effect that Norris had told his class, at least, that welding should not take place near a gas tank and that the gas tank should be placed ten feet away from the car while welding. Respondents argue that under the evidence in this case the jury was entitled to draw an inference that the students voluntarily assumed a risk with knowledge of a dangerous situation. . . . We are convinced that under the evidence in the instant case it was error for the court to give instructions on assumption of risk. Paul Dutcher and Dennis Rehe were properly in the shop in pursuit of their regular studies, they went from the point where they had been instructed in the technique of removing valves from an engine to the place where they could grind those valves, and stopped for a moment to observe the work of Donald Saunders. It appears that they were prompted either by a legitimate interest in the work of Donald, or mere youthful curiosity, and there is nothing to show that they knew anything about the dangerous proximity of the gas tank to the torch or appreciated the danger of an explosion.

We do not believe that the record would support a finding that the boys knew and appreciated the extent of the risk involved. . . .

The appellants next contend that the court committed prejudicial error in refusing to give their proposed instruction on required care and supervision of the use of a dangerous instrument. The parties agree that this instruction was based on the testimony sought to be obtained from Vernon W. Bailey, teacher of auto mechanics at Napa College, in regard to practices used in a Napa school. The trial court sustained objections to his testimony and in stating its ruling of the objection said, "do not let us from Napa come over here and persuade you that our regulations are

better than yours." Respondents contend that the proposed instruction should not have been given because it found no support in the record.

Appellants contend that it was error to disallow this testimony and that the judge's remark above was prejudicial. It appears from the record that appellants sought testimony from Bailey as to the particular practice at his school and the judge properly sustained the objection to such testimony upon the ground that this was not expert testimony as to general custom and usage but as to particular instances and therefore not admissible.

Inasmuch as there was no evidence upon which to base the instruction offered by appellants there was no error in refusing to give it. . . .

The final instruction complained of by appellants reads as follows:

"The acts of the defendants herein complained of must be connected with the act of Donald Saunders in coming to the fifth period class and of burning a hole in his automobile in proximity to his gasoline tank, and it must not only appear that the injury complained of in the present cases were the natural and probable consequence, or negligent or unlawful act, if any, of the defendants, but that it ought to have been foreseen in the light of the attendant circumstances that Donald Saunders would follow the course of conduct that he did with the resulting injuries that are complained of. One may not be held responsible for those consequences following from an act which could not have been anticipated by a reasonably prudent person. In order to find the defendants liable in the present cases, you must find that the defendants were charged with the duty of anticipating as a matter of ordinary consequence of their negligence, if any, that Donald Saunders would commit the acts performed by him."

We believe that this instruction should not have been given and that it would tend to confuse and mislead the jury. It is properly subject to the objection that it is in the main argumentative and is the type of formula instruction that should not be given. We believe that a court should instruct a jury in simple, clear, and concise language as to the law applicable to the case and should leave the matter of argument to counsel for the respective parties. . . .

While the giving of this instruction would not constitute reversible error, we hold that it should not have been given.

Case note. The board based its defense on the theory of "assumption of risk." This theory rarely is adequate defense in actions for damages on account of injuries sustained by young people. Assumption of risk is based on the assumption that the injured knew of the dangerous condition and nevertheless chose to accept the risk. Many courts say that even when pupils know that a condition is dangerous they do not always know the extent of the danger and therefore the theory of assumption of risk is inapplicable.

Luce v. Board of Education of Village of Johnson City, 2 A.D.
(2d) 502, 157 N. Y. S. (2d) 123 (New York, 1956) *aff'd* (memorandum opinion) 3 N. Y. (2d) 792, 143 N. E. (2d) 797 (1957).
[Pupil injury in state which has abrogated common-law immunity.]

The judgment, based upon jury verdicts, awards damages to each
plaintiff against all three defendants resulting from personal injuries sustained by the infant plaintiff on November 16, 1953, while participating
in a physical education class in an elementary school. The accident occurred while the infant plaintiff, then eleven years of age, was participating
in a game called "jump the stick relay" in a physical education class conducted and supervised by the defendant, Katharine Denton, a physical
education teacher. The defendant Leola Holcomb was the supervising
principal of the elementary school in which the accident occurred. The
school was one of the schools under the jurisdiction of the defendant
Board of Education.

The infant plaintiff had suffered two previous fractures of her right
forearm in accidents unrelated to her school activities, one in 1949 and
one in 1950. The 1950 fracture necessitated an open reduction which left
a noticeable scar on her forearm, and when she returned to school in the
fall of 1950 her arm was in a cast and she did not participate in gymnasium
class activities for some time, although she attended the classes. She was
excused from participating because of a doctor's certificate that her
physical condition did not permit such activity. During the school term
in which the accident here involved occurred there was no such doctor's
certificate presented, and it appears that the attending physician had given
his permission that the infant plaintiff participate in physical education
classes in general. There is evidence, however, that the child's mother
had advised the principal and the defendant teacher that because of her
previous injuries, the child should not participate in "rough games," and
the mother testified that she advised both of these defendants that the
child should not participate in any activity or game in which she might
be caused to fall.

The general theory of negligence urged by plaintiffs is that, having or
being chargeable with knowledge of her physical condition due to the
previous accidents, the principal and teacher should not have directed or
permitted the infant plaintiff to participate in the game resulting in
her fall because the consequences were reasonably foreseeable.

It is urged that the Board is liable for its own negligence in failing to
adopt necessary rules for the governing of its gymnasium classes, its
principals and teachers, and rules relating to the limitation of activity by
children with physical defects. Section 1709, subdivision 2, of the Education Law gives the Board the power and imposes the duty, "To establish
such rules and regulations concerning the order and discipline of the
schools, in the several departments thereof, as they may deem necessary
to secure the best educational results." Our attention is also called to the
following provision in subdivision 13 of the same section: "To have in
all respects the superintendence, management and control of said union
free schools. . . ." We do not think that by this language the Legislature

intended to impose upon the Board of Education a duty to make and assume the direct responsibility of enforcing rules which reach down into each of the numerous class rooms and classes of a complex school system and to provide in detail the type of activities and the qualification of individuals for participation therein. In a modern school system composed of several schools, each with many and varied classes, supervised in general by a superintendent and immediately supervised by many trained and competent teachers, such a requirement would be impractical and unrealistic. It would be entirely impossible for a board of education to adopt and enforce rules which would cover every detail of activity and every individual situation which might arise. The judgment against the Board of Education should be reversed and the complaint dismissed as to it.

The defendant Leola Holcomb was the supervising principal of the elementary school where the accident happened. Her duties, too, were administrative, supervisory, and general in nature. She was responsible for the assignment of class rooms, for discipline in the school, and administrative supervision over the teachers in the school. It does not appear that she had any authority, let alone duty, to personally supervise or to direct the nature of activities or limit the participation of any pupil in a physical education class. The physical education department was a separate arm of the Board of Education, operating in all of the schools. Mrs. Denton, the physical education teacher in immediate charge here, was an agent of the physical education department. It is a matter of common knowledge that in modern times the educational and competency requirements of such a teacher are high. Of necessity the detailed activities of each class and of each student therein must be left to such supervising teacher. As observed in Thompson v. Board of Education, 280 N.Y. 92, 96, 19 N.E.2d 796, 797: "Appellant [a principal] could not personally attend to each class at the same time, nor was any such duty imposed upon him." The fact that the defendant Holcomb knew of the infant plaintiff's previous injuries, or that the mother had requested her to relieve the child of some gymnasium activities, does not impose liability upon her under the circumstances here. It does not appear that the principal had the power or authority to direct the detailed conduct of a physical education class, or to substitute her judgment for that of Mrs. Denton as to the risks of a particular game to a particular pupil, and it does appear that Mrs. Denton, the teacher in immediate charge had the same information and request directly from the mother. The evidence does not sustain a finding of negligence on the part of the defendant principal, and the judgment against her should be reversed and the complaint dismissed.

The defendant Denton was the physical education teacher in immediate charge and supervision of the class and of the infant plaintiff at the time of the accident. She was under a duty to exercise reasonable care to prevent injuries and to assign pupils to such activities as were within their abilities, and to properly and adequately supervise the activities. The failure to do so constitutes actionable negligence on the part of the teacher. Govel v. Board of Education, supra; LaValley v. Stanford, 272 App.Div. 183, 70 N.Y.S.2d 460. The questions of her knowledge of the pre-existing physical condition of the infant plaintiff, the foreseeability of the conse-

quences, and the risks involved in the game being played, and the ultimate question of whether she exercised reasonable care, are questions of fact for determination by jury. However, the question of the negligence of the defendant Denton was submitted to the jury in conjunction with the questions of negligence of the other two defendants and the jury returned a verdict against all three. Such a consideration of the collective liability of all defendants could very well have confused the issue of negligence of the defendant Denton alone, which we have determined was the jury question. The judgment against the defendant Denton should be reversed and a new trial ordered.

Case note. The trial court's judgment was reversed and a new trial ordered because the trial court had submitted the question of negligence to the jury without distinction between the board, the principal, and the teacher in charge. The appellate court held that the board was not liable; nor was the principal; but the teacher could be.

Molitor v. Kaneland Community Unit District No. 302, 18 Ill. (2d) 11, 163 N. E. (2d) 89 (Illinois, 1959) *cert. den.* 362 U. S. 968 (1959). [Suit allowed to extent of insurance in common-law state.]

Plaintiff, Thomas Molitor, a minor, by Peter his father and next friend, brought this action against Kaneland Community Unit School District for personal injuries sustained by plaintiff when the school bus in which he was riding left the road, allegedly as a result of the driver's negligence, hit a culvert, exploded and burned. . . .

Defendant's motion to dismiss the complaint on the ground that a school district is immune from liability for tort was sustained by the trial court, and a judgment was entered in favor of defendant. Plaintiff elected to stand on his complaint and sought a direct appeal to this court. . . .

In his brief, plaintiff recognizes the rule, established by this court in 1898, that a school district is immune from tort liability, and frankly asks this court either to abolish the rule *in toto,* or to find it inapplicable to a school district such as Kaneland which was organized through the voluntary acts of petition and election by the voters of the district, as contrasted with a school district created *nolens volens* by the State.

With regard to plaintiff's alternative contention, we do not believe that a logical distinction can be drawn between a community school district . . . and any other type of school district, insofar as the question of tort liability is concerned. . . .

Thus we are squarely faced with the highly important question—in the light of modern developments, should a school district be immune from liability for tortiously inflicted personal injury to a pupil thereof arising out of the operation of a school bus owned and operated by said district? . . .

Surveying the whole picture of governmental tort law as it stands in Illinois today, the following broad outlines may be observed. The General

Assembly has frequently indicated its dissatisfaction with the doctrine of sovereign immunity upon which the Kinnare case was based. Governmental units, including school districts, are now subject to liability under the Workmen's Compensation and Occupational Disease Acts. . . . The State itself is liable, under the 1945 Court of Claims Act, for damages in tort up to $7,500 for the negligence of its officers, agents or employees. . . . Cities and villages have been made directly liable for injuries caused by the negligent operation of fire department vehicles, and for actionable wrong in the removal or destruction of unsafe or unsanitary buildings. . . .

[The court pointed out that the Illinois School Code authorizes school bus insurance and requires all such policies to include a waiver of the defense of governmental immunity.] Thus, a person injured by an insured school district bus may recover to the extent of the insurance while one injured by an uninsured school district bus cannot recover under the Kinnare doctrine.

Defendant contends that the quoted provision of the School Code constitutes a legislative determination that the public policy of this State requires that school districts be immune from tort liability. We can read no such legislative intent into the statute. Rather, we interpret that section as expressing dissatisfaction with the court-created doctrine of governmental immunity and an attempt to cut down that immunity where insurance is involved. The difficulty with this legislative effort to curtail the judicial doctrine is that it allows each school district to determine for itself whether, and to what extent, it will be financially responsible for the wrongs inflicted by it. . . .

It is a basic concept underlying the whole law of torts today that liability follows negligence, and that individuals and corporations are responsible for the negligence of their agents and employees acting in the course of their employment. The doctrine of governmental immunity runs directly counter to that basic concept. What reasons then, are so compelling as to allow a school district, as a quasi-municipal corporation, to commit wrongdoing without any responsibility to its victims, while any individual or private corporation would be called to task in court for such tortious conduct? . . .

The original basis of the immunity rule has been called a "survival of the medieval idea that the sovereign can do no wrong." . . .

We are of the opinion that school district immunity cannot be justified on this theory. . . .

The other chief reason advanced in support of the immunity rule in the more recent cases is the protection of public funds and public property. . . .

We do not believe that in this present day and age, when public education constitutes one of the biggest businesses in the country, that school immunity can be justified on the protection-of-public-funds theory. . . .

We conclude that the rule of school district tort immunity is unjust, unsupported by any valid reason, and has no rightful place in modern day society.

Defendant strongly urges that if said immunity is to be abolished, it should be done by legislature, not by this court. With this contention we must disagree. The doctrine of school district immunity was created by this court alone. Having found that doctrine to be unsound and unjust under present conditions, we consider that we have not only the power, but the duty, to abolish that immunity. . . .

We have repeatedly held that the doctrine of *stare decisis* is not an inflexible rule requiring this court to blindly follow precedents and adhere to prior decisions and that when it appears that public policy and social needs require a departure from prior decisions, it is our duty as a court of last resort to overrule those decisions and establish a rule consonant with our present day concepts of right and justice. . . .

For the reasons herein expressed, we accordingly hold that in this case the school district is liable in tort for the negligence of its employee, and all prior decisions to the contrary are hereby overruled.

Case note. Judges and text writers almost unanimously express dissatisfaction with the governmental immunity rule. In this opinion are cited a number of statements of this sort from these sources. However, though expressing disapproval judges usually follow the rule and declare that any abrogation of a common-law rule must be done by the legislature. There are few courts which have been convinced by the reasoning of many text writers that a judge-made rule can be changed by a judge without legislative action. Courts frequently overrule precedents; it is difficult to understand why they have been reluctant to do so in this particular area of governmental immunity.

Sources of Further Information

47 Am. Jur. "Schools" secs. 56, 57, 61.
78 C.J.S. "Schools and School Districts" secs. 153, 238, 318-322.
A.L.R. "Schools" Topic Nos. 25 and 45.
American Digest System "Schools and School Districts" Key Nos. 18, 88, 89, 147.

Work Sheet

1. Has your state enacted legislation to protect teachers who may be sued in tort actions by injured pupils?

2. Has your school board promulgated rules and regulations especially designed to prevent accidents to pupils?

3. If you teach any subject in which there may be inherent dangers for pupils, have you prepared and posted a warning thereof?

4. Has your state by statute modified the traditional common-law rule of governmental immunity?

5. If so, have your state courts interpreted it strictly or liberally?

6. If there is no legislation, has there been any tendency on the part of your state courts to relax the common-law rule?

7. Is there a "safe-place" statute applicable to school buildings in your state?

8. Has legislation been enacted to provide compensation of any kind to injured pupils in transportation? In athletics? In other school activities?

9. If so, what is the nature of the compensation so provided?

10. Is there what might be called an "attractive nuisance" in the neighborhood of your school? How could it be guarded so as to prevent injuries to pupils?

11. Are school buses in your district insured? Does the policy carry an endorsement waiving the defense of governmental immunity?

12. Has any pupil been injured recently in your school? If so, collect the facts and analyze the case to determine whether there might have been a charge of negligence against the teacher connected with the injury, if any, even though no suit was brought by the injured pupil. Could the injured pupil have had redress against the school board under any theory at all?

APPENDIXES

Appendix A.

HOW TO FIND SCHOOL LAW
(LEGAL RESEARCH TOOLS)

In the following pages directions will be given for legal research on school-law topics, particularly those included in this text, by use of legal research tools. Descriptions of these tools must, of necessity, be brief; photostatic copies of pages from some of the law books serve as illustrations. However, only by actually working with these devices can their real value be learned.

Constitutions

The Federal Constitution and the constitution of the particular state are usually placed at the beginning of each state code of general laws. The Federal Constitution appears in the United States Code also.

Some editions of these constitutions are annotated; others are not. An index to the constitutional provisions may be included in the index to statutory provisions, or a separate index to each constitution may be given.

Although it is occasionally possible to obtain a compilation in one volume of constitutional provisions of all states, these compilations go out of date; and, aside from the undesirability of using a secondary source, it is safer to use the state constitution included in each of the latest state code of laws, because this copy will contain all amendments to date.

State Statutes

Almost every state department of education publishes from time to time a compilation of state laws relating to education. Some of these publications appear infrequently and are difficult to use without further search for later enactments. Supplements may be issued between dates of complete compilations, but search through a half dozen or more pamphlets is a tedious task and one which is subject to error unless done very carefully.

There is a more serious objection to using some state department publications. These compilations of state school laws in some states are arranged in a sequence and numbered differently from the arrangement used in the state code of general laws for the particular state. This practice was more general a few years ago than at present. It is undesirable because, when the state department issues the school law codified according to its own departmental numerical plan, legal research tools applicable to the codification of the official state code cannot be used.

However, a number of state departments now publish the school laws using the codification of the official state code. In such cases, section 1198, for example, in the state department publication is identical with section 1198 of the state code of general laws. Then the devices of legal research may be used as easily with the state department publication as with the state code, provided it is not too far out of date for use as a point of departure. Some state department publications use both their own and the official codification numbers to identify each section, in which case the state department numbers can be ignored in legal research.

One point in favor of using state department publications on school law is their availability to educators. However, warning should be made that before any such bulletin is used it should be examined to ascertain its codification plan. Usually the preface explains the numbering system of the bulletin.

In view of the variation in usability among state department publications of school laws, it is recommended that state codes of general laws be used wherever available, either instead of the state department publication or in connection with it. State codes are more frequently published in practically every state, and are usually kept currently up to date by cumulative supplements or pocket parts; they are more completely indexed usually; they are arranged and numbered in a way which allows the use of legal research tools to be described later.

Some states recompile general statutes after each legislative session (usually every odd year). Those with pocket parts do not issue new compilations until the pocket parts become too bulky to be included in the cover of the publication. A few states have neither pocket parts nor frequent recompilations, but these instances are rare.

The publications having pocket parts are especially useful. In the back cover of each of these volumes is a pocket in which is inserted

at frequent intervals the new laws and amendments to the statutes included in the bound part of the volume, coordinated into the codification scheme. If the edition is annotated, the pocket part includes annotations to cases which have interpreted the statutes in the bound part of the volume, as well as any statutory changes, the sections being identified by their numbers. Thus, the pocket parts keep the compilation up to date.

For enactments later than the latest code, supplement, or pocket part, session laws must be used. In most states, only the last session need be cited to session laws, since pocket parts, or supplements, or revisions of the entire code bring the statutes up to within a year or two of any given date.

Most compilations of general statutes are annotated. Volumes which are annotated contain, commonly under each section of the law, the history of the statute or the section and citations to court cases in which it has been mentioned.

Exhibit 1 shows a copy of page 148 from the *Annotated Code of Maryland*. The page number is at the bottom of the page. However, page numbers are not usually used in statute citations. For example, if one were referring to the Maryland law on suspension and expulsion of pupils, the citation would be to section 131, not to page 148. At the top of the page it may be seen that sections 130-133 are shown on this page.

The school laws of Maryland are compiled in Article 77. The Maryland Code uses "articles" for main headings which are on the level called "titles" in most statutory compilations.

At the end of each section, in parentheses, are citations to former codes containing identical or similar provisions. This is the "legislative history" of the section. Almost all statutory compilations include legislative history even though other types of annotations may not be included. The Maryland Code does include other types of annotations: cross references and citations to court decisions in which each section has been interpreted. The value of statutory annotations can be seen easily from this example. Although, of course, different states follow different styles, the Maryland Code is typical.

Shepard's Citations to Statutes. To find out what has happened to a statute since the date of the official state code publication, one turns to Shepard's Citations to Statutes. To find cases more recent than those included in the annotated statutes, or those for any reason omitted from the annotations, if any, or in a state where the code

participation as if they were teachers employed in the public schools, subject to all the conditions, limitations and restrictions imposed by § 127 of this article. (An. Code, 1951, § 123; 1939, § 110; 1939, ch. 399.)

CHAPTER 9. PUPILS

§ 130. Admission.

All white youths between the ages of six and twenty-one years shall be admitted into such public schools of the State, the studies of which they may be able to pursue; provided, that whenever there are grade schools, the principal and the county superintendent shall determine to which school pupils shall be admitted. (An. Code, 1951, § 124; 1939, § 111; 1924, § 114; 1912, § 63; 1904, § 59; 1888, § 54; 1872, ch. 377; 1916, ch. 506, § 63.)

Cross reference.—See note to § 1 of this article.

The effect of the decision in Brown v. Board of Education, 347 U. S. 483, 74 S. Ct. 686, 98 L. Ed. 873, was to strike the word "white" out of this section. Robinson v. Board of Education, 143 F. Supp. 481.

Individual Negro children now have the right to apply under this section for admission to a particular school, and from the decision of the county superintendent on such application an appeal lies to the State Board. Whether the refusal of such an application would also give an immediate right to file proceedings in a State court to determine any question of law involved, or to file proceedings in this court to review any alleged deprivation of constitutional rights, might depend upon

the reason or reasons for such refusal. Robinson v. Board of Education, 143 F. Supp. 481.

And when denied admission have an adequate administrative remedy.—Colored children denied admission to the school of their choice have an adequate administrative remedy by way of application to the county superintendent for admission, and appeal to the State Board from any decision of the county superintendent adverse to their application. Robinson v. Board of Education, 143 F. Supp. 481.

Formerly, separation of races was valid where equal facilities provided.—See Williams v. Zimmerman, 172 Md. 563, 192 A. 353.

Cited in Boyer v. Garrett, 88 F. Supp. 353, aff'd in 183 F. (2d) 582.

§ 131. Suspension and explusion.

The district board of school trustees shall have power, to suspend and expel pupils for cause; provided, that an appeal shall be to the county superintendent, whose decision shall be final. (An. Code, 1951, § 125; 1939, § 112; 1924, § 115; 1912, § 64; 1904, § 60; 1888, § 55; 1872, ch. 377; 1916, ch. 506, § 64.)

§ 132. Attendance in adjoining district.

Children living remote from the school of the district in which they reside may attend school in an adjoining district, with the consent of the county superintendent of schools. (An. Code, 1951, § 126; 1939, § 113; 1924, § 116; 1912, § 65; 1904, § 61; 1888, § 56; 1872, ch. 377; 1916, ch. 506, § 65.)

§ 133. Vaccination.

Every child before being admitted to any public school shall produce a certificate from a regular physician that he has been properly vaccinated. (An. Code, 1951, § 127; 1939, § 114; 1924, § 117; 1912, § 66; 1904, § 62; 1888, § 57; 1872, ch. 377.)

Cross references.—See § 134 et seq. As to State vaccine agency, see article 43, § 68 et seq. As to duties of teachers relative to vaccination of pupils, see article 43, § 74.

Exhibit 1. Photostatic copy of page 148 in Volume 7 of the *Annotated Code of Maryland*. Reproduced with permission of the publisher and copyright owner, The Michie Company, Charlottesville, Va.

is not annotated, the same citator is used. With one or two exceptions, every state is covered by this periodical device for finding changes in laws and citations to cases where the statute has been mentioned by a court in connection with particular facts. By using Shepard's Citations to Statutes one may discover every instance where any particular section of any law has been affected by subsequent legislation and every instance where it has been cited, applied, or construed by the courts.

The method used in these citators is merely the listing of the section numbers of the statutes with reference to the later enactments and the court decisions, each preceded by an abbreviation which tells the story of what happened in each instance. These abbreviations[1] cover many situations, a few of which are listed herewith:

A (amended) means that the statute was amended.

Ad (added) means that a new section was added without affecting the numbering of the old section.

R (rejected or repealed) means that an existing statute has been abrogated.

S (superseded) means that new legislation was substituted for an existing statute but the old statute was not expressly abrogated.

U (unconstitutional) means that the court has declared the statute unconstitutional.

C (constitutional) means that the court has upheld the constitutionality of the statue.

V (void or invalid) means that the court has declared the statute invalid.

Some of these abbreviations may be seen in Exhibit 2 which shows page 139 (see lower left-hand corner) from *Shepard's Massacuhsetts Citations*. The part of the volume to be used in "Shepardizing" statutory provisions is always identified by the name of the code at the top of the page in the citator.

Sections of the Massachusetts laws may be identified by the larger numbers in bold-face type preceded by the section symbol. From this example, it may be seen that section 24A of Chapter 74 was amended by Chapter 154 of the 1958 session laws, while a new section—31B—was added in 1960 by Chapter 481 of the session laws. Also, section 16 of Chapter 78 was repealed by Chapter 429 of the 1960 session laws.

In addition to showing what has happened to each section of the statutes by subsequent legislatures, Shepard's citators show where each

---

[1] Reproduced with permission of the publisher and copyright owner, Shepard's Citations, Inc., Colorado Springs, Colo.

Massachusetts—Massachusetts General Laws Annotated Ch. 81

§ 4
A1960C 403
§ 4A
A1960C 403
§ 4B
A1960C 403
§ 5
A1960C 403
§ 6
A1960C 403
§ 7
A1958C 605
A1959C 246
L1959C 477
A1959C 592
A1960C 403
§ 8
A1959C 246
A1960C 403
§ 9
R1958C 605

Ch. 74

335Mas 493
140NE 474
1958C518§3
1960C330§3
§ 1
"Agricultural Education"
335Mas 491
140NE 470
"Industrial Education"
335Mas 491
140NE 470
"Vocational Education"
335Mas 493
140NE 470
§ 24A
A1958C 154
§ 31B
Ad1960C481
§ 42B
A1958C 243
§ 42C
Ad1958C538

Ch. 75

335Mas 493
140NE 474
'56-57AG 45
§ 1
'56-57AG 45
§ 5A
'56-57AG 45
§ 13
A1960C 526
'57-58AG 49
§ 24
'56-57AG 46
§ 26
335Mas 447
140NE 487
§ 27
1958C 456
§ 28
L1958C 456

§ 32
Ad1960C493

Ch. 75A

335Mas 493
140NE 474
§ 2
'56-57AG 82
§ 12
A1958C 538
A1960C 563

Ch. 75B

Ad1960C543
§ 1
Ad1960C543
§ 2
Ad1960C543
§ 3
Ad1960C543
§ 4
Ad1960C543
§ 5
Ad1960C543
§ 6
Ad1960C543
§ 7
Ad1960C543
§ 8
Ad1960C543
§ 9
Ad1960C543
§ 10
Ad1960C543
§ 11
Ad1960C543
§ 12
Ad1960C543
§ 13
Ad1960C543
§ 14
Ad1960C543
§ 15
Ad1960C543
§ 16
Ad1960C543
§ 17
Ad1960C543
§ 18
Ad1960C543
§ 19
Ad1960C543
§ 20
Ad1960C543

Ch. 76

§ 1
'56-57AG 66
§ 5
'56-57AG 67

Ch. 77

44MQ(2)119
§ 13
Rs1960C 313

Ch. 78

Rp1960C429

§ 10
et seq.
38BUR386
§ 16
R1960C 429
§ 17
R1960C 429
§ 18
R1960C 429
§ 19
A1960C 429

TITLE XIII

Ch. 79

L1958C 603
335Mas 80
138NE 609
335Mas 620
142NE 348
335Mas 723
142NE 327
336Mas 56
142NE 391
336Mas 137
143NE 220
336Mas 448
146NE 488
337Mas 308
149NE 227
338Mas 218
154NE 606
338Mas 662
157NE 209
1959AS 734
158NE 349
1959AS1019
159NE 342
1959AS1243
161NE 759
1959AS1287
162NE 266
1960AS 132
164NE 138
1960AS 589
165NE 748
1960AS 759
166NE 904
170NE 355
174FS 454
1958C 212
1958C232§2
1958C242§1
1958C 250
1958C297§4
1958C 353
1958C 371
1958C 384
1958C 418
1958C 420
1958C 472
1958C 473
1958C 474
1958C518§6
1958C 524
1958C 531
1958C532§5
1958C 563
1958C 587
1958C598§5
1958C606§5
1958C 652
1958Res [C 148
1959C 172
1959C 212
1959C 291
1959C 377
1959C 601
1960C 23
1960C 66
1960C 68
1960C 308
1960C 418
1960C440§4
1960C 450
1960C543§4
1960C635§4
1960C 710
1960 p 575
§ 1
et seq.
1959AS 733
158NE 348
1959AS1287
162NE 265
1960AS 589
165NE 747
§ 1
E1958C 603
335Mas 624
142NE 350
38BUR415
§ 3
E1958C 603
A1959C 626
335Mas 622
142NE 349
44MQ(3) 23
§ 4
E1958C 603
§ 6
335Mas 190
138NE 769
§ 7
174FS 453
§ 8
E1958C 603
A1959C 626
A1960C 49
335Mas 622
142NE 349
174FS 454
44MQ(3) 23
§ 8A
Ad1959C626
44MQ(3) 23
§ 9
E1958C 603
335Mas 623
142NE 347
336Mas 130
143NE 216
44MQ(2) 15
§ 10
E1958C 603
335Mas 624
142NE 347
336Mas 54
142NE 390
336Mas 137
143NE 220
338Mas 218
154NE 605
44MQ(2) 15
§ 12
E1958C 603
A1959C 626
335Mas 81
138NE 609
335Mas 193
138NE 769
335Mas 374
140NE 212
335Mas 598
141NE 384
335Mas 625
142NE 351
335Mas 724
142NE 328
336Mas 54
142NE 390
336Mas 131
143NE 217
338Mas 49
153NE 623
338Mas 218
154NE 605
338Mas 662
157NE 209
1959AS1021
159NE 342
1960AS1092
169NE 904
1960AS1133
170NE 324
162FS 484
44MQ(2) 15
44MQ(3) 24
§ 13
E1958C 603
§ 14
E1958C 603
335Mas 190
138NE 769
335Mas 622
142NE 349
335Mas 723
142NE 327
336Mas 55
142NE 390
336Mas 134
143NE 216
337Mas 433
149NE 905
338Mas 360
155NE 171
1959AS1477
162NE 777
1960AS1133
170NE 324
174FS 453
44MQ(3) 23
§ 16
et seq.
E1958C 603

§ 16
335Mas 622
142NE 349
336Mas 130
143NE 216
174FS 454
§ 22
336Mas 57
142NE 392
174FS 453
44MQ(2) 18
§ 24
et seq.
336Mas 446
146NE 486
§ 32
336Mas 57
142NE 392
1959AS1477
162NE 777
§ 33
1959AS1478
162NE 777
§ 35
335Mas 81
138NE 610
338Mas 48
153NE 623
44MQ(2) 19
§ 37
Rs1960C 298
335Mas 601
141NE 384
1960AS1133
170NE 325
§ 38
44MQ(3) 24
§ 39
A1959C 626
44MQ(3) 23
§ 40
E1958C 606
1958C598§5
§ 41
E1958C 603
§ 42
E1958C 603
§ 43
E1958C 603
§ 44A
E1958C 603
335Mas 598
141NE 381
1960AS 405
165NE 113
§ 44B
336Mas 133
143NE 218
§ 45
174FS 453

Ch. 80

1958C 250
1958C 563
1959C 291
1960C 23
1960C 308
1960C 450

§ 1
L1960C 589
1959C 39
§ 2
L1960C 589
1959C 39
§ 12
337Mas 467
150NE 276
§ 13
A1960C 248
1959C 47

Ch. 80A

1958C242§1
1958C 624
1959C 172

TITLE XIV

Ch. 81

335Mas 625
142NE 351
'56-57AG 91
§ 7
335Mas 625
142NE 351
336Mas 131
143NE 220
338Mas 223
154NE 608
1959AS1021
159NE 342
272F2d 430
44MQ(2) 18
§ 7A
A1960C 183
337Mas 310
149NE 225
§ 7C
335Mas 79
138NE 609
335Mas 625
142NE 351
336Mas 131
143NE 220
1959AS1019
159NE 342
272F2d 430
'56-57AG 91
44MQ(2) 18
§ 7D
'56-57AG 91
§ 7F
Ad1958C582
§ 7G
Ad1960C710
§ 12
335Mas 1
138NE 276
§ 14
1960AS 562
166NE 219
§ 21
335Mas 78
138NE 609
'56-57AG 91

139

Exhibit 2. Photostatic copy of page 139, *Massachusetts Citations, Cases and Statutes*, February, 1961. Reproduced with permission of the publisher and copyright owner, Shepard's Citations, Inc., Colorado Springs, Colo.

section has been cited by a court; *e.g.*, section 21 of Chapter 81 has been cited in 335 Mass. 78, 138 N.E. (2d) 609 and on page 91 of the 1956-57 volume of attorney general's opinions. Unless there is a symbol in front of these references to cases, it means merely that the court referred to that section. If the court, for example, held that a section is constitutional, the reference would be preceded by a "C."

These examples show the practical value of Shepard's Citations to Statutes. (Citators contain citations to the constitution, to state statutes, and to court decisions in the same volume for each state, usually, but they are separately treated in the citators and discussed separately here. In a few states there are separate volumes for statutes and court decisions.)

State department publications of school law which do not use the codification of the state compilation of laws cannot be used with the citators. It was for this reason that recommendation was made that state codes be used for legal research rather than state department publications, unless the state department bulletin follows the same numbering system as is used in the state code.

For laws enacted after the date of the official state code, annual session laws are used and a section of Shepard's Citations to Statutes is devoted to citations to session laws, by years, in the same way that citations to the state code sections are shown in Exhibit 2.

State Law Index. Until 1949, the Library of Congress issued biennially an index to state legislation arranged by subject matter. It was the only publication of its kind where statutory material was compiled by subject matter. Unfortunately no appropriation was made by Congress in 1949 for the continuance of this work and the last issue covers the 1947-1948 biennium. Therefore, statutes must be researched by each state separately. Nowhere is to be found an index to statutes from all states.

Court Decisions

Appellate courts, in some states the intermediate as well as the highest court, record their opinions for future reference and these records are available to the public in the form of so-called "reports." Almost every state publishes its own series of reports. In Exhibit 2 many notations may be found referring to cases reported in the Massachusetts reports, as was mentioned.

If one is interested in a problem at large, he will want to read cases on the subject outside his own state. Thousands of cases are reported each year and without mechanical devices to segregate the cases in point, the task would be impossible. There are several such devices, to be described below.

The American Digest System. The American Digest System is a series of digests of cases from 1658 to date. There are eight units, as follows:

1956 to date: General Digest, Third Series;
1946 to 1956: Sixth Decennial Digest (36 volumes);
1936 to 1946: Fifth Decennial Digest (49 volumes);
1926 to 1936: Fourth Decennial Digest (34 volumes);
1916 to 1926: Third Decennial Digest (29 volumes);
1906 to 1916: Second Decennial Digest (24 volumes);
1896 to 1906: First Decennial Digest (25 volumes);
1658 to 1896: Century Digest.

Cases in each of these units are arranged in the same order according to subject matter. "Schools and School Districts" is in its alphabetical setting. Within each topic the subject matter is logically outlined and each item in the outline is given a number; this number is called the key number. As an illustration of the detail used in classifying the cases for the American Digest System, the outline of topics on "Schools and School Districts" is here reproduced in part.[2] The arabic number in front of each subtopic is its key number.

I. Private Schools and Academies. (1-8).
II. Public Schools. (9-178).
   A. Establishment, School Lands and Funds, and Regulation in General. (9-20).
   B. Creation, Alteration, Existence, and Dissolution of Districts. (21-44).
   C. Government, Officers, and District Meetings. (45-63).
   D. District Property, Contracts, and Liabilities. (64-89.19).
   E. District Debt, Securities, and Taxation. (90-111).
   F. Claims against District, and Actions. (112-126).
   G. Teachers. (127-147).
      127. Eligibility in general.
      128. Teachers' institutes.
      129. Certificate or license.
      130. _____In general.
      131. _____Requisites to appointment or employment.

---

[2] Reproduced with permission of the publisher and copyright owner, West Publishing Company, St. Paul, Minn.

132. _____Revocation.
133. Employment in general.
133.1. Selection and appointment.
133.2. _____Nomination by district boards.
133.3. _____Recommendation by superintendent of schools.
133.4. _____Civil service laws and examinations.
133.5. Term of employment in general.
133.6. Permanent tenure.
133.7. _____Constitutional and statutory provisions in general.
133.8. _____Purpose of statutes.
133.9. _____Construction and operation of statutes.
133.10. _____Teachers and persons entitled in general.
133.11. _____Length of service and probation.
133.12. _____Substitute and supply teachers.
133.13. _____Schools affected.
133.14. Leave of absence.
133.15. Reappointment.
134. Contracts of employment.
135. _____Making, requisites, and validity.
    (1). Authority to contract in general.
    (2). Authority to bind successors.
    (3). Requisites and validity in general.
    (4). Formal requisites.
    (5). Ratification and estoppel.
136. _____Construction and operation.
137. _____Performance or breach.
138. _____Remedies for enforcement.
139. Resignation and abandonment.
140. Suspension, removal, and reassignment.
141. _____In general.
    (1). In general.
    (2). Authority to remove or discharge in general.
    (3). Contracts reserving right.
    (4). Grounds for removal or suspension.
    (5). Proceedings and review.
    (6). Reinstatement.
142. _____Actions for damages.
143. Compensation.
144. _____In general.
    (1). Right to compensation in general.
    (2). Effect of closing of school because of contagious disease.
    (3). Effect of removal, suspension, or abandonment of employment.
    (4). Rate or amount of compensation.
    (5). Payment, and orders therefor.
145. _____Actions.
146. Pensions.
147. Duties and liabilities.

H. Pupils, and Conduct and Discipline of Schools.
 148. Nature of right to instruction in general.
 148½. Aid to indigent children.
 149. Eligibility.
 150. _____In general.
 151. _____Race or color.
 152. _____Age.
 153. _____Residence.
 154. _____Assignment or admission to particular schools.
 155. Proceedings to compel admission.
 156. Health regulations.
 157. In general.
 158. _____Vaccination.
  (1). In general.
  (2). Existence of epidemic.
 159. Payment for tuition.
 159½. Transportation of pupils to and from schools or provisions in lieu thereof.
 160. Compulsory attendance.
 161. Truants and truant officers and schools.
 162. School terms, vacations, and holidays.
 163. Grades or classes and departments.
 164. Curriculum and courses of study.
 165. Religious instruction and reading of Scriptures.
 166. Textbooks.
 167. _____Selection or adoption and change.
 168. _____Duty to furnish.
 169. Control of pupils and discipline in general.
 170. Rules and regulations.
 171. _____Authority to make.
 172. _____Reasonableness and validity.
 172½. _____Construction and operation.
 173. Violation of rules and offenses.
 174. Punishment.
 175. _____In general.
 176. _____Corporal punishment.
 177. _____Expulsion or suspension.
 178. Graduation, and diploma or certificate.

Thus, the American Digest System constitutes a device for finding all of the cases on a point among the thousands of cases reported each year. The System consists of short digests of each case arranged in the order of the outline of topics. Exhibit 3 shows a page from Volume 26 in which "Schools and School Districts" is to be found in the sixth Decennial Digest, covering the period 1946-1956. The number of the subtopic in the outline is identified by a tiny key in front of it, and for this reason it is referred to as the "key number." At the beginning of each digest is the name of the state in bold-face type.

At the end of each digest is the citation to the case, its name, and where it may be found.

Exhibit 3 shows the digests of *all* cases decided between 1946 and 1956 in which the topic "Selection and appointment" of teachers—key number 133.1—was an issue. The first case listed under this key number arose in New York and was decided in the Supreme Court of the United States. It was *Adler v. Board of Education of City of New York* which may be read at 72 S. Ct. 380 or at 342 U.S. 485, or at 96 L. Ed. 517. This digest is followed by the digest of a case from Alabama and cases from other states are listed alphabetically by states.

The American Digest System includes a Table of Cases which gives for each case the exact title, alphabetically listed, and all the places where it may be found to be read, also the topic and the key numbers of every point of law decided in each case and whether it has been affirmed, reversed, or modified. From the Table of Cases, then, the key numbers of a familiar case may be noted, and other cases can be found in the digests by looking for those identified by the same key numbers.

There is also a subject matter index to the American Digest System. It is called the "Descriptive Word Index." This index uses nonlegal terms as well as legal terminology and contains innumerable cross references. Key numbers identify the references, and it is possible to discover by this index under what key number a point has been digested.

Any particular case contains more than one point which is indexed with a key number. For example, an action by a dismissed teacher for reinstatement might be indexed under Removal, Compensation, Contract, and Mandamus. Each of these points has a different key number. Therefore, in the Descriptive Word Index and in the digests themselves, the case may be indexed in more than one place depending upon the various points involved in the case. In the reports of actual opinions, however, the case appears only once in each report although headnotes at the beginning before the opinion itemize the points of law involved under all the key numbers.

From the American Digest System one compiles a bibliography of cases for further study. The digests in the American Digest System aid in determining whether a particular case is likely to be in point; they may be used in classifying cases to fit into a topical outline to be followed in the research study. But, this is just the first step in

⟨⧈⟩133 SCHOOLS & SCHOOL DIST. 26–6th D—1578

Act of 1939, P.L. 482, as amended by the Act of 1947, P.L. 646.—Welland v. Stull, 16 Cambria 249.

Pa.Com.Pl. The number of teachers to be hired is a matter for the internal management of the board of school directors under the supervision of the Department of Public Instruction; and unless the School Code contains a plain mandate requiring the employment of a specified number of teachers on a basis of calculated units, the court may not interfere with the discretion of the board exercised in accordance with advice from the Department of Public Instruction.—Caperelli v. Winton Borough, School Dist., 53 Lack.Jur. 269.

The fact that the state by mathematical computation based on the number of pupil-days provides state aid on the basis of calculated reimbursement units does not warrant the court in holding that the school district must employ the number of teachers necessary to fill a mathematical quota authorized because the school district is entitled to such reimbursement units.—Caperelli v. Winton Borough, School Dist., 53 Lack.Jur. 269.

Pa.Com.Pl. Although the term "professional employee" includes teachers actively assigned to continuous classroom work, it is not exclusive as to such assignments.—McAndrew v. Throop Borough, School Dist. of, 56 Lack.Jur. 201.

Wash. Teachers are employees of district which employs them, and are not public or state officers.—State ex rel. Mary M. Knight School Dist. No. 311, Mason County v. Wanamaker, 281 P.2d 846.

W.Va. Statute prescribing method of employment of teachers in schools of a county school district is exclusive, and nomination by County Superintendent is an indispensable prerequisite to execution of a valid teaching contract between the County Board of Education and a teacher. Code, 18-4-10(2, 3) as amended 18-5-4 as amended 18-7-1 as amended.—Cochran v. Trussler, 89 S.E. 2d 306.

⟨⧈⟩133.1. Selection and appointment

U.S.N.Y. School authorities have right and duty to screen officials, teachers and employees as to their fitness to maintain integrity of schools as part of ordered society.—Adler v. Board of Ed. of City of New York, 72 S.Ct. 380, 342 U.S. 485, 96 L.Ed. 517.

In employment of officials and teachers for school system, state may properly inquire into company they keep and, when determining fitness and loyalty of such persons, may consider organizations and persons with whom they associate.—Adler v. Board of Ed. of City of New York, 72 S.Ct. 380, 342 U.S. 485, 96 L.Ed. 517.

Ala. The "administrative functions" exercised by a board of education in public school system include the hiring of teachers, their assignment in the school system, and the management and control of school property.—State ex rel. Steele v. Board of Ed. of Fairfield, 40 So.2d 689.

Fla. Power to select and nominate teachers for public schools is vested in the trustees.—State ex rel. Lawson v. Cherry, 47 So.2d 768.

Ill.App. No person has the right to demand to be retained as a teacher, and School Board has absolute right to decline to employ an applicant for any reason.—Halfacre v. Board of Ed. of School Dist. No. 167, 73 N.E.2d 124, 331 Ill.App. 404.

District School Board of Education was entitled to reject application for a teacher's position without giving any reason therefor, notwithstanding that

applicant was the only applicant for the position holding a valid teacher's certificate.—Halfacre v. Board of Ed. of School Dist. No. 167, 73 N.E.2d 124, 331 Ill.App. 404.

Ky. An illegal appointment as high school principal could not serve as foundation of appointee's claim to continued employment. KRS 160.380.—Beverly v. Highfield, 209 S.W.2d 739, 307 Ky. 179.

Mass. The powers of school committee include the employment of janitors and custodians as well as teachers and the absolute right to fix their salaries, and no other officer has authority over the maintenance of schoolhouses. G.L. (Ter.Ed.) c. 71, §§ 37, 68 as amended.—Molinari v. City of Boston, 130 N.E.2d 925.

Mont. Under statute, no person can be employed to teach in public schools without a contract with board of school trustees, and so-called teachers' tenure act does not eliminate necessity of having a contract; the only effect of tenure act being to renew teacher's existing contract for another year by operation of law after election for third consecutive year unless notice specified in statute is given. Rev.Codes 1935, § 1015, subd. 2; § 1075.—Eastman v. School Dist. No. 1 of Lewis and Clark County, 180 P.2d 472, 120 Mont. 63.

N.Y.App.Div. A petition filed in 1946 for declaration that petitioner was a regular member of faculty of city college of New York with full tenure was not filed late insofar as it sought to compel performance of duty which the Board of Higher Education had not refused to perform, but was filed late insofar as petitioner sought to review propriety of determination in 1942 that eligible lists of former high school teachers would not be applicable for positions in municipal colleges. Education Law, § 1143-c. subd. 9; Civil Practice Act, § 1286.—Trilling v. Board of Higher Ed. of City of New York, 67 N.Y.S.2d 572, 190 Misc. 52.

N.C. Election of a principal or teacher by school committee of district in a county administrative unit has no validity until such election has been approved by both the county superintendent of schools and county board of education. G.S. §§ 115-117, 115-354.—Iredell County Bd. of Ed. v. Dickson, 70 S.E.2d 14, 235 N.C. 359.

Resolution adopted by county board of education in meeting assembled after close of school term supporting any action taken by district school committee in electing a principal for specified school undertook to give district school committee carte blanche in the premises, and not to confer retroactive approval on previously attempted dismissal or rejection of principal. G.S. §§ 115-354, 115-359.—Iredell County Bd. of Ed. v. Dickson, 70 S.E.2d 14, 235 N.C. 359.

Re-election of principal by school committee of district in a county administrative unit without approval of county superintendent of schools or county board of education was without any validity in law and hence under statute, principal's contract of employment automatically continued in force for ensuing year, though he failed to give notice to county superintendent of schools of acceptance of renewed employment within 10 days after notice of re-election. G.S. §§ 115-37, 115-354.—Iredell County Bd. of Ed. v. Dickson, 70 S.E.2d 14, 235 N.C. 359.

N.Y.Sup. The determination of Board of Higher Education of City of New York, upon abolishing high school which had been operated to prepare students for entrance into college of City of New York, that preferred lists established upon abolition of the high school should not be deemed applicable to positions in municipal colleges was

discretionary with the board. Education Law, § 1143-c, subd. 9.—Trilling v. Board of Higher Ed. of City of New York, 67 N.Y.S.2d 572, 190 Misc. 52.

Where Board of Higher Education of City of New York upon abolishing high school which had been operated to prepare students for entrance to City College established preferred eligible list pursuant to statute which required such lists to be established for three years, and during such period no one was appointed to any educational unit in disregard of the list, a former teacher in high school was not entitled as matter of right to appointment to faculty of city college. Education Law, § 1143-c. subd. 9.—Trilling v. Board of Higher Ed. of City of New York, 67 N.Y.S.2d 572, 190 Misc. 52.

Ohio Com.Pl. Statutory provision that if a clerk of a board of education is absent from any meeting of board, members present shall choose one of their number to serve in his place pro tempore, provision that clerk shall record proceedings of each meeting and provision that on a motion to adopt a resolution to employ a superintendent or teacher, clerk of board shall publicly call roll of members composing board and enter on records names of those voting aye and names of those voting no, and mandatory and noncompliance therewith by a board invalidates its proceedings. Gen.Code, §§ 4834-1 to 4834-3.—Schafer v. Board of Ed. of Alliance City School Dist., Stark County, 94 N.E.2d 112.

The words "to employ" a superintendent or teacher in statute providing that, on a motion to adopt a resolution to employ a superintendent or teacher, clerk of board shall publicly call roll of members composing board and enter on records names of those voting aye and names of those voting no, embody and encompass words "not to employ," "to accept or not to accept a resignation" and "to retain or not to retain" a superintendent of schools. Gen.Code, § 4834-1.—Schafer v. Board of Ed. of Alliance City School Dist., Stark County, 94 N.E.2d 112.

Pa.Com.Pl. The employment of a teacher as a "professional employee" of a school district must be made, and salary fixed, by the affirmative vote of the majority of all the members of the board of directors, duly recorded on the minutes, showing how each member voted.—Felix v. Fairfield Tp. School Dist., Bd. of Directors, 32 West. 207.

Wash. Under statute providing for employment of school teachers by school boards, the Legislature has left question of employment solely within discretion of school board and applicant, and no district can be forced to enter into a contract of employment with teacher against will of majority of board of directors, nor can applicant be forced to teach school in any district against her will. RCW 28.58.100(4).—State ex rel. Mary M. Knight School Dist. No. 311, Mason County v. Wanamaker, 281 P.2d 846.

⟨⧈⟩133.2. —— Nomination by district boards

Fla. Board of trustees of school district had no discretion under statute to reject recommendation of county superintendent and refuse to nominate district supervising principal to board of public instruction for reappointment, except for good cause shown. F.S.A. §§ 230.01 et seq., 230.33(7) (c), 230.43(1), 231.35.—Armistead v. State ex rel. Smyth, 41 So.2d 879.

The board of trustees for each school district is vested by Constitution with the power to nominate teachers for the district. F.S.A.Const. art. 12, § 10.—Armistead v. State ex rel. Smyth, 41 So.2d 879.

Exhibit 3. Photostatic copy of page 1578 in Volume 26 of the *Sixth Decennial Digest*. Reproduced with permission of the publisher and copyright owner, West Publishing Company, St. Paul, Minn.

making a legal study. The digests are only these short paragraphs on each point in the case, as shown in Exhibit 3. In order to know their application, it is necessary to read the entire opinion of the court. in the reports. The holding of a case cannot be cited on the basis of the digests alone. Doing so is an error of many inexperienced school-law researchers. The opinion must be read in its entirety.

Court opinions may be found in the state reports, in the National Reporter System, or possibly in the Annotated Reports which are to be described later.

National Reporter System. The National Reporter System includes all cases from all courts of record in all states and gives the actual opinion of the court in each. Using the National Reporter System, it is possible to read all the cases in all the states on a particular point. The System is divided into nine geographical sections, for publication and citation purposes:

The Atlantic Reporter, abbreviated "Atl." or "A. (2d)," covers Maine, New Hampshire, Vermont, Connecticut, New Jersey, Pennsylvania, Delaware, and Maryland.

The Northeastern Reporter, abbreviated "N.E." or "N.E. (2d)," covers Massachusetts, Rhode Island, New York, Ohio, Indiana, and Illinois.

The Southeastern Reporter, abbreviated "S.E." or "S.E. (2d)," covers Virginia, West Virginia, North Carolina, South Carolina, and Georgia.

The Southern Reporter, abbreviated "So." or "So. (2d)," covers Florida, Alabama, Mississippi, and Louisiana.

The Southwestern Reporter, abbreviated "S.W." or "S.W. (2d)," covers Kentucky, Tennessee, Missouri, Arkansas, and Texas.

The Pacific Reporter, abbreviated "Pac." or "P. (2d)," covers Montana, Wyoming, Idaho, Kansas, Colorado, Oklahoma, New Mexico, Utah, Arizona, Nevada, Washington, Oregon, and California.

The Northwestern Reporter, abbreviated "N.W." or "N.W. (2d)," covers Michigan, Wisconsin, Iowa, Minnesota, North Dakota, South Dakota, and Nebraska.

The National Reporter System also includes the Supreme Court Reporter covering cases decided in the Supreme Court of the United States, the Federal Reporter covering cases decided in the Federal Circuit Courts of Appeals and the Federal Supplement covering cases decided in the lower federal courts. New York State is reported

not only in the Northeastern Reporter but in the New York Supplement which is another series of the National Reporter System covering certain New York courts only.

Several volumes in each reporter series are issued each year. Prior to the publication of each volume, the cases are published in weekly bulletins with paper bindings, called "Advance Sheets." These weekly bulletins enable one to read a case without waiting for the publication of the reporter in its bound form. With the use of the Advance Sheets a problem may usually be followed to within a month of any current date. It takes at least a month for a decision to be released by the court, processed, and reported in the weekly bulletins.

The case material in this textbook is excerpted from the court decisions which are reported in the state reports and in the National Reporter System. The latter need not be illustrated at this point since it is identical to that material. It may be mentioned, however, that at the beginning of each decision editors of the National Reporter System have inserted digests of points in the case, reproduced from the American Digest System (see Exhibit 3). These digests at the beginning of each case in the National Reporter System are not part of the court's opinion unless they are shown separately under the heading of "Syllabus of the Court." Usually the name of the judge who wrote the opinion appears at the beginning of the opinion; any language preceding this point is not part of the opinion.

Annotated Reports. Since there are many cases on some problems, one may wish to read only the leading cases, and omit those which involve identical problems and are decided on the basis of the decisions in leading cases. The Annotated Reports make this possible. It is a series of selected cases from all states. Cases dealing with purely local law are eliminated as are also decisions on problems already well settled. The cases included are those which are new or deal with questions on which there is conflict of legal opinion. Some other cases are included because they represent outstanding legal reasoning or review the authorities on a question.

The Annotated Reports consist of seven series including early English and American decisions. Except for historical studies, only the latest series need be used in school-law research; that is, the *American Law Reports* (abbreviated "A.L.R.") which began in 1919. About six volumes appear each year. Alphabetical indexes are furnished as well as indexes to cases and to annotations.

The word "annotations" is here used in a different sense than formerly in this text. The name of this series of law books, Annotated Reports, is taken from notes which follow most of the cases reported. These notes are called annotations. This series is used primarily because of the annotations, although it can be used for reading of the opinion also. The annotations review the substance of what has been decided in other cases on the same point.

Indexes to A.L.R. Annotations are so well done that the numerical system is of secondary importance. However, it does facilitate research if one can scan for a particular topic by number. The outline of topics used by the editors of A.L.R. follows:[3]

    I. IN GENERAL
   II. SCHOOL DISTRICTS, IN GENERAL
  III. PROPERTY AND BUILDINGS
  IV. LIABILITY OF SCHOOL DISTRICT OR AUTHORITIES
   V. CONTRACTS; FUNDS AND EXPENDITURES; INDEBTEDNESS
  VI. SCHOOL TAXES
 VII. ADMINISTRATIVE OFFICERS AND BOARDS
VIII. PUBLIC MEETINGS; ELECTIONS
  IX. TEACHERS AND PRINCIPALS

    Sec. 30 Generally.
    Sec. 31 Selection, appointment, and term of employment.
    Sec. 32 Contracts of employment.
    Sec. 33 _____Power of school authorities to bind successors by.
    Sec. 33.5 Tenure and tenure statutes, generally.
    Sec. 34 Qualification, generally.
    Sec. 35 License or certificate.
    Sec. 36 _____As requisite to appointment or employment.
    Sec. 37 _____Revocation or suspension.
    Sec. 38 Compensation.
    Sec. 39 _____While school is closed.
    Sec. 41 Transfer.
    Sec. 42 Suspension; dismissal; resignation; reinstatement.
    Sec. 43 _____Grounds and procedure for.
    Sec. 44 _____Actions for damages for wrongful suspension or dismissal.
    Sec. 45 Liability of.
    Sec. 48 Pensions and retirement funds. [See Pensions and Retirement Funds, sec. 7.]

   X. PUPILS
    Sec. 49 Generally.
    Sec. 50 Admission generally; residence.

---

[3] Reproduced with permission of the publishers and copyright owners, The Lawyers Co-operative Publishing Company, Rochester, N. Y., and Bancroft-Whitney Company, San Francisco, Calif.

Sec. 51 Scholarships.

Sec. 52 Separation or discrimination by reason of race, color, or religion.

Sec. 55 Health regulations.

Sec. 57 _____Vaccination or inoculation.

Sec. 58 Transportation of.

Sec. 59 Compulsory attendance.

Sec. 60 Control over; patriotic ritual; discipline.

Sec. 61 Secret societies; fraternities and sororities.

Sec. 62 Suspension or expulsion; reinstatement.

Sec. 63 Graduation; right to diploma.

XI. TEXTBOOKS; SUPPLIES AND EQUIPMENT

Sec. 64 Textbooks.

Sec. 65 Supplies and equipment.

XII. INSTRUCTION; CURRICULUM

Sec. 66 Generally.

Sec. 67 Sectarianism; religious teaching.

Sec. 68 Thrift system and instruction.

Sec. 69 Physical education; athletics.

XIII. PRIVATE AND PAROCHIAL SCHOOLS

Some annotations are lengthy, and all except the shortest ones are preceded by an outline of the annotation. An example of an outline of an annotation on a school-law case is given below. It follows the report of the case *Mitchell v. Consolidated School District,* ___ Wash. (2d) ___, 135 P. (2d) 79. The annotation is cited 146 A.L.R. 625. The outline at the beginning of the annotation is shown here:[4]

Annotation (p. 625-638)
Transportation of school pupils at expense of public
[Schools #58]

I. Power to provide transportation in the absence of express statute, 625.

II. Constitutionality of statutes expressly providing for transportation:

a. Generally, 625.

[No later decisions herein.]

b. Objection of diversion of school funds, 626.

c. Classification, discrimination, uniformity, 627.

d. Other objections, 628.

III. Powers, duties, and rights under statutes:

a. Extent of power conferred:

1. Generally, 629.

2. Place or character of school, 629.

---

[4] Reproduced with permission of the publishers and copyright owners, The Lawyers Co-operative Publishing Company, Rochester, N. Y., and Bancroft-Whitney Company, San Francisco, Calif.

3. Outside school activities, 631.
   [No later decisions herein.]
b. Discretionary or mandatory, 631.
c. Abuse of discretion, 633.
d. Who entitled to transporation, 633.
e. Measuring distance, 633.
   [No later decisions herein.]
f. Sufficiency of transporation:
   1. Part-way transportation, 633.
   2. Character of conveyance, 634.
   3. Shelters, 634.
      [No later decisions herein.]
g. Contracts for transportation, 634.
h. Matters relating to remedy, 638.
   [No later decisions herein.]
i. Miscellaneous, 638.

This annotation supplements those in 63 A.L.R. 413 and 118 A.L.R. 806.

This annotation covers the problem of pupil transportation exhaustively so far as case law is concerned; any topics not directly related to the items of the outline are cross-referenced to other annotations. The annotation in 146 A.L.R., outline of which is quoted above, reviews all the judicial authorities since the former annotations on the subject and shows the existing current state of the law. Notice that in this annotation no decisions are included under several subtopics which had been reviewed in the former annotations. This means that since the former annotations there have been no decisions involving these points.

Annotations such as this example are extremely useful in obtaining a general understanding of a point, or in gathering together loose ends of a topic after having read many, and possibly conflicting, cases.

Whenever a new decision warrants it, an annotation is published to bring the entire topic up to date. In the example, the previous annotation was 118 A.L.R. 806, and, before that, 63 A.L.R. 413. Thus by tracing back the several annotations on a topic it is possible to study the history of a problem over the years. The same outline is used in each annotation on a particular topic, but information found in one annotation is not repeated in a subsequent one.

Shepard's Citations to Cases. When a bibliography of cases has been made from the American Digest System, and the judicial opinions have been read in the state reports or in the National Reporter System, and the annotations on the topic, if any, studied in the Annotated Reports, the next question is whether there have been later

cases which followed, disapproved, modified, or reversed these decisions. Shepard's Citations to Cases is the tool used for this purpose.

Each time any case is cited in another decision, Shepard's Citations make note of that fact with appropriate abbreviations to indicate what happened. A few examples of these abbreviations are listed here: [5]

a (affirmed) means that the same case was affirmed on appeal.

D (dismissed) means that appeal of the same case was dismissed.

m (modified) means that the same case was modified on appeal.

r (reversed) means that the same case was reversed on appeal.

j (dissenting opinion) means that the citation is found in the opinion of dissenting judges.

o (overruled) means that the court expressly rejected the ruling in the cited case as being no longer controlling.

With these abbreviations in mind, study of Exhibit 4 will show the usefulness of Shepard's Citations. One section of the state citator is devoted to court decisions. The geographical areas of the National Reporter System are also separately published in the form of citations to cases such as in Exhibit 4.

The page exhibited includes cases in volumes 155 and 156 of the Northeastern Reporter, Second Series. The numbers, such as—682—, refer to the page in the respective volume. Occasionally, an opinion is so short that two cases appear on the same page of the reporter; this situation is illustrated by the first two cases in Exhibit 4. The small "s" before 155 N. E. (2d) 494 under Case 1 indicates that another opinion in the first case on page 682 of volume 155 of the Northeastern Reporter, Second Series, may be found on page 494 of that volume. The parentheses around 168 OS 470 means that this case appears on page 470 of volume 168 of the state reports as well as on page 682 of the Northeastern Reporter. Case 2 on page 682 of volume 155 was affirmed in a case which may be found on page 311 of volume 160 of the Northeastern Reporter, Second Series. The case appearing on page 6 of volume 156 of the Northeastern Reporter, Second Series, is connected with another case which may be found on page 476 of volume 125 of the Northeastern Reporter, Second Series, as indicated by the symbol "cc." The case, 156 N.E. (2d) 190 was dismissed at 147 N.E. (2d) 856, was affirmed at 156 N.E. (2d) 190,

---

[5] Reproduced with permission of the publisher and copyright owner, Shepard's Citations, Inc., Colorado Springs, Colo.

NORTHEASTERN REPORTER, 2d SERIES — Vol. 156

—682— Case 1 (168OS 470) s155NE 494	**—798—** Case 2 (338Mas460) **—800—** (338Mas790)	**—853—** (5NY134) (182S2d 1) s160S2d 152 s171S2d 717	s177S2d 696 s158NE 122 s185S2d 259 s159NE 697 s188S2d 211	**—868—** Case 1 (5NY871) (182S2d 21) s154NE 138	s153NE 733 s179S2d 103 164NE 721 196S2d 703 166NE 862	s142NE 747 f163NE 5576 **—6°—** (20IIA266) cc125NE 476
—682— Case 2 a160NE 311	**—801—** (338Mas792)	166NE 5321 199S2d 536	s161NE 740 s191S2d 956	s179S2d 859 s158NE 124	200S2d 72 168NE 519	**—9—** (20IIA259) **—12—**
—686— (106OA 488) D153NE 674 s144NE 501	**—803—** (338Mas465) 46Æ 404s **—805—**	185S2d 949 185S2d 990 190S2d 601 196S2d 789	s170S2d 979 **—863—** Case 1 (5NY861)	s185S2d 262 s159NE 704 s188S2d 222	203S2d 73 (338Mas518) 162NE 263	(20IIA311) **—13—** (20IIA282)
—690— (107OA 473)	**—806—** (338Mas791) 25Æ 364s (338Mas463)	199S2d 155 201S2d1005 203S2d 498 203S2d 993	**—865—** Case 2 (182S2d 14) s159NE 211 s186S2d 668 s168S2d 937	Case 2 (5NY871) (182S2d 21) **—868—**	26Æ 610s **—874—** (338Mas794) **—876—**	s150NE 581 **—16—** (20IIA271) **—21—**
—698— (108OA229) **—702—** (108OA 457)	**—859—** Case 1 (5NY858)	s174S2d 487 **—863—** Case 2	Case 3 (5NY871) (182S2d 22)	29Æ 731s **—879—**	(338Mas514) 158NE 1482 **—24—**	114So2d 434 **—131—** (168OS 461)
—708— D158NE 379 s155NE 1497	**—808—** (338Mas790)	162NE 119 162NE 219 162NE 2813 (182S2d 9) s174S2d 230	(5NY862) (182S2d 15) s188S2d 184	s159NE 677 s188S2d 184 s160NE 128	(338Mas401) **—82—** (338Mas795)	(338Mas531) 158NE 3467 162NE 2798	p164NE 417 167NE 3363 **—136—**
—709— (108OA 514) **—713—** 18Æ 352s	**—809—** (20IIA224) 163NE 1232 **—814—**	s176S2d 957 **—859—** Case 2 (5NY859)	s170S2d 852 **—864—** (5NY863) (182S2d 16)	s188S2d1001 s168NE 705 s203S2d 900 s361US 874	**—884—** (168OS 391) 50Æ1029s 69Æ1383n	165NE 3912 **—30—** (338Mas507) **—34—**	(168OS 478) **—138—** D163NE 177 D168NE 876
—736— 14Æ1242s **—745—** 158NE 2164 14Æ 224s	**—815—** (20IIA306) (20IIA235) **—819—**	(182S2d 9) s163NE 670 s194S2d 922 s177S2d 880 s178S2d 621	s173S2d 927 **—865—** Case 1 (5NY865) (182S2d 17)	s 4LE 113 s 80SC 137 **—868—** Case 4	**—889—** (338Mas488) (168OS 482) 159NE 1229 169NE 1456	13Æ1409s **—38—** (338Mas796)	**—153—** (107OA 166) **—155—** (106OA 544)
—754— (338Mas473) 158NE 1142 164NE 1311 167NE 1758	(20IIA309) (20IIA309) **—821°—** (20IIA244) r162NE 428	s160—859 s157S2d 391 s162S2d 80 s171S2d 674 **—865—** Case 2	(5NY871) (182S2d 22) s174S2d 447 **—869—** Case 1	**—897—** (168OS 445) 158NE 1570 163NE 2782 **—898—**	(338Mas795) **—41—** (338Mas542) 165NE 5107	**—156—** s154NE 87 **—159—** 15Æ 170s
—758— (338Mas435) 160NE 3113 **—762—** (338Mas442) s143NE 196	37Æ 7s **—825—** (20IIA310) **—826—** (20IIA306) **—827—**	s140NE 875 s159S2d 983 s158NE 855 s186S2d 284 s150S2d 34 s325S2d 427 s168S2d 307	(5NY867) (182S2d 18) s153NE 729 s179S2d 97 s170S2d 423	(5NY871) (182S2d 22) s153NE 734 s179S2d 105 s166S2d 492	(168OS 410) s153NE 711 **—904—** (168OS 471) s153NE 190	42Æ1319s **—44—** (338Mas494) 60Æ1146s **—49—**	34Æ 372s **—162—** **—164—** (106OA 541) **—170—**
—767— (338Mas791) 29Æ 911s **—768—** (338Mas793) 22Æ1176s	(20IIA288) 165NE 2740 71Æ 91n 71Æ 418n 71Æ 161n **—829—**	s169S2d 897 s174S2d 970 s176S2d 938 s176S2d 946 s178S2d 636 **—861—** Case 1	**—866—** Case 1 (5NY869) (182S2d 18) s148NE 315 s171S2d 104	s175S2d1016 s359US 1004 s 3LE 1032 s 79SC 1143 **—869—** Case 2	q164NE 7165 f166NE 4229 **—909—** (168OS 418) f167NE 1784 **—917—**	168NE 1276 21Æ 611s Ore 341P2d 118 **—52—**	169NE 662 **—175—** 155NE 1525 **—176—** D147NE 856
—770— (338Mas421) 166NE 5700 **—775—** (338Mas368)	(20IIA311) **—830—** (20IIA201) **—832—** (20IIA303) **—833—**	Case 1 (5NY859) (182S2d 12) s161NE 217 s190S2d1005 s175S2d 422	s154NE 564 s180S2d 308 s167S2d 425 s168S2d 607 **—866—** Case 2	(5NY872) (182S2d 23) s154NE 570 s180S2d 316 s175S2d 557	(168OS 398) 53Æ 850s **—922—** (168OS 481) **—923—** (168OS 468)	(338Mas547) 157NE 8883 158NE 141 166NE 5921 168NE 869 **—57—**	a156NE 190 s358US 283 s 3LE 312 s 79SC 297 **—190—** D147NE 856
158NE 5495 158NE10495 d162NE 1831 Wis 99NW 160 **—781—** (338Mas792)	(20IIA192) **—838—** (20IIA307) a163NE 523 **—839°—** (20IIA305) **—841—**	s177S2d1010 s178S2d 620 **—861—** Case 2 (5NY860) (182S2d 13) s174S2d 947	(5NY870) (182S2d 19) s177S2d1018 **—867—** Case 1 (5NY870)	**—870—** Case 1 (5NY874) (182S2d 24) s154NE 574 s180S2d 322	s360US 907 s 3LE 1258 s 79SC 1286 s361US 856 s 4LE 98 s 80SC 47	(338Mas520) 18Æ1010s **—61—** (338Mas554) 162NE 2787 27Æ1348s	s156NE 176 s163NE 383 s358US 283 s 3LE 312 s 79SC 297 **—198—**
—782— (338Mas793) 24Æ 194s **—783—** (338Mas481) 163NE 9266	r163NE 89 s362US 968 s 4LE 900 s 80SC 955 68Æ1448n	**—862—** Case 1 (5NY860) (182S2d 13) s156NE 921 s175S2d 579	(182S2d 20) s157NE 717 s184S2d 841 s176S2d 240 **—867—** Case 2	s170S2d1010 s175S2d1010 s359US 994 s 3LE 982 s 79SC 1127 165NE 174	**—925—** (106OA 517) s151NE 797 s154NE 83 s155NE 468 21Æ 643s	(5NY142) (182S2d361) s162S2d 833 s171S2d 715 204S2d 569	a164NE 759 **—202—** D154NE 822 s359US 983 s 3LE 984 s 79SC 940
—787— (338Mas468) **—791—** (338Mas450) 157NE11222 164NE 5316 167NE 156	**—844—** (20IIA370) **—847—** (20IIA308) **—848°—** (20IIA332)	s359US 997 s 3LE 985 s 79SC 1132 **—862—** Case 2 (5NY861)	(182S2d 20) s159NE 206 s186S2d 661 s175S2d 20 **—867—** Case 3	197S2d 155 **—870—** Case 2 (5NY875) (182S2d 25) s173S2d 665	(20IIA365) s175S2d 862 1888S2d 800 203S2d 223 **—87—**	**—71—** (5NY147) (182S2d365) **—222—** (20IIA297) 16Æ 3s **—225—**
—798— Case 1 (338Mas793) 46Æ 9s	166NE 1621 49Æ 797s **—859°—** (20IIA304)	(182S2d 14) s151NE 90 s174S2d 658 s152NE 657	(182S2d 21) s158NE 512 s185S2d 822	s175S2d 154 191S2d 886 203S2d 280 **—871—** (5NY876) (182S2d 26)	Vol. 156 **—1°—** (20IIA292) **—4°—** (20IIA279)	163NE 4579 168NE10210 168NE11210	(20IIA336) 163NE 1108 **—229—** Case 1 (20IIA477) *Continued*

* Illinois Appellate Court Cases when Certiorari or Leave to Appeal Denied

Exhibit 4. Photostatic copy of page 483 of the *Northeastern Reporter Citator*, January 1961. Reproduced with permission of the publisher and copyright owner, Shepard's Citations, Inc., Colorado Springs, Colo.

and went to the Supreme Court as shown by the three references to reports of opinions of that Court.

Corpus Juris Secundum. Corpus Juris Secundum, abbreviated "C.J.S.," is the second series of a many-volumed publication of case law principles reported in encyclopedic form. Textual matter provides a running account, and copious footnotes give citations to cases in point. The material is classified according to subject matter and the topic "Schools and School Districts" appears in volumes 78 and 79. Pocket parts keep *Corpus Juris Secundum* up to date.

Each subject in *Corpus Juris Secundum* is outlined in detail at the beginning of its treatment, and each subtopic in the outline is given a number which is used in the discussion to identify the subtopic. There are 512 subtopics in "Schools and School Districts," a few of which are given herewith:[6]

   I. DEFINITIONS AND CLASSIFICATION OF SCHOOLS, secs. 1-2.
  II. PRIVATE SCHOOLS, secs. 3-11.
 III. PUBLIC SCHOOLS, secs. 12-512.
    A. In General, secs. 12-15.
    B. School Lands and School Funds, secs. 16-22.
    C. School Districts and other Local School Organizations, secs. 23-82.
    D. Administration, Government, and Officers, secs. 83-143.
    E. Agents and Employees, secs. 144-153.
    F. Teachers, Principals, and Superintendents, secs. 154-238.
      1. *In General,* secs. 154-169.
      2. *Selection, Appointment, or Election,* secs. 170-182.
      3. *Contracts of Employment,* secs. 183-197.
      4. *Assignment and Transfer,* secs. 198-199.
      5. *Change of Status,* secs. 200-217.
      6. *Compensation, Board and Lodging, and Pensions,* secs. 218-236.
      7. *Duties and Liabilities,* secs. 237-238.
    G. Property, Contracts, and Liabilities, secs. 239-322.
    H. Fiscal Management, Debts, Securities, and Taxation, secs. 323-413.
    I. Remedies of Taxpayers in General, secs. 414-422.
    J. Presentation and Allowance of Claims, secs. 423-427.
    K. Actions, secs. 428-444.
    L. Pupils, and Conduct and Discipline of Schools, secs. 445-508.
      1. *Admission and Attendance of Pupils,* secs. 445-482.

---

[6] Reproduced with permission of the publisher and copyright owner, The American Law Book Company, Brooklyn, N. Y.

the certificate for use in that county[50] and to make it exempt from collateral attack.[51]

§ 168. —— Conclusiveness as Evidence; Collateral Attack

A teacher's certificate is prima facie evidence of the teacher's qualifications, and of the fact that the members of the board or committee issuing such certificate have properly performed their duty as to the manner and requisites of their issuing it. In the absence of fraud it cannot be collaterally impeached.

A teacher's certificate is prima facie evidence of the teacher's qualifications[52] and of the fact that the members of the board or committee issuing such certificate have properly performed their duty as to the manner and requisites of their issuing it.[53] In the absence of fraud it cannot be collaterally impeached,[54] as, for example, in a suit by a teacher to recover wages after being dismissed,[55] or after destruction of the school by fire and failure of the

board to provide other quarters,[56] or in a suit between contestants to try title to the office of state superintendent of public instruction[57] or county superintendent of schools.[58]

§ 169. Attendance at Teachers' Institute

Attendance at a teachers' institute may be necessary before the teacher can be lawfully permitted to teach.

Where the statute so provides, attendance at a teachers' institute for the period designated is necessary before the teacher can be lawfully permitted to teach[59] unless the teacher has been excused therefrom by a proper school official,[60] which excuse may be given orally in the absence of statutory requirement to the contrary.[61] A statute which provides for the collection of annual fees from applicants for teachers' certificates for the support of teachers' institutes is valid.[62]

2. SELECTION, APPOINTMENT, OR ELECTION

§ 170. In General

Appointment is generally a prerequisite to employment as a teacher, principal, or superintendent; and the matter of appointment of such school employees is, subject to constitutional restrictions, within the power and control of the legislature.

Appointment, in the broad sense of being chosen, selected, or designated to occupy the position of teacher, principal, or superintendent, by the proper

authorities in accordance with all statutory requirements, is generally a prerequisite to employment in such capacity.[63] The matter of appointment of such school employees is, subject to constitutional restrictions, within the power and control of the legislature.[64] The usual rules of statutory construction govern the construction of statutes relating to the appointment of teachers and other instructional employees.[65]

---

50. Neb.—State v. Grosvenor, 27 N.W. 728, 19 Neb. 494.

51. Neb.—State v. Grosvenor, supra.

52. Kan.—Strange v. School Dist. No. 97, 295 P. 672, 132 Kan. 268.
Tenn.—Corpus Juris quoted in State ex rel. Clement v. Dodson, 83 S.W. 2d 558, 169 Tenn. 178.
Wyo.—Corpus Juris quoted in State ex rel. Pape v. Hockett, 156 P.2d 299, 305, 61 Wyo. 145.
56 C.J. p 377 note 4.

53. Tenn.—Corpus Juris quoted in State ex rel. Clement v. Dodson, 83 S.W.2d 558, 169 Tenn. 178.
Wyo.—Corpus Juris quoted in State ex rel. Pape v. Hockett, 156 P.2d 299, 305, 61 Wyo. 145.
56 C.J. p 377 note 5.

54. Tenn.—Corpus Juris quoted in State ex rel. Clement v. Dodson, 83 S.W.2d 558, 169 Tenn. 178.
Wyo.—Corpus Juris quoted in State ex rel. Pape v. Hockett, 156 P.2d 299, 305, 61 Wyo. 145.
56 C.J. p 377 note 6.

55. Tenn.—Corpus Juris quoted in State ex rel. Clement v. Dodson, 83 S.W.2d 558, 169 Tenn. 178.
Wyo.—Corpus Juris quoted in State

ex rel. Pape v. Hockett, 156 P.2d 299, 305, 61 Wyo. 145.
56 C.J. p 377 note 7.

56. Tenn.—Corpus Juris quoted in State ex rel. Clement v. Dodson, 83 S.W.2d 558, 169 Tenn. 178.
Wis.—Clune v. Buchanan School Dist. No. 3, 166 N.W. 11, 166 Wis. 452, 6 A.L.R. 736.

57. N.D.—McDonald v. Nielson, 175 N.W. 361, 43 N.D. 346.
Tenn.—Corpus Juris quoted in State ex rel. Clement v. Dodson, 83 S.W. 2d 558, 169 Tenn. 178.
Wyo.—Corpus Juris quoted in State ex rel. Pape v. Hockett, 156 P.2d 299, 305, 61 Wyo. 145.

58. N.D.—Wendt v. Waller, 176 N. W. 930, 46 N.D. 268.
Tenn.—Corpus Juris quoted in State ex rel. Clement v. Dodson, 83 S.W. 2d 558, 169 Tenn. 178.
Wyo.—Corpus Juris quoted in State ex rel. Pape v. Hockett, 156 P.2d 299, 305, 61 Wyo. 145.

59. W.Va.—Capehart v. Graham Dist. Board of Education, 95 S.E. 838, 82 W.Va. 217.
Revocation of certificate for failure to attend see supra § 165.

60. W.Va.—Capehart v. Graham Dist. Board of Education, supra.

61. W.Va.—Capehart v. Graham Dist. Board of Education, supra.

62. Mich.—Hammond v. Muskegon School Board, 67 N.W. 973, 109 Mich. 676.

63. N.J.—Moriarity v. Board of Education of City of Garfield in Bergen County, 42 A.2d 465, 133 N.J. Law 73, affirmed 46 A.2d 734, 134 N.J.Law 356.
N.Y.—Nicol v. New York City Board of Education, 211 N.Y.S. 749, 125 Misc. 678.
Pa.—Potts v. School Dist. of Penn. Tp., 193 A. 290, 127 Pa.Super. 173.
W.Va.—Rowan v. Board of Education of Logan County, 24 S.E.2d 583, 125 W.Va. 406.
Contracts of employment see infra §§ 183-187.

64. Ill.—Groves v. Board of Education of Chicago, 10 N.E.2d 403, 367 Ill. 91 appeal dismissed 58 S.Ct. 746, 302 U.S. 122, 82 L.Ed. 1085, rehearing denied 58 S.Ct. 763, 303 U.S. 669, 82 L.Ed. 1125.

65. Statutes construed
(1) Statute conferring power to appoint a superintendent of schools

---

Exhibit 5. Photostatic copy of page 993 in Volume 78 of *Corpus Juris Secundum*. Reproduced with permission of the publisher and copyright owner, The American Law Book Company, Brooklyn, N. Y.

2. *School Terms, Classification of Pupils, and Instruction,*
   secs. 483-492.
3. *Control of Pupils and Discipline,* secs. 493-505.
4. *Graduation, Scholarships, and Diplomas,* secs. 506-508.
   M. Miscellaneous Criminal Offences, secs. 509-512.

The sections under each of these major topics are outlined with
considerable detail. In the body of the volume, each subtopic is discussed as is exemplified in Exhibit 5. The pocket parts which keep
Corpus Juris Secundum up to date show subsequent cases according
to the footnote numbers in the bound volume.

Study of Exhibit 5 together with the outline reproduced in part
should indicate the type of information available in *Corpus Juris
Secundum.* Footnotes in *Corpus Juris* (the first edition) are not repeated in *Corpus Juris Secundum* and the original edition will not be
completely superseded for historical studies.

American Jurisprudence. American Jurisprudence is the second
edition of *Ruling Case Law* which is encyclopedic in style similiar to
both editions of *Corpus Juris* but it contains only the leading cases
whereas *Corpus Juris* and *Corpus Juris Secundum* are all-inclusive.
Volume 24 of *Ruling Case Law* contained the material on "Schools,"
but since it was published in 1919, it is of no practical use today.

Following is an outline of the topics included in *American Jurisprudence.*[7] Not only may this outline be compared with the outline
of *Corpus Juris Secundum,* previously shown; the actual material in
the two encyclopedias may also be compared. Exhibit 6 shows a page
from *American Jurisprudence* and Exhibit 5 showed a page from
Corpus Juris Secundum.

    I. INTRODUCTORY. (1-11).
   II. SCHOOL DISTRICTS. (12-28).
  III. ADMINISTRATIVE OFFICERS AND BOARDS. (29-47).
  IV. CONTRACTS IN GENERAL. (48-55).
   V. TORT LIABILITY. (56-61).
  VI. SCHOOL PROPERTY AND BUILDINGS. (62-75).
 VII. TAXATION. (76-82).
VIII. SCHOOL FUNDS AND EXPENDITURES. (83-107).
  IX. TEACHERS AND OTHER EMPLOYEES. (108-145).
       A. In General. (108-113).
       B. Employment and Compensation in General. (114-126).
       C. Teachers' Tenure Statutes. (127-145).

---

[7] Reproduced with permission of the publishers and copyright owners, The
Lawyers Co-operative Publishing Company, Rochester, N. Y., and Bancroft-
Whitney Company, San Francisco, Calif.

one is not justified in relying upon representations relating to facts of which he has a better knowledge than the party making the representations[14] is likewise applicable to contracts of this nature.[15]

Where, by statute, an oath of allegiance to the Federal and state Constitutions and of fidelity to duty is required to be embodied in a teacher's contract of employment, the oath will be deemed to have been embodied in the contract where it was administered on the occasion and at the time when the contract was executed, and a statement subscribed by the teacher, embodying the oath, is found below the signature of the parties to the contract.[16]

§ 116. —With School Board Member or Wife of Member.—In agreement with the elementary principle that a member of a school board may not enter into a contract with the board in which he has a personal interest,[17] a school board cannot contract with one of its own members to teach the school.[18] But in jurisdictions where the earnings of the wife are her separate property, a school board may contract to employ the wife of a member as a teacher,[19] although in states where the earnings of the wife constitute part of the community property of which the husband has the control and management,[20] the decisions are to the contrary.[1]

§ 117. —Extending beyond Term of Board; Contracts Beginning in Subsequent Term.—In contrast with the general rule applicable to contracts by

year, were informed by the superintendent of schools that the school budget did not admit of their paying the amount of salary named in the contract were precluded by their delay from rescinding the contract because of the principal's misrepresentation as to the amount of the budget, even if otherwise entitled to rely on such misrepresentations as a fraud justifying the rescission, where, for over two months, they did nothing to repudiate the contract, but permitted the principal to prepare for the school term, and finally to enter upon his duties when school opened on August 30, the notice terminating the contract not having been served upon him until September 20, it being then too late to secure another position. Weir v. School Dist. 200 Wash 172, 93 P(2d) 308, 123 ALR 1057.

14 See 23 Am Jur 947, FRAUD AND DECEIT, § 146.

15 Weir v. School Dist. 200 Wash 172, 93 P(2d) 308, 123 ALR 1057.

School directors were not justified in relying upon misrepresentations by one whom they employed as principal, that he had consulted the county superintendent and was advised by her that the school budget had been approved and that the district would be able to pay him the amount named in the contract, upon which misrepresentations they predicated fraud as justification for termination of the contract, where they were themselves the persons who tentatively were to determine and express the needs and abilities of the district, and they knew that the approval of the budget lay with the county superintendent and the reviewing board and were told repeatedly by the superintendent that they would not have money enough to pay so large a salary as that named in the contract. Ibid.

16 June v. School Dist. 283 Mich 533, 278 NW 676, 116 ALR 581 (stating further that

such a requirement will be given a reasonable construction).

The lack of a jurat to such an oath does not render the employment contract fatally defective so as to preclude its enforcement. June v. School Dist. 283 Mich 533, 278 NW 676, 116 ALR 581. Anno: 116 ALR 587.

17 See supra, § 49.

18 Scott v. School Dist. 67 Vt 150, 31 A 145, 27 LRA 588.

The reason for the rule is clearer when it is considered that it is the duty of the board to remove a teacher when necessary; it is fundamental that a man shall not be a judge in his own case. Ibid.

The inclusion, however, by a county superintendent of schools of his own name in a list of approved teachers of the county does not invalidate a subsequent contract employing him as a teacher, where the superintendent does not himself employ the teachers but merely submits a list of names to the board of education, which is the employing authority. White v. Board of Education, 117 W Va 114, 184 SE 264, 103 ALR 1376.

19 Thompson v. School Dist. 252 Mich 629, 233 NW 439, 74 ALR 790. Anno: 74 ALR 792.

A contract employing as a teacher the wife of a school board member whose concurrence is necessary in order to bind the district is not within the meaning of a statute declaring it to be illegal for any member of a board of education "to be personally interested in any way, directly or indirectly, in any contract with the district in which he holds office," where the earnings of a married woman are her separate property. Thompson v. School Dist. 252 Mich 629, 233 NW 439, 74 ALR 790.

20 See 11 Am Jur 196, COMMUNITY PROPERTY, § 34.

1 Anno: 74 ALR 795.

Exhibit 6. Photostatic copy of page 378 in Volume 47 of *American Jurisprudence*. Reproduced with permission of the publishers and copyright owners, The Lawyers Co-operative Publishing Company, Rochester, N.Y., and Bancroft-Whitney Company, San Francisco, Calif.

X. PUPILS; ADMISSION, ATTENDANCE, DISCIPLINE,
AND PUNISHMENT. (146-188).
   A. In General. (146-150).
   B. Right to Attend Schools. (151-155).
   C. Compulsory Attendance. (156-159).
   D. Transportation of Pupils. (160-166).
   E. Disciplinary Regulations. (167-172).
   F. Discipline and Punishment. (173-188).
XI. HEALTH REGULATIONS. (189-199).
XII. COURSES OF INSTRUCTION, TEXTBOOKS, AND
SUPPLIES. (200-207).
XIII. SECTARIANISM IN SCHOOLS. (208-215).
XIV. RACE SEGREGATION. (216-219).
XV. PRIVATE SCHOOLS. (220-229).

Corpus Juris Secundum and *American Jurisprudence* both use the same style of presentation: textual material with copious footnotes giving citations to cases illustrating the statements of principles in the text on the upper part of the page. The chief difference between them is in the scope of material included. Most topics are more extensively treated in *Corpus Juris Secundum* than in *American Jurisprudence.*

However, for the purpose of research in school-law problems, *American Jurisprudence* may be adequate coverage. Choice between these two encyclopedias will depend upon the purpose of the investigator's study. If an exhaustive piece of research is contemplated, *Corpus Juris Secundum* will provide a greater fund of information than *American Jurisprudence.* On the other hand, *American Jurisprudence* is sufficient for most research in school law by school administrators, teachers, or others who are not concerned with technical niceties and distinctions of interest to lawyers.

Summary

Many lawyers are of the opinion that one without legal training should not touch a law book. They are as jealous of their prerogatives as a physician of his instruments, and rightly so. This appendix has been included in this text because students of education have attempted to search legal problems affecting the public schools in connection with graduate study requirements. In so doing they have on occasion used secondary sources which are possibly unreliable or

antiquated; they have quoted statutes that have been repealed or possibly declared unconstitutional; they have cited court decisions which have been overruled. It is safer to instruct a layman how to use technical instruments than to leave them unguarded for indiscriminate use by the zealous but untaught. If students of education are to learn school law, they should know how to find it.

Appendix B.

GLOSSARY OF LEGAL TERMS

Action. An ordinary proceeding in a court by which one party prosecutes another for the enforcement or protection of a right, the redress of a wrong, or the punishment of a public offense. In common language, a "suit," or "lawsuit."

Action at law. Court action in a law case, as distinguished from equity.

Actionable. That which furnishes legal grounds for an action. Sometimes a court will say "The action will lie," meaning that the circumstances are such that there is a ground for court action.

Ad litum. Latin, meaning for the purpose of the suit, usually used when minors are, in fact, the plaintiffs. Because they are minors they must sue "by next friend," referring to parent or guardian who is plaintiff for the purpose of the suit.

Allegation. Statement in pleadings, setting forth what the party expects to prove.

Allege. To state, assert, or charge; to make an allegation.

Amicus curiae. "Friend at court"—one who volunteers or is requested to give information to the court regarding some matter of law in regard to which the judge is doubtful or mistaken; one who has no right to appear in a case but is allowed to file a brief or enter into the argument because of an indirect interest.

Annotation. Notes or commentaries in addition to the principal text. A book is said to be annotated when it contains such notes.

Appellant. The party who takes an appeal from one court to another.

Appellee. The party against whom an appeal is taken.

Arbitrary. Not supported by fair cause and without reason given.

Arbitration. Submission of a controversy, usually in labor disputes, for determination. *See* Mediation.

Assault. An attempt to beat another, without touching him. *See* Battery.

Attractive nuisance. A condition, instrumentality, machine, or other agency, dangerous to young children because of their inability to appreciate its danger although they may be expected to be attracted to it. *See* Nuisance.

Avoid a contract. To cancel and make the contract void.

Battery. An unlawful beating or other wrongful physical violence inflicted on another without his consent. The offer or attempt to commit a battery is an assault. There can be an assault without a battery; battery always includes assault. The two words are usually used together.

Bill. A written complaint filed in a court.

Bill of attainder. An act of the legislature inflicting a penalty (technically capital punishment) without conviction in judicial proceedings. Loosely used to include all legislation imposing a penalty applicable to acts not considered a crime when committed.

Breach of contract. Failure without legal excuse to perform part or the whole of a contract.

Certificate. A document designed as notice that some act has been done, or some event occurred, or some legal formality complied with; evidence of qualification.

Citations. References to law books. A citation includes the book where the reference is found, the volume number, and section or page numbers. A uniform system of abbreviations in case law has been adopted, but statutory materials differ from state to state according to the official designation accepted by the legislature.

Citations, judicial. References to court decisions. Citations in the case materials in this text refer to official state reports and to the National Reporter System. The volume number precedes the abbreviation of the reporter, and the page number follows it. In parentheses is the name of the state where the decision was rendered, and its date. A complete judicial citation includes everywhere that the case may be found, but for school-law work complete parallel citations are unnecessary.

Citations, statutory. References to statutes; where the statute may be found in publicly available form. Statutory citations in this text include the name of the volume, the title and/or chapter, and the section number(s) quoted.

Civil action. One brought to recover some civil right, or to obtain redress for some wrong.

Class bill or suit. A case in which one or more in a numerous class, having a common interest in the issue, sue in behalf of themselves and all others of the class.

Closed shop. Term in labor law meaning that worker must be a member of the union as a condition precedent to employment. *See* Union shop.

Code. A compilation of statutes, scientifically arranged into chapters, subheadings, and sections, with a table of contents and index.

Codification. Process of collecting and arranging the laws of a state into a code.

Collateral attack. An attempt to destroy the effect of a judgment by reopening the merits of a case or by showing reasons why the judgment should not have been given, in an action other than that in which the judgment was given; that is, not in an appeal.

Common Law. As used in this text, legal principles derived from usage and custom, or from court decisions affirming such usages and customs, or the acts of Parliament in force at the time of the American Revolution, as distinguished from law created by enactment of American legislatures.

Concurrent jurisdiction. Two courts having the same authority.

Concurring opinion. An opinion written by a judge who agrees with the majority of the court as to the decision in a case, but has different reasons for arriving at that decision.

Consideration in contracts. The inducement, usually an amount of money.

Constitution. The supreme organic and fundamental law of a nation or state, establishing the character and conception of its government, laying the basic principles to which its internal life is to be conformed, organizing the government, and regulating, distributing, and limiting the functions of its different departments, and prescribing the extent and manner of the exercise of sovereign powers.

Contract. An agreement upon sufficient consideration, to do or not to do a particular thing; the writing which contains the agreement of the parties, with the terms and conditions, and which serves as proof of the obligation.

Contract action. An action brought to enforce rights under a contract.

Credibility of witnesses. Worthiness of belief of testimony of witnesses.

Criminal action. Proceeding by which a party charged with a crime is brought to trial and punishment.

Damages. Pecuniary compensation or indemnity which may be recovered in court by the person who has suffered loss or injury to his person, property, or rights through the unlawful act, or omission, or negligence of another.

De facto officer. One who is in actual possession of an office without lawful title; as opposed to a *de jure* officer.

De jure officer. One who has just claim and rightful title to an office, although not necessarily in actual possession thereof.

Declaratory relief. A judgment which declares the rights of the parties or expresses the opinion of the court on a question of law, without ordering anything to be done.

Decree. Order of court of equity announcing the legal consequences of the facts found.

Defendant. The party against whom relief or recovery is sought in a court action.

Defendant in error. Defendant in appellate court when the "appeal" is for review on writ of error.

Defense. That which is offered and alleged by the defendant as a reason in law or fact why the plaintiff should not recover.

Demurrer. Allegation by one party that other party's allegations may be true but, even so, are not of such legal consequence as to justify proceeding with the case.

Dictum. Statement of a legal principle by a court, which principle is not necessitated by the facts or the law of the case; because such statements are not directly in point, they are not controlling precedents, though often persuasive.

Directory. An instruction of no obligatory force and involving no invalidating consequences for its disregard.

Dismissed for want of equity. Case dismissed because the allegations in the complaint have been found untrue, or because they are insufficient to entitle complainant to the relief sought.

Dissenting opinion. The opinion in which a judge announces his dissent from the conclusions held by the majority of the court.

Divisible contract. One which can be separated into two or more parts not necessarily dependent on each other nor intended by the parties to be so.

Discrimination, unconstitutional. The effect of a statute which confers particular privileges on a class arbitrarily selected and for whom no reasonable distinction can be found.

Due process. The exercise of the powers of government in such a way as to protect individual rights.

Ejusdem generis. Of the same kind, class, or nature. In statutory construction the *ejusdem generis* rule is that, where general words follow an enumeration of words of a particular and specific meaning, the general words are not interpreted in their widest sense but as applying to persons or things of the same general kind or class as those specifically mentioned.

Emancipation of child. Surrender of the right to care, custody, and earnings of a child by its parents who at the same time renounce parental duties.

Enforceable contract. Any contract not void or voidable because defective.

Enjoin. To require a person, by writ of injunction from a court of equity, to perform, or to abstain or desist from, some act.

Equitable relief. Decree in court of equity.

Equity. As used in this text, the field of jurisprudence differing in origin, theory, and methods from the common law.

Estop. To prevent.

Estoppel. A bar raised by the law which prevents a man from alleging or denying a certain fact because of his previous statements or conduct.

Ex post facto. After the fact. An ex post facto law is one passed after an act which retrospectively changes the legal consequences of that act. The Federal Constitution prohibits the passage of ex post facto laws, referring to criminal laws only. *See* Bill of attainder and Retroactive.

Ex rel. Abbreviation for *ex relatione,* meaning on relation or information. For the purpose of this text, it need be explained only as designating a type of court action.

Exception. In civil procedure, a formal objection to the action of the court when it refuses a request or overrules an objection, implying that the party excepting does not acquiesce in the court's ruling and may base an appeal thereon.

Executed contract. A completed contract as opposed to one which is executory.

Executory contract. An incompletely performed contract; something yet to be done in the future.

Governmental immunity. Immunity from tort actions enjoyed by governmental units in common-law states.

Hearing on the merits. Trial on the substance of a case as opposed to consideration of procedure only.

Hearsay evidence. Testimony given by a witness who relates what others have told him or what he has heard said by others, rather than what he knows personally.

In loco parentis. In place of the parent; charged with some of the parents' rights, duties, and responsibilities.

In re. Concerning. When used in a title of a court case, it merely designates a type of case.

Indivisible contract. One which forms a whole, the performance of every part a condition precedent to bind the other party; as opposed to a divisible contract which is composed of independent parts the performance of any one of which will bind the other party only as far as it goes.

Information. An accusation against a person.

Infringement. An encroachment upon or invasion of one's rights.

Injunction. A prohibitive writ issued by a court of equity forbidding the defendant to do some act he is threatening, or forbidding him to continue doing some act which is injurious to the plaintiff and cannot be adequately redressed by an action at law.

Injunction, temporary. An injunction granted at the beginning of a suit to restrain the defendant from doing some act, the right to which is in dispute, and which may be discharged or made permanent according to the result of the case after the rights of the parties are determined.

Invalid. Not binding; lacking in authority.

Ipso facto. By the fact itself.

Judgment. Decision of the court, usually that part involving the payment of damages.

Judgment-proof. Said of those against whom a judgment has been rendered even though they are not in financial condition to pay it.

Laches. Omission to assert a right for an unreasonable and unexplained length of time, under circumstances prejudicial to the adverse party.

Law. (1) System of principles or rules of human conduct. In this sense it includes decisions of courts as well as acts of legislatures. (2) An enactment of a legislature, a statute.

Legal disability. Lack of legal capacity to perform an act.

Legal power. The right or ability to do some act.

Liability. Legal responsibility.

Liquidated damages. A specific sum of money stipulated by the parties by bond or contract as the amount of damages to be recovered by one party for breach of the agreement by the other.

Majority opinion. The statement of reasons for the views of the majority of the members of the bench in a decision in which some of them disagree.

Majority rule. A legal principle upheld by the majority of decisions on the question, when there is a lesser number of decisions to the contrary on the same issue.

Malfeasance. Commission of an unlawful act, applied to public officers and employees. *See* Misfeasance and Nonfeasance.

Mandamus. A writ to compel a public body or its officers to perform a duty.

Mandatory. Compulsory, referring to a command for which disregard or disobedience is unlawful.

Mediation. Attempt to reconcile differences, usually in labor disputes. *See* Arbitration.

Minority rule. The principle upheld by some courts on an issue which has been decided to the contrary by the majority of courts.

Misdemeanor. An offense lower than a felony and usually punishable by fine, or imprisonment otherwise than in a penitentiary.

Misfeasance. Improper performance of a lawful act. *See* Malfeasance.

Nonfeasance. Omission to perform a required duty.

Nolens volens. With or without consent.

Nonsuit. Judgment against a plaintiff when he is unable to prove a case, or when he neglects to proceed to the trial of a case after it has been put in issue.

Nuisance. A continuous condition or use of property in such a manner as to obstruct proper use of it by others lawfully having right to use it, or the public.

Parol-evidence rule. Oral evidence as to matters not contained in a written contract or other instrument is not admissible.

Persuasive value. Influence of decisions of one jurisdiction in another jurisdiction.

Petition. Written application or prayer to the court for the redress of a wrong or the grant of a privilege or license.

Petitioner. The one who presents a petition to the court; same as plaintiff in other kinds of cases.

Plaintiff. Person who brings an action; he who sues by filing a complaint.

Plea in abatement. An objection to the place, method, or time of plaintiff's assertion of a claim, without disputing the justice of the claim.

Pleadings. Formal papers filed in court action including complaint by plaintiff and defendant's answer, showing what is alleged on one side and admitted or denied on the other side.

Plenary. Complete power, usually applied to legislatures over matters within their entire jurisdiction; applicable also to any public officer who has unqualified power in a designated matter.

Police power. As used in this text, legislative power to enact laws for the comfort, health, and prosperity of the state; for the general welfare of the people concerned.

Power. The authority to do something expressly or impliedly granted.

Prayer. The part of the petition in which petitioner requests the court to grant the relief sought.

Precedent. A decision considered as furnishing an example or authority for an identical or similar case afterward arising on a similar question of law.

Prima facie case. A case in which the evidence is so strong that the adverse party can overthrow the evidence only by sufficient rebutting evidence.

Privies of parties. Persons connected with mutual interest in the same action.

Quantum meruit. An implication that the defendant had promised to pay plaintiff as much as he reasonably deserved for work or labor.

Quasi-. As if, or almost as if it were, *e.g.*, quasi-judicial act of a school board in holding a hearing before dismissal of a teacher.

Quo warranto—information in the nature of a quo warranto. Method of trying title to a public office.

Ratification. Confirmation of a transaction by one who before ratification had the optional right to relieve himself of its obligation.

Regulations. Rules for management or government.

Relator. One on whose complaint certain writs are issued; for all practical purposes, the plaintiff.

Relief. The redress or assistance which a complainant seeks from the court; not properly applied to money damages.

Remand a case. To send the case back to the court from which it came for further proceedings there, after an appellate decision.

Res adjudicata. A matter judicially decided.

Rescission of contract. Cancellation or abrogation by the parties, or one of them.

Respondent. Defendant in certain kinds of cases.

Restrain. To prohibit from action; to enjoin.

Retroactive. A law which creates a new obligation on considerations already past, or destroys or impairs former privileges. Not all retroactive laws are unconstitutional.

Right. A power or privilege in one person against another.

Scienter. Knowingly; defendant knew the circumstances leading to his injury. Used chiefly in loyalty laws.

Stare decisis. Principle that when a court has made a declaration of a legal principle it is the law until changed by competent authority; upholding of precedents within the jurisdiction.

Statute. Act of the legislature.

Stipulation. (1) A particular provision in an agreement; (2) an agreement between counsel concerning business before a court.

Subpoena. Process commanding a witness to appear and testify.

Sufficiency of evidence. Evidence adequate in character, weight, or amount to justify legal action sought.

Tenure. In its general sense, mode of holding an office or position, especially with respect to time.

Tort. Legal wrong committed upon the person, reputation, or property of another, independent of contract.

Ultra vires. Acts beyond the scope of authority.

Union shop. Term in labor law meaning that, although nonmembers of the union may be employed, they must join the union within a designated time or face dismissal.

Validity. Legal sufficiency in contradistinction to mere regularity.

Vested right. A right which has so completely and definitely accrued or settled in a person that it cannot be cancelled or impaired.

Void. Ineffectual, having no legal force or binding effect; said of a contract so defective that nothing can cure it.

Voidable. That which may be avoided or declared void; as to contracts, a defective instrument which can be cured by ratification by the one who could have avoided it.

Waive. To renounce or abandon a right.

Waiver. Intentional and voluntary relinquishment of a known right.

Without prejudice. No rights or privileges will be considered waived or lost.

Writ in vacation. Court order issued during intermission of court session.

Writ of error. Appellate court orders lower court to submit record of an action on which the lower court has reached a final judgment, so that the appellate court may examine the alleged errors of the lower court.

Appendix C.

SELECTED BIBLIOGRAPHY

Secondary sources are not recommended for legal research work. Even when reliable, most such publications are written in such a way as to be out of date after a relatively short time has elapsed. For this reason, a bibliography of books or periodicals dealing with school law is not provided in this text as is customary in textbooks on other educational subjects. References are given to a few current books only, and mention made of where new and up-to-date publications may be obtained in the future. The best source of information, however, are those law books mentioned in Appendix A. From statutes and court decisions, the original sources of school-law material, the investigator may define his problem and analyze it according to his purposes and interests. Secondary sources should be used for background only.

The *Cumulative Catalog*, the *Educational Index*, and the *Legal Periodical Index*, of course, may be examined to discover new publications in the field of school law and these sources should not be neglected in any research project. However, not every word in print is based upon an adequate foundation, and publications should be scrutinized carefully before being accepted as authority.

The National Education Association publishes annual compilations of new laws and court decisions. It also issues analyses of school-law topics. Occasionally a National Education Association report covers a broad area, one such being *The Teacher and the Law* (School Law Series, Research Monograph 1959-M3. 92 p.).

Lee O. Garber has compiled case-law digests annually for the past eleven years under the title *Yearbook of School Law* (e.g., *1960 Yearbook of School Law*. Danville, Illinois: the Interstate Printers & Publishers, Inc. 1960. 184 p.). These Yearbooks contain an annotated bibliography of selected publications in school law, and, also, special articles on selected school-law topics.

337

There are several old books on particular school-law subjects which, regardless of date of publication, are still useful for the study of general principles so long as the student is aware that there have been statutory changes and subsequent court decisions which should be investigated apart from the book. In some instances even the general principles have been altered by the courts since publication of the book. One of these publications is *Liability for School Accidents* by Harry N. Rosenfield (Harper & Brothers, 1940. 220 p.).

The National Organization on Legal Problems in Education (NOLPE) sponsors publication of symposiums by its members who are especially qualified in school law. To date three such symposiums have been published, all by the Anderson Company of Cincinnati, Ohio. They are *The Law and the Superintendent*, edited by Robert L. Drury (1958. 339 p.), *An Evaluation of Existing Forms of School Laws with Recommendations for Their Improvement*, edited by Madaline Kinter Remmlein and Martha L. Ware (1959. 253 p.), and *The Law and the School Principal*, edited by Reynolds C. Seitz and Marlin M. Volz (1961. 266 p.).

For the law of a particular state and its interpretation, the state department of education is undoubtedly the best source. These departments issue many special bulletins, at least in some states. Especially where the chief state school officer is endowed with statutory authority to interpret the school law, these state department of education bulletins have considerable importance. School law of interest to teachers in particular states has been explained in simplified language; *e.g.*, *The Law and the Teacher in Pennsylvania*, by Lee O. Garber (University of Pennsylvania, Educational Service Bureau. 1955. 97 p.). Garber has cooperated with school-law specialists in the preparation of similar books for teachers in several other states.

Some of the newer publications of general coverage in school law are listed below.

Edwards, Newton. *The Courts and the Public Schools.* (2nd Ed.) Chicago: University of Chicago Press, 1955. 622 p.

Garber, Lee O. (Ed.) *Law and the School Business Manager.* Danville, Ill.: The Interstate Printers & Publishers, Inc., 1957. 331 p.

Gauerke, Warren E. *Legal and Ethical Responsibilities of School Personnel.* Englewood Cliffs, N. J.: Prentice-Hall. 1959. 302 p.

Hamilton, R. R. and Mort, P. R. *The Law and Public Education.* (2nd Ed.) New York: Foundation Press, 1959. 641 p.

Hamilton, R. R. and Reutter, E. Edmund, Jr. *Legal Aspects of School Board Operation.* New York: Bureau of Publications, Teachers College, Columbia University, 1958. 199 p.

Kramer, Robert (Ed.) "School Pupils and the Law." *Law and Contemporary Problems.* 20:1-195. 1955.

Nolte, M. Chester, and Linn, John Phillip, *School Law for Teachers.* Danville, Ill.: The Interstate Printers & Publishers, Inc., 1963. 343 pp.

Remmlein, Madaline Kinter. *Law of Public School Administration.* New York: McGraw-Hill Book Co., 1953. 271 p.

Spurlock, Clark. *Education and the Supreme Court.* Urbana, Ill.: University of Illinois Press, 1955. 252 p.

It must be repeated, however, that secondary sources are not the best sources in school-law research. The statutes and judicial interpretations of them should form the groundwork upon which a study may be framed through reference to other authoritative opinions.

INDEX*

A

Age limits for school attendance, 195
Alabama, court decision in, 270-271
Antifraternity rules, 269-270, 274-276
Antinepotism, 6, 10-12, 20
Appeal from school-board decisions, 187-191
  statutory provisions for, 53, 188-189
Appointment of teachers, 3-21, 59
  without discrimination on basis of sex, 16-18
  from eligibility lists, 5, 15-19
  of husband and wife in same school system, 77-79
  of non-citizens, 3
  of part-time teacher in tenure area, 51-53
  statutory provisions for, 5-6
Arkansas, continuing-contract law in, 29
  court decision in, 210-215
Assault on pupil, 268-269, 270-271, 329
Attendance, 195-226
  compulsory, 196, 216-217
  free, 196, 203-206
  home instruction as substitute for, 202-203
  at nonpublic schools, 199-201
  statutory provisions for, 198-199

B

Bible reading, 251, 257-260
Butte, Mont., collective bargaining agreement, 93-95

C

California, abrogation of governmental immunity in, 282-283
  court decisions in, 63, 77-79, 111-113, 202-203, 290-293
  minimum salary law in, 98
  statutory provisions regarding pupil injuries in, 282-283
Case law, definition of, xxi-xxii
Certification of teachers, 3-21, 59
  definition of, 3, 330
  prerequisite to employment, 4, 7, 8-9
  statutory provisions for, 5-7
Chambers v. Davis et al., 102
Chicago v. Chicago, 279
Child-benefit theory, 235-242, 251-253
Church schools (See Parochial schools)
Civil procedure, xxv-xxvii
Closed shop, 86-96
Collective bargaining by teachers' associations, 85-96
Colorado, statutory provisions on excusable homicide in, 269
Common law, abrogation of, xxiv
  application of, xxii
  definition of, 330
  (See also Defamation of character; Immunity from tort action)
Compulsory attendance (See Attendance)
Conduct of pupils, control of, 267-276

---

*Statutory provisions used as illustrations are indexed under their subject matter and under the state of their enactment, without citations. They are listed with complete citations, by states, on pages xiii-xiv.

Court decisions referred to in notes are indexed and those of the United States Supreme Court, by name only without citations. Citations may be found on the pages indicated. Court decisions of other courts quoted as examples are not indexed by name, only by subject matter and by state in which rendered. They are listed alphabetically with full citations on pages xv-xvii.

341

Connecticut, court decisions in, 89-93, 107-111, 288-289
Constitution, Federal, xix, xx
  Bill of Rights, xix
  Fifth Amendment, 43, 63-69
  First Amendment, 59-60, 247
  Fourteenth Amendment, xix, 59
  (*See also* Vested rights of teachers, and specific situations in which these various Amendments were applied, *e.g.*, Released-time programs)
  Tenth Amendment, xix
Constitutionality of antifraternity rules, 274-276
  of Bible reading in public schools, 247, 257-260
  of curriculum restrictions, 253-257
  effect of, generally, xx-xxi
  of flag-salute requirements, 217-226
  of free textbooks for nonpublic-school pupils, 251-252
  of minimum salary laws, 97
  of released-time programs, 260-265
  of salary discriminations on basis of race, 99-101
  of statute compelling attendance at public schools, 199-201
  of tenure laws, 27
  of transportation of nonpublic-school pupils, 235-242
Constitutions, states, xix, xx, xxi
  (*See also* specific situations in which state constitutions were applied, *e.g.*, to tenure laws)
Contract actions distinguished from tort actions, xxvi
Contracts, breach of, 23
  definition of, 331, 332, 333
  impairment of (*See* Vested rights of teachers)
Contracts for employment of teachers, 23-57, 31, 37-39
  consideration for, 97, 331
  continuing, 25
    distinguished from tenure, 25, 28, 43-45
    statute on, 29
  forms for, 24
  penalty clause in, 73-74
  ratification of, 25, 335
  (*See also* Appointment of teachers; *Quantum meruit;* Tenure)

Corporal punishment of pupils, 267-271
  statutory provisions regarding, 268-269
Cruelty to children, laws forbidding, 268-269
Curriculum, 245-266
  in private schools, 253-255
  statutory requirements for, 249-251, 255-257

D

Declaratory judgment, 20, 331
De facto officer, definition of, xxix, 331
Defamation of character, 129-139
  of pupils by teachers, 133-134
  statutory provisions regarding, 134-135
  of teachers, 129-133
  suits for, 135-139
Delaware, court decision in, 206-209
Delegation of powers, to local school boards, xxi
  to local superintendent, 5
  to state board of education, xx
Discipline of pupils, 267-276
Dismissal of teachers, 23-72
  board procedure in, 27
  for cause, xxiv
  under continuing-contract law, 43-45
  during contract term, 23-25
  without due process, 41-43, 66-69
  probationary teachers, 48-51
  tenure teachers, 45-47, 26-29, 32-36
District of Columbia, court decision in, 208
  workmen's compensation law in, 143-147

E

Ejusdem generis, definition of, xxiii, 332
Eligibility lists, appointment from, 5, 15-19
Employees distinguished from officers, xxix-xxx
Employment of teachers (*See* Appointment of teachers; Contracts for employment of teachers; Eligibility lists; Probationary teachers; Tenure)

Engel v. Vitala, 260
Expulsion and suspension of pupils, 267, 217-226, 271-276

F

Federal Constitution (*See* Constitution, Federal)
Flag-salute requirement, constitutionality of, 217-226
Florida, court decisions in, 8-9, 185-187
leave-of-absence law in, 120-122

G

Gable *et al.* v. Raftery *et al.*, 189
Garner *et al.* v. Board of Public Works of Los Angeles, 63
Georgia, court decisions in, 13-14, 137-139, 271-274
law providing appeal from school-board decisions in, 188
Governmental immunity, xxiv, 143, 279-281, 283, 332

H

Health certificates required of pupils, 196, 271-274
of teachers, 179-181
Heyland v. Wayne Independent School District No. 5 of Wayne Township, xxix

I

Illinois, court decisions in, 87-89, 171-173, 260-261, 296-298
Immunity from tort action (*See* Governmental immunity)
In loco parentis, 267, 332
Indiana, court decisions in, 54-56, 124-126
law forbidding cruelty to children in, 269
statute on residences of teachers, 182
Instruction in evolution, 255-257
in moral and spiritual values, 262
sectarian, 246-247, 257-265
in subjects not permitted in public schools, 246, 253-255
Insurance, effect of on court actions, 231, 280-281, 283-284, 286-288, 296-298
power of school board to carry, 280

statutory provisions for athletic teams, 284
for state payments in lieu of insurance coverage, 231-232
for transportaions coverage, 283
Iowa, court decision in, 148-149

J

Judicial process (*See* Procedure, court; Civil procedure)
Jury, functions of, xxvi

K

Kansas, court decisions in, 203-205, 206-209
Kentucky, court decisions in, 7-8, 115-116, 135-137, 232-233
transportation law in, 228

L

Law, definition of, xix, 333
Leaves of absence of teachers, 119-127
involuntary, 120, 124-127
reinstatement after, 119
right to, 119, 122-124
statutory provisions for, 120-122
Legal disability of teachers, 7-8
Letters of recommendation for pupils from teachers, 134
for teachers from principals or superintendents, 134
Liability (*See* Immunity from tort action; Insurance; Negligence; Governmental immunity)
Libel (*See* Defamation of character)
Louisiana, court decisions in, 122-124, 251-252, 274-275
Loyalty of teachers, 3, 59-72
requirements to testify as to, 60-63, 66-72
statutory provisions on, 60-63

M

Maryland, state-adopted contract form in, 37-39
state department of education anti-fraternity rule in, 269-270
Massachusetts, court decisions in, 19-20, 101-102, 102-104
minimum salary law in, 98-99
statutory provisions regarding teachers' political activities, 185

Medical treatment of pupils by teachers, 285-286
Minersville v. Gobitis, 217-226
Minnesota, court decisions in, 41-43, 257-259
Montana, court decisions in, 43-45, 45-47, 93-95

N

Nebraska, court decision in, 253-254
Negligence, contributory, 278
  definition of, 277
  principles of, 277-279
  of school-board members personally, 283
Nepotism (See Antinepotism)
Nevada, statutory provisions regarding insurance for athletic teams in, 284
New Hampshire, collective bargaining authority, 86
  court decision in, 82-84
New Jersey, court decisions in, 53-56, 190-191, 235-242
  law forbidding corporal punishment in, 268-269
  statutory provisions regarding curriculum prescriptions, 249-250
New Mexico, court decision in, 286-288
New York, anti-strike law, 75-76
  court decisions in, 15-16, 16-18, 51-52, 64-65, 66-69, 105-107, 114-115, 153-155, 180-181, 262-265, 294-296
  law abrogating governmental immunity in, 281
  law for appeal from school-board decisions in, 188-189
  teachers' retirement law in, 165-171
North Carolina, health requirements for teachers, 179-180
  law providing compensation to pupils injured in transportation in, 231-232

O

Officer, de facto (See De facto officer)
  de jure distinguished from de facto, xxix
  distinguished from employee, xxix-xxx
Ohio, court decision in, 149-151
  textbook law in, 247-249

Oklahoma, compulsory attendance law in, 198-199
  law providing for transportation insurance in, 283
Oregon, court decision in, 199-201

P

Parochial schools, curriculum, 253-255
  textbooks at public expense, 251-253
  transportation of pupils of, at public expense, 235-242
Parties in court actions, identity of, xxvii
Penalty for failure to complete contract, 73-74
Pennsylvania, court decisions in, 48-51, 69-71, 182-184, 216-217, 285
  statutory provisions regarding Bible reading, 251
  tenure law in, 31-36
Pensions distinguished from retirement benefits, 171-174
Pensions (See Retirement of Teachers)
Plessy v. Ferguson, 208
Presumptions, xxi, xxiv, 19
Private schools (See Attendance at nonpublic schools; Parochial schools)
Probationary teachers, 26
Procedure, court, xxv-xxvii
Public funds for private-school pupils (See Parochial schools)
Pupil injuries, 277-299
  immunity of school board, 279-281, 284, 286-288
    abrogation of, by court decision, 279, 296-298
    by law, 282-283
  liability for, of individual board members, 283
  of negligent teachers, 277-279, 290-293
  of principals, 294-296
  by medical treatment of teachers, 285-286
  nuisance, as exception to governmental immunity, 288-290, 334
  payments for, by state claims agencies, 231-232
  as pure accidents, 277
  safe-place statutes, 280
  save-harmless statutes, 281
  (See also Insurance)

Q

Quantum meruit, definition of, 8, 334

R

Race discrimination among teachers, 99-101
Race segregation of pupils (*See* Segregation of pupils by races)
Released-time programs, 247, 260-265
Religious freedom, 216-217, 217-226
Religious garb, teachers wearing, 262
Religious instructions (*See* Instruction, sectarian; Parochial schools)
Res adjudicata, application of, 189
definition of, 335
Research in school law (*See* Sources of school law)
Residence of pupils for school attendance, 195, 203-206
Resignation of teachers, 73-84
Retirement of teachers, 161-177
on disability, 151-155
increasing benefits after, 164, 174-176
pension distinguished from retirement fund for, 171-174
rescinding application for, 153-155
statutory provisions for, 152-153, 165-171

S

Salaries, 97-117
dependency allowances, 102-105
discriminations in, on basis of marital status, 95-96, 97
of race, 98, 99-101
of sex, 97, 101-102
for extra duties, 105-107
increases of, 107-111, 111-114, 114-115
minimum salary laws, 97, 98-99
constitutionality of, 97
reduction of, 53-54, 115-116
Salary schedules, 97
Schempp v. Abington Township School District, 259
School board, conduct of business of, 5
effect of change in personnel of, xxviii
fiscal independence, 111
legal status of, xxvii-xxix
School districts, legal status of, xxi, xxvii-xxix
School supplies free to nonpublic-

school pupils, 251-253
Scienter, definition of, 63, 335
Secret societies forbidden to pupils, 269-270, 274-276
Sectarian education (*See* Instruction, sectarian; Parochial schools)
Segregation of pupils by races, 197, 206-216
Slander (*See* Defamation of character)
Social security program, disability benefits in, 155-159
generally, 161
statute on, 156-159
Sources of school law, xix-xxii, 303-327, 337-339
constitutions, xix-xx, 303
court decisions, 309-327
American Digest System, 310-315
American Jurisprudence, 324-326
American Law Reports, 316-319
Annotated Reports, 316-319
Corpus Juris, 322-324, 326
National Reporter System, 315-316
Shepard's Citations to Cases, 319-322
statutes, xx-xxi, 303-305, 306, 309
Shepard's Citations to Statutes, 305-309
State Law Index, 309
South Carolina, court decision in, 206-209
examination of teachers prerequisite to certification, 4
State board of education, regulations of, xx, xxi, 37-39, 227, 245, 269, 269-270
State ex rel. Barney v. Hawkins, xxx
State ex rel. Halloway v. Sheats, xxx
Statutes, construction of, xxii-xxv
effective date of, xxiv
federal, xx, 143-147, 156-159
invalid, xxi
parts of, xxii
state, xx-xxii (*See also* subjects of and states enacted in)
codification of, xxii, 330
Strikes by teachers, 74-76, 79-84
Superintendent, power to appoint teachers, 5
Supreme Court of the United States, decisions quoted from
Adler *et al.* v. Board of Education, 64-65

Beilan v. Board of Public Education, 69-71
Brown et al. v. Board of Education (and other segregation cases), 206-209
Cochran v. Louisiana State Board of Education, 251-252
Cooper v. Aaron, 210-215
Dodge v. Board of Education of Chicago, 171-173
Everson v. Board of Education of Ewing Township et al., 235-242
Hughes et al. v. Caddo Parish School Board et al., 274-275
Illinois ex rel. McCollum v. Board of Education of School District No. 71, Champaign County, Illinois, 260-261
Indiana ex rel. Anderson v. Brand, 54-56
Meyer v. State of Nebraska, 253-254
Phelps v. Board of Education of West New York, 53-54
Pierce v. Society of Sisters; Pierce v. Hill Academy, 199-201
Slochower v. Board of Higher Education, 66-69
West Virginia State Board of Education v. Barnette, 217-225
Zorach et al. v. Clauson et al., 262-265
Suspension of pupils (See Expulsion and suspension of pupils)

T

Taxpayers' interests, 19-20
Teachers, health requirements of, 179-181
injuries and other disabilities, 141-160
legal status, xxix-xxx
political activities of, 184-187 (See also Loyalty)
residence requirements of, 181-184
Tennessee, court decision in, 255-257
Tenure, acquisition of, 48-51, 77-79
definition of, 25-26, 335
distinction between legislative and contractual status under, 28, 53-57
loss of, 36, 75-76
statutory provisions for, 29-30, 31-36
constitutionality of, 27
Textbooks, 245-246, 247-249

free, for nonpublic-school pupils, 251-253
uniform adoption, 245
Transportation of pupils, 227-243
free for nonpublic-school pupils, 235-242
insurance coverage for, 228-231
statutory provisions regarding, 228-231, 283
suits to compel, 232-235
Tudor v. Board of Education and Gideon International, 259-260
Tuition, 195-196, 203-206

U

United States statutes, xx, 143-147, 156-159
Utah, court decision in, 10-12

V

Vaccination of pupils, 196, 271-274
Vested rights of teachers, definition of, 335
to increments in salary schedules, 97-98
under retirement laws, 164, 171-173
under tenure laws, 54-57
Virginia, court decisions in, 99-101, 206-209
law for employment of teachers in, 5-6
state board of education regulation for suspension of pupils in, 269

W

Washington, teachers' retirement law in, 152-153
West Virginia, court decision in, 217-225
Whitfield v. East Baton Rouge Parish School Board, 289
Wieman v. Updegraff, 64
Williamson v. Board of Education of Woodward, 8
Wilson et al. v. Abilene Independent School District, 276
Wisconsin, court decisions in, 174-175, 233-235
law on libel in, 134-135
Workmen's compensation benefits, 141-151
claims by teachers, 148-151
statutory provisions for, 143-147
Wright v. Board of Education of St. Louis, 276